Who Cares for America's Children?

Child Care Policy for the 1990s

Cheryl D. Hayes, John L. Palmer, and
Martha J. Zaslow, Editors

Panel on Child Care Policy

Committee on Child Development Research and
Public Policy

Commission on Behavioral and
Social Sciences and Education

National Research Council

WITHDRAWN

NATIONAL ACADEMY PRESS
Washington, D.C.   1990

National Academy Press • 2101 Constitution Avenue, N.W. • Washington, D.C. 20418

NOTICE: The project that is the subject of this report was approved by the Governing Board of the National Research Council, whose members are drawn from the councils of the National Academy of Sciences, the National Academy of Engineering, and the Institute of Medicine. The members of the committee responsible for the report were chosen for their special competences and with regard for appropriate balance.

This report has been reviewed by a group other than the authors according to procedures approved by a Report Review Committee consisting of members of the National Academy of Sciences, the National Academy of Engineering, and the Institute of Medicine.

The work that provided the basis for this volume was supported by the Ford Foundation, the Foundation for Child Development, and the U.S. Department of Health and Human Services.

Library of Congress Cataloging-in-Publication Data

Who cares for America's children? : child care policy for the 1990s /
    Cheryl D. Hayes, John L. Palmer, and Martha J. Zaslow, editors :
    Panel on Child Care Policy, Committee on Child Development Research
    and Public Policy, Commission on Behavioral and Social Sciences and
    Education, National Research Council.
        p.   cm.
    Includes bibliographical references.
    ISBN 0-309-04032-9
    1. Child care—United States. 2. Child care—Government policy-
  -United States. 3. Child care services—Government policy—United
    States. I. Hayes, Cheryl D. II. Palmer, John Logan. III. Zaslow,
    Martha J. IV. National Research Council (U.S.). Panel on Child
    Care Policy.
    HQ778.7.U6W53 1990   90-5813
    362.7—dc20   CIP

Cover: A collage of drawings done by children from the Stoddert After School Program, Washington, D.C., and the Clara Barton School-Aged Extended Day Center, Bethesda, Maryland.

iii

Contents

WITHDRAWN

v

Honorable Louis Sullivan
Secretary
U.S. Department of Health and Human Services
Washington, D.C.

Dear Mr. Secretary:

We are pleased to forward *Who Cares for America's Children?*, the report of the Panel on Child Care Policy. The report was prepared at the request of and with support from the Department of Health and Human Services, with additional support from the Ford Foundation and the Foundation for Child Development.

This report is an important statement on child policy issues. It has been prepared by a distinguished group of professionals with diverse backgrounds in pediatrics, public policy, business, education, economics, psychology, and other social science fields.

The panel was impressed with research showing the importance of close parental involvement with children in the first year of life. In its fifth recommendation, in recognition of the need for close and early parent-child interaction and the shortage of quality infant care programs, the panel recommends mandating the option of unpaid, job-protected leave for employed parents of infants up to one year of age.

As the panel chair notes in his preface, "appropriate public and private policies toward child care ultimately must reflect differing value orientations as much as the weight of scientific evidence and analysis." At least in the near term, there is unlikely to be a clear public consensus on parental leave issues. We believe that further review will be necessary to resolve the matter. We anticipate that such studies will recognize the undoubted burdens that are convincingly documented here to families and children of the current absence of such a provision. But they will also need to consider in fuller detail the very real burdens to individual firms, to the nature of hiring decisions, and to the economy at large that uniform federal mandating of such leave would entail and how they would be allocated. These are issues that should now be addressed with a different array of specialists than those represented on the current panel.

Very truly yours,

Robert McC. Adams, Chairman
Commission on Behavioral and
Social Sciences and Education
National Research Council

Frank Press
Chairman
National Research Council

Preface

One has had only to follow the news media in recent years, or to be the parent of a young child, to know that child care has become an issue of great concern in America. The social revolution that has transformed American family life over the past several decades has had many repercussions, but none more important than those that affect the care and rearing of our children. As a consequence, a subject that as recently as a generation ago was strictly regarded as a private family matter is today the focus of intense public debate and, increasingly, of public policies.

While there is general agreement that the current U.S. system of child care is inadequate and that child care policies should promote the healthy development of children, there is little social consensus beyond this. How important is parental care relative to nonparental care? What specific kinds of care are needed by children of different ages and of various social, economic, and cultural backgrounds? How available and affordable is such care in out-of-home settings? What is the appropriate role of parents, of governments, of employers, and of other institutions in ensuring that children receive such care? These are but some of the important issues that must be better understood, if the nation is to respond effectively to what some have characterized as a crisis in child care.

The Panel on Child Care Policy was convened under the auspices of the National Research Council's Committee on Child Development Research and Public Policy to collect, integrate, and critically assess data and research that bears on these issues. Our efforts were financed by the Ford Foundation, the Foundation for Child Development, and the U.S. Department of Health and Human Services. This diverse group of sponsors sought a comprehensive review of knowledge concerning the costs, effects, and feasibility of alternative child care policies and programs to assist federal, state, and local decision makers—as well as decision makers in the private sector—who, in the coming years, will set the course for government and employer involvement in the provision, financing, and regulation of child care services. This report contains the major findings of this review and the panel's consequent recommendations for future data collection and research and for directions for policy and program development.

The magnitude of our task was obviously large and the allotted time to carry it out short. Fortunately, we were blessed in several respects. Our sponsors' key staff, Betsy Ussery, Associate Commissioner of Head Start in the Office of Human Development Services, Heidi Sigal of the Foundation for Child Development, and Shelby Miller of the Ford Foundation, were all that one could wish—supportive and generous but nonintrusive. The various members of the panel embodied a wide range of essential scholarly and practical perspectives and, to the last, were exceedingly generous with their time and goodwill.

The National Research Council provided us with very able staff assistance. The leadership and contributions of Cheryl Hayes, the study director, in particular, were invaluable at every stage of the process, from the initial formulation of the study through to the drafting and redrafting of the final report. In addition to her overall responsibility for managing the study, Cheri worked with the working group on service delivery and assumed primary responsibility for drafting chapters 1, 2, 6, 9, and 10 of this report. The contributions of other members of the staff were also significant to the outcome of the study. Martha J. Zaslow, senior research associate/consultant, worked with members of the working group on the policy implications of child care research to prepare a detailed scholarly review of the child development research on child care and assumed primary responsibility for drafting chapters 3, 4, and 5 of this volume. Brigid O'Farrell, senior research associate, worked with the members of the working group on the child care market and assumed primary responsibility for drafting chapters 7 and 8. Pat N. Marks, research associate, worked with the working group on standards, regulations, and enforcement and assumed primary responsibility for the state data collection, as well as for preparation of all the tables and figures in the report. April Brayfield, consultant, worked with Pat Marks to gather and analyze the state data. Michelle Daniels, administrative secretary, managed all of the details associated with the panel's meetings and prepared the manuscript for publication. Eugenia Grohman, the CBASSE associate director for reports, edited the manuscript and managed its formal review.

Finally, numerous individuals outside the panel and its immediate staff also contributed in important ways to the success of the study. Several scholars prepared background papers and analyses that were critical to the panel's deliberations: Teresa Kohlenberg and Frederick Jarman of the University of Massachusetts Medical School, a detailed review of the research on illness and injury in child care; Lorelei Brush, a paper on the projected costs of expanding Head Start; Roberta Barnes of the Urban Institute, simulation projections of the costs of proposed alternative child care policies; Linda Waite and Arlene Leibowitz of the Rand Corporation, a paper on the effects of child care on women's labor force participation and fertility; Rachel Connelly of the University of Vermont, a paper on the child care market; Sheila Kamerman and Alfred Kahn of the Columbia University School of Social Work, an overview of international comparisons of child care policies. Drs. Kamerman and Kahn also organized and cochaired the panel's workshop on cross-national perspectives on child care policy. Many other social science scholars, health and early childhood professionals, federal, state, and local policy officials, representatives of community organizations, businesses, and labor unions from the United States and abroad participated in the panel's five workshops and generously contributed their knowledge, experience, and ideas (see Appendix C). In addition, several individuals were invaluable sources of information and comment that aided the panel and staff in preparing this report, most especially Howard Hayghe at the Bureau of the Census, Lindsay Chase-Landsdale at the George Washington University Medical School, Deborah Phillips at the University of Virginia, Peggy Connerton of the Service Employees International Union, Marcy Whitebook at the Child Care Employee Project, Norton Grubb at the University of California at Berkeley, and Douglas Besharov at the American Enterprise Institute.

As is the case with so many important issues currently facing our country, appropriate public and private policies toward child care ultimately must reflect differing value orientations as much as the weight of scientific evidence and analysis. Nowhere was this more evident than in the deliberations and conclusions of our panel. Nevertheless, panel members were unanimous in their conviction that we are currently investing far too little in the care of our children for the future health of our nation as a whole. Scientific evidence and analysis are persuasive on this point, and they illuminate fruitful avenues of remedy. We trust that this will be evident to the readers of the pages that follow.

John L. Palmer, *Chair*
Panel on Child Care Policy

The National Academy of Sciences is a private, nonprofit, self-perpetuating society of distinguished scholars engaged in scientific and engineering research, dedicated to the furtherance of science and technology and to their use for the general welfare. Upon the authority of the charter granted to it by the Congress in 1863, the Academy has a mandate that requires it to advise the federal government on scientific and technical matters. Dr. Frank Press is president of the National Academy of Sciences.

The National Academy of Engineering was established in 1964, under the charter of the National Academy of Sciences, as a parallel organization of outstanding engineers. It is autonomous in its administration and in the selection of its members, sharing with the National Academy of Sciences the responsibility for advising the federal government. The National Academy of Engineering also sponsors engineering programs aimed at meeting national needs, encourages education and research, and recognizes the superior achievements of engineers. Dr. Robert M. White is president of the National Academy of Engineering.

The Institute of Medicine was established in 1970 by the National Academy of Sciences to secure the services of eminent members of appropriate professions in the examination of policy matters pertaining to the health of the public. The Institute acts under the responsibility given to the National Academy of Sciences by its congressional charter to be an adviser to the federal government and, upon its own initiative, to identify issues of medical care, research, and education. Dr. Samuel O. Thier is president of the Institute of Medicine.

The National Research Council was organized by the National Academy of Sciences in 1916 to associate the broad community of science and technology with the Academy's purposes of furthering knowledge and advising the federal government. Functioning in accordance with general policies determined by the Academy, the Council has become the principal operating agency of both the National Academy of Sciences and the National Academy of Engineering in providing services to the government, the public, and the scientific and engineering communities. The Council is administered jointly by both Academies and the Institute of Medicine. Dr. Frank Press and Dr. Robert M. White are chairman and vice chairman, respectively, of the National Research Council.

Executive Summary

In the United States over the past decade and a half, as in other developed countries, mothers' entry and attachment to the labor force has changed the allocation of child care and childrearing tasks. The majority of children now have working mothers, and as a result, child care increasingly includes market services provided in an array of out-of-home settings. Since the mid-1970s, care outside the home by unrelated adults has become an increasingly common experience for very young children and for older children during the hours when they are not in school. Child care is no longer simply a protective or remedial service for poor youngsters or those from troubled families; it is an everyday experience for children from all economic classes. What was until recently treated strictly as a private family matter has become a topic of widespread public debate and public policy.

In light of these dramatic demographic and economic changes, in 1987 the National Research Council's Committee on Child Development Research and Public Policy established under its auspices the Panel on Child Care Policy to critically review and assess knowledge concerning the costs, effects, and feasibility of alternative child care policies and programs as a basis for recommending future directions for public- and private-sector decision making. Over a 2-year period, with support from the Administration for Children, Youth, and Families in the U.S. Department of Health and Human Services, the Foundation for Child Development, and the Ford Foundation, the panel has gathered, integrated, and reviewed existing data and research on trends in work, family, and child care; the implications of child care for child health and development; the delivery and regulation of services; and the costs and effects of alternative child care policies and programs.

FINDINGS AND CONCLUSIONS

On the basis of its review and deliberations, the panel has reached seven general findings and conclusions that underlie its recommendations:

1. Existing child care services in the United States are inadequate to meet current and likely future needs of children, parents, and society as a whole. For some families, child care services are simply unavailable; for many others, care may be available, but it is unaffordable or fails to meet basic standards of quality. The general accessibility of high-quality, affordable child care has immediate and long-term implications for the health and well-being of children, parents, and society as a whole. Developmentally appropriate care, provided in safe and healthy environments, has been shown to enhance the well-being of young children. It enables parents who need or want to work outside the home to do so, secure in the knowledge that their children are being well provided for. It can contribute to the economic status of families and enhance parents' own personal and career development. And since today's children are tomorrow's adult citizens and workers, their proper care and nurturance will pay enormous dividends to society as a whole.

2. Of greatest concern is the large number of children who are presently cared for in settings that do not protect their health and safety and do not provide appropriate developmental stimulation. Poor-quality care, more than any single type of program or arrangement, threatens children's development, especially children from poor and minority families. Quality varies within and across programs and arrangements provided under different institutional auspices. High-quality and low-quality care can be found among all types of services, whether they are provided in the child's home or outside it, in schools, child care centers, or family day care homes, in programs operated for profit or those operated not for profit.

3. Irrespective of family income, child care has become a necessity for the majority of American families. Yet specific gaps in current programs and arrangements mean that many children and families lack access to services. Families with infants and toddlers, those with children with disabilities, those with mildly or chronically ill children, those with school-age children, and those in which parents work nontraditional schedules often have particular difficulty arranging appropriate child care services.

4. Arranging quality child care can be difficult, stressful, and time-consuming for all families. However, the problems are inevitably compounded for low-income families who lack time, information, and economic resources. For these families, the choices are often more limited, and the consequences of inadequate care are likely to be more severe. Therefore, in addressing specific child care needs, public policies should give priority to those who are economically disadvantaged.

5. The most striking characteristic of existing child care services is their diversity. The current system is an amalgam of providers, programs, and institutional auspices that have little interconnectedness and do not share a sense of common purpose or direction. This diversity is at once a source of strength and a challenge to the development of a more coherent system that meets the needs of all children and all families. On the positive side, the diversity means that parents seeking child care outside their homes have a range of programs and arrangements from which to choose. On the negative side, the diversity means that the costs, availability, and quality of care vary substantially. Preserving parents' choices in the care and rearing of their children is essential; however, it has to be balanced against the need to plan and coordinate services in a way that ensures their quality and accessibility to all families who need them.

6. There is no single policy or program that can address the child care needs of all families and children. The nation will need a comprehensive array of coordinated policies and programs responsive to the needs of families in different social, economic, and cultural circumstances and to children of different ages, stages of development, and with special needs.

7. Responsibility for meeting the nation's child care needs should be widely shared among individuals, families, voluntary organizations, employers, communities, and government at all levels. Americans place a high priority on individuals' values and on the rights of parents to raise their children according to their own beliefs. Therefore, all child care policies should affirm the role and responsibilities of families in childrearing. Governments, community institutions, and employers should support rather than detract from that role.

GOALS OF A CHILD CARE SYSTEM

The panel has identified three overarching policy goals that should guide the future development of the child care system in the United States:

- achieve quality in out-of-home child care services and arrangements;
- improve accessibility to quality child care services for families in different social, economic, and cultural circumstances; and
- enhance the affordability of child care services for low- and moderate-income families.

Achieving all three of these goals is critical to the development of an improved child care system in which all children and families have access to affordable programs and arrangements that meet fundamental standards of quality and parents have increased choice in combining child care and employment. In the absence of fiscal constraints, these goals are not mutually exclusive, nor do they necessarily reflect competing priorities; in the current environment, however, pursuing them simultaneously will inevitably involve some difficult tradeoffs.

RECOMMENDATIONS FOR CHILD CARE POLICIES AND PROGRAMS

On the basis of its review of the scientific evidence and the panel's best assessment of the costs, effects, and feasibility of selected alternative policy and programmatic actions, the panel recommends five immediate steps to improve the child care system in the United States. The first three will require substantially augmenting current government allocations for child care—by $5 to $10 billion annually. The other two can be implemented at much more modest cost, much of which could be borne by the private sector.

> 1. **The federal government, in partnership with the states, should expand subsidies to support low-income families' use of quality child care programs and arrangements.**

For many parents in or near poverty, problems with child care can be a barrier to becoming and staying employed. Therefore, child care must be a central component of any policy to help poor families achieve economic self-sufficiency through employment. Several specific funding mechanisms are available to channel support for low-income child care, including: (1) changing the dependent care tax credit to meet the needs of low-income families; (2) expanding the earned income tax credit or converting the personal tax exemption for children to a refundable credit; (3) providing additional support for the purchase of services through grant programs such as the Social Services Block Grant program; and (4) allocating additional support for child care and early childhood education provided by the public school systems.

The panel is neutral as to the specific funding mechanisms for channeling general support for low-income child care. Each of the policy alternatives presents tradeoffs among the three goals of quality, accessibility, and affordability. While scientific evidence and policy analysis can highlight these tradeoffs, choosing among the goals, and therefore among the policy instruments, is the role of the political process.

> 2. **In partnership with the states, the federal government should expand Head Start and other compensatory preschool programs for income-eligible 3- and 4-year-olds who are at risk of early school failure.**

Over two decades of experience with the federally funded Head Start program and major evaluation studies provide convincing evidence of the effectiveness of high-quality comprehensive early childhood education. These programs provide economically disadvantaged and at-risk preschool children an early educational experience that improves their chances of later academic success. Accordingly, the panel concludes that the Head Start program should be expanded to serve all income-eligible 3- and 4-year-olds in need of comprehensive child development services. In addition, Head Start programs should be integrated with community child care programs to provide extended-day care for children whose parents are employed. They should also be coordinated with other public and private school and child care programs serving children in low-income families and children with disabilities in this age group to ensure that appropriate services are accessible to all children and families who need them. For low-income children who do not require intensive comprehensive child care programs that combine health, education, and social services, publicly provided compensatory education programs should be expanded.

3. **Governments at all levels, along with employers and other private-sector groups, should make investments to strengthen the infrastructure of the child care system.**

The panel urges several specific steps to strengthen the infrastructure of the child care system:

a. **expand resource and referral services;**
b. **improve caregiver training and wages;**
c. **expand vendor-voucher programs;**
d. **encourage the organization of family day care systems; and**
e. **improve planning and coordination.**

Improving the accessibility of quality child care to low- and moderate-income families will depend in part on developing a child care system that meets the needs of all children and families. Improving the capacity of the system to match consumers and providers, to offer information and referral to parents, to provide training and technical assistance to family day care providers, and to support effective planning and coordination of policies, programs, and resources at all levels would enhance the quality and accessibility of services to all families.

4. **The federal government should initiate a process to develop national standards for child care.**

An extensive and growing body of scientific research and best professional practice has established the importance of child care quality for child development. Based on existing knowledge, it is possible to specify reasonable ranges for standards to govern many important features of child care, including staff/child ratios, group size, caregiver qualifications, and the configuration of physical space.

Staff/Child Ratios   Research shows that the staff/child ratio is most critical for infants and young toddlers (0 to 24 months). For those youngest children, the ratio should not exceed 1:4. For 2-year-olds, acceptable ranges are 1:3 to 1:6; for 3-year-olds, 1:5 to 1:10; and for 4- and 5-year-olds, 1:7 to 1:10.

Group Size   Children benefit from social interactions with peers; however, larger groups are generally associated with less positive interactions and developmental outcomes. Acceptable ranges are a maximum of 6 to 8 children during the first year of life, 6 to 12 for 1- and 2-year-olds, 14 to 20 for 3-year-olds, and 16 to 20 for 4- and 5-year-olds.

Caregiver Training and Experience   Caregivers in child care centers, family day care homes, and school-based programs should have specific training in child development theory and practice. In addition, research shows that more years of general education contribute to caregiver performance and children's developmental outcomes.

Physical Space and Facilities   Space should be well organized, orderly, differentiated, and designed for children's use. Specific activities should have assigned areas within a child care center or family day care home (e.g., an art table, a dramatic play corner, a block-building corner, a reading corner). Facilities and toys should be age appropriate for the children using them.

Current state regulations vary dramatically, and few reflect existing knowledge about the dimensions of quality that are essential to protect children's health and safety and to stimulate social and cognitive development. Unfortunately, there are few economic or political incentives for the states to take this step. Thus, incentives must also be created to encourage state involvement: for example, linking federal funding to compliance with national standards. Accordingly, the panel recommends that the federal government establish a national-level task force to bring together representatives of the states, the relevant professional organizations, service providers, and appropriate federal agencies to review current knowledge from child development research and professional practice to develop national standards for the provision of child care services and preschool education.

5. **The federal government should mandate unpaid, job-protected leave for employed parents of infants up to 1 year of age.**

In light of scientific evidence on the importance of establishing strong relationships between parents and children in the early months of life and the greater likelihood that these enduring relationships will develop when parents have time and emotional energy to devote to their young children, the panel urges that the federal government mandate unpaid, job-protected leave for employed parents of infants up to 1 year of age. Clearly, public policies should also stimulate the development of quality child care programs for infants and toddlers. However, in light of existing knowledge from child development research and the shortage of quality infant and toddler care programs, national child care policy should also offer parents the option of remaining at home to care for their own children.

Even among those who agree that parental leave policies should be implemented, there is little consensus about whether leaves should be paid or unpaid and, if paid, at what level of wage replacement, for what period of time, at whose cost, and with what assistance for the particular problems of small employers. Our conclusion, based on a review of the available research and the panel's professional judgment, is that, in the long term, policies should provide paid leave with partial income replacement for up to 6 months and unpaid leave for up to an additional 6 months, with job-related health benefits and job guarantees during the year.

We recognize, however, that the costs to employers and governments will make the implementation of paid parental leave impossible in the near term. Accordingly, as a first step, we recommend that the federal government mandate that employers ensure unpaid, job-protected leave, with continued health benefits, for up to 1 year for all parents who prefer to remain at home following the arrival of a new baby. We acknowledge that without wage replacement, parental leave will not be a viable option for many families, and we look forward to the eventual implementation of policies to provide paid leave.

In sum, in keeping with the panel's objective of enhancing families' choices among child care arrangements for infants, parental leave—as well as quality out-of-home care—should be an option regardless of parents' economic status.

Who Cares for America's Children?

Child Care Policy for the 1990s

I

Introduction

1

Child Care in a Changing Society

The United States, along with most other industrialized countries, has experienced a social revolution during the past quarter century. Since the mid-1960s, more and more women, including those with children, have entered and remained in the paid work force. Their employment has been accompanied by falling birth rates, rising divorce rates, and older ages at marriage. Together these trends have had dramatic effects on the roles of men and women and on the form and function of families. Scholars, commentators, and public leaders alike have expressed amazement about the scope of social change in U.S. society and concern about its consequences for parents, for children, for employers, and for the nature of work and family life. Since the late 1980s, a major focus of this concern has been on the care and rearing of American children. There is growing recognition that if parents are to manage productive roles in the labor force and at the same time fulfill their roles within the family, a substantial social response is required. An issue that a generation ago was strictly regarded as a private family matter is today the subject of public discussion and public policy.

In 1988 more than 10.5 million children under age 6, including nearly 6.6 million infants and toddlers under age 3, had mothers in the labor force. Another 18 million children between the ages of 6 and 13 had working mothers, and the numbers are expected to rise into the 1990s (Bureau of Labor Statistics, 1988). Using U.S. Department of Labor data, Johnston and Packer (1987) project that by 1995 roughly two-thirds of all new labor force entrants will be women, and 80 percent of those in their childbearing years are expected to have children during their work life (Scarr et al., 1988). Many children of working mothers are and will continue to be cared for by their parents, siblings, or other relatives, but a growing proportion receive care from unrelated adults in their own homes, in their caregivers'

3

homes, in schools, and in organized child care facilities (Bureau of the Census, 1987). As a result, concern about the quality, availability, and affordability of nonparental child care has become a widespread national priority. What was traditionally viewed by most Americans as a problem of the poor has in the 1980s become a fact of everyday life for the majority of U.S. children and their families. Child care is now an essential aspect of domestic life and of the economic structure of the country.

Although there is broad consensus that society should promote the healthy development of the next generation and minimize potentially harmful conditions, there is less agreement about what kinds of care are best for children of different ages and for those who are living in different social, economic, and cultural circumstances. There is, similarly, little agreement about who should provide care and who should pay for it. Debate over the appropriate role of government, employers, and parents themselves has intensified in recent years and has led to numerous proposals from leaders of both political parties and a broad array of special interest groups to address the increasing need for child care support and services.

Although they differ greatly in their specifics, these proposals share the fundamental recognition that child care is costly, whether it is provided by parents, other family members, or unrelated caregivers and whether it is privately or publicly financed. For parents, usually mothers, who stay at home to care for their own children, there are "opportunity costs": the forgone income and work experience that employment outside the home would have yielded. For working parents, the purchase of child care services entails significant cash outlays. Quality care—care that is developmentally enriching and protective of physical health and safety—is generally more costly than minimally adequate or poor-quality care. And quality care has been shown to compensate for disadvantaged family environments and to promote better intellectual and social development for some children than they would have experienced only in their homes (McCartney et al., 1985; Ramey et al., 1985). For children who do not receive adequate care, the short-term costs are often manifested in a variety of poor social, emotional, and cognitive outcomes; behavioral difficulties; and health problems, especially for those from poor and disorganized home environments. The long-term costs, to the extent that they have been documented, are measurable in poor skills development, dropping out of school, reduced earnings, antisocial behavior, and even economic dependency.

For society, a commitment to quality child care will inevitably entail substantial resources, which in the current context implies monetary costs that must be borne by parents, employers, taxpayers, or some combination of them. Until recently, however, the high costs of child care were largely invisible in an economic sense. The labor of a mother caring for her own child is not counted as productive economic activity in calculations of the gross national product; in contrast, one parent caring for the children of others is counted if it involves monetary expenditures. It is this transfer of money that has become more commonplace and has focused attention on the costs of child care in recent years.

Another powerful aspect of the debate over child care policy is the growing recognition that children are a valuable national resource. Declining fertility and a growing demand for skilled labor in the United States have drawn increasing attention to children. Pragmatic observers call attention to the fact that a smaller proportion of young workers will have to support a larger proportion of nonworking old people over the next several decades. They argue, therefore, that it is in society's self-interest to support the development and optimize the productivity of each child. There is evidence of growing public concern about whether children are receiving appropriate social and cognitive stimulation and about whether they are physically safe and emotionally nurtured. Despite the strong conviction of most Americans that government should not intervene in the family except in the most extreme circumstances, they also believe in high standards for childrearing. Although these de facto standards will not dictate child care policy, they may provide a basis for national action.

What public policy ought to be, of course, rests in part on assessments of the costs and benefits of quality child care and the costs of inadequate care. It also depends on consideration of who reaps the benefits and who should pay the costs. What level of quality is "good enough"? Who should make that judgment? Should childless individuals and families subsidize the costs of child care and childrearing? Should employers help bear these costs for their employees? To what extent and in what ways should government play a role in the care of children whose parents work outside the home and those whose parents remain at home?

CONTEXT OF THE DEBATE

The United States, unlike most Western industrialized countries, lacks a clear public child care policy. Issues concerning the care and rearing of children are complex, controversial, and they touch on closely held values. Virtually everyone holds definite views about how children should be nurtured. For this reason, any debate over child care policy inevitably raises a number of fundamental political, ideological, and developmental concerns.

For some people, the overriding concern is mothers' labor force participation regardless of the availability and affordability of child care. Despite broader social and economic trends over the past two decades, some regard mothers' working outside the home as a menacing threat to traditional family values. They argue that a mother's care for her children is preferable, that daily care by adults other than a child's own mother significantly risks the social and emotional well-being of the child and weakens mother-child attachment. Fears that "institutionalized" child care will lead to abnormal withdrawal and maladjustment have caused some people to completely oppose employment of mothers of young children and out-of-home care arrangements.

Others, however, believe that changing patterns of maternal employment are the inevitable consequence of broader social trends, including U.S. economic conditions, gender equity in the workplace, feminism, changing family forms and patterns of marriage, changing education and work patterns, and the declining standard of living in single-income families even if both parents are present. Public policy and programs, they suggest, should be neutral about whether or not mothers enter or remain in the paid labor force, but they should be aimed at optimizing the health and development of children whose mothers do work by ensuring accessibility to quality child care services. The costs of providing appropriate care for young children, they contend, are far less than the costs of ameliorating the predictable long-term negative consequences for children who are not well cared for.

Still others argue that public policies should be aimed at enhancing women's labor force participation and career opportunities. For mothers of young children, child care is an essential condition of employment. Particularly for low-income mothers, many of whom are the single heads of their households, the availability and affordability of child care may be a significant determinant of whether they seek job training and employment or receive support from Aid to Families with Dependent Children. As increasing numbers of middle-class mothers have entered the labor force over the past 15 years, concern about the employability and economic self-sufficiency of poor mothers has become more salient. There is growing recognition on the part of many who urge "workfare" (working as a condition of receiving welfare) that such change cannot occur without adequate child care support. Indeed, the intention that low-income women, including those with children, should acquire job skills and enter the work force was a powerful force in the passage of the 1988 Family Support Act.

In addition, there are many who argue that comprehensive early child development programs—including education, social services, medical and dental care, and nutrition—are needed to give children from low-income and otherwise disadvantaged backgrounds the kinds of social skills and pre-academic experiences that will adequately prepare them for early schooling. Programs such as Head Start, they contend, have been instrumental in fostering the early academic success of many poor and minority children, regardless of the labor force status of their mothers. Such initiatives represent fundamental investments in human capital that have far-reaching social and economic benefits to the individuals, their families, and society. In the context of the current policy debate, there are questions about whether Head Start–type programs can and should be adapted to meet the child care needs of low-income working parents and their children.

Widespread disagreement about the nature of the child care problem has created confusion and conflict over what to do about it. Political leaders, program planners, early childhood professionals, as well as parents themselves appear divided over what the primary goals should be: to provide safe and developmentally appropriate care for all children whose parents work outside the home; to enhance the employability and career opportunities of women, including women who are the mothers of young children; to provide incentives for mothers on welfare to seek education and job training and accept positions in the work force that will help them achieve economic self-sufficiency and reduce welfare dependency; or to provide comprehensive early childhood services for disadvantaged children to ameliorate the negative consequences of deprivation and to enhance their readiness for entry into regular elementary education programs.

Historically, the care and rearing of children was regarded as a private family affair, not as a public responsibility. Americans held as a fundamental tenet the right of parents to raise their children according to their own values and beliefs. Government involvement in the family domain consistently provoked controversy except when parents were clearly unable or unwilling to provide the necessary care, nurturing, and supervision. Child protection, not child care, was regarded as an appropriate public role. This view provided a meager basis for legitimizing child care and child development as an item on the public agenda, and it discouraged far-reaching designs, such as the defeated Comprehensive Child Development Act of 1972 (see Hayes, 1982). In 1971, despite congressional support, President Nixon rejected efforts to launch an ambitious federal child care program. In his veto message, he charged that the proposed program threatened the sanctity of the American family and promoted communal approaches to childrearing. Decisions concerning child care policy, especially at the federal level, were played out in highly value-laden debates about state intrusion in family life (Hayes, 1982; Phillips, 1988; Steiner, 1981). Child care has once again become a significant public concern in the late 1980s, and debate about the appropriate balance of public- and private-sector responsibility continues. Indeed, it now goes beyond the availability, affordability, and quality of care for children in out-of-home care and includes consideration of the appropriate public role in enhancing the economic feasibility of mothers staying at home to care for their own children.

The diversity of child care arrangements adds to the complexity of the issue and has worked against the development of a national policy. Child care is not a monolithic service system. It includes an array of professional providers and program types, such as child care centers, family day care and group homes, public and private nursery schools, prekindergartens and kindergartens, Head Start programs, and before and after school programs, as well as informal arrangements such as relative care, in-home babysitting, and nanny care. To some extent, this diversity reflects both the varied preferences and the limited options of parents in different social, economic, and cultural circumstances. Concern that a federal child care law would limit parents' flexibility and choice in making the arrangements they believe best meet their own needs and their children's has often been cited as an argument against support for categorical service programs.

Disagreement and division within the professional service-provider community has also hampered efforts to develop a coherent child care policy. Historically, child care traces its roots in two separate traditions, social welfare and early childhood education. Child care as a component of the social welfare system has been regarded as a custodial and protective service for children whose parents worked, attended school, or needed out-of-home care themselves. Beginning with the charitable day nurseries that were established during the last quarter of the nineteenth century for poor immigrant children, such programs have served poor and dependent children. In contrast, early childhood education programs have provided comprehensive services for young children with an emphasis on cognitive growth and the development of social competence. Nursery schools and kindergartens were often initiated at the urging of middle-class parents concerned about providing academic and social enrichment to their children. These child-centered institutions were predicated on a belief that early learning will result in later cognitive gains and better school performance. Other child-oriented programs drawing on and expanding this model, most notably Head Start, were initiated by the federal government in the late 1960s to provide similar preschool experiences for low-income children. The early childhood field has developed in this mixed tradition, and unfortunately little has changed to unite the divergent public images of care and education. Many knowledgeable observers argue that it has resulted in a dichotomy that, at best, hampers effective program planning, coordination, and advocacy, and at worst, creates a two-tiered system that segregates poor children from their middle- and upper middle-income peers (Cahan, 1988; Kagan, 1988; Phillips and Zigler, 1987).

The lack of a clear public child care policy in the United States also stems in part from the fact that child care is intimately related to a number of other social policy issues about which there has been disagreement: women's participation in the labor force, welfare and workfare, compensatory early childhood education, and the special protection of children at risk of developmental delay or damage. Unlike some other emotion-ally charged issues that have strongly united constituencies (such as gun control), the child care issue has had a crowded field of political players with divergent and often contradictory interests. These key individuals and organizations have rarely spoken with a unified voice. As a result, the child care issue has generally been characterized by vagueness. As Woolsey noted (1977:128): "To specify objectives clearly—what form of care, for which children, financed through which institutional structures, employing what sort of staff, would undermine team spirit and is thus avoided."

Moreover, despite the magnitude of the child care issue, there is a lack of detailed information about the costs, benefits, and feasibility of alternative policies and programs. Understanding of trends in mothers' labor force participation, the social and economic structure of families, and the developmental effects of supplemental care has advanced significantly in recent years, but knowledge of the effects and effectiveness of formal and informal, public- and private-sector responses to the child care needs of working families has not kept pace. In part, this is because the system of services is so diverse. Many kinds of child care arrangements are difficult to study, and systematic data at the national level are lacking. In part, inadequate empirical knowledge also reflects the fact that child care has not, until very recently, been an issue of national or even state-level priority. During much of the 1980s, federal research dollars were not allocated to national studies of child care. In addition, however, deeply conflicting concepts of the role of child care and its effects on children, parents, and society have made it difficult for researchers to frame questions and interpret data in ways that provide checks and balances over their own values and biases on these issues.

For many American families in the 1980s and for the foreseeable future, mothers' employment and their earnings are not a luxury. They are essential to maintain an adequate standard of living or simply to escape poverty. For many employers, women with children comprise a significant and growing component of their work force. Recruitment, retention, and productivity in many firms increasingly depend on the availability of supports and services to assist employees in managing their family responsibilities. In light of this reality, many observers conclude that, as a society, the United States may be ready to make the necessary adjustments to bring the separate worlds of work and family life closer together.

CROSS-NATIONAL CONTEXT

The United States was not alone in experiencing dramatic social changes during the past two decades. By the mid-1970s, labor force participation was the modal pattern for adult women in most Western industrialized countries. As in the United States, women's increasing role in the paid work force made the tensions between work and family life more visible and universal. Although the policy responses have varied among countries, cross-national researchers and advocates often point out that the United States "lags" behind the rest of the developed world in its efforts to address the child care needs of working parents and their children (Kamerman and Kahn, 1981; Scarr et al., 1988). Some countries have based their policies and programs on facilitating women's employment; others stress the child development focus of their initiatives. Regardless of their primary objectives, however, child care has come to be viewed as a public responsibility in many European countries, Canada, and Israel. These nations have invested heavily in child care, and they seem prepared to continue to do so. Despite a decade of fiscal constraints, none has curtailed its child care subsidies, and several are now moving to expand their commitments (Kamerman, 1988).

Almost all industrialized countries other than the United States have established maternity/parenting policies that permit working parents to remain at home for a period of time after childbirth to recover physically and to care for their infants. These policies allow parents (natural and adoptive) to take leave without forfeiting either their employment or their income. The primary differences among countries that have adopted maternity/parenting leave policies is the length of the leave (from 6 months to 3 years), the level of wage replacement (from 25 to 75 percent), and the inclusion of fathers as well as mothers (see Kamerman, 1988; Moss, 1988).

Almost all the European countries, as well as Canada and Israel, have acknowledged the importance and value of early childhood education for 3- to 5-year-olds and have taken steps to make these programs available to all children regardless of their mothers' work status. Primarily aimed at enhancing children's socialization and school readiness, these programs also provide child care services for the children of working mothers. Increasingly, these programs are universal, free, and publicly funded, and they are often publicly operated as well. Even though they are not mandatory, they are used by all children whose parents can secure a place. Even in those countries that have established child care systems separate from the educational system, early childhood programs stress age and developmentally appropriate programming for all children regardless of whether their mothers are in the paid labor force or not (Kamerman, 1988; Moss, 1988).

Among most industrialized nations, there is also growing recognition of the need to expand the supply of child care services for children under age 3. As in the United States, concern about the availability of infant care has been accompanied by concern about the quality and cost of such care.

The demand for child care arrangements for very young children appears to exceed the current supply in many countries, but only Sweden and Finland have announced any significant commitment to expand services. Indeed, there is a growing trend in Europe to extend parenting leaves in some form to encourage one parent to remain at home until a child is 18 months, 2 years, or even 3 years of age (Kahn and Kamerman, 1987). This type of policy, which began first in Hungary, has emerged in several Western European countries as well, including France, Finland, Germany, and Austria. The extraordinarily high costs of purchasing satisfactory out-of-home infant care, a deep-seated conviction that very young children are best cared for by their mothers, and an effort to encourage low-skilled women to stay out of the labor force in periods of high unemployment have all been cited as rationales for extending parental leaves as an alternative to expanding organized out-of-home infant care (Kamerman, 1988).

It is important to note that several countries have adopted these types of parental leave and child care initiatives as a complement to broader family policies that provide child or family cash allowances and in-kind benefits or both. These benefits are designed to supplement the income of low-income families with very young children so that married women with employed husbands can elect not to enter the labor force without suffering economic hardship. At the same time, however, the benefit is available to families in which both parents work or a single parent (usually the mother) is employed. In France and other countries that provide child and family allowances, there may be an implicit pronatalist objective, although, to date, parental leave has not been associated with noticeable increases in birth rates. Overall, family allowances have been successful in redistributing money from individuals and families with no children to those with children, and have benefited low-income families in a way that does not require mothers' employment (Kamerman and Kahn, 1981).

What are the implications of the experiences of other industrialized countries for the development of an appropriate social response to the growing need for child care supports and services in the United States? The United States is clearly different than many other countries because of its size and the social, economic, and cultural diversity that characterizes its population. The political process and social welfare traditions are also significantly different. The challenge for U.S. policy makers is to fashion policies and programs that fit the social and economic climate that values children and supports family life. Accordingly, regardless of whether there are direct lessons to be learned from the experiences of other countries, there are relevant points of comparison that can inform the continuing policy debate.

THE PANEL'S STUDY

This study by an interdisciplinary panel, established under the auspices of the National Research Council's Committee on Child Development Research and Public Policy, was supported by the U.S. Department of Health and Human Services, the Foundation on Child Development, and the Ford Foundation. Over a 2-year period, the panel, through a set of working groups, has sought to gather, integrate, and critically assess data concerning the implications of child care services for child development; regulations, standards, and enforcement; the child care market; and the child care delivery system as a basis for recommending future directions for policy and program development. Each working group commissioned background papers, conducted analyses of available data, and convened a workshop involving an array of researchers, policy makers, employers, providers, consumers, and child care advocates to gather information, identify significant issues, and highlight differing political, ideological, and intellectual perspectives. In addition, the panel gathered data to develop state profiles of the child care system.

Child care policies and programs, and the issues that underlie them, touch upon deeply felt values. No review of existing research will ultimately resolve disputes arising from different political and ideological orientations. Scientific data and analysis are only some of the relevant inputs in the policy-making process. Nevertheless, a broad interdisciplinary synthesis of what is known about the developmental implications of supplementary care and a dispassionate assessment of what is known about the supply of and demand for different types of services—and the factors affecting their costs, quality, and delivery—will serve several important purposes. First, it will help clarify the issues, sharpen awareness of crucial decision points, and focus attention on the tradeoffs and complementarities among different positions. Second, it will bring together, in one source, the many types of information that policy makers, service providers, and researchers regularly need. Third, it will identify gaps in existing knowledge. Finally, and perhaps most importantly, such a review of available evidence will provide a useful contribution to the continuing debate and it will suggest promising directions for future policy and program initiatives.

Objectives of Child Care:
A Framework for the Study

Any analysis of the child care issue in this country must recognize the different yet interrelated purposes of relevant policies and programs. At the most abstract and simplistic level, these objectives are threefold: to promote the health and well-being of children, to enhance the employability of their parents, and to improve the economic health and productivity of the nation at large.

Although these objectives overlap, they are not always congruent. Promoting the health and development of children requires that the care they receive protects their physical health and safety and stimulates their social and cognitive growth. The quality of the physical environment, the child care provider, and the interactions between children and their adult caregivers significantly influence children's health and developmental outcomes. Enhancing the employability of parents requires that child care services be available in convenient locations and during the hours when parents work or participate in education and job training programs. It also requires that these services be affordable so that parents who want or need to work outside their homes can bear the economic burden of doing so. Finally, improving the economic health and productivity of the nation requires a strong, reliable work force now and in the future, which means that public investments should enhance the productivity and economic self-sufficiency of U.S. citizens. It is in the interest of society as a whole for today's workers who are parents to have the ability to manage their employment and family responsibilities and for the children who are tomorrow's workers to be well-prepared for the roles they will be expected to fill.

In the absence of fiscal constraints, achieving quality in child care, improving access, and enhancing affordability, especially for low-income families, are not inconsistent or incompatible goals. However, in light of current economic realities in the United States, formulating child care policies will inevitably involve tradeoffs. Improving the quality of out-of-home child care services will raise the costs of care. Higher costs will have to be passed on to consumers in the form of higher fees or partially or wholly offset by employers or government. Without such subsidies, raising the price of care will likely make it unaffordable to many families, especially those with low incomes. Faced with a shrinking consumer market, many providers will be forced to decrease their services or to close their doors, thereby reducing the supply of child care services and making them inaccessible to families who are unable to pay. Accordingly, public policies to improve child care will have to balance concerns for the quality, accessibility, and affordability of programs and arrangements.

These three fundamental goals of child care policy provide a framework for examining the needs and interests of children, parents, and society as a whole; for relating knowledge concerning the health and developmental consequences of out-of-home child care to knowledge concerning the functioning of the current child care system; and for assessing the costs, effects, and feasibility of alternative proposals to improve it.

Structure of the Report

In the remaining nine chapters of this report, we review what is known about the costs and effects of child care quality, the nature of existing programs and arrangements, and their accessibility to children and families in different social and economic circumstances, as well as the affordability of different types and quality of care to families with different levels of income. These chapters are grouped in four sections. The second chapter of this introductory section summarizes trends in work, family structure and income, and child care and their implications for the supply and demand for alternative child care programs and arrangements.

Section II presents what is known about the relationship between child care and child development, which has implications for the way in which policies are structured and services are provided. Chapter 3 traces the development of child care research. Chapter 4 reviews what is known about the quality of care and children's developmental needs at different ages and stages of development. Chapter 5 highlights knowledge concerning the best practices for safeguarding children's health and safety and for the design and implementation of child care services.

Section III presents what is known about the current child care system in the United States and assesses current and proposed policies and programs in terms of their effects on quality, availability, and affordability. Chapter 6 examines the delivery system for child care and early childhood education programs. Chapter 7 focuses on public policies and programs at the federal and state levels, as well as employer policies and benefit programs. Chapter 8 addresses issues concerning the tradeoffs between quality, availability, and affordability and what is known about the extent to which each would be affected by proposed policies.

Finally, Section IV presents the panel's recommendations. Chapter 9 outlines directions for future data collection and research. Chapter 10 presents the panel's priorities for future policy and program development.

REFERENCES

Bureau of the Census
    1987   *Who's Minding the Kids?* Current Population Reports, Series P-70, No. 9. Washington D.C.: U.S. Department of Commerce.
Bureau of Labor Statistics
    1988   Marital and Family Characteristics of the Labor Force: March 1988. Unpublished data. U.S. Department of Labor, Washington, D.C.
Cahan, E.D.
    1988   Poverty and the Care and Education of the Preschool Child in the United States, 1820-1965. Paper prepared for the National Resource Center for Children in Poverty, Columbia University.

Hayes, C.D., ed.
  1982   *Making Policies for Children: A Study of the Federal Process.* Committee on
          Child Development Research and Public Policy, Commission on Behavioral and
          Social Sciences and Education, National Research Council. Washington, D.C.:
          National Academy Press.
Johnston, W.B., and A.H. Packer
  1987   *Workforce 2000: Work and Workers for the 21st Century.* HI-3796-RR. Indianapo-
          lis: Indiana Hudson Institute.
Kagan, L.
  1988   Current reforms in early childhood education: Are we addressing the issues?
          Young Children 43(2):27-32.
Kahn, A.J., and S.B. Kamerman
  1987   *Child Care: Facing the Hard Choices.* Dover, Mass.: Auburn House.
Kamerman, S.B.
  1988   Child Care Policies and Programs: An International Overview. Paper prepared
          for the Panel on Child Care Policy, Workshop on International Perspectives on
          Child Care, August 9, 1988. National Research Council, Washington, D.C.
Kamerman, S.B., and A.J. Kahn
  1981   *Child Care, Family Benefits, and Working Parents.* New York: Columbia University
          Press.
McCartney, K., S. Scarr, D. Phillips, and S. Grajek
  1985   Day care as intervention: Comparisons of varying quality programs. *Journal of
          Applied Developmental Psychology* 6:247-260.
Moss, P.
  1988   Comment From a European Community Perspective. Paper prepared for the
          Panel on Child Care Policy, Workshop on International Perspectives on Child
          Care, August 9, 1988. National Research Council, Washington, D.C.
Phillips, D.A.
  1988   With a Little Help: Children in Poverty and Child Care. Paper prepared
          for the Conference on Poverty and Children, Lawrence, Kansas, June 20-22.
          Department of Psychology, University of Virginia.
Phillips, D.A., and E. Zigler
  1987   The Checkered History of Child Care Regulation. In E. Rothkopf, ed., *Review
          of Research in Education* (Vol. 14). Washington, D.C.: American Education
          Research Association.
Ramey, C.T., D.M. Bryant, and T.M. Suarez
  1985   Preschool compensatory education and the modifiability of intelligence: A
          critical review. In D. Detterman, ed., *Current Topics in Human Intelligence.*
          Norwood, N.J.: Ablex.
Scarr, S., D.A. Phillips, and K. McCartney
  1988   Facts, Fantasies, and the Future of Child Care in America. Unpublished paper.
          Department of Psychology, University of Virginia.
Steiner, G.
  1981   *The Children's Cause.* Washington, D.C.: The Brookings Institution.
Woolsey, S.H.
  1977   Pied piper politics and the child-care debate. *Daedalus* 106(2):127-145.

2

Trends in Work, Family, and Child Care

The experience of growing up in the United States is likely to be different for children in the late 1980s and the 1990s than it was for children several decades ago. Although a significant proportion still live in a traditional two-parent family (including both natural and stepparent families) in which the father is the wage earner and the mother is the homemaker, most do not. Since 1970, significant social, demographic, and economic changes have altered the form and the function of many American families, with consequent effects on the daily experiences of children. More children than at any time since the Great Depression live in families with only one parent, usually their mothers. More children than ever before live in families in which their mothers, as well as their fathers, work outside the home. Children are more likely than any other age group in the United States to be living in poverty, and if they live in a single-parent family in which the mother is unemployed, they are almost certain to be poor. Moreover, today more children than ever before spend time in the care of adults other than their parents.

These dramatic trends have been the subject of popular media attention and scholarly inquiry, and they have significant implications for child care issues. Recent shifts in labor force participation—particularly among women with children—in family structure, in family income, and in the settings in which children are cared for and reared are clearly related, but there is little definitive evidence of causal links (Kamerman and Hayes, 1982). Undoubtedly, a complex variety of social, economic, cultural, and ideological factors contributed to these changes in American families, and they are not easily disentangled. Our purpose in describing these trends in not to imply direct cause-and-effect relationships, but instead to identify

16

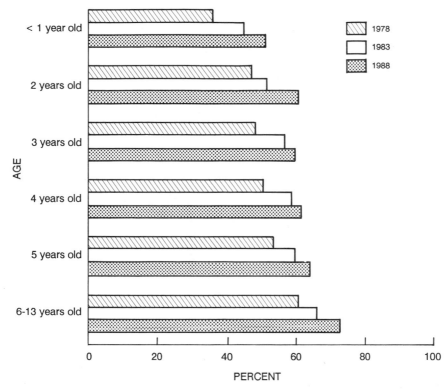

FIGURE 2-1 Labor Force Participation Rates of Mothers by Age of Youngest Child, 1978-1988. Source: Data from Bureau of Labor Statistics, *News*, September 7, 1988. Washington, D.C.: U.S. Department of Labor.

significant associated patterns of change in U.S. society that have created the current context for child care policy.

LABOR FORCE PARTICIPATION

The past decade and a half have witnessed an unprecedented increase in the labor force participation of mothers with young children. Between 1970 and 1988 the proportion of women with children under age 6 who were in the work force rose from 30 to 56 percent. Today approximately 10.5 million children under age 6, including 6.6 million infants and toddlers under age 3, have working mothers (see Figure 2-1). In 1987, for the first time, more than one-half of all mothers with babies 1 year old or younger (approximately 1.9 million) were working or looking for work (Bureau of Labor Statistics, 1988). Women with school-age children are even more likely to be working or looking for work outside their homes. In 1988, more

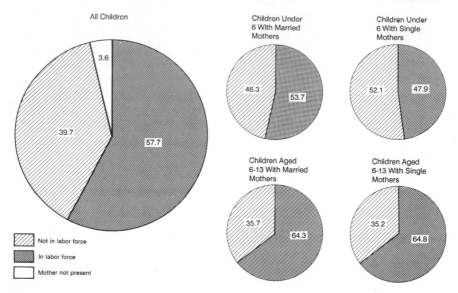

FIGURE 2-2   Children Under Age 13 by Mothers' Labor Force Participation and Marital Status, 1988. Source: Unpublished data from Bureau of Labor Statistics, Marital and Family Characteristics of the Labor Force: March 1988. U.S. Department of Labor, Washington, D.C.

than 72 percent of those whose youngest child was between the ages of 6 and 13 were in the labor force. Approximately 16 million children, or more than 60 percent of all children in this age group, had working mothers (see Figure 2-2), and the numbers are expected to rise in the 1990s (Bureau of Labor Statistics, 1988).

The most dramatic change in labor force participation has been among mothers in two-parent families: between 1970 and 1987 this proportion jumped from 39 percent to 61 percent. Indeed, just since 1980 the labor force participation rate for married mothers has increased by 13 percentage points. Although in another era many of these women would have left the labor force when they married or had children, they are now continuing to work. Those with school-age children are more likely to be employed than those with preschool-age children; however, the rate of increase in labor force participation of women has been greatest among those with very young children, an astounding 25 percent increase since 1980. Today, nearly 55 percent of married mothers with children under age 4 are in the work force (see Figure 2-3). Mothers who delay childbearing until after age 25 and those with 4 or more years of college education are more likely to be in the labor force than are younger mothers and those with less than 12 years of schooling (Bureau of the Census, 1988a).

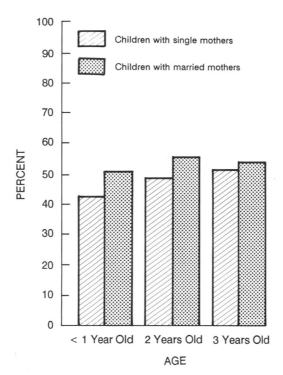

FIGURE 2-3   Children Under Age 4 With Working Mothers, by Child's Age and Mother's Marital Status, 1988. Source: Unpublished data from Bureau of Labor Statistics, Marital and Family Characteristics of the Labor Force: March 1988. U.S. Department of Labor, Washington, D.C.

Although there has been a notable decline in family size generally, the number of children in a family is closely linked to the extent to which mothers work. Among families with only one child, about three-quarters of the mothers in single- and two-parent families were employed in 1987. By contrast, less than one-half of mothers with four children, regardless of marital status, and only one-quarter of single mothers with five or more children were working outside their homes (Bureau of Labor Statistics, 1988). The causal relationship between family size and mothers' labor force participation is complex and difficult to sort out.

Historically, low-income and unmarried mothers have had higher labor force participation rates than other women (Grossman, 1978, 1983). Because these women constitute a greater proportion of black than white mothers, black women traditionally have been more likely to be working or looking for work outside their homes than white women. Although the past 15 years have seen a rise in the labor force participation of low-income and unmarried women, the most dramatic increase has been among middle-class married mothers, especially those with young children. As a result, the proportion of black children and white children under 6 with working mothers was approximately equal in the late 1980s (see Figure 2-4). If the current trend continues, the proportion of white children with working mothers is likely to exceed that of black children by the mid-1990s (Hofferth and Phillips, 1987). Among single-parent families, white mothers are far more likely than black or Hispanic mothers to be in the labor force and to be employed. For women who are single parents who are in the labor force, unemployment is particularly high among black women with preschool-age children: at 26.8 percent in 1988, their jobless rate was over twice as high as that of white mothers with preschoolers and more than three times that of Hispanic mothers with very young children (Bureau of Labor Statistics, 1988).

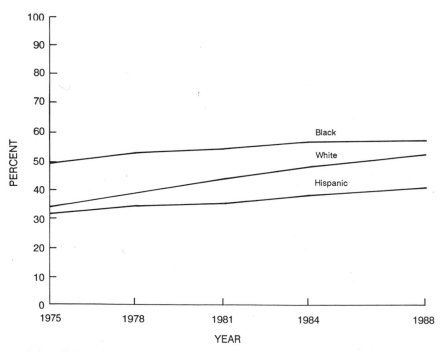

FIGURE 2-4 Children Under Age 6 With Mothers in the Labor Force, by Race or Ethnicity, 1975-1988. Source: Unpublished data from Bureau of Labor Statistics, Marital and Family Characteristics of the Labor Force: March 1975, March 1978, March 1981, March 1984, and March 1988. U.S. Department of Labor, Washington, D.C.

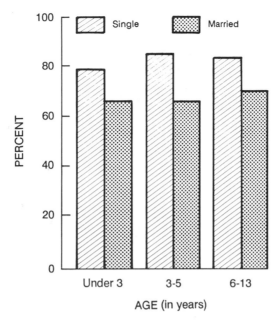

FIGURE 2-5 Full-Time Work of Employed Mothers, by Marital Status and Age of Child, 1988. Source: Unpublished data from Bureau of Labor Statistics, Marital and Family Characteristics of the Labor Force: March 1988. U.S. Department of Labor, Washington, D.C.

Of the total number of employed mothers with children under age 13 (about 16 million) in 1988, approximately 72 percent worked full time. A greater proportion of working mothers who are single parents than of mothers with husbands present were employed full time. In addition, women with school-age children were somewhat more likely to work full time than women with preschoolers. As indicated in Figure 2-5, it appears that marital status rather than the age of the child determines whether a mother who is employed works full or part time.

Although women's labor force participation in the United States has increased in almost every decade since 1890, the dramatic increase in the number of mothers working outside the home during the past decade represents a fundamental change in the day-to-day life of many American women. It is attributable in part to the baby-boom generation coming of age and in part to the dramatic increase during the 1960s and the 1970s in the proportion of women who chose (or were obliged) to seek paid work (Kamerman and Hayes, 1982; Reskin and Hartmann, 1986). This change is undoubtedly linked to broader changing social, cultural, ideological, and economic conditions in the United States. The economic growth of the

1960s and the mid-1980s, increases in the number of available jobs, growing legal pressures to assure women equal access to the workplace, the resurgence of the feminist movement, and the availability of effective contraception have all removed barriers to women entering the job market and remaining in it. Such factors as the declining income and job opportunities of young men (especially for those who lack skills) (Wilson, 1987) and the mechanization of the household are also undoubtedly relevant (O'Neill, 1980). Regardless of their motivation to go to work, however, mothers' employment has been accompanied by changes in family structure, and mothers' earnings have brought about changes in patterns of family income (Kamerman and Hayes, 1982).

FAMILY STRUCTURE

Between the Great Depression and 1970, approximately 90 percent of American children lived in families with both parents present. In 1987 only about 75 percent of children ages 6 to 17 and 81 percent of children under age 6 lived in two-parent families. Although the proportion of children living with neither parent has remained relatively stable throughout the twentieth century at 3 to 5 percent, the proportion living with only one parent has increased dramatically since 1970 (Bureau of the Census, 1988b; see also Figure 2-6). Most of these children live in families maintained by mothers; less than 3 percent live only with their fathers. While most white and Hispanic children live with two parents, more than one-half of all black children do not. Despite differences in the prevalence of children living with only one parent, rates of growth in the formation of mother-only families have been similar for whites, blacks, and Hispanics. During the 1960s and 1970s, the number of children living only with their mothers rose between 35 and 40 percent per decade for all groups (Garfinkel and McLanahan, 1986).

The increasing number of children in single-parent families reflects a rapidly rising divorce rate among adult mothers and a rising rate of childbearing among unmarried women, particularly among adolescents (Hayes, 1987; Kamerman and Hayes, 1982). Approximately one-half of all marriages in the United States now end in divorce, and approximately 40 percent of all white babies and almost 90 percent of all black babies of teenage mothers are born to unmarried women. Even when adolescent marriages occur, they are characterized by instability, and the children of teenage mothers can be expected to spend a substantial period of their early life in a single-parent family (Hayes, 1987). Perhaps the most striking feature of the growth of mother-only families over the past generation has been the difference between blacks and whites: for whites, the increase was

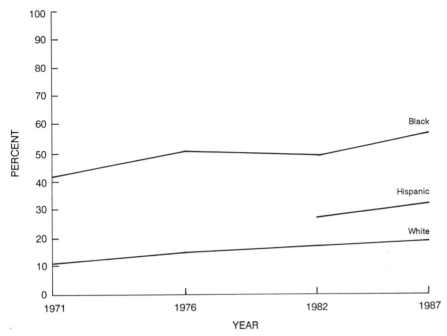

FIGURE 2-6 Children Under 18 Living With Only One Parent, by Race or Ethnicity, 1971-1987. Source: Data from Bureau of the Census, *Marital Status and Living Arrangements*, Current Population Reports, Series P-20: 1971, No. 225; 1976, No. 306; 1982, No. 380; 1987, No. 423. Washington, D.C.: U.S. Department of Commerce.

due primarily to marital dissolution; for blacks, the increase was due primarily to unmarried childbearing (Garfinkel and McLanahan, 1986). The combined result of these trends is that more than one-half of all white children and three-quarters of all black children born in the 1970s and 1980s are expected to live for some portion of their formative years with only one of their parents (Bureau of the Census, 1979; Cherlin, 1981; Hofferth, 1985).

Rising rates of single parenthood, like rising rates of mothers' labor force participation, are part and parcel of a series of complex social and economic trends in the United States during the past generation. The growth of the feminist movement, emerging educational and career opportunities for women, the rising age of marriage, the declining employment of young men, and declining standards of living for one-income families have all undoubtedly contributed. Changes in family structure, coupled with changes in mothers' employment, have significant implications for the economic well-being of American families and for the care and rearing of children.

FAMILY INCOME

The social and economic environment in which children are reared substantially influences their health and well-being, as well as their education, later employment, and family formation. The economic status of children usually reflects the economic status of their parents. Those who live in mother-only families and those who are black or Hispanic disproportionately live in families whose incomes are below the U.S. median family income and often below the poverty level.

The period since 1970 has been characterized by erratic changes in patterns of family income (Levy, 1987): real median income increased in the early 1970s, declined in the recessionary period from 1973 to 1975, and then rose in alternate years during the second half of the decade. Recession in the 1980-1982 period caused another more significant decline that has been balanced by growth during the economic recovery of the mid-1980s. The result of these ups and downs is that median family income for families with children in the United States—$30,721 in 1988—was less than 7 percent higher than the 1970 level after adjusting for inflation (Bureau of the Census, 1988c).

Throughout the decade of the 1970s, the average annual growth rate for family income was virtually zero; since 1980, the average annual growth rate has been only 0.8 percent per year. In comparison, the average annual growth rate was between 3.0 and 3.3 percent during the 1950s and 1960s. Even though more U.S. families have two earners, family income has remained fairly level. In addition to the slow economic growth of the past decade and a half, the increase in the number and proportion of mother-only families exerted a downward influence on overall median family income, as shown in Figure 2-7 (Bureau of the Census, 1987a). Significantly, however, although median income stagnated during the 1970s and increased only modestly during the early and mid-1980s, average family size also fell, creating a rise in per capita income levels within families.

These income trends have significant implications for the economic well-being of children. Many economists argue that, on average, U.S. children were better off in the 1980s than they were in the 1960s, primarily because of rising family incomes prior to 1973 and the smaller number of children in most American families (Easterlin, 1987; Haveman et al., 1988). A variety of economic measures—including children's mean and median per capita income, financial wealth, fungible wealth, and assets that yield access to services—support this conclusion (Haveman et al., 1988). Nevertheless, this economic profile of the average American child does not capture the growing disparity among families with children. Levels of income and assets among nonwhite children, though greater than in the 1960s, remain far below those of white children, and especially for minority

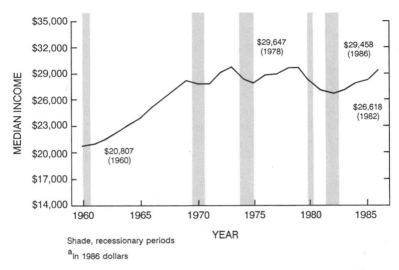

FIGURE 2-7   Median Family Income, 1960-1986. Source: Bureau of the Census (1987), *Money Income of Households, Families, and Persons in the United States: 1986.* Current Population Reports, Series P-60, No. 159. Washington D.C.: U.S. Department of Commerce.

children in single-parent families. Overall, the level of economic inequality as measured by income and assets has increased substantially over the past generation (Cherlin, 1988; Haveman et al., 1988; Minarik, 1988).

Children whose mothers were in the labor force were more economically secure in 1987 than children of nonworking mothers, regardless of race or family structure. As indicated in Figure 2-8, median income of married-couple families with children under 13 was $34,267 in 1988; the income of mother-only families with children under 13 was only $8,305. Although the overall earnings of white, black, and Hispanic mothers is not substantially different, levels of median income in two-parent, two-earner families vary significantly by race and Hispanic origin, largely because the average earnings of white husbands is greater than those of black or Hispanic husbands (Bureau of the Census, 1988c).

Although their earnings are significantly lower than their husbands' earnings, working women make a substantial contribution to family income. Between 1960 and 1986, the average proportion of income earned by the wife in a two-parent family rose from approximately 20 percent to 30 percent. Although this proportion varied significantly depending on work experience, occupation, education, and full- or part-time employment, wives who worked full time all year contributed on average almost 40 percent of family income in 1986; those who worked part time or who worked full

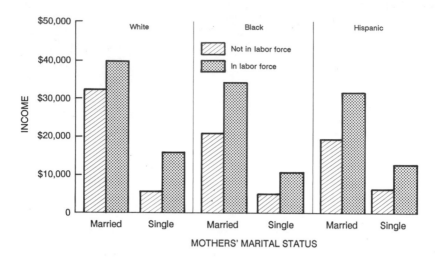

FIGURE 2-8   Median Family Income for Families With Children Under 13, by Employment and Marital Status of Mother, 1988. Source: Unpublished data from Bureau of Labor Statistics, Marital and Family Characteristics of the Labor Force: March 1988. U.S. Department of Labor, Washington, D.C.

time for 26 weeks or less contributed about 12.5 percent (Bureau of Labor Statistics, 1987).

Children in mother-only families in which the mother was working were better off than those in families in which the mother did not work. However, they were not on average as well off as children in two-parent families, regardless of the mother's labor force participation. In mother-only families in which the mother worked, the median family income in 1986 was less than one-half that of all married-couple families with children. Moreover, it was less than $4,000 above the poverty level for a nonfarm family of four ($11,203) (Bureau of the Census, 1987a). Although white children in mother-only families were marginally better off than black or Hispanic children in mother-only families, all children in mother-only families were significantly less economically well off than their peers in two-parent families.

Children in mother-only families in which the mother was not employed were generally living below the poverty level. The median income in such families was only $5,211 in 1988 (Bureau of the Census, 1988c). In 1986 nearly 12.7 million children, more than one of every five children under 18 in the United States, lived in families with an income below the official poverty level (Bureau of the Census, 1987b). The poverty rate for children, although lower in 1988 than in 1960, had increased significantly from 1970 to 1988. As might be expected, children in mother-only families were significantly more likely to be poor than those in two-parent families—59 percent compared with 10 percent. Black or Hispanic children are more likely to live in poverty than are white children: more than 45 percent of black children under 18 and more than 39 percent of Hispanic children were living in poverty in 1987, compared with less than 15 percent of white children. Among black or Hispanic children in mother-only families, the poverty rates are even higher: more than 68 percent of black children and 70 percent of Hispanic children, compared with 46 percent of white children, were poor in 1987 (Bureau of the Census, 1988c; see also Figure 2-9). This difference is largely attributable to the higher rates of labor force participation among white mothers who are the heads of their households.

In the United States in the late 1980s, children were the poorest group. In contrast to the late 1960s when the majority of poor children lived in two-parent families with an employed head, today more than one-half of all poor children live in mother-only families, and in most of these families the mother is not employed.

Children in two-parent families benefit from higher levels of family income. Whether children live in mother-only families or two-parent families, however, they are materially better off if their mothers are working than if they are not (Kamerman and Hayes, 1982). In mother-only families, women's employment frequently means the difference between

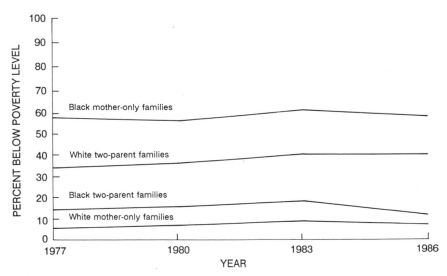

FIGURE 2-9 Poverty Status of Families With Children Under 18, by Race and Family Structure, 1977-1986. Source: Data from Bureau of the Census (1987), *Poverty in the United States: 1986.* Current Population Reports, Series P-60, No. 160. Washington, D.C.: U.S. Department of Commerce.

poverty and an adequate existence and between independence and dependence on public assistance. For the most part, mother-headed families are able to survive on their own economically only if the mother has regular employment (Masnick and Bane, 1980).

THE CARE OF CHILDREN

As more mothers have decided to enter or remain in the labor force since 1970, families have increasingly come to rely on adults outside the immediate family to care for their children. Approximately two-thirds of children under age 5 whose mothers work receive care for some portion of time each week from individuals other than their parents, grandparents, and siblings (or themselves) (Bureau of the Census, 1987c). In 1985, the most recent year for which these data are available, approximately 8 percent of mothers of young children who worked also managed the full-time care of their children. Typically these women were employed as private household workers or as child care workers, positions that allowed them to work and care for their children simultaneously. About 16 percent of all children under school age were cared for by their fathers. Father care is especially common in two-parent families where parents work different shifts or have otherwise alternating work schedules. Grandparents and other relatives cared for 24 percent of children under age 5 in the child's home or in the relative's home. And approximately 6 percent were cared for in their own homes by a nonrelative. The rest, more than 46 percent of the children in this age group with working mothers, were cared for outside their own home, either in the home of a nonrelative caregiver or in an organized child care facility. The use of organized child care facilities has increased substantially since the late 1970s. In 1985, as shown in Figure 2-10, 24 percent of all preschool children (approximately 1.9 million) received their primary care in day care centers, nurseries, preschools, or kindergartens (Bureau of the Census, 1987c).

Not surprisingly, of the 18.5 million grade-school-age children (5 to 14 years old) whose mothers were employed, about 75 percent were either in kindergarten or grade school most of the hours that their mothers were at work, and the school was their primary caretaker. Among school-age children who were not in school most of the hours that their mothers work, fathers were the principal caregiver. Many married parents who manage this kind of arrangement work different shifts (Presser, 1988a; Presser and Cain, 1983). In 1985 the most common arrangement for the children of full-time working mothers was care in the child's own home (42 percent) or in another home (24 percent) by a relative or nonrelative. Only about 7 percent of children in this age group were in organized child care programs.

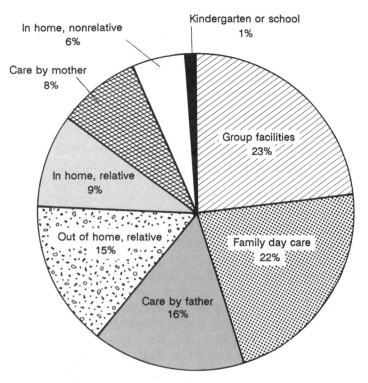

FIGURE 2-10 Primary Child Care Arrangements Used by Employed Mothers With Children Under Age 5, Winter 1984-1985. Source: Data from Bureau of the Census (1987) *Who's Minding the Kids?* Current Population Reports, Series P-70, No. 9. Washington, D.C.: U.S. Department of Commerce.

Children in self-care are frequently referred to as latchkey children (because many of them wear their house keys around their necks). Estimates of the number of latchkey children have ranged from a low of 1.4 million as measured by the Bureau of the Census in the mid-1980s to a high of 15 million as measured by Zigler (1983). For 1984-1985, the most recent year for which data are available, the Survey of Income and Program Participation (SIPP) found that an estimated 2.1 million school-age children were in self-care, approximately 18 percent of those with working mothers. Older children were far more likely than younger ones to care for themselves during out-of-school hours—approximately 25 percent of 11- to 13-year-olds compared to only 5 percent of 5- to 7-year-olds (Bureau of the Census, 1987c; Cain and Hofferth, 1987). The number of hours per week that children were reported to be in self-care varied from 1 to 20 or more. Children of full-time working mothers were more likely than those of part-time working mothers to be in self-care, 21 percent compared with 12 percent (Bureau of the Census, 1987c; Cain and Hofferth, 1987). Presumably, this difference is because many mothers who work part time arrange their schedules to be at home with their children during nonschool hours.

Considerably different patterns of child care use can be found among mothers according to their weekly work schedule. The demands for child care services of families with full-time working mothers cannot normally be met by other household members or relatives who have job and career commitments requiring them to work full time themselves. As a result, full-time working mothers tend to place their preschool children in child care outside the child's own home and with nonrelatives rather than with family members or relatives in the child's home. Preschoolers of full-time working mothers in 1985 were less likely to be cared for at home than were children of part-time working mothers, 24 percent compared with 42 percent. Child care by fathers was less frequent in families with mothers who worked full time than in those with mothers who worked part time, 11 percent compared with 24 percent (Bureau of the Census, 1987c).

It is not only how many hours but also *which* hours mothers (and fathers) are employed that affect the type of child care arrangement they use, including father care. More than 12 percent of full-time employed married mothers and nearly 22 percent of part-time employed married mothers work other than a regular day schedule. Father care is very prevalent under these conditions, accounting for nearly 39 percent of children whose mothers are employed evenings or nights full time, and more than 66 percent of children whose mothers are employed evenings or nights part time (Presser, 1986). Similarly, when fathers work evenings or nights and mothers work days, father care is especially high (Presser, 1988a).

The principal difference between the child care arrangements used by married and unmarried mothers with preschool children is the availability of the father to serve as caregiver (typically by working different hours). Only about 2 percent of young children of unmarried mothers are cared for by their fathers while their mothers work, compared with about 19 percent of children of married mothers. Even though children of unmarried mothers are less frequently cared for by their fathers, the proportion who are cared for in their own home is not substantially different than for children of married mothers. Grandparents appear to play a larger role in the care of preschool age children of unmarried mothers than of married mothers, about 16 percent compared with 3 percent (Bureau of the Census, 1987c). About one-third of grandmothers who provide child care are otherwise employed. This situation is about twice as common among unmarried as among married mothers (Presser, 1988b).

As dramatically increasing numbers of mothers of infants and toddlers have chosen to work outside the home, the care of their very young children has become a special concern. SIPP data describing the child care arrangements used by families with children under age 3 show that care by relatives is most common. As shown in Table 2-1, among families with babies less than 1 year old in 1985, more than 18 percent relied on care by the child's father; grandparents or other relatives cared for approximately 28 percent of infants with working mothers. Seventy-eight percent of infants were cared for either in their own homes or in another home; only about 14 percent were cared for in organized child care facilities. However, it is notable that this latter proportion represents a significant increase over the 5 percent of infants who were reported to be in organized child care facilities in 1982 (Bureau of the Census, 1987c).

The use of organized child care facilities for preschool children has increased significantly since these data were first collected by the Bureau of the Census in 1958. In 1985, 25 percent of working mothers who had a child under age 5 used a child care center, nursery, preschool, or kindergarten as their primary form of care while they worked, compared with 13 percent in 1977. Given the dramatic rise in the number of working mothers with young children during this period, it is important to note that the number as well as the proportion of preschool children attending organized child care programs increased substantially. In 1985, approximately 1.9 million children were in this form of care, compared with 871,000 in 1977 (Bureau of the Census, 1987c).

The growing use of organized child care facilities during the 1970s and 1980s must be viewed in the broader context of the rising enrollment among preschool-age children in programs providing educational enrichment. Whether or not their mothers work, increasing numbers of 3- and 4-year-old children are spending some portion of their day or week in a group program intended to supplement their home experience. An estimated 29 percent of 3-year-olds and 49 percent of 4-year-olds were enrolled in preschool programs (distinct from child care centers) in 1986, compared with only 5 percent and 16 percent, respectively, in 1965 (U.S. Department of Education, 1986). Although the young children of working mothers are more likely than the children of nonworking mothers to be enrolled in preschool enrichment programs, enrollment among all children in this age group has grown.

The characteristics of children and their families help determine the form of care that parents will choose. Black children under age 5 are more likely than white or Hispanic children to be in organized child care facilities and significantly more likely to be in child care centers than in nursery or preschool programs. Women who are single parents are more likely to choose child care centers rather than nursery or preschool programs, if

TABLE 2-1 Primary Child Care Arrangements Used by Mothers of Children Under 15, by Age of Child, 1984-1985 (numbers in thousands)

Type of Child Care Arrangement	Total		Under 1 Year		1 and 2 Years		3 and 4 Years		5 to 14 Years	
	Number	Percent	Number	Percent	Number	Percent	Number	Percent	Number	Percent
Number of children	26,455	100.0	1,385	100.0	3,267	100.0	3,516	100.0	18,287	100.0
Care in child's home	2,699	17.8	516	37.3	1,068	32.7	950	27.0	2,164	11.8
By father	2,496	9.4	252	18.2	528	16.2	502	14.3	1,214	6.6
By grandparent	712	2.7	102	7.4	208	6.4	157	4.5	244	1.3
By other relative	804	3.0	44	3.2	147	4.5	115	3.3	498	2.7
By nonrelative	687	2.6	118	8.5	185	5.7	176	5.0	208	1.1
Care in another home	3,801	14.4	563	40.6	1,368	41.9	1,089	31.0	782	4.3
By grandparent	1,138	4.3	174	12.6	361	11.0	298	8.5	305	1.7
By other relative	467	1.8	70	5.1	130	4.0	167	4.7	100	0.5
By nonrelative	2,196	8.3	319	23.0	877	26.8	624	17.7	377	2.1
Organized child care facilities	2,411	9.1	195	14.1	563	17.2	1,131	32.2	523	2.8
Day care or group care center	1,440	5.4	116	8.4	401	12.3	625	17.8	298	1.6
Nursery school or preschool	971	3.7	79	5.7	162	5.0	506	14.4	225	1.2
Kindergarten or grade school	13,815	52.2	--	--	--	--	61	1.7	13,753	75.2
Child cares for self	488	1.8	--	--	--	--	--	--	488	2.7
Parent cares for child[a]	1,245	4.7	112	8.1	267	8.2	285	8.1	581	3.2

[a]Includes mothers working at home or away from home.

Source: Data from Bureau of the Census (1987c).

they place their children in organized out-of-home facilities. Mothers with 4 or more years of college education and those holding managerial or professional positions appear to prefer organized child care programs to more informal arrangements in their own home or in another home. Mothers with less than a high school education and those in service jobs are much less likely to choose organized child care facilities. In part this reflects the fact that women in service positions are more likely to work evening or night shifts and therefore may be more able to rely on husbands or other relatives as caretakers. In addition, the lower annual earnings of women in service positions may affect their ability to pay for organized child care services (Bureau of the Census, 1987c).

Parents' use of child care arrangements often becomes more extensive and complicated when there is more than one child in the family. Supplementing school and preschool programs with one or more other forms of organized or informal child care services appears to be commonplace in many families. Included among these arrangements may be in-home care by a relative or a nonrelative; out-of-home care by relatives, friends, neighbors, or other paid caretakers; and special arrangements when a usual routine is disrupted. Children under compulsory school age are especially likely to experience multiple forms of care by multiple caretakers during the course of a normal week if their parent(s) are employed. A recent survey of child care use in three cities showed that approximately one-quarter of preschool-age children are cared for in more than one arrangement. For the large majority, secondary arrangements are care by relatives or informal arrangements with friends, neighbors, or other nonrelatives. Secondary arrangements are more likely than primary child care arrangements to be located in the child's own home. However, children whose primary arrangement is care by relatives are less likely to have a secondary arrangement (Kisker et al., 1988). Although little is known about the variations in "packaging of care arrangements" for families in different social and economic circumstances, it appears to be becoming more prevalent in many families (Kamerman and Hayes, 1982).

The extent to which parents' use of different types of child care arrangements reflects their preferences or their range of options is difficult to determine. Surveys that have questioned parents about their satisfaction with current arrangements show that the majority are satisfied and do not desire a change (Kisker et al., 1988; Travers et al., 1982). Parents indicate that convenience, location, and cost are primary determinants of these selections. However, expressed preferences for center-based care seem to be increasing among mothers of children at all ages. The shift appears to be related, at least in part, to parents' desire to encourage and enhance their children's learning experiences. Available evidence suggests that mothers who prefer center care base their preference on the belief that children learn more in more educational settings (Atkinson, 1987; Kisker et al., 1988).

In contrast to the general population, recipients of Aid to Families with Dependent Children (AFDC) express stronger preferences for family day care (by nonrelatives) than child care centers. In one recent study, in-home care by a nonrelative was rated most satisfactory by low-income mothers receiving AFDC, even though they perceived their children to be less happy in family day care than in center care (Sonenstein and Wolf, 1988). The reasons underlying these stated preferences are not clearly understood. As we discuss in Chapter 8, however, there is some evidence to suggest that supply constraints, which exist for everyone, are particularly strong for many low-income families: the cost of center care limits its accessibility. Poor single parents are even more constrained in their choices. They frequently face not only the high (to them) cost of center care but the unavailability of a spouse with whom to share child care responsibilities. Furthermore, the option for low-income parents to rely on other relatives has also diminished as grandmothers, aunts, and extended family members have increased their own labor force participation in recent years (Kisker et al., 1988; Sonenstein and Wolf, 1988).

IMPLICATIONS OF CHILD CARE FOR WOMEN'S EMPLOYMENT AND FERTILITY

Changing patterns of women's employment and family structure have profoundly influenced the use of supplemental child care services in the United States. At the same time, the availability and affordability of child care services appear to have significant effects on mothers' decisions to enter, reenter, or remain in the labor force, with consequent effects on decisions concerning fertility. A growing body of research shows that the ease with which women can arrange for the care of their children, their satisfaction with the arrangement, the amount they must pay, as well as their wages and job satisfaction affect a calculation of their gains from employment (Leibowitz and Waite, 1988; Sonenstein and Wolf, 1988).

An important factor affecting a mother's decision to work is the amount she must pay for child care relative to what she can earn. For many employed mothers, the cost of child care is a major household budget item. In 1985, the national median weekly child care expenditure was $38 per child per week overall, and it was $42 per week for preschool-age children (Bureau of the Census, 1987c). However, the amount families pay for child care varies dramatically by the type of care they choose and the geographic area in which they live.

The lack of child care clearly keeps some women from working at all and inhibits their ability to pursue education or job training. Poorly educated women with little work experience earn low wages, and unless they can find subsidized, affordable, or free child care, employment may not make economic sense to them. Some analysts have argued that this constraint explains why employment rates among high school dropouts and young unmarried mothers have actually declined over the past decade while employment rates for better educated women have jumped (O'Connell and Bloom, 1987; Sonenstein and Wolf, 1988). If true, this phenomenon has both short- and long-term consequences: women who remain out of the labor force fail to develop job skills through work experience and on-the-job training. They thus forgo the growth in earnings that accompanies experience, and over time, their training and skills depreciate from lack of use (Mincer and Ofek, 1982).

Child care is not only a constraint on entry into employment for low-income women, it can also constrain sustained employment. In order for a mother, especially a single parent, to maintain consistent labor force participation, her child care arrangements must be dependable. In a 1985 Current Population Survey sample, 6 percent of employed mothers reported that they had lost time from work in the past month because of the failure of child care arrangements. Over a year's time, the proportion of women reporting lost time would be substantially higher (Bureau of the Census, 1987c; Sonenstein and Wolf, 1988).

Among mothers who have some discretion about when and how much they work outside the home, the availability and affordability of "adequate child care" also affect decisions to seek employment. A mother's labor force participation necessarily reduces her time and energy for home production activities, including child care, transportation, housework, and shopping. Earnings may be used to replace these functions. Lazaer and Michael (1980) estimated that because of lost home production and the expenses directly related to employment, two-parent families with an employed mother require 25 to 30 percent more income to maintain the same standard of living as a comparable family in which the mother works only at home. Child care is the most essential home production activity, and it is most expensive and time-consuming when children are very young. As children get older, they require less parental time, thus shifting the costs and benefits of mothers' employment (Oppenheimer, 1974). The clear implication is that in families in which a mother's income is not essential to basic subsistence, her decision concerning whether to work outside the home will be significantly influenced by the net economic gain from her earnings. Because many women work in occupations that pay relatively low wages (Reskin and Hartmann, 1986), the incentive to work will depend heavily on their husbands' income. The more their husbands earn, the less likely that women with young children will enter, reenter, or remain in the labor force unless they can find "adequate child care at an acceptable price" (Leibowitz and Waite, 1988).

That the availability and affordability of child care pose constraints on women's employment is supported in national survey data and a variety of smaller studies. In 1982, 26 percent of mothers of preschool children who were not in the labor force reported that they would be looking for work if they could find satisfactory child care, and 16 percent of employed mothers reported that they were constrained in their work hours by the availability of satisfactory child care. Substantially more unmarried mothers (45 percent) than married mothers (22 percent) indicated that they would work if child care were available at a reasonable cost. Women with family incomes over $25,000 were least likely to express such intentions (O'Connell and Rogers, 1983). More recent data from the youth cohort of the National Longitudinal Survey of Labor Market Experience, which oversamples low-income and minority women, confirms findings from the Current Population Survey (Leibowitz and Waite, 1988). Similarly, a recent GAO study of AFDC recipients found that 60 percent of the respondents reported that a lack of child care prevented them from participating in current work programs, although only 17 percent said it was a very significant barrier (U.S. General Accounting Office, 1987). Confirmatory evidence also comes from several smaller studies that indicate that some women with low earnings find employment profitable only because they have access to free or very low-cost care from relatives (Leibowitz et al., 1988) and that the cost and availability of child care services constrain the number of hours they work (Mason, 1987).

Women who find it difficult or costly to combine work and motherhood may have to choose between them in some sense. Traditionally, most women who chose motherhood stayed out of the labor force when they had young children. More recently, a significant and rapidly growing proportion of women are continuing to work after marriage and after giving birth. Employed women have historically had smaller families than women who work only in the home. Scholars have debated whether low fertility permits employment or whether employment leads to low fertility. Research suggests that, in the long term, women tailor their childbearing to their work and career goals, but in the short run the demands of a new baby reduce labor supply (Cramer, 1980; Hout, 1978; Leibowitz et al., 1988; Waite and Stolzenberg, 1976).

Both fertility and expected family size decrease with increasing commitment to the labor force. Among women aged 18 to 34, the fertility rate for those who were employed in 1987 was 890 per 1,000 women, compared with 1,673 per 1,000 for those who were not in the labor force. Similarly, the lifetime birth expectation for working women was 1,967 per 1,000 women, compared with 2,320 per 1,000 for women who were not in the labor force. Even more striking is the difference in the proportion of women who expect to remain childless: 11.3 percent of employed women and 5.7 percent of women who were not in the labor force (Bureau of the Census, 1988b). Presser and Baldwin (1980) found that women with children under age 5 who reported that they were constrained in work by child care were generally more likely to expect to have no more children than were women of comparable employment status who reported no child care constraints. This finding suggests that some women who feel constrained in their employment choices by lack of child care (or lack of affordable child care) resolve this dilemma by having fewer children (Leibowitz and Waite, 1988). Other research supports this contention, but the effects appear to be quite modest (Blau and Robins, 1986; Mason, 1987). To the extent that child care costs and availability affect the timing of childbearing or women's completed family size, these constraints could affect later economic well-being as well. Hofferth (1984), for example, found that women who waited until at least age 30 to begin having children and those with smaller families were better off at retirement age than those who had a first birth earlier and those with relatively large families.

Families in which the mother is employed benefit directly from her earnings. The income she generates contributes directly to her own support and that of her family. As discussed above, that income is essential to basic subsistence and economic independence in many mother-only families. In two-parent families it may be used to provide enrichment for children through enhanced educational opportunities. In addition, mothers' employment often improves families' access to health care, if health insurance benefits are provided or subsidized by the employer (Leibowitz and Waite, 1988). Moreover, women themselves gain in long-term earning power from continuous employment while their children are young. Work experience, together with job tenure, is an important determinant of current earnings. Mothers who enter the work force or remain employed after childbearing increase their current income, and they enhance their opportunities to earn more in the future. To the extent that child care poses a constraint on women's employment, it decreases their long-term earnings potential and may, in the short term, threaten the economic well-being of their families.

FUTURE TRENDS

The dramatic demographic and economic trends of the 1970s and the 1980s seem likely to continue into the 1990s. Although specific patterns and rates of change in mothers' labor force participation, children growing up in single-parent families, and children who will require care outside their own homes are dependent on a variety of factors, there is general

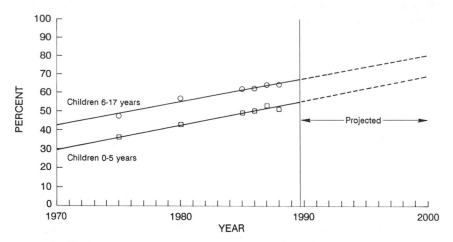

FIGURE 2-11   Children With Mothers in the Labor Force, 1970-2000. Source: Projections prepared by Kristin Moore, Child Trends, Inc. Data from House Select Committee on Children, Youth, and Families, *U.S. Children and Their Families: Current Conditions and Recent Trends* (1989), based on data from Bureau of Labor Statistics, Current Population Survey, March 1988.

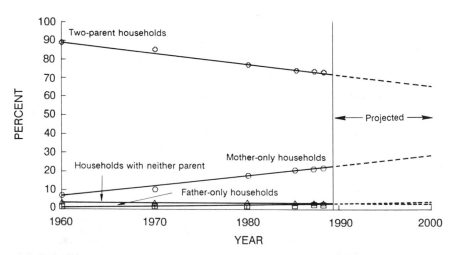

FIGURE 2-12   Composition of Households With Children Under 18, 1960-2000. Source: Projections prepared by Kristin Moore, Child Trends, Inc. Data from House Select Committee on Children, Youth, and Families (1989), *U.S. Children and Their Families: Current Conditions and Recent Trends*, based on Bureau of Labor Statistics, Current Population Survey, March 1988.

agreement that the trends of the past decade and a half will not be reversed in the near future.

Straight-line projections of the proportion of children with mothers in the labor force suggest that by 2000 approximately 80 percent of school-age children and 70 percent of preschool-age children will have mothers who are working or looking for work outside their homes (see Figure 2-11). Demographers also project that if current patterns continue, one-third of all U.S. children will live in single-parent families by 2000 (see Figure 2-12). Among minority children, the proportions are likely to be considerably larger. One can predict with some certainty that many of these children will require care from adults other than their parents. The growing proportion of children living with only one parent, usually their mothers, coupled with the rising labor force participation of extended family members who were once available to provide child care, suggests that the demand for out-of-home child care services will continue to increase well into the 1990s.

REFERENCES

Atkinson, A.M.
    1987   A comparison of mothers' and providers' preference and evaluations of day care services. *Child and Youth Care Quarterly* 16(1):35-47.
Blau, D.M., and P.K. Robins
    1986   Fertility, Employment and Child Care Costs: A Dynamic Analysis. Paper presented at meetings of the Population Association of America, San Francisco.
Bureau of the Census
    1979   *Divorce, Child Custody, and Child Support.* Current Population Reports, Series P-23, No. 84. Washington, D.C.: U.S. Department of Commerce.
    1987a   *Money Income of Households, Families, and Persons in the United States: 1986.* Current Population Reports, Series P-60, No. 159. Washington, D.C.: U.S. Department of Commerce.
    1987b   *Poverty in the United States, 1986.* Current Population Reports, Series P-60, No. 160. Washington, D.C.: U.S. Department of Commerce.
    1987c   *Who's Minding the Kids?* Current Population Reports, Series P-70, No. 9. Washington D.C.: U.S. Department of Commerce.
    1988a   *Fertility of American Women: June 1987.* Current Population Reports, Series P-20, No. 427. Washington D.C.: U.S. Department of Commerce.
    1988b   *Marital Status and Living Arrangements: March 1987.* Current Population Reports, Series P-20, No. 423. Washington, D.C.: U.S. Department of Commerce.
    1988c   *Money Income and Poverty Status in the United States: 1987.* Current Population Reports, Series P-60, No. 161. Washington, D.C.: U.S. Department of Commerce.
Bureau of Labor Statistics
    1987   Marital and Family Characteristics of the Labor Force: March 1987. Unpublished data. U.S. Department of Labor, Washington, D.C.
    1988   Marital and Family Characteristics of the Labor Force: March 1988. Unpublished data. U.S. Department of Labor, Washington, D.C.

Cain, V., and S.L. Hofferth
    1987   Parental Choice of Self Care for School-Age Children. Paper presented at the
            annual meeting of the Population Association of America, Chicago.
Cherlin, A.J.
    1981   *Marriage, Divorce, Remarriage.* Cambridge, Mass.: Harvard University Press.
    1988   The family. In I. Sawhill, ed., *Challenge to Leadership: Economic and Social
            Issues for the Next Decade.* Washington, D.C.: The Urban Institute.
Cramer, J.C.
    1980   Fertility and female employment: Problems of causal direction. *American
            Sociological Review* 45:167-190.
Easterlin, R.A.
    1987   Struggle for relative economic status. In R.A. Easterlin, ed., *Birth and Fortune:
            The Impact of Numbers on Personal Welfare,* 2nd ed. Chicago, Ill.: University of
            Chicago Press.
Garfinkel, I., and S.S. McLanahan
    1986   *Single Mothers and Their Children: A New American Dilemma.* Washington,
            D.C.: The Urban Institute.
Grossman, A.
    1978   *Children of Working Mothers, March 1977.* Special Labor Force Report 217,
            Bureau of Labor Statistics. Washington, D.C.: U.S. Department of Labor.
    1983   *Children of Working Mothers, March 1982.* Special Labor Force Report, Bureau
            of Labor Statistics. Washington, D.C.: U.S. Department of Labor.
Haveman, R., B.L. Wolfe, R.E. Finnie, and E.N. Wolff
    1988   Disparities in the well-being among U.S. children over two decades: 1962-1983.
            In J. Palmer, T. Smeeding, and B. Torrey, eds., *The Vulnerable.* Washington
            D.C.: The Urban Institute.
Hayes, C.D., ed.
    1987   *Risking the Future: Adolescent Sexuality, Pregnancy, and Childbearing.* Panel
            on Adolescent Pregnancy and Childbearing, Committee on Child Development
            Research and Public Policy, Commission on Behavioral and Social Sciences and
            Education, National Research Council. Washington, D.C.: National Academy
            Press.
Hofferth, S.L.
    1984   Long-term economic consequences for women of delayed childbearing and
            reduced family size. *Demography* 21(2):141-155.
    1985   Updating children's life course. *Journal of Marriage and the Family* 47:93-116.
Hofferth, S.L., and D.A. Phillips
    1987   Child care in the United States: 1970-1995. *Journal of Marriage and the Family*
            49:559-571.
Hout, M.
    1978   The determinants of marital fertility in the U.S., 1968-1970: Inferences from a
            dynamic model. *Demography* 15:139-160.
Kamerman, S.B., and C.D. Hayes, eds.
    1982   *Families That Work: Children in a Changing World.* Panel on Work, Family,
            and Community, Committee on Child Development Research and Public Policy,
            Commission on Behavioral and Social Sciences and Education, National Research
            Council. Washington, D.C.: National Academy Press.
Kisker, E.E., R. Maynard, A. Gordon, and M. Strain
    1988   The Child Care Challenge: What Parents Need and What Is Available in
            Three Metropolitan Areas. Draft report. Mathematica Policy Research, Inc.,
            Princeton, N.J.

Lazaer, E.P., and R.T. Michael
    1980   Real income equivalents among one-earner and two-earner families. *American Economics Review* 70(2):203-208.
Leibowitz, A., and L.J. Waite
    1988   The Consequences for Women of the Availability and Affordability of Child Care. Paper prepared for the Panel on Child Care Policy.
Leibowitz, A., L.J. Waite, and C. Witsberger
    1988   Child care for preschoolers: Differences by child's age. *Demography* 25(2):205-220.
Levy, F.
    1987   *Dollars and Dreams: The Changing American Income Distribution.* New York: Russell Sage Foundation.
Masnick, G., and M.J. Bane
    1980   *The Nation's Families: 1960-1990.* Boston: Auburn House.
Mason, K.O.
    1987   The Perceived Impact of Child Care Costs on Women's Labor Supply and Fertility. Population Studies Center Research Report No. 87-110, University of Michigan.
Minarik, J.L.
    1988   Family incomes. In I. Sawhill, ed., *Challenge to Leadership: Economic and Social Issues for the Next Decade.* Washington, D.C.: The Urban Institute.
Mincer, J., and H. Ofek
    1982   Interrupted work careers. *Journal of Human Resources* 17:3-24.
O'Connell, M., and D.E. Bloom
    1987   *Juggling Jobs and Babies: America's Child Care Challenge.* Population Trends and Public Policy Series, No. 12. Washington, D.C.: Population Reference Bureau, Inc.
O'Connell, M., and C.C. Rogers
    1983   *Child Care Arrangements of Working Mothers: June 1982.* U.S. Bureau of the Census, Current Population Reports, Series P-23, No. 129. Washington, D.C.: U.S. Department of Commerce.
O'Neill, J.
    1980   Trends in the labor force participation of women. Pp. 28-38 in C.D. Hayes, ed., *Work, Family, and Community: Summary Proceedings of an Ad Hoc Meeting.* Washington, D.C.: National Academy Press.
Oppenheimer, V.
    1974   The life cycle squeeze: The interaction of men's occupational and family life cycles. *Demography* 11:227-246.
Presser, H.B.
    1986   Shift work among American women and child care. *Journal of Marriage and the Family* 46(3):551-563.
    1988a   Shift work and child care among young dual-earner American parents. *Journal of Marriage and the Family* 50(February):3-14.
    1988b   Some Economic Consequences of Child Care Provided by Grandmothers. Unpublished paper. Department of Sociology, University of Maryland.
Presser, H.B., and W. Baldwin
    1980   Child care use and constraints in the United States. Pp. 295-304 in Anne Horberg, ed., *Women and the World of Work.* New York: Plenum.
Presser, H.B., and V.S. Cain
    1983   Shift work among dual-earner couples with children. *Science* 219:876-879.

Reskin, B.F., and H.I. Hartmann, eds.
  1986   *Women's Work, Men's Work: Sex Segregation on the Job.* Washington, D.C.:
         National Academy Press.
Sonenstein, F.L., and D.A. Wolf
  1988   Caring for the Children of Welfare Mothers. Paper presented at the annual
         meeting of the Population Association of America, New Orleans, La., April
         21-23, 1988.
Travers, J., R. Beck, and J. Bissell
  1982   Measuring the outcomes of day care. In J. Travers and R. Light, eds.,
         Learning from Experience: *Evaluating Early Childhood Demonstration Programs.*
         Washington, D.C.: National Academy Press.
U.S. Department of Education
  1986   *Pre-School Enrollment: Trends and Implications.* Publication No. 065-000-0276-1.
         Washington, D.C.: U.S. Department of Education.
U.S. General Accounting Office
  1987   *Welfare: Income and Relative Poverty Status of AFDC Families.* GAO/HRD 88-9.
         Washington, D.C.: U.S. Government Printing Office.
Waite, L.J., and R.M. Stolzenberg
  1976   Intended childbearing and labor force participation among young women:
         Insights from nonrecursive models. *American Sociological Review* 41:235-252.
Wilson, W.J.
  1987   *The Truly Disadvantaged: The Inner City, the Underclass, and Public Policy.*
         Chicago: University of Chicago Press.
Zigler, E.
  1983   Latchkey children: Risks and alternatives. Testimony on school-age day care for
         Senate Children's Caucus Policy Forum. *Congressional Record* 129(June 21):88.
         Washington, D.C.: U.S. Government Printing Office.

II

Child Care and
Child Development

3

The Effects of Child Care

Chapters 3 through 5 review what has been learned about the lives of children in child care from research, clinical practice, and work with young children. In Chapter 3 we trace successive phases of child care research, which have moved to increasingly complex and fruitful questions about child care. In Chapter 4 we highlight the particular dimensions of child care quality (e.g., group size, ratio) that are most important to children's development. And in Chapter 5 we review what is known about how child care can support children's physical health and psychological development.

PROCESSES OF CHILD DEVELOPMENT

Before turning to these issues of child care and children's development, however, it is useful to outline briefly several basic principles about development that underlie the ensuing discussion. These principles emerge from and reflect important areas of agreement in different scientific disciplines that shed light on children's development, notably developmental psychology, clinical work with children, and research in early education.

First, children's development is multiply determined: by sources within the child, such as temperament, neurological integrity, and impairment; by factors in the child's immediate environment, such as quality of relationships and interactions with parents and quality of out-of-home care; and by factors in the child's larger social environment, including the immediate neighborhood and the broader culture. These factors do not operate separately but interact in a complex fashion to influence developmental outcomes. Child care must therefore be viewed as one of many sources of influence on children's development and one that interacts in complex ways with numerous others.

Second, children are not only influenced by their immediate and broader environments, but also shape these environments. Development reflects the transactional processes—or mutual influences of child and environment. In child care settings, for example, children are influenced by caregiver and peer behaviors, and they also selectively relate to certain teachers and peers.

Third, children's development involves the biological, cognitive, and socioemotional domains. Although development in these domains is interrelated, progress across domains does not occur uniformly. Rather, children may advance or lag in one domain but not others. It is therefore important to consider the development of children in child care in specific domains, rather than to view patterns of influence as equally affecting all domains.

Fourth, children's physiological, cognitive, and socioemotional needs differ markedly by developmental level. Consideration of the age of a child is fundamental to understanding the differing needs of children in child care settings.[1]

Finally, the nature of environmental influences on children is best thought of as probabilistic. Recent research and practice with children posits risk factors, conditions or events that increase the probability of negative or less than optimal developmental outcomes, and protective factors, conditions or events that increase the probability of positive or optimal developmental outcomes. Risk and protective factors are thought to influence development most often by interacting with other sources of influence on a child's development. Child care could function as a protective factor, a risk factor, or a relatively neutral factor for particular developmental domains.

In short, the relationship between child care and child development is complex. In light of this complexity, it is not surprising that there are no perfect studies and few that are conclusive about the relationship between child care and child development. Nonetheless, the cumulative weight of evidence from empirical studies, clinical work, and professional practice is sufficient to draw some conclusions that can serve as provisional guides to program and policy. The rest of this chapter and the next two review that evidence.

---

[1] In this chapter, and indeed throughout this volume, *infants* refers to children in the first year of life, *toddlers* to those 13 to 36 months, *preschool age* to those 3 to 5 years old, and *school age* to those 6 years or older. We note, however, that there is some variation across researchers and legislators in the precise demarcations used for these developmental periods. Where a particular study, author, standard, or regulation uses age demarcations that differ from ours, we note the discrepancy and specify the intended age of the children.

EVOLUTION OF CHILD CARE RESEARCH

Marked social changes that impinge on the lives of families and children have often sparked an initial wave of psychological research that asks, "Is this harmful to children?" It has been the case repeatedly that this initial wave of research, which might be called the "alarm phase," does not address questions of sufficient subtlety or complexity to illuminate the impact of the social change. Typically, in the evolution of the research, the alarm phase gives way to a second research phase that examines the demographic shift in a more differentiated manner.

The research on maternal employment (a "sister" literature to that on child care that is not restricted to young children receiving a particular form of supplemental care) illustrates this evolution. Researchers and practitioners responded decades ago to the striking increases in rates of maternal employment by asking whether or not children were adversely affected by daily separations and nonmaternal care. But the great complexity in the research findings from those early studies indicated that it was not enough to ask about potential harm. Some children clearly benefited from their mothers' employment. Furthermore, it did not appear that maternal employment was a unitary phenomenon with uniform implications (Bronfenbrenner and Crouter, 1982; Hoffman, 1979). Rather, its impact on children was related to a number of child characteristics (e.g., age and sex), family characteristics (e.g., father involvement with children, mothers' role satisfaction, and extended family support), and factors beyond the family (e.g., culture) (Zaslow et al., *in press*). Research restricted to a status strategy—mother *is* or *is not* employed—gave way to research focusing on mechanisms and processes, the factors associated with differing outcomes of maternal employment for children.

The research on child care is following a similar pattern of evolution (Belsky, 1984; Phillips, 1988). A first wave of studies asked whether the increasing rates of participation of young children in family day care and center care was cause for alarm. Did the development of children in supplemental child care differ from that of children cared for by parents? The accumulating evidence, however, has forced a shift in the research focus. Child care was not found to be inherently or inevitably harmful. Rather, it was found to vary greatly as an environment for children, and children's development was linked to the variation. A second wave of child care research, still in progress, examines children's development in light of variations in the environment of child care.

According to Phillips (1988), the major focus of a third wave of child care research is beginning to emerge. This phase will view the home and child care environments as linked and mutually influential. Children's development is beginning to be understood in light of experiences across the two care settings.

Each successive wave of child care research reflects progressively greater conceptual complexity and methodological refinement. Yet the question central to each wave remains important, even as the new questions emerge. That is, the waves of research overlap and complement one another, rather than supplanting each other.

It is important to continue to ask how the development of children reared at home and in child care settings differs (the question focal to the first wave of research), even as questions are asked about the implications of poor-quality care in comparison to care that is adequate or of high quality (second wave) and about the joint impact of the child's home and the child care settings (third wave). Although there are methodological weaknesses as well as strengths in each research wave, we view each phase as using research approaches appropriate to the central question being addressed. We begin, however, not with the first wave, but one step further back, in the research on maternal deprivation.

ROOTS OF CHILD CARE RESEARCH:
MATERNAL DEPRIVATION

The alarm phase of research in child care has its roots in the substantial body of clinical and empirical studies of children experiencing maternal deprivation and institutionalization (long or short stays in residential facilities for children). It was not only initially considered possible that child care might belong on a continuum with the institutionalization of children, but actually explicitly stated that this was the case. The influential 1951 World Health Organization Expert Committee on Mental Health concluded on the basis of the work of John Bowlby (1951), that "day nurseries" constituted a form of maternal deprivation with permanent negative effects on children (Rutter, 1981a).

Studies of short-term (hospitalization, short-stay residential nursery) and long-term (long-stay residential nursery, institutionalization) parent-child separations, many of them rooted in the psychoanalytic tradition, do indicate problems in children's development (e.g., Freud and Burlingham, 1944, 1973; Goldfarb, 1943; Provence and Lipton, 1962; Ribble, 1965; Robertson and Robertson, 1971; Spitz, 1945; Wolkind, 1974). These problems range from acute distress syndrome, associated with short periods in care, to conduct disorders, problems in forming relationships, and intellectual deficits, associated with longer term care (Rutter, 1981a). In particular, "an institutional upbringing which involves multiple changing caretakers has been shown to lead to important social deficits and problems in interpersonal relationships" (Rutter, 1981a:154). But does the accumulated evidence regarding weeks or years completely away from parents indicate that child care should be considered together with this grouping of studies, as a form of maternal deprivation?

Rutter's (1979, 1981a) reassessments of the theory and research into maternal deprivation are extremely helpful in extracting those elements of early views of maternal deprivation (particularly those of Bowlby) that the research evidence has sustained and those elements that have required revision. According to Rutter, there have been two important and lasting contributions of the early work on maternal deprivation. First, that work identified deplorable conditions in short- and long-term residential settings for children. In response, there have been widespread changes in those conditions. Second, studies responding to that work have resulted in an understanding of experiences that are necessary for young children's normal development.

Above all, that research showed that young children need to develop enduring relationships with a limited number of specific individuals, relationships that are characterized by affection, reciprocal interaction, and responsiveness to the particular and highly individualized cues of the infant and young child, and that the child's environment has to provide sufficient opportunity for stimulation (Rutter, 1981a, summarizes the evidence). It is in the context of familiar relationships that children make their major developmental advances in communication and understanding in the first years. The growth of language and social understanding depends on the child's social exchanges with familiar, responsive others (Bruner, 1983; Dunn, 1988; Lock, 1978; Trevarthen, 1977).

In other respects, other early conclusions on maternal deprivation have required revision in light of subsequent research (Rutter, 1979, 1981a). Perhaps most central, the initial work emphasized the child's need to become attached to the *mother* in particular, and to be cared for in his or her own home, for healthy subsequent development. For example, Bowlby's early statements viewed the mother-child bond as different from all other relationships (Bowlby, 1951). Subsequent work has not confirmed this exclusive emphasis on the mother-child relationship. Rather, the evidence indicates a normal tendency for children to form multiple simultaneous attachments (Chibucos and Kail, 1981; Dunn, 1983). These attachments tend to be hierarchical, with one attachment (often to the mother) most significant to the child (Rutter, 1981b). However, mothers are not the only caregivers who can provide the essential experiences for healthy early development. Children can benefit from "multiple mothering" *if* it provides affection, warmth, responsiveness, and stimulation in the context of enduring relationships with a reasonably small number of caregivers (according to Rutter [1981a], four or five caregivers), who have come to know and be able to respond to the child's individual needs and style.

Accordingly, researchers no longer believe that the effects of institutionalization on children are solely the result of disruption of the mother-child relationship. In the more complex and differentiated view of institutionalization that has evolved, it is now understood that some of the more serious developmental problems follow not from interruption of a mother-child relationship, but from an initial lack of any such relationship. Furthermore, the effects of residential care vary according to the setting's provision of enduring relationships and stimulation; according to the child's physical status (e.g., nutrition, pre- and postnatal complications); and to the family circumstances surrounding the institutionalization, particularly family discord. Thus, the nature and circumstances of the separation in combination with the characteristics of the child determine its implications rather than the single fact of mother-child separation (Rutter, 1979, 1981a; Wolkind, 1974).

Of particular importance in the present context, Rutter's reassessment of the maternal deprivation research concludes that child care does *not* fall on a continuum with institutionalization (Rutter, 1981a:154):

> [T]here is a world of difference between institutional care without any parental involvement and day care in which the mother remains a key figure who continues to actively participate in looking after the child. For these reasons, little weight can be attached to the results of *residential* group care as a basis for assessing the probable sequelae of group *day* care.

In sum, infants and young children tend to form several attachments to a small number of selected individuals. A healthy environment for child development does include at least one secure attachment, but does not necessarily require care exclusively by a mother. Rather, environments that provide stable, warm, responsive, and stimulating relationships with several caregivers, if these relationships are limited in number, can encourage healthy psychological development. Child care differs fundamentally from institutionalization and should not be considered part of the same phenomenon simply on the grounds of mother-child separation. Yet when child care environments fail to provide those elements found to be essential to normal development—and instead involve a large number of caregivers, frequent changes in caregivers, lack of responsiveness to the child as an individual, and lack of social and cognitive stimulation—they can be expected to have negative implications for development.

FIRST WAVE OF CHILD CARE RESEARCH:
DEVELOPMENT OF CHILDREN IN CHILD CARE AND
THOSE REARED AT HOME

The impetus for the first wave of empirical, systematic child care research, then, was the concern that young children would be harmed by daily separations from their mothers. As it became clear that mother-child separations and daily participation in child care did not have the drastic negative implications that the maternal deprivation construct predicted, important questions nevertheless remained: Did the development of children in supplemental child care differ from that of home-reared children in meaningful if less marked ways? Were there *subgroups* of children whose development was enhanced by the child care experience? Were there *subgroups* of children whose participation in child care was associated with any degree of risk for development?

Several comprehensive reviews of the first wave of child care research by Belsky and colleagues (Belsky, 1984; Belsky and Steinberg, 1978), Clarke-Stewart and Fein (1983), and Rutter (1981b) have addressed these questions and provide extensive documentation, summarized below. Consistent with the assumptions about development presented in the preface to these chapters, we assume that the impact of child care differs by domain of development. As such, we present the major findings separately for the areas of intellectual and social development. However, we cannot present findings separately by developmental level because researchers have made surprisingly little effort to differentiate the outcomes for children exposed to child care according to child age. The evidence rests largely on a mosaic of cross-sectional studies, rather than on longitudinal studies aimed at documenting the changes and consistencies in children's needs in child care as they get older. The major exception to this pattern is that the infancy period has been singled out for particular focus. But the years from toddlerhood through school age are rarely discussed in the child care literature with an assumption of changing developmental needs.

A further limitation in this wave of child care research in the United States that is important to note is its very heavy reliance on studies of center care, rather than the demographically more prevalent family day care. In this respect much can be learned from the European research, which has more consistently encompassed family day care as well as center care in its attempts to examine the impact of child care experience versus parental care (e.g., Cochran, 1977; Lamb, Hwang, Bookstein, et al., 1988; Lamb, Hwang, Broberg, and Bookstein, 1988).

Intellectual Development

On measures of intellectual development, reviews of the evidence conclude that "children in day care centers do as well as those at home

. . . or that they do better, at least for a time or on some measures" (Clarke-Stewart and Fein, 1983:965).

Social class is an important factor in understanding the findings for cognitive development among children in child care (Belsky, 1984; Belsky and Steinberg, 1978). Studies of more economically advantaged children in community-based child care find either no differences in cognitive development related to child care participation or more advanced development among these youngsters. Studies of economically disadvantaged children in high-quality child care intervention programs, however, consistently find more advanced cognitive development in day care children than in home-reared children. These children do not show the declines found for their home-reared counterparts from disadvantaged families on tests of intellectual development.

Although Belsky's reviews (Belsky, 1984; Belsky and Steinberg, 1978) conclude that, overall, middle-class child care and home-reared children do not differ on indices of intellectual development, Clarke-Stewart and Fein (1983) diverge in their assessment of the research, pointing to indications of superior scores on cognitive indices in some studies of children attending community-based child care programs (e.g., Doyle, 1975; Rubenstein et al., 1981). Thus, for more economically advantaged children in community-based programs, the most consistent conclusion appears to be that child care attendance does not have *negative* implications for cognitive development.

In children from disadvantaged families, measures of IQ (that are language dependent) typically decline beginning in the second year of life (see Slaughter [1983] for discussion of this pattern and the types of measures on which it occurs). Reviews of the evidence on early intervention programs for children at risk for this decline indicate that such programs are effective in preventing or slowing the decline. Bryant and Ramey (1987), for example, in an excellent recent review of this evidence, restricted their examination to methodologically adequate experimental studies of early intervention programs and considered the role of child's age at entry, duration and intensity of intervention program, nature of educational activities, and whether the child or parents were primary targets of the intervention. They conclude that program effectiveness was most closely linked with the child's (or family's or both) *extent* of contact with the intervention program and that "the most improvement in intellectual development occurs when children attend day care and families receive parent training or other services" (Bryant and Ramey, 1987:71). Interventions were found to be effective irrespective of whether they were initiated during infancy, early childhood, or the preschool years. And the type of educational emphasis and the curriculum were not closely linked with outcomes.

Findings of the early intervention programs indicate that gains on measures of intellectual development are temporary rather than permanent (evidence summarized by Clarke-Stewart and Fein, 1983; Haskins, 1989). However, longitudinal evaluations of early intervention that include outcome measures in addition to IQ show some persistent effects. For example, in one longitudinal analysis of 10- to 17-year-olds who had attended early intervention programs, although group differences on IQ did not persist, differences on measures of school-related behavior did: children who had participated in intervention programs were less likely to repeat a grade in school and less likely to be referred for special education than those who had not participated (Darlington et al., 1980; Lazar et al., 1982).

Recent research also indicates that when an intervention program is continued into the elementary school years, complementing the child's regular school participation, differences can be sustained. Horacek and colleagues (1987:762) found that "children who participated in both [a] preschool program and [a] school-age support program performed better in school than the group that had only preschool" intervention, even though the intervention at school age was of limited intensity. Thus, children at risk for school failure may benefit most from a combination of early *and* sustained intervention.

Haskins (1989), in reviewing the findings on the impact of early intervention programs, urges a distinction between model intervention programs (e.g., those considered in the Bryant and Ramey [1987] review) and Head Start. Haskins points out that both types of programs yield "significant and meaningful gains" on measures of intellectual performance by the end of the first year of intervention, but it is only for the model programs that there is evidence of strong positive effects on the later school-related behavior variables. He suggests several possible explanations for this difference in the findings for model early intervention programs and Head Start. Since data collection has been far more extensive and systematic for the model programs, the long-term effects of Head Start may be undetected by the fewer and less rigorous Head Start outcome studies. However, there are fundamental program differences that could underlie the difference in longer term implications of the two kinds of programs: Head Start encompasses sites ranging substantially in quality; while model programs are consistently high quality. Furthermore, Head Start selects for participation the most disadvantaged children and families, but draws *control* groups from those remaining on the waiting list and who are thus relatively less disadvantaged. Work by Lee and colleagues (1988) suggests that particularly because of Head Start selection practices the impact of Head Start may be systematically underestimated in studies.

Haskins (1989), while apologizing for the tendency of social scientists to call for more research, notes the particular need for methodologically rigorous longitudinal studies of Head Start. We concur that Head Start, a federally supported, comprehensive early child development intervention, with strong evidence of short-term benefits in the intellectual domain, should be the focus of carefully planned longitudinal studies that track a broader array of social, emotional, and cognitive outcomes.

Social Development

Attachment

In studying the socioemotional development of children in child care, researchers have been concerned about the nature of mother-child relations. Do children in supplemental care show patterns of attachment similar to those of home-reared children? What happens to children who enter child care during the developmental period (the first year of life), when the attachment to mother is forming? Before turning to the evidence on child care and security of attachment, we briefly consider the attachment construct.

The Attachment Construct: Definition and Assessment The term "attachment," as used in the psychological research, has its roots in the work of Bowlby (1969, 1973, 1980). Bowlby stressed two central functions of an infant's enduring relationship with its mother: the provision of a "secure base" from which the infant could explore the environment and the provision of a "haven of safety" to return to when stressed or distressed (see Campos et al. [1983] for a discussion of the evolution of the attachment construct). The security of the infant with the mother, that is the use of the mother both as a secure base and a haven of safety, has been widely evaluated using an assessment known as the Ainsworth "strange situation" (Ainsworth et al., 1978). In this laboratory situation, infant behavior toward its mother is observed in a sequence of eight episodes involving introduction to a novel situation in the presence of the mother, behavior toward a female stranger in the presence and absence of the mother, infant behavior when left alone in the novel setting, and reunion behaviors with the mother. The components of the strange situation (unfamiliar setting, unfamiliar though friendly adult, separation, and reunion) were devised in keeping with Bowlby's view that attachment behaviors would be most readily observed in a context in which the baby is stressed or aroused.

The Ainsworth strange-situation assessment, as it has been widely used, distinguishes three qualitatively different patterns of attachment (although recent work raises the possibility of a fourth category). In this assessment, infants rated as securely attached "tend to seek proximity to, and contact with, attachment figures. . . . Moreover, such infants manifest clear preferences for their caretakers over the stranger" (Campos et al., 1983:863). Approximately two-thirds of middle-class American infants observed in the strange situation (Campos et al., 1983) are categorized as securely attached; while one-third are rated insecurely attached in one of two ways. "Anxious-avoidant" infants "conspicuously avoid their caretaker during the reunion episodes, fail to cling when held, and tend to treat the stranger the same way as, or sometimes more positively than, their caretaker" (Campos et al., 1983:862). "Resistant" or "ambivalently attached" infants "tend to resist interaction and contact with their caretaker, yet they also manifest contact- and proximity-seeking behavior. [These] infants seek proximity and contact before separation, moreover, which may inhibit their exploration of the novel environment" (Campos et al., 1983:863).

A body of research relates these three patterns of attachment both to antecedents (particularly the nature of the mother-infant interaction) and asks whether the pattern of attachment is predictive of aspects of development. Features of mother-infant interaction related to the differing patterns of attachment are the mother's interest in and availability for interaction with the infant, as well as the emotional tone of interactions. Work by Ainsworth and colleagues with a middle-class sample (summarized in Ainsworth et al., 1978) indicates that mothers of securely attached infants were more effective in soothing and interpreting infant signals, that they participated in more face-to-face interaction with their infants, and that they were more affectionate and emotionally positive with the infants. By contrast, mothers of anxious-avoidant babies were more irritable and rejecting in their interactions, and mothers of resistant infants were more inept and insensitive to signals. Subsequent work has continued to differentiate mother-infant interactions according to pattern of attachment, but the particular differentiating features have not always been identical nor has the differentiation been unambiguous or strong (see evaluation by Campos et al., 1983).

Campos and colleagues (1983) conclude that the evidence that the strange-situation classification predicts developmental status is more robust than that it has unambiguous roots in early interaction. Thus, for example, children categorized as securely attached as infants have been reported to be subsequently more compliant and cooperative (e.g., Matas et al., 1978), more sociable with peers (Pastor, 1981) as well as more competent with peers (Waters et al., 1979), and to engage more effectively in carrying out cognitive tasks (e.g., Matas et al., 1978).

Before asking whether participation in child care is related to security of attachment as assessed in the strange situation, it is important to call attention to concerns expressed in the literature about the use of this assessment. These concerns relate both to the strange-situation classifications in general and to the application of this procedure specifically to children who have experienced frequent separations from their mothers because of maternal employment (Campos et al., 1983:869):

> So widely accepted is the system of Ainsworth et al. (1978) for classifying individual differences in the Strange Situation that few have stopped to ask whether [its] trichotomy constitutes a valid way of clustering individual differences. . . .

Indeed, an evaluation of the research carried out by Campos and colleagues asks (1983:872) whether it is "justifiable to equate 'security of attachment with Strange-Situation classification.'" For example, they note a wide range in reports examining the stability of an attachment classification over time, including reports that only approximately one-half of a sample retains the same classification over time (e.g., Thompson et al., 1982). In addition, they note the possibility that behavior in the (stressful) strange situation may be a reflection not only of the history of mother-infant interactions, but also of the baby's temperamental characteristics, including how easily the infant becomes distressed and is comforted, characteristics that "may be evident long before the attachment relationship is built" (Campos et al., 1983:868). Campos and colleagues question the original attachment groupings and the manner in which they were determined. Finally, they point to widely divergent proportions of infants categorized as insecure and secure in attachment in studies carried out beyond the United States (e.g., the work of Grossman et al. [1981] reporting a higher proportion of German infants showing anxious-avoidant attachment). Such differences raise the possibility of important cultural or experiential differences among infants in the strange situation, particularly the extent to which the baby finds the experience stressful.

In keeping with this perspective on the cross-cultural data, other researchers have questioned the equivalence of the strange-situation assessment for infants whose mothers have rarely parted from them in comparison with infants who are accustomed to daily departures. Clarke-Stewart (1989) in particular questions whether this procedure is "psychologically equivalent" for infants of homemaker and employed mothers. She notes that it is much less likely for the child of an employed mother to see as unusual or stressful the experiences of a novel play setting, being left by the mother with a female stranger or being comforted by her, and reunion with the mother. Clarke-Stewart (1989:267) concludes that "we need to assess infants' attachment using procedures that are not biased by differential familiarity and potentially differential stressfulness."

Because of these questions, the panel regards the data on security of attachment among children who have participated in child care with some caution. The almost exclusive reliance on the strange-situation procedure offers one advantage in that one can look at comparable data across studies (Clarke-Stewart, 1989). Yet, at the same time, there has been a tendency among some researchers to uncritically accept the validity of the strange-situation classification, even though questions remain about its equivalence for samples with different care histories.

Security of Attachment and Participation in Day Care The findings on security of attachment and child care participation are best summarized separately for children who begin child care in the first year of life or later. For the somewhat older children, attendance in a child care program does not appear to alter the hierarchy of attachments (Rutter, 1981a,b). Most children do develop attachments to stable caregivers and seem to gain security from their presence (Howes et al., 1988). Yet, most children consistently prefer proximity, interaction with, and comfort from their mothers (see Rutter [1981b] for evaluation of this evidence). Therefore, daily hours apart do not alter mothers' primary role in the lives of children in child care.

For these somewhat older children, the months following entry into child care may involve "transient distress" that manifests itself in the mother-child relationship (Belsky, 1984). However, beyond this adaptation period, there are no marked differences in the quality of attachment to mother for children in nonparental care and home-reared children in this age range. In evaluating these findings, it is important to recall that having a mother who is a homemaker does not ensure secure attachment or optimal mother-child interactions. As noted above, a nontrivial proportion of toddlers with homemaker mothers show "insecure" attachments as assessed in the strange situation (Richters and Zahn-Waxler, 1988; Thompson, 1988). Furthermore, being a homemaker has been found to be associated with depression among working-class women in England (Brown and Harris, 1978), and depression in the mother, in turn, is associated with problems in preschool children.

Among children who begin their child care attendance for more than 20 hours per week during the first year of life, researchers now agree that, while a majority show secure attachments to their mothers when tested in the strange situation, a higher proportion of the remainder show anxious-avoidant attachment to their mothers than do home-reared infants (Barglow et al., 1987; Belsky, 1988; Belsky and Rovine, 1988; Schwarz, 1983).

There is agreement that infants who start full-time child care in their first year are more likely to show this pattern of attachment, but there is no consensus about what it means (Belsky, 1988; Clarke-Stewart, 1989; Richters and Zahn-Waxler, 1988; Thompson, 1988). Some researchers contend that it reflects an undesirable pattern in the infant-mother relationship that may have negative implications for later development (Belsky, 1988; Belsky and Rovine, 1988); others conclude that the pattern is a manifestation of other factors, such as patterns of self-selection, which distinguish families that do and do not use child care for infants, a different but healthy adaptation in infants of employed mothers, or a reflection of the methodological issues noted above.

Rutter (1981b) and Clarke-Stewart (1989) both emphasize the possibility of self-selection factors distinguishing between families that rely on parental care and those that rely on child care. Perhaps the most revealing studies on psychological factors that differentiate between mothers who choose to be homemakers or choose to be employed have been carried out by Hock and colleagues. For example, Hock and colleagues (1980), looking at a group of mothers of newborns all of whom *planned* to be homemakers, found differences between those who carried out this plan and those who changed plans and resumed employment. Three months after the births of their children the mothers who resumed employment expressed less positive attitudes about the maternal role and greater difficulty with infant fussiness. Hock and colleagues (1984) found that in the newborn period, mothers expecting to be homemakers differed from those expecting to return to employment in terms of how strongly they believed that it is important for babies to be cared for exclusively by their mothers and in their home orientations. Such differences may have implications for the development of infant-mother attachment. For example, the tendency of mothers returning to employment to experience infant fussiness as more aversive may imply that they are less responsive to their infants' distress or less effective responding to it. Both patterns, as noted above, have been linked with the emergence of insecure attachments. Similarly, Crockenberg (1981:862) found that "the adequacy of the mother's social support is clearly and consistently associated with security of infant-mother attachment" and with higher rates of avoidance and anxious attachment when mothers have little social support. Perhaps mothers who remain home with their infants have better networks of support. Indeed, such a factor could contribute to their decisions to be homemakers.

Researchers have also raised the possibility that findings of higher rates of anxious-avoidant attachment in infants of employed mothers may simply indicate a healthy adaptation by infants to child care: such infants may show greater autonomy from their mothers or less distress in the assessment situation because they are accustomed to separations (Clarke-Stewart, 1989; Clarke-Stewart and Fein, 1983). A further possibility (although one that Clarke-Stewart [1989] evaluates as not supported by available data) is that higher rates of insecure attachment in infants who have attended child care are linked to poor-quality early care. Perhaps most important, studies to date have not yet followed day care children showing anxious-avoidant attachment to assess directly the stability of the pattern or its developmental implications.

Stress and Parenting During the First Year   The fact that negative findings concerning attachment pertain specifically to children who participate in full-time child care during the first year of a child's life have led some researchers to ask whether stresses unique to this period are indeed taking a toll on parent-infant relations. Research in the United States has long debated the *extent* of disruption to parents and to the marital relationship when a baby is born (e.g., Dyer, 1963; Hobbs and Cole, 1976; LeMasters, 1957), but it is clear that the birth of a child involves rapid readjustment within the family that is both stressful and positive. Employed women in particular tend to experience an intensification of "role overload" (too much expected given dual roles) and "role conflict" (internal conflict about the relative importance of work and family roles) with the birth of a child (Moen, 1989).

Brazelton (1986) has questioned whether mothers' early return to employment, when added to the stresses of parenting an infant, may limit the time and energy mothers and infants have to establish a pattern of mutual communication and sensitivity to cues. Furthermore, he points to possible obstacles affecting the mother's ability to develop strong positive feelings for and about the infant when she needs to cope with frequent separations and shares her baby's care with another caregiver.

Observations of parent-infant interaction in the first year of life suggest that infants in middle-class families in which the mother is employed are engaged in somewhat less playful interaction with their parents than infants with homemaker mothers (Zaslow et al., 1989). Further research suggests that secure attachment may not be used in the same way by infants in families with employed mothers as it is in families with homemaker mothers. Vaughn and colleagues (1985) found that security of attachment in infancy was an excellent predictor of later socioemotional development in children whose mothers were homemakers, but it did not predict later socioemotional competence in children whose mothers returned to work when their babies were very young.

Clarke-Stewart (1989) notes several ways in which stresses unique to combining employment and care of an infant might be associated with increased rates of anxious-avoidant attachment. Anxious-avoidant attachment, as noted above, may be rooted in a rejecting quality to mother-infant interactions. Clarke-Stewart (1989:270) points out that "the increased stress of handling two full-time jobs, work and motherhood, [could] lead to more rejection of every additional burden, including the baby." Alternatively, a perception of rejection by the baby might not be a reflection of the mother's feelings about the baby, but simply her inaccessibility because the tasks facing her when she returns home compete for her time and attention with the baby.

Clarke-Stewart notes several studies that relate attitudinal or personality factors among employed mothers (e.g., desire for motherhood, psychological integration, anxiety, and dissatisfaction) and security of attachment in their infants (Benn, 1986; Farber and Egeland, 1982; Owen and Cox, 1988). It is possible that higher rates of anxious-avoidant attachment among infants in child care are related to higher proportions of employed mothers feeling anxious, stressed, or overburdened. Findings from Sweden point out that providing greater flexibility in employment roles may reduce the stress that many employed mothers experience. Moen (1989) indicates that reports of daily fatigue and psychological stress by mothers in Sweden are related to the recent birth of a first child. The use of parental leave or the reduction of hours of employment to a part-time schedule significantly reduce both indicators of stress. Moen also notes that mothers experience significantly greater stress than fathers in Sweden, despite the availability of employment and leave options.

These findings, taken together, have implications for evaluating parental leave policies in the United States. We must distinguish between what the data permit us to say with some certainty, and where there are problems with the evidence. We can say with some certainty that U.S. mothers of infants, who are also employed full time, experience overload and stress. Furthermore, we know that factors reflecting psychological distress among employed mothers are related to the emergence of insecure attachment in their infants. Researchers agree that infants of mothers who resume full-time employment in the first year of their infants' lives show higher rates of anxious-avoidant attachment to their mothers. Finally, there is evidence from Sweden that parental leave or reduction in hours of parental employment can reduce stress in mothers. In the United States, evidence suggests that it is only full-time employment, not part-time work, that is associated with the pattern of anxious-avoidant attachment in infants.

Yet there is no research to date that puts these pieces of evidence together to establish paths of influence. That is, there is no research in the United States examining directly the effect of a period of parental leave or reduced hours of employment on stress among mothers, on the quality of mother-infant relations, or on rates of secure and insecure attachment among their infants. Furthermore, as we have noted, there are important questions about the single assessment of the mother-infant relationship that has been widely used and particularly about its use with children who have participated in out-of-home child care.

Support for a parental leave policy in the United States at the present time cannot be built on definitive data about its implications for infants, mothers, and families. It can, however, rest on a set of individual findings sufficient to raise concerns about stress in employed-mother families with infants and its possible implications for children.

Summary of Findings on Attachment and Child Care   For children beginning child care after the first year of life, there is little indication of differences in the mother-child relationship beyond an initial adaptation period. Children beginning full-time child care within the first year, however, show higher rates of anxious-avoidant attachment to their mothers than other children. The interpretation and implications of this pattern need to be further scrutinized. In particular, it should be a high priority in future research both to examine the use of the strange-situation assessment in infants of employed mothers and to substantially extend assessment of the mother-infant relationship beyond this single measure. Research is also needed on the context in which anxious-avoidant attachment arises among infants of employed mothers; to trace the development of infants of employed mothers with differing attachment ratings; and to directly assess the impact of parental leave on stress among mothers in the United States and on the quality of the mother-infant relationship.

Relationships With Peers and Adults

Child care researchers have observed and documented the social relations of children in child care (as opposed to home-reared children) in two areas other than the mother-child relationship: relations with peers and with other adults. The results suggest that child care children orient somewhat more strongly to peers and somewhat less strongly to adults than their home-reared counterparts (Belsky, 1984; Belsky and Steinberg, 1978; Clarke-Stewart and Fein, 1983; Rutter, 1981b).

This peer orientation appears to have positive as well as negative correlates. Positively, studies indicate greater complexity and reciprocal perceptiveness in the peer interactions of children in child care. In summarizing this evidence, Clarke-Stewart and Fein (1983:959) conclude that children with experience in early childhood programs "have been observed to be more popular, ... to form relationships with other children more often ... and more positively or agreeably. ..." Negatively, "a number of studies have documented the tendency of children in early childhood programs to be more antisocial with peers" (Clarke-Stewart and Fein, 1983:959). It is important to note that the measures used in studies do not unambiguously indicate whether the more frequent peer conflict reflects hostile or angry behavior in a clinically problematic range, heightened aggression within a normal range, or simply positive assertiveness. One interpretation of these findings is that "with greater peer exposure comes greater peer interaction, which is more likely to be both positive and negative in quality" (Belsky, 1984:13).

Several studies have reported children in child care to be less cooperative with adults (Haskins, 1985; Rubenstein and Howes, 1983; Schwarz et al., 1974). Schwarz and colleagues (1974), for example, found child care experiences to be associated with greater physical and verbal conflict among preschoolers, as well as with less cooperation with adults. Belsky (1984), in reviewing the findings on child care and cooperation with adults, raises the possibility that problems may be a reflection of particular experiences of children in particular child care settings: that is, the effects may be program specific. He notes that while the Swedish research does show more advanced peer relations among children in child care, there is no indication in this research of differences in children's cooperation with adults. Such differences, then, may be a result of specific experiences in child care, rather than an inevitable result of child care participation.

Social Competence

Clarke-Stewart and Fein (1983) conclude that, in addition to differences in the nature of their relationships with adults and with peers, children in child care show differences in more general social attributes or characteristics. In particular, they found the evidence to indicate that children in child care show greater social competence. Thus, for example, in work by Clarke-Stewart (summarized in Clarke-Stewart and Fein [1983]), child care children scored higher than home-reared children on a rating of social competence that encompassed indices of awareness of social norms, appropriate independence, friendliness, responsiveness, and social confidence. Other studies reviewed by Clarke-Stewart and Fein show differences in the dimensions of social cognition (social problem solving, perspective taking, understanding of emotional labels and sex roles) and of behavior in social situations (self-confidence, self-sufficiency, assertiveness, tendency to be outgoing, helpfulness). In interpreting these findings, Clarke-Stewart and Fein hypothesize that children develop greater social competence in part from the skills required to interact with a range of different peers.

There have been few attempts to evaluate the overall socioemotional adjustment of children in child care as opposed to home-reared children. In particular, the use of clinical measures of adjustment, of known psychometric properties, has been and continues to be rare in studies of children in child care programs. Therefore, it is difficult to say whether differences observed between the social behaviors and attributes of children in child care and home-reared children reflect variations within the normal range or whether from a clinical perspective child care children show indications of more or less adequate overall adjustment. Similarly, research to date has not addressed the possibility that participation in child care settings has distinct implications for the socioemotional development of minority group children. For example, are child care programs that incorporate multicultural perspectives associated with more positive cultural identification? Do such program emphases have implications for other aspects of socioemotional development in minority group children or for their later adaptation to elementary school? Thus, while there are indications of greater social competence among children in child care, the evidence available to date regarding the overall socioemotional development of children in child care is extremely limited.

Methodological Issues

The first wave of child care research is characterized by a group comparison strategy: the development of children in child care is compared with that of home-reared children. As child care research has progressed, there has been growing awareness of methodological issues inherent in this approach. This awareness has led both to methodological refinement in studies continuing to use a group contrast approach and to the emergence of a second wave of studies using a different approach.

One major methodological issue in the first wave of research is the possibility that group differences are not rooted in the child care experiences, but rather reflect other ongoing differences among child care children and home-reared children and their families (Belsky, 1984). Such differences may be relevant to some "outcomes." Perhaps, for example, parents who enroll their children in child care are in part responding to an already stronger motivation in their children to interact with peers rather than adults. Perhaps there are differences in the nature of parent-child interactions between these groups. Researchers using the two-group approach have called for increased use of random assignment to care settings and the use of home-reared control groups drawn from child care waiting lists, in order to control for possible preexisting tendencies (Cochran, 1977; Lamb, Hwang, Bookstein et al., 1988), and for examination of behavior in child care children and their families prior to entry into child care (Lamb, Hwang, Bookstein et al., 1988; Roopnarine and Lamb, 1978).

Another methodological issue in these studies is that child care samples have been drawn primarily from high-quality, often university-based, model programs. Although these studies can show, for example, whether child care under optimal circumstances involves alteration in the mother-child relationship, they cannot show whether differences occur for the majority of children who attend community-based child care. The increasing inclusion of community-based programs in research using the group comparison approach has forced an awareness of the wide range of experiences of children in child care.

As we have noted, the large majority of studies using a group comparison approach have focused on center care. Thus, there are relatively few data pertaining to the far more widespread family day care. Also, there is very little information on whether participation in child care, particularly community-based care, has differential implications, either salutary or stressful, for children from minority cultural, ethnic, and racial groups. And, also as noted, the first-wave studies to date are most often cross-sectional rather than longitudinal and thus fail to yield a picture of differential implications of child care participation (beyond the infancy period) in relation to child age.

Finally, researchers have also noted that the group comparison strategy generally fails to tie findings to particular processes or experiences. Child care in the United States seems to enhance both positive and negative behaviors with peers, but what specifically are the features that do so? Are such effects related to caregiver emphasis on guidance in social interactions? To other specific qualitative features of the program, such as group size or ratio? The first wave of child care research points to the need both to search for associations between child outcomes and particular features of the child care environment and for refinements in studies using the group comparison approach.

Summary

One can conclude with some certainty from the first wave of research that child care participation is not inevitably or pervasively harmful to children's development. Indeed, in certain respects, children benefit from experiences in child care. Beyond this broad statement, more detailed conclusions from the first wave of child care research need further scrutiny as methodological refinements become more widespread among studies using the group comparison strategy, notably as studies use sample selection or assignment procedures to control for self-selection and as a wider range of community-based child care settings, including family day care settings, is included in research. At present, however, some conclusions about development among child care participants are possible.

In the area of cognitive development, there is no evidence that child care participation has negative effects among middle-class children. Furthermore, high-quality cognitive enrichment child care programs have positive implications for intellectual development among low-income children at risk for declining IQ scores.

In the area of socioemotional development, the evidence points to a pattern of greater overall social competence in children with child care experience. Children in child care show a pattern of peer interactions that is richer and more complex, but also characterized by more conflict. Children in child care tend to show a shift in social orientation toward peers and away from adults. For children beginning full-time child care in the first year of life (though not for those starting later or less than full time), there are differences in the pattern of their attachment to their mothers. This finding is open to a range of interpretations, however, that will need to be resolved through further research.

THE SECOND WAVE OF CHILD CARE RESEARCH: VARIATION IN CHILD CARE QUALITY AND CHILDREN'S DEVELOPMENT

As child care research moved beyond model programs to include community-based family day care and center care, it became increasingly clear that child care programs and arrangements are extremely heterogeneous. They vary from minimally structured and custodial environments to highly structured and enriched environments. The actual teacher/child ratio for 3- or 4-year-old children in centers ranges from 1 teacher per 5 to 1 per 24 (Vandell and Powers, 1983). Toys and educational materials can be abundant and in good condition or limited and ragged. Caregiving staff can have college degrees in child development or have no college education or training pertinent to children. There may be low rates of turnover and good continuity of relationships between particular caregivers and children or high rates of staff turnover and poor continuity of relationships. Family day care providers may be isolated from resources and support or part of a supportive network. Directors may make use of or generate resources in the community for preventive mental health work with children and families or may not do so. Parents may feel that they collaborate with their child care providers in the care of their children or they may feel criticized and excluded. Does this variation in child care quality have implications for children's development? The second wave of research asks: Does quality of care have an influence on children's development while they are in care? Are there any implications of child care quality that persist into the elementary school years?

The research uses three approaches to measuring quality. In many studies, a global or summary measure is used. Researchers distinguish between high- and low-quality care (or high, medium, and low) based on a composite picture of such factors as staff/child ratios, caregiver training, organization of space, and daily routine. A widely used composite measure is the Harms and Clifford (1980) Early Childhood Environment Rating Scale. The second approach is to focus on individual components of overall quality in relation to outcomes. In such an approach, a specific component of quality, such as staff/child ratio or group size, is examined in relation to development. The third approach is to examine not the physical or structural features of child care related to quality (e.g., group size, staff/child ratio), but rather to define quality in terms of children's experiences in care. Thus, caregiver verbal behavior or empathic behavior may be related to child development.

In contrast to earlier studies, the strategy in this second wave of research has been largely naturalistic in that it involves the study of correlates of quality variation as it actually occurs in community-based (rather than model) child care. To anticipate the discussion of methodological issues for this wave of research (as well as of our assessment of the needs for future research in Chapter 9), an understanding of quality would be strengthened if the naturalistic approaches to quality were more often complemented with studies involving random assignment and manipulation of quality variables. Although most studies do control for key family background variables, the possibility remains that ongoing characteristics of the families or children themselves may affect both their placement in care of varying quality and child outcomes. Again, to anticipate, the third wave of child care research is beginning to grapple with these issues.

Because the second wave of research is still very much in progress, the panel commissioned a detailed review of the relevant findings. The following summary draws extensively on that review (Zaslow, 1988) and on one by Phillips and Howes (1987). Our discussion here centers on the issue of whether there is evidence that quality of care (as defined in any of the three ways indicated above) matters for contemporaneous or later development. By contrast, our discussion of quality of care in Chapter 4 attempts to specify which of the structural dimensions of quality have the strongest associations with children's development.

Quality and Contemporaneous Development

Overall, quality of care has been found to be associated with children's cognitive as well as social development when developmental status is assessed at the same time as quality of child care. These findings hold for samples that are diverse both as to family background and type of care received.

Cognitive Development

Analyzing the cognitive and language data from a study of center care in Bermuda, McCartney (1984:251) concluded that, overall, center quality "appears to have a profound effect on language development." A summary measure of quality significantly predicted children's scores on several accepted assessments of language skills, including the revised Peabody Picture Vocabulary Test (PPVT) , the Preschool Language Assessment Instrument, the Adaptive Language Inventory, and, for a subsample, ratings of free speech in a communication task. Furthermore, the total number of caregiver utterances to children predicted children's scores on the Adaptive Language Inventory and free-speech samples, whereas conversations initiated by children with their peers were a negative predictor of three of the four language measures.

In the National Day Care Study of center care in the United States (Ruopp et al., 1979), children's change in scores from fall to spring on the Preschool Inventory (PSI), a school readiness test, and the PPVT, were related to center group size, teacher qualifications, and center orientation. In smaller groups, children made greater gains on both measures. In centers in which caregivers had child-related training or education, children made greater gains on the PSI. Finally, children showed greater gains on test scores in centers where staff cited cognitive development as a goal and where the focus was on individual development rather than group experience.

As in the study by McCartney (1984), cognitive development in children in the National Day Care Study was related to observed caregiver behaviors. In centers with lower gains in PSI scores and thus less advanced development, caregivers showed less individual attention to children, engaged children in more open-ended and fewer structured activities, and interacted with children more often in large than in medium-sized groups. Greater gains in scores on the PPVT were related to interactions occurring with individual children and with medium-sized groups, with more teacher management of activities, and more social interaction with children.

Findings reported by Goelman and Pence (1987a) extend the cognitive findings to family day care settings. Studying care quality in Victoria, Canada, they found quality of care to be much more variable in family day care than in center care, and a "much more potent predictor of children's language development than quality in centers" (Goelman and Pence, 1987a:99). Total quality scores predicted children's PPVT language scores as well as their scores on the Expressive One-Word Picture Vocabulary Test.

Social Development

Quality of care is also predictive of children's concurrent social development from toddlerhood through the preschool years. For example, Anderson and colleagues (1981) noted that the behavior of 2 1/2-year-olds in a laboratory observation differed according to the level of involvement of the center caregivers with the children. With highly involved caregivers, children showed behavior suggestive of secure attachment: more initial exploration in an unfamiliar room; more physical, visual, and vocal contact with the caregiver; and selective orientation to the caregiver rather than a stranger after a period of time alone in the laboratory playroom.

Howes and Olenick (1986) contrasted the compliance and self-regulatory behaviors of toddlers in high- and low-quality center care. Observations indicated that children in the low-quality settings were less compliant and more resistant. In laboratory observations, children from low-quality centers were less likely to regulate their behavior in a situation requiring restraint. McCartney and colleagues (1982) found ratings of center quality to be related to preschoolers' social as well as cognitive development. In centers in Bermuda with lower overall quality, children were given lower ratings on sociability and considerateness, using the Classroom Behavior Inventory. Children in centers with less adult talk to individual children were found to be less adult oriented, and the language environment of centers also predicted ratings of child considerateness. Extending the findings to family day care, Clarke-Stewart (1987) reported less optimal social development in children whose caregivers less often engaged them in conversation and less often touched them, read to them, or gave them directions.

A study carried out in Sweden (Lamb, Hwang, Broberg, and Bookstein, 1988), however, does not support the prediction that high-quality care is associated with greater social or personality maturity. In that study, quality of care was related in inconsistent and contradictory ways with outcome measures. For example, children who were observed to be more sociable both with peers and unfamiliar adults were in out-of-home child care (both center and family day care) that was rated lower in *both* positive and negative events occurring in child care as observed using the Belsky and Walker checklist. Similarly, regarding a measure of personality maturity, quality of out-of-home care was significantly predictive, but not in the expected direction: out-of-home care of lower quality (as measured by the Belsky and Walker checklist) was associated with greater maturity. Lamb and colleagues urge caution in generalizing to child care in the United States from these findings. They note, in particular, that all out-of-home care in Sweden is of exceptionally high quality by comparison with that in the United States. They raise the possibility that the limited quality variation tapped by their measures is not sufficient for an assessment of the implications of care quality and underlies the contradictory findings. They conclude that consistently high-quality care in Sweden "makes this culture a poor choice for research emphasizing the quality of out-of-home care" (Lamb, Hwang, Broberg, and Bookstein, 1988:39). Interestingly, social skills as well as personality maturity in that study were positively predicted by time spent in out-of-home care. Thus, more time spent in (uniformly high-quality) Swedish family or center day care positively predicted social development, whereas variation within this limited quality range was not a predictor of social development in a consistent manner.

Overall, then, the findings for social development, as for cognitive development, support the prediction that care quality is related to measures of development.

Longitudinal Correlates of Child Care Quality

Five studies have been carried out in the United States that relate quality of child care at one age to later development. Two of the studies focus on the quality of care during toddlerhood and predict development at age 3 (Carew, 1980; Golden et al., 1978);[2] the other three studies examine quality of care during the preschool years in relation to development in kindergarten or later (Howes, 1988; Howes, in press, a; Vandell et al., 1988). Each of these studies supports the hypothesis that quality of care has continuing effects. The findings again pertain to family day care as well as center care and to samples of children from differing family backgrounds. Because of their particular relevance for policy, we note especially the findings extending beyond the preschool years.

In a prospective study by Howes (1988), children's social and cognitive development was assessed at the end of first grade in a high-quality model elementary school in light of the quality and stability of the children's previous child care experiences. The sample was diverse both in ethnicity and socioeconomic status: the ethnicity and socioeconomic status (SES) of children in the school were selected to match the distributions in the U.S. population. The children had attended 81 different center care and family day care settings. Assessment of the children's development occurred after 3 years in the lab school and encompassed teacher ratings of the child's academic progress and school skills, and parent ratings of behavior problems. With family characteristics controlled, higher quality of earlier child care was predictive of better academic progress and school skills and fewer behavior problems in boys and of better school skills as well as fewer behavior problems in girls.

Howes (in press, a) has also reported on analyses from a further study examining age of entry (before or after first birthday) and quality of child care (high or low) in relation to social and cognitive devel-

---

[2] The studies by Carew (1980) and Golden and colleagues (1978) are good examples of how waves of day care research have not been entirely separate, but rather overlap. Both studies present results pertinent both to the first wave (group comparisons) and to the second (quality variation).

opment in the toddler and preschool periods and in kindergarten. Quality of child care was predictive of later social outcomes but not of cognitive outcomes. Looking particularly at outcomes during kindergarten, lower quality child care predicted more child hostility and less task orientation as rated by teachers. Children who entered care *before* their first birthdays and experienced poor-quality care received less positive teacher ratings on distractibility and considerateness in kindergarten.

Vandell and colleagues (1988) found that the quality of center care (high or low) that children received at age 4 affected their observed and rated social behavior in three-way peer interactions at age 8. Controlling for social class, higher quality care at age 4 for this white middle-class sample significantly predicted friendlier peer interactions, more positive affect, greater social competence, and better conflict negotiations. Higher quality care at age 4 was negatively correlated with unfriendly interactions, solitary play, and designations of the child as shy. This study also found significant relations between children's observed activities in child care at age 4 (as opposed to overall quality of care at age 4) and their social functioning at age 8. For example, more positive interaction with caregivers at age 4 was related to ratings of the child at age 8 as more socially competent, peer accepted, empathic, and capable of negotiating conflicts and frustration.

The longitudinal evidence now extends only through the early years of elementary school; it is as yet limited to a small set of studies; and it has not yet eliminated the possibility that further variables may explain the correlations between quality of care and child development. Nevertheless, it is consistent in finding that the quality of center and family day care that children experience in the preschool years is associated with measures of later development.

Methodological Issues

An important strength of the research on child care quality is its ability to go beyond the model day care programs and more closely describe child care as it actually is experienced by the majority of U.S. children. These studies encompass samples that vary by ethnicity and socioeconomic status, and their findings pertain to family day care as well as center care. As a result, the research on quality clearly permits generalizations beyond white middle-class children in university programs. The use of longitudinal research strategies also reflects an important strength in this wave of research.

A problem in this wave of research, however, pertains to the way in which quality is measured. From a policy perspective, the most useful way to assess quality is through specific, potentially regulatable, program characteristics such as group size, caregiver/child ratio, caregiver training, and educational material available. Many of the studies of quality rely instead on global or summary measures. It is impossible to separate the particular program features to determine which are most strongly or causally related to children's development. Thus, the existing research on quality often addresses the broad questions—Does quality matter to both immediate and longer term development?—rather than the specific question of *which* aspects of quality matter most (see Chapter 4). In a similar vein, the research on quality is limited in its usefulness in the policy arena in that it has not, as yet, considered effect sizes. For example, the magnitude of improvements on particular child outcomes cannot be associated with specific increments in quality.

As the research has proceeded, a further methodological issue has emerged, that of the relationship between measures of quality and family characteristics. Higher quality care has been found to be associated with family economic and psychological characteristics in a number of studies. Just as the methodological issues that emerged in the first wave of child care research gave rise to the second wave, this key issue is sparking the emergence of a third wave of studies. How and why are family and child care measures linked?

Summary

The second wave of child care research strongly supports a key conclusion: child care quality is important to children's development.

The strength of the second-wave research to date is that it is very broadly based. The linkage between child care quality and children's development has been documented using a variety of approaches to define quality; samples of varying socioeconomic status; both family day care and center day care settings; and cognitive as well as socioemotional measures of children's development. Furthermore, there are now indications that quality of care in the preschool years continues to have implications for children's development into the early school years.

Further methodological progress in the second wave of child care research can be expected in several important areas: wider use of research strategies involving manipulation of selected quality dimensions; more efforts at disentangling the component features of quality to examine their relative contributions; and attempts to determine the magnitude of improvement in children's development associated with measured improvements in quality. A further methodological issue is already the focus of substantial interest, that of the association between family characteristics and the quality of care a child receives.

TOWARD A THIRD WAVE OF CHILD CARE RESEARCH: THE LINKAGES BETWEEN FAMILY AND CHILD CARE ENVIRONMENTS

Two types of evidence indicate that family and child care environments are related: findings showing linkages between child care quality and family SES and findings showing associations between child care quality and family social and psychological characteristics.

Child Care Quality and Family Social and Psychological Characteristics

Not all studies relating SES variables (e.g., parental education, occupation, income) and quality of care report the two to be significantly related (see, e.g., Howes, 1983; Howes and Olenick, 1986; McCartney et al., 1982). Those that do report a relationship indicate that higher SES is associated with better quality care (e.g., Anderson et al., 1981; Goelman and Pence, 1987b; Holloway and Reichhart-Erickson, 1988; Kontos and Fiene, 1987) or that in lower income samples very low SES is associated with higher quality care, most likely because of the availability of government subsidies (Ruopp et al., 1979). Thus, Anderson and colleagues (1981) found middle-class parents of children in "high physical quality" centers to be better educated, and Goelman and Pence (1987a) found that children from low-resource families (single mothers with little education, low-status occupation, and low incomes) disproportionately enrolled in low-quality centers. Yet, in the National Day Care Study (Ruopp et al., 1979), in centers receiving some federal funds, children in classes with better staff/child ratios tended to be from poorer neighborhoods, to have less-educated mothers, and to come from single-parent families. In general, it appears that in the absence of government subsidies, higher quality child care and higher SES are correlated.

Recent studies go beyond socioeconomic factors to point to differences in family values and behaviors that are associated with differences in child care quality. For example, Howes and Olenick (1986) report that families using low-quality center care had higher scores on a measure of "complexity" (parents live apart, work requires travel, long work hours, weekend work, split shift), a variable that can be interpreted to mean family stress. Furthermore, parents of children in high-quality child care were found to be more involved and invested in child compliance. Howes and Stewart (1987) found that families that could be characterized as "nurturing and supported" by a social network had children in higher quality care; more "restrictive and stressed" families had children in lower quality care. In the study of center care in Bermuda, two family background variables were found to be significantly correlated with center quality: the value the family placed on social skills (as measured by parental reports) was positively related to the quality of the child care arrangement; the value the family placed on conformity (again measured through parental reports) was negatively correlated with quality (McCartney, 1984; Phillips et al., 1987). A partial replication within the United States for this result is reported by Kontos and Fiene (1987): center quality in the state of Pennsylvania was positively associated with the value the family placed on prosocial behavior.

Howes (in press, b), in an excellent discussion of the issues, notes that family variables and the quality of care may have mutual influences over a period of time. A stressed family, for example, may not be able to persevere in a search for higher quality care and may place a child in a lower quality setting. Experiences in such a setting then influence the child's development (perhaps, for example, with regard to compliance), which in turn may increase stress levels in the home. Such patterns of mutual influence between school and family have been identified in older children, especially boys (Patterson, 1986).

The Link Between Child Care Quality and Family Variables

Given the interrelated nature of family and child care quality measures, recent research has asked whether the quality of care has an impact separate from family economic and psychological variables. Evidence that family variables and the quality of care, separately, contribute to development is of two kinds: correlational studies in which care quality continues to predict child development with family variables controlled, and research designs involving random assignment to different child care situations.

Studies using correlational designs have consistently concluded that family and quality of care variables are important contributors. Howes and Stewart (1987), for example, examined the role of family characteristics (factor scores describing families as "nurturing and supported" or "restrictive and stressed") and quality of child care in predicting the level of children's play with objects, peers, and adults. Each set of variables significantly predicted level of play with the other set of variables controlled. McCartney (1984) concluded that the quality of center care was as predictive of children's language skills as family background variables.

As research using the strategy of controlling for correlated family variables progresses, one can anticipate the assessment of a wider range of family variables and the use of direct observation of family processes, rather than reliance on self-report measures. An excellent recent example of progress in both respects can be seen in the work of Owen and Henderson (1989). In this study, child care quality at age 4 was found to be related to several measures of mother-child and father-child interaction as observed at 12 months: children in higher quality care at age 4 had shown less negative affect at 12 months and had parents who had been rated as more sensitive and positive. However, even with these early observational measures controlled, children in higher quality care at age 4 were observed to show more advanced social skills.

A study by McCartney and colleagues (1985) goes beyond a correlational design to ask what happens to children of lower socioeconomic status, compared with more advantaged children, when they are in center care of higher overall quality. In this study, the social and cognitive development of children attending a government-run center for low-income children in Bermuda was compared with the development of children attending eight private child care centers on the island.

The children at the government centers had mothers not only with lower occupational status, but also with lower verbal IQ scores than mothers in the comparison group. At the same time, the overall quality of the government center was the highest of the centers as measured by the Early Childhood Environment Rating Scale. Analysis of the developmental status of the children in the government center with children of the same age attending all other child care programs indicated higher scores for those in the government center on measures of language development, intelligence, and task orientation, as well as on indices of sociability and considerateness. The authors comment that the findings "are especially convincing because the comparison group consists of children of higher SES . . . " (McCartney et al., 1985:251).

Studies involving random assignment of children to groups varying as to quality of care provide the most rigorous examination of whether quality has an impact independent of family factors. Experimental designs, which randomly assign children to differing child care situations, are a widely used strategy in studies of early intervention for children from disadvantaged families. In a recent review of that evidence, Bryant and Ramey (1987) identified assessments of 17 early intervention programs that involved random assignment to intervention or no-intervention groups. They restricted their attention to studies involving such designs in light of concerns about the failure, in other studies, "to ensure adequately the initial equivalence of educationally treated and untreated (control) groups" (Bryant and Ramey, 1987:35). The crucial finding from that review is that the program benefits, as measured by IQ scores, were most closely related to the intensity of contact (amount and breadth) a child had with the intervention program. This pattern, identified by looking across studies, has also been found within a study that systematically varied children's extent of contact with an intervention program (Horacek et al., 1987). This dose-response relationship in experimentally oriented research permits us to conclude with confidence that programs involving high-quality care have positive implications for children, independent of family background factors.

Although designs involving randomization are widely used in early intervention studies, they are as yet rarely used in studies of variation in quality in community-based child care programs. A notable exception illustrates the feasibility and usefulness of such a strategy in studying quality. One substudy within the National Day Care Study (NDCS) (Ruopp et al., 1979) was carried out in the Atlanta public school system and involved random assignment of children, within child care centers, to classrooms varying systematically on quality factors. This substudy confirmed the findings of the overall NDCS that children's growth on cognitive measures from fall to spring was linked most closely to the quality component of group size in child care centers.

Studies of variation in child care quality in community-based care appear to be at an early and descriptive phase, documenting naturally occurring variation and its correlates. Such a descriptive phase appears both important and necessary (e.g., it revealed the family-quality associations), and it will be especially important in future work on dimensions of quality to follow the path of the intervention studies and the NDCS in using experimental designs.

The conclusion best supported by the existing research is that children who are cared for in both child care and the family are influenced by both. As the research in this new wave progresses, an increasingly clear picture will emerge of how care in one environment can offset or complement care in the other. One example of this more complex conceptualization comes from recent research by Howes and colleagues (1988). In that study, toddlers with insecure attachments to *both* mother and caregiver showed the least ability to engage in interactions with caregivers while in child care. Children with insecure attachments to their mothers but secure attachments to caregivers showed behaviors indicating that the relationship with the caregiver was compensatory: "These children appeared more socially competent than the children who failed to form compensatory secure relationships with alternative caregivers (1988:415)." The social behavior of toddlers in child care was thus a reflection of relationships both at home and in the child care setting.

As research progresses, consideration of indirect as well as direct effects can also be expected. That is, not only are children directly influenced by both of their care settings, but child care can have implications for parents that in turn influence children. Thus, for example, Parker and colleagues (1987) found that mothers who participated in the supportive activities offered by Head Start reported fewer psychological symptoms, more feelings of mastery, and greater satisfaction with the current quality of life at the end of a year. The researchers note that such changes in the mothers may well have implications for children: "In addition to the direct effects on children of Head Start, future research should also examine the potentially positive *indirect* effects on children stemming from the enhanced parental well-being that parents' involvement in Head Start programs produces" (Parker et al., 1987:232). Similarly, Edwards and colleagues (1987) found participation in a high-quality infant day care program to be associated with changes over time in parent-infant interaction. Parents of center children diverged over time from other parents in such behaviors as playing with, holding, and touching their babies. The authors relate the increases in those behaviors among the parents to the child-centered orientation and behavior of the center caregivers. Indeed, the changes in parental behavior mirrored observed caregiver behaviors. It will be important, then, in future work to examine further the implications for parents of their children's participation in programs of varying quality and to complete the picture by determining the indirect effects of these influences on children.

Summary

Work reveals that a child's experiences at home and in a child care setting are not separate and unrelated experiences: they are very much linked. Although family and care quality factors are not independent, both sets of factors contribute to children's development: that is, children who experience care both in child care settings and in the home show the influence of both.

Thus far, the major focus of the third wave of research has been to document that a child's placement in child care of higher or lower quality in part reflects family psychological and socioeconomic factors. In the absence of subsidies or interventions, families that are more stressed, both psychologically and economically, are more likely to use lower quality care. The United States thus has a group of children in double jeopardy: the children in greatest need of high-quality care to offset stress at home often receive low-quality care.

Increasingly thorough and rigorous research on the joint contributions of home and child care factors to children's development can be expected. For example, a few studies now identify and control for a wide range of family factors in considering the impact of care quality, but future work on this issue will have to incorporate views of the family-day care linkage that go well beyond the finding that family factors influence choice of care quality. For example, how care quality influences family stress levels and parent-child interaction needs to be examined.

CONCLUSIONS

The research on child care is evolving, and our evaluation of the evidence points to the continuing need to address issues of methodology. Even as it stands, however, the existing evidence from each of the research stages we have identified provides the basis for broad conclusions:

- Child care participation is not a form of maternal deprivation. Children can and do form attachment relationships to multiple caregivers, if the number of caregivers is limited, the relationships enduring, and the caregivers are responsive to the individual child.
- Child care is not inevitably or pervasively harmful to children's development. Indeed, the evidence points to aspects of development for which child care is beneficial.
- The quality of child care—in either family day care or center care— is important to children's development, whatever their socioeconomic levels and whether one looks at cognitive or socioemotional development.
- Children from families enduring greater psychological and economic stress are more likely to be found in lower quality care settings. Thus, there are children in the United States, especially those from low-income families, in double jeopardy from stress both at home and in their care environments.

There is no strong basis in our review for urging parents toward or away from enrolling children in child care settings, although we do find unresolved questions concerning full-time care in the first year of life. Rather, our review strongly directs attention to the issue of child care *quality* and its impact on children's development. Accordingly, the next chapter addresses in greater detail two key questions: What are the components of care quality? What are the thresholds demarcating high- and low-quality care on these dimensions?

REFERENCES

Ainsworth, M.D.S., M. Blehar, E. Waters, and S. Wall
1978 *Patterns of Attachment*. Hillsdale, N.J.: Erlbaum.
Anderson, C.W., R.J. Nagle, W.A. Roberts, and J.W. Smith
1981 Attachment to substitute caregivers as a function of center quality and caregiver involvement. *Child Development* 52:53-61.
Barglow, P., B.E. Vaughn, and N. Molitor
1987 Effects of maternal absence due to employment on the quality of infant-mother attachment in a low-risk sample. *Child Development* 58:945-954.
Belsky, J.
1984 Two waves of day care research: Developmental effects and conditions of

quality. Pp. 1-34 in R.C. Ainslie, ed., *The Child and the Day Care Setting: Qualitative Variations and Development*. New York: Praeger.

1988   The "effects" of infant daycare reconsidered. *Early Childhood Research Quarterly* 3:235-272.

Belsky, J., and M. Rovine

1988   Nonmaternal care in the first year of life and the security of infant-parent attachment. *Child Development* 59:157-167.

Belsky, J., and L. Steinberg

1978   The effects of daycare. *Child Development* 49:929-949.

Benn, R.K.

1986   Factors promoting secure attachment relationships between employed mothers and their sons. *Child Development* 57:1224-1231.

Bowlby, J.

1951   *Maternal Care and Mental Health*. Geneva: World Health Organization.

1969   *Attachment and Loss, Vol. 1, Attachment*. New York: Basic Books.

1973   *Attachment and Loss, Vol. 2, Separation*. New York: Basic Books.

1980   *Attachment and Loss, Vol. 3, Loss*. New York: Basic Books.

Brazelton, T.B.

1986   Issues for working parents. *American Journal of Orthopsychiatry* 56:14-25.

Bronfenbrenner, U., and A.C. Crouter

1982   Work and family through time and space. Pp. 39-83 in S.B. Kamerman and C.D. Hayes, eds., *Families That Work: Children in a Changing World*. Panel on Work, Family, and Community, Committee on Child Development Research and Public Policy, Commission on Behavioral and Social Sciences and Education, National Research Council. Washington, D.C.: National Academy Press.

Brown, G., and T. Harris

1978   *Social Origins of Depression: A Study of Psychiatric Disorders in Women*. London: Tavistock.

Bruner, J.

1983   *Child's Talk*. New York: Norton.

Bryant, D.M., and C.T. Ramey

1987   An analysis of the effectiveness of early intervention programs for high-risk children. Pp. 33-78 in M. Guralnick and C. Bennett, eds., *The Effectiveness of Early Intervention for At-Risk and Handicapped Children*. New York: Academic Press.

Campos, J.J., K.C. Barrett, M.E. Lamb, H.H. Goldsmith, and C. Stenberg

1983   Socioemotional development. Pp. 783-915 in P.H. Mussen, ed., *Handbook of Child Psychology, Vol. 2*. New York: Wiley.

Carew, J.

1980   Experience and the development of intelligence in young children at home and in day care. *Monographs of the Society for Research in Child Development* 45(6-7):Serial No. 187.

Chibucos, T., and P. Kail

1981   Longitudinal examination of father-infant interaction and infant-father interaction. *Merrill-Palmer Quarterly* 27:81-96.

Clarke-Stewart, K.A.

1987   Predicting child development from child care forms and features: The Chicago study. Pp. 21-42 in D.A. Phillips, ed., *Quality in Child Care: What Does Research Tell Us?* Washington, D.C.: National Association for the Education of Young Children.

1989   Infant day care: Maligned or malignant? *American Psychologist* 44:266-274.

Clarke-Stewart, K.A., and G.G. Fein
   1983   Early childhood programs. Pp. 917-999 in P.H. Mussen, ed., *Handbook of Child Psychology, Vol. 2.* New York: Wiley.
Cochran, M.
   1977   A comparison of group and family child-rearing patterns in Sweden. *Child Development* 48:702-707.
Crockenberg, S.
   1981   Infant irritability, mother responsiveness, and social support influences on the security of infant-mother attachment. *Child Development* 52:857-865.
Darlington, R.B., J.M. Royce, A.S. Snipper, H.W. Murray, and I. Lazar
   1980   Preschool programs and the later school competence of children from low-income families. *Science* 208:202-204.
Doyle, A.
   1975   Infant development in day care. *Developmental Psychology* 11:655-666.
Dunn, J.
   1983   Sibling relationships in early childhood. *Child Development* 54:787-811.
   1988   *The Beginnings of Social Understanding.* Cambridge, Mass.: Harvard University Press.
Dyer, E.D.
   1963   Parenthood as crisis: A re-study. *Marriage and Family Living* 25:196-201.
Edwards, C.P., M.E. Logue, S.R. Loehr, and S.B. Roth
   1987   The effects of day care participation on parent-infant interaction at home. *American Journal of Orthopsychiatry* 57:116-119.
Farber, E.A., and B. Egeland
   1982   Developmental consequences of out-of-home care for infants in a low-income population. Pp. 102-125 in E.F. Zigler and E.W. Gordon, eds., *Day Care: Scientific and Social Policy Issues.* Boston: Auburn House.
Freud, A., and D.T. Burlingham
   1944   *Infants Without Families; The Case for and Against Residential Nurseries.* New York: International Universities Press.
   1973   *Infants Without Families; Reports on the Hampstead Nurseries, 1939-1945.* New York: International Universities Press.
Goelman, H., and A.R. Pence
   1987a   Effects of child care, family, and individual characteristics on children's language development: The Victoria Day Care Research Project. Pp. 89-104 in D.A. Phillips, ed., *Quality in Child Care: What Does Research Tell Us?* Washington, D.C.: National Association for the Education of Young Children.
   1987b   Some aspects of the relationship between family structure and child language in three types of day care. Pp. 129-146 in D. Peters and S. Kontos, eds., *Annual Advances in Applied Developmental Psychology, Vol. 2.* Norwood, N.J.: Ablex Publishing Corp.
Golden, M., L. Rosenbluth, M.T. Grossi, H.J. Policare, H. Freeman, Jr., and E.M. Brownlee
   1978   *The New York City Infant Day Care Study.* New York: Medical and Health Research Association of New York City.
Goldfarb, W.
   1943   The effects of early institutional care on adolescent personality. *Journal of Experimental Education* 12:106-129.
Grossman, K.E., K. Grossman, F. Huber, and U. Wartner
   1981   German children's behavior towards their mothers at 12 months and their fathers at 18 months in Ainsworth's Strange Situation. *International Journal of Behavioral Development* 4:157-181.

Harms, T., and R.M. Clifford
 1980   *Early Childhood Environment Rating Scale.* New York: Teachers College Press.
Haskins, R.
 1985   Public school aggression among children with varying day-care experience. *Child Development* 56:689-703.
 1989   Beyond metaphor: The efficacy of early childhood education. *American Psychologist* 44:274-282.
Hobbs, D.F., and S.P. Cole
 1976   Transition to parenthood: A decade replication. *Journal of Marriage and the Family* 38:723-731.
Hock, E., K. Christman, and M. Hock
 1980   Factors associated with decisions about return to work in mothers of infants. *Developmental Psychology* 16:535-536.
Hock, E., M.T. Gnezda, and S.L. McBride
 1984   Mothers of infants: Attitudes toward employment and motherhood following birth of the first child. *Journal of Marriage and the Family* 46:425-431.
Hoffman, L.W.
 1979   Maternal employment: 1979. *American Psychologist* 34:859-865.
Holloway, S.D., and M. Reichhart-Erickson
 1988   The relationship of day-care quality to children's free play behavior and social problem solving skills. *Early Childhood Research Quarterly* 3:39-54.
Horacek, H.J., C.T. Ramey, F.A. Campbell, K.P. Hoffmann, and R.H. Fletcher
 1987   Predicting school failure and assessing early intervention with high-risk children. *Journal of the American Academy of Child and Adolescent Psychiatry* 26:758-763.
Howes, C.
 1983   Caregiver behavior and conditions of caregiving. *Journal of Applied Developmental Psychology* 4:99-107.
 1988   Relations between early child care and schooling. *Developmental Psychology* 24:53-57.
 in press, a Can age of entry and the quality of infant child care predict behaviors in kindergarten? *Developmental Psychology.*
 in press, b Current research in early day care: A review. In S. Chehrazi, ed., *Balancing Working and Parenting: Psychological and Developmental Implications of Day Care.* New York: American Psychiatric Press.
Howes, C., and M. Olenick
 1986   Family and child influences on toddlers' compliance. *Child Development* 57:202-216.
Howes, C., and P. Stewart
 1987   Child's play with adults, toys, and peers: An examination of family and child care influences. *Developmental Psychology* 23:423-430.
Howes, C., C. Rodning, D.C. Galluzzo, and L. Myers
 1988   Attachment and child care: Relationships with mother and caregiver. *Early Childhood Research Quarterly* 3:403-416.
Kontos, S., and R. Fiene
 1987   Child care quality, compliance with regulations, and children's development: The Pennsylvania study. Pp. 57-80 in D.A. Phillips, ed., *Quality in Child Care: What Does Research Tell Us?* Washington, D.C.: National Association for the Education of Young Children.
Lamb, M.E., C.-P. Hwang, F.L. Bookstein, A. Broberg, G. Hult, and M. Frodi
 1988   Determinants of social competence in Swedish preschoolers. *Developmental Psychology* 24:58-70.

Lamb, M.E., C.-P. Hwang, A. Broberg, and F.L. Bookstein
   1988   The effects of out-of-home care on the development of social competence in
           Sweden: A longitudinal study. *Early Childhood Research Quarterly* 3:379-402.
Lazar, I., R.B. Darlington, H. Murray, J. Royce, and A. Snipper
   1982   Lasting effects of early education: A report of the Consortium for Longitudinal
           Studies. *Monographs of the Society for Research in Child Development* 47(2-
           3):Serial No. 195.
Lee, V.E., J. Brooks-Gunn, and E. Schnur
   1988   Does Head Start work? A 1-year follow-up comparison of disadvantaged
           children attending Head Start, no preschool, and other preschool programs.
           Developmental Psychology 24:210-222.
LeMasters, E.E.
   1957   Parenthood as crisis. *Marriage and Family Living* 19:352-355.
Lock, A., ed.
   1978   *Action, Gesture, and Symbol.* New York: Academic Press.
Matas, L., R. Arend, and L.A. Sroufe
   1978   Continuity of adaptation in the second year: The relationship between quality
           of attachment and later competence. *Child Development* 49:547-556.
McCartney, K.
   1984   Effect of quality of day care environment on children's language development.
           Developmental Psychology 20:244-260.
McCartney, K., S. Scarr, D. Phillips, and S. Grajek
   1985   Day care as intervention: Comparisons of varying quality programs. *Journal of
           Applied Developmental Psychology* 6:247-260.
McCartney, K., S. Scarr, D. Phillips, S. Grajek, and J.C. Schwarz
   1982   Environmental differences among day-care centers and their effects on children's
           development. Pp. 126-151 in E.F. Zigler and E.W. Gordon, eds., *Daycare:
           Scientific and Social Policy Issues.* Boston: Auburn House.
Moen, P.
   1989   *Working Parents: Transformations in Gender Roles and Public Policies in Sweden.*
           Madison: University of Wisconsin Press.
Owen, M., and M. Cox
   1988   Maternal employment and the transition to parenthood. Pp. 85-119 in A.E.
           Gottfried and A.W. Gottfried, eds., *Maternal Employment and Children's Devel-
           opment: Longitudinal Research.* New York: Plenum.
Owen, M.T., and V.K. Henderson
   1989   Relations Between Child Care Qualities and Child Behavior at Age 4: Do
           Parent/Child Interactions Play a Role? Paper presented at the meetings of the
           Society for Research in Child Development, Kansas City, April.
Parker, F.L., C.S. Piotrkowski, and L. Peay
   1987   Head Start as social support for mothers: The psychological benefits of
           involvement. *American Journal of Orthopsychiatry* 57:220-233.
Pastor, D.L.
   1981   The quality of mother-infant attachment and its relationship to toddlers' initial
           sociability with peers. *Developmental Psychology* 17:326-335.
Patterson, G.R.
   1986   Performance models for antisocial boys. *American Psychologist* 41:432-444.
Phillips, D.
   1988   Quality in Child Care: Definitions at the A.L. Mailman Family Foundation,
           Inc. Paper presented at symposium on dimensions of quality in programs for
           children. White Plains, New York, June.

Phillips, D.A., and C. Howes
    1987   Indicators of quality in child care: Review of research. Pp. 1-20 in D.A. Phillips,
            ed., *Quality in Child Care: What Does Research Tell Us?* Washington, D.C.:
            National Association for the Education of Young Children.
Phillips, D.A., S. Scarr, and K. McCartney
    1987   Dimensions and effects of child care quality: The Bermuda study. Pp. 43-56
            in D.A. Phillips, ed., *Quality in Child Care: What Does Research Tell Us?*
            Washington, D.C.: National Association for the Education of Young Children.
Provence, S., and R.C. Lipton
    1962   *Infants in Institutions: A Comparison of Their Development With Family-Reared
            Infants During the First Year of Life.* New York: International Universities Press.
Ribble, M.A.
    1965   *The Rights of Infants: Early Psychological Needs and Their Satisfaction* (2nd ed.).
            New York: Columbia University.
Richters, J.E., and C. Zahn-Waxler
    1988   The infant day care controversy: Current status and future directions. *Early
            Childhood Research Quarterly* 3:319-336.
Robertson, J., and J. Robertson
    1971   Young children in brief separations: A fresh look. *Psychoanalytic Study of the
            Child* 26:264-315.
Roopnarine, J.L., and M.E. Lamb
    1978   The effects of day care on attachment and exploratory behavior in a strange
            situation. *Merrill-Palmer Quarterly* 24:85-95.
Rubenstein, J.L., and C. Howes
    1983   Social-emotional development of toddlers in day care: The role of peers and
            individual differences. In S. Kilmer, ed., *Early Education and Day Care*, Vol. 3.
            Greenwich, Conn.: JAI Press.
Rubenstein, J.L., C. Howes, and P. Boyle
    1981   A two-year follow-up of infants in community-based day care. *Journal of Child
            Psychology and Psychiatry* 22:209-218.
Ruopp, R., J. Travers, F. Glantz, and C. Coelen
    1979   *Children at the Center: Final Results of the National Day Care Study.* Boston:
            Abt Associates.
Rutter, M.
    1979   Maternal deprivation, 1972-1978: New findings, new concepts, new approaches.
            Child Development 50:283-305.
    1981a   *Maternal Deprivation Reassessed.* Middlesex, England: Penguin Books.
    1981b   Social-emotional consequences of daycare for preschool children. *American
            Journal of Orthopsychiatry* 5:4-28.
Schwarz, J.C.
    1983   Infant day care: Effects at 2, 4, and 8 years. Paper presented at the meeting
            of the Society for Research in Child Development, Detroit.
Schwarz, J.C., R.G. Strickland, and G. Krolick
    1974   Infant day care: Behavioral effects at preschool age. *Developmental Psychology*
            10:502-506.
Slaughter, D.T.
    1983   Early intervention and its effects on maternal and child development. *Mono-
            graphs of the Society for Research in Child Development* 48(4):Serial No. 202.
Spitz, R.A.
    1945   Hospitalism: An inquiry into the genesis of psychiatric conditions in early
            childhood. *Psychoanalytic Study of the Child* 1:53-74.

Thompson, R.A.
1988   The effects of infant day care through the prism of attachment theory: A critical appraisal. *Early Childhood Research Quarterly* 3:273-282.
Thompson, R.A., M.E. Lamb, and D. Estes
1982   Stability of infant-mother attachment and its relationship to changing life circumstances in an unselected middle class sample. *Child Development* 53:144-148.
Trevarthen, C.
1977   Descriptive analyses of infant communicative behaviour. In H.R. Schaffer, ed., *Studies in Mother-Infant Interaction.* London: Academic Press.
Vandell, D.L., and C.P. Powers
1983   Day care quality and children's free play activities. *American Journal of Orthopsychiatry* 53:493-500.
Vandell, D.L., V.K. Henderson, and K.S. Wilson
1988   A longitudinal study of children with day-care experiences of varying quality. *Child Development* 59:1286-1292.
Vaughn, B.E., K.E. Deane, and E. Waters
1985   The impact of out-of-home care on child-mother attachment quality: Another look at some enduring questions. In I. Bretherton and E. Water, eds., *Growing Points of Attachment Theory and Research. Monographs of the Society for Research in Child Development* 50(1-2):Serial No. 209.
Waters, E., J. Wippman, and L.A. Sroufe
1979   Attachment, positive affect, and competence in the peer group: Two studies in construct validation. *Child Development* 50:821-829.
Wolkind, S.
1974   The components of "affectionless psychopathy" in institutional children. *Journal of Child Psychology and Psychiatry* 15:215-220.
Zaslow, M.J.
1988   The Quality of Care. Paper prepared for the Panel on Child Care Policy, Committee on Child Development Research and Public Policy, Commission on Behavioral and Social Sciences and Education, National Research Council, Washington, D.C.
Zaslow, M.J., F.A. Pedersen, J.T.D. Suwalsky, and B.A. Rabinovich
1989   Maternal employment and parent-infant interaction at one year. *Early Childhood Quarterly* 4:459-478.
Zaslow, M.J., B.A. Rabinovich, and J.T.D. Suwalsky
in press From maternal employment to child outcomes: Preexisting group differences and moderating variables. In J. Lerner and N. Galambos, eds., *Maternal Employment in the Childrearing Years.* New York: Garland Press.

4
Quality of Child Care: Perspectives of Research and Professional Practice

DEFINING QUALITY

In the previous chapter we concluded that, in general, quality of care has an impact on children's development. Is it possible to be more specific, to identify the dimensions of quality that are most closely linked with the development of day care children?

Researchers who have gone beyond summary measures (a center's quality is "high" or "low") to identify particular qualitative dimensions in child care settings have generally focused on one of two approaches to defining or measuring quality: children's daily experiences in care (e.g., Anderson et al., 1981; Carew, 1980) or specific structural features of the care environment, such as group size, ratio, caregiver training, available space, and equipment (e.g., Berk, 1985; Fosburg, 1981; Ruopp et al., 1979). Of these two approaches, the one that most closely links day care participation with developmental outcomes is that focusing on children's experiences (Belsky, 1984; Bredekamp, 1986). Children's development is particularly closely associated with caregiver-child interactions. For example, the comprehensive study of child care centers carried out on the island of Bermuda showed that one aspect of interaction, caregiver speech to children, was the strongest predictor of development (McCartney et al., 1982).

If children's daily experience in child care is key, what is the role of structural features? They appear to support and facilitate more optimal interactions (Belsky, 1984). In the National Day Care Study (NDCS), for example, structural features of the environment were associated with caregiver and child behaviors observed in centers (Ruopp et al., 1979). Observed behaviors in turn were predictive of gains children made in a year on measures of cognitive development. Although environmental features cannot ensure that more optimal patterns of interaction will occur, they can increase the likelihood of responsive and stimulating interactions and thus of closer to optimal developmental outcomes.

The distinction between structural and interactive dimensions of quality made in research is useful in differentiating between the two arenas in which efforts can be made to enhance the quality of child care: government regulations and professional standards.

Regulations establish minimum standards that are enforceable by state licensing authorities. Most regulations aim at structural dimensions of quality. For example, in a survey of state regulations for child care centers carried out for the panel, we found that all states regulate staff/child ratios and the square footage per child of indoor space in child care centers. Many states further specify training required of center staff (directors, teachers, and assistants) and square footage available per child outdoors (see Appendix A). Although many state regulations consider such factors as the nature of *disciplinary* interactions permitted (i.e., corporal punishment), the focus of regulations is generally not on the interactive aspects of quality.

In contrast, professional standards cover structural features and interactive aspects of child care quality.[1] Unlike regulations, professional standards specify *goals* for quality care.

The accreditation criteria of the National Academy of Early Childhood Programs of the National Association for the Education of Young Children (NAEYC), for example, go beyond structural features such as group size and ratio to include criteria for quality interactions among staff and children, as well as for staff-parent interaction. The NAEYC accreditation criteria include the following statements regarding staff-child interactions (National Association for the Education of Young Children, 1984:8):

> Staff interact frequently with children. Staff express respect for and affection toward children by smiling, holding, touching, and speaking to children at their eye level throughout the day. . . . Staff are available and responsive to children; encourage them to share experiences, ideas, and feelings, and listen to them with attention and respect.

These criteria were developed on the basis of a review of research and of approximately 50 evaluation documents (i.e., program standards in localities), as well as the judgments of 175 early childhood specialists. To

---

[1] Appendix B summarizes four professional standards of quality: the accreditation criteria of the National Academy of Early Childhood Programs of the National Association for the Education of Young Children; the Early Childhood Environment Rating Scale; the National Black Child Development Institute's safeguards; and the Child Welfare League of America's standards for day care service. It also presents the criteria for quality given in two sets of requirements for receipt of federal funds: the Federal Interagency Day Care Requirements and the Head Start performance standards.

date, 675 child care centers in 47 states have completed the process of self-study and external observation necessary for accreditation. Research with the observation component of the accreditation program has supported the reliability and validity of the assessment of interactions in early childhood settings and underscored the importance of staff-child interactions in evaluations of program quality (Bredekamp, 1986).

Federal and state legislative efforts to ensure the quality of care that children receive in child care centers and family day care have primarily addressed regulatable aspects of care. Accordingly, we summarize below the evidence regarding the structural aspects of quality. The NAEYC accreditation program serves as a reminder, however, that it is possible to delineate well-grounded guidelines for high-quality interactions in early childhood programs and that child care professionals view such guidelines as attainable. Although focusing on the "regulatable aspects" of quality in the following discussion, we affirm Morgan's (1982) view that regulations and standards are important in improving the quality of child care services.

RESEARCH FINDINGS ON STRUCTURAL ASPECTS OF QUALITY

Conclusions regarding the structural aspects of quality rest on the complementary perspectives of research and professional practice. Research has examined empirically the question of which features of center and family day care settings are most closely associated with children's development, but there is an important gap in the existing research: with few exceptions, it has not addressed the question of acceptable versus unacceptable ranges on the key structural dimensions. At what point, for example, does group size become too large to support development? Research has determined whether a structural feature is important; however, determining where "to draw the line" between what is acceptable and what is unacceptable comes from standards developed for professional practice.

The existing body of research on the structural dimensions of quality identifies three important sets of variables: major policy variables (identified in the National Day Care Study), i.e., group size, ratio, and caregiver qualifications;[2] additional variables (which pertain to both family and center

---

[2]The NDCS (Ruopp et al., 1979) defined *group size* in a day care center as the total number of children present in or assigned to a class or to a principally responsible caregiver; *ratio* in center day care as the number of caregivers divided by group size; and *caregiver qualifications* in terms of total years of education, whether or not a caregiver had child-related training, and years of experience in day care. *Child-related training* was defined as presence or absence of special training received by caregivers in high school, junior college, vocational or technical school, college, or graduate school that was directly related to young children (in such fields as day care, early childhood education, child development, child psychology, or elementary education). Child-related training almost always involved a combination of field work and classroom instruction.

day care), i.e., caregiver stability, structure or curriculum, and space and equipment; and factors specific to family day care, i.e., licensing and age mix of children. In this chapter, after evaluating the evidence for these three sets of variables, we identify several other aspects of quality that have not received extensive research attention, notably, overall center size, parent involvement, and sensitivity to the cultural ethnic and racial backgrounds of children. We also consider professional standards on acceptable ranges on the key structural dimensions of quality.

Group Size, Ratio, Qualifications:
The Iron Triangle

The NDCS (Ruopp et al., 1979) proposed that the debate on quality focus on three variables that it called the policy variables. These three variables, recently redubbed the "iron triangle" (Phillips, 1988) are group size, caregiver/child ratio, and caregiver qualifications. The NDCS (Ruopp et al., 1979; Travers et al., 1979) concluded that of the three key policy variables, group size had the most consistent and pervasive effects on teacher and child behavior in child care centers and on children's gains on cognitive tests from fall to spring. In that study, ratio was clearly important for infants and toddlers, but had less effect on preschoolers. Of the three aspects of caregiver qualifications considered—education, training in child development, and experience in child care—only specialized training in child development had consistent positive correlations with development for preschoolers.

Much of the subsequent research on structural aspects of quality has continued to focus on these three key variables. That research affirms in part the conclusions of the NDCS. For group size, the findings are consistent concerning the benefits of smaller groups. For caregiver/child ratio, the findings are mixed: the findings on ratio for infants and toddlers are more consistent than the findings for preschoolers. For caregiver qualifications, research confirms the importance of both child-related training and overall education.

Group Size

Findings concerning group size clearly pertain to both family day care and center care. In family day care settings, larger groups are associated with less positive patterns of interaction (Fosburg, 1981; Howes, 1983; Howes and Rubenstein, 1985;[3] Stith and Davis, 1984), and less advanced

---

[3]Howes and Rubenstein (1985) present their findings in terms of ratio, but in their study ratio and group size are the same for family day care.

development (Clarke-Stewart, 1987). In center care settings, larger groups have again been reported to be associated both with less positive interaction patterns (Howes, 1983; Howes and Rubenstein, 1985) and developmental outcomes (Holloway and Reichhart-Erickson, 1988; though see also Clarke-Stewart, 1987; Kontos and Fiene, 1987).

A decade ago, the NDCS (Ruopp et al., 1979) pointed out that despite findings concerning the importance of group size, this structural aspect of quality was not consistently regulated, but ratio, which was found to be a less important structural feature, was. The report urged wider inclusion of group size in child care regulations. Our survey of state regulations shows that 10 years later, while group size in family day care is regulated in all but 3 states, only 20 states and the District of Columbia regulate size for all the age groups we examined in child care centers. Five other states regulate group size only for infants. Group size continues to be a dimension of quality in which important research findings have not influenced policy.

Ratio

In family day care, ratio is usually synonymous with group size; therefore the findings summarized here focus on center care. In the NDCS, ratio did not have widespread correlates for preschoolers, but it was important in predicting the daily experiences of infants and toddlers. Higher ratios (i.e., more children per adult caregiver) were found to be associated with more distress in infants as well as toddlers. For infants, it was also associated with more child apathy and with more situations involving potential danger to the child.

In further research involving infants and toddlers, ratio does appear to be an important factor. Howes (1983), for example, found that in centers with lower ratios for toddlers, caregivers were better able to facilitate positive social interactions and to foster a more positive emotional climate. In another study involving toddlers, Howes and Rubenstein (1985) found that children in groups with more children per adult engaged in significantly less talk and play behavior. Most recently, lower ratios have been found to be associated with a higher incidence of secure attachment to caregivers by toddlers (Howes et al., 1988).

Like the findings of the NDCS, the subsequent research on ratios for preschool-age children is not consistent. Howes and Rubenstein (1985) found ratio to be important in predicting caregiver and child behaviors in center child care, and Holloway and Reichhart-Erickson (1988) found that children spent less time in solitary play in classes with better ratios. Yet, McCartney (1984) did not find better ratio to be a positive predictor of child language development, and Clarke-Stewart (1987) reports that children from classes with more children per teacher were *more* cooperative with peers and adults in an observation setting.

Thus, it appears that ratio is particularly important for infants and toddlers. Further research is needed to clarify the mixed findings for preschoolers. Would differentiating between equal ratios in groups of varying sizes make a difference? The NDCS, for example, suggested that in larger groups with several teachers, lead teachers tend to manage classroom activities and direct other teachers rather than interact directly with the children. The NDCS continues to stand alone in attempting to study ratio and group size as related variables. More work of this kind is needed.

Ratio is nearly universally regulated by states (see Appendix A), with all but one state specifying ratios. However, there is substantial variation in what states view as acceptable ratios for children of different ages. For example, California and the District of Columbia require a 1:4 staff/child ratio for infants up to 1 year of age, whereas Georgia accepts a ratio of 1:7 for infants. Similarly, for children of 3 years, North Dakota specifies a ratio of 1:7, whereas Arizona, North Carolina, and Texas permit more than twice this number, 1:15. The substantial range in ratios in regulations, particularly for infants, contradicts the research on optimal ratios for the youngest children.

Qualifications

The NDCS (Ruopp et al., 1979; Travers et al., 1979) concluded that for preschoolers the key caregiver qualification variable was child-related training. It was associated with more caregiver social interaction with children, with more cooperation and task persistence among children, and with less time children spent uninvolved in activities. However, three issues qualify the basic conclusion that child-related training is central. First, the correlations among the different components of staff qualifications—child-related training, years of education, and experience—while moderate, were "high enough to warrant caution in interpreting individual effects" (Ruopp et al., 1979:37). Second, the findings again differed by age of child: for example, for infants and toddlers, overall education, rather than child-related training, showed positive correlates. Third, the *ranges* of caregiver education and training may be important to the findings in any one study. For example, the NDCS involved caregivers with an average of 2 years of education beyond completion of high school, but other studies, reaching different conclusions (e.g., Berk, 1985; see below), involved caregivers with college educations.

Findings from the National Day Care Home Study (NDCHS) (Fosburg, 1981) on family day care strongly support the NDCS findings concerning child-related training. Caregiver training had strong and positive effects in all three types of family day care homes studied: sponsored, regulated, and unregulated. For example, in sponsored and regulated family day care homes, training was associated with more teaching, helping, and dramatic play and with less activity that did not involve interacting with children. Training was found to be a predictor of caregiver behavior in further studies of this type of care by Howes (1983) and Rosenthal (1988). Yet findings from other studies point to positive correlates of caregiver overall education. Berk (1985) found caregiver education to be the most important predictor of caregiver communicative behavior with children in child care centers, with the distinction being made between caregivers with high school only and those with at least 2 years of college. Education predicted caregiver behavior with infants in the NDCS (Ruopp et al., 1979) and some caregiver behaviors in family day care (Fosburg, 1981). The evidence, then, points to positive correlates of both caregiver education and training specific to child development. We note, however, that the two studies of national scope (the NDCS focusing on center care and the NDCHS focusing on family day care) are in agreement in showing a stronger impact of training specific to child development.

There is little indication that the third approach to measuring qualifications, greater caregiver experience, is positively associated with either interactions or outcomes (Howes, 1983; Rosenthal, 1988). Indeed, Ruopp and colleagues (1979) found less cognitive and social stimulation of infants and more apathy among infants and toddlers with more experienced caregivers, and Kontos and Fiene (1987) did not find caregiver experience considered alone to be a predictor of child outcomes.

Two approaches in future research would greatly clarify the role of caregiver qualifications. First, no study to date has involved random assignment of caregivers to receive different training or education experiences. Such an approach would help eliminate the possibility that caregivers with more and less training or education already differ in ways that would have implications for the development of children in their care. Second, there is a need for greater specificity in defining both training and education. For example, is the key aspect of training the experience of supervised teaching, of coursework, or of something else? Although the research affirms the importance of caregiver qualifications, states do not consistently regulate this dimension of child care. Indeed, only 27 states and the District of Columbia require preservice training for teachers in child care centers, and only about one-quarter of the states require preservice training for family day care providers.

Summary

From the existing research we conclude that group size is an important determinant of children's development in child care settings, and that the ratio of staff to children in centers is particularly important for infants and toddlers. Further study is needed on the relationship between ratio and group size. While both caregiver training specific to child development and caregiver overall education are associated with outcomes among children in child care, the two existing national studies point to caregiver training as the more important factor.

Existing state regulations do not reflect these research findings. A minority of states regulates group size for all ages in child care centers. Ratios, while consistently regulated, vary substantially, with some states permitting a single caregiver to care for seven babies. And only a little more than one-half of the states require preservice training for center teachers. There are, then, serious gaps in the regulation even of these three so-called "regulatable" dimensions of child care quality.

Stability, Structure, Facilities:
Beyond the Iron Triangle

Recent research has moved beyond the iron-triangle variables to identify additional characteristics of child care environments that foster children's development. The evidence points, in particular, to the importance of caregiver stability and continuity, structure of daily routine, and adequacy of physical facilities. Caregiver stability is not directly regulatable, but it is a structural feature of quality that could probably be affected by higher salaries for caregivers.

Caregiver Stability and Continuity

Chapter 3 summarized the research pointing to children's needs for enduring relationships with particular caregivers. In both family day care and center care, these needs are more adequately fulfilled if children do not experience frequent changes of caregivers caused by staff turnover or families changing their child care arrangements. In center care, these needs are further assured when children become involved with particular caregivers among the several caregivers to whom they are exposed. (In Chapter 5, we discuss in more detail findings pointing to the importance of enduring relationships among particular children in child care).

The number of changes a child experiences in child care arrangements has implications for both short- and long-term development. Multiple changes in child care arrangements have been found to be associated with higher rates of insecure attachment to mother (see Chapter 3) both in a highly stressed, lower income sample (Vaughn et al., 1980) and in a middle-class sample (Suwalsky et al., 1986). Howes and Stewart (1987) found that when children in family day care experience a greater number of different child care arrangements, they demonstrate lower levels of complexity in their play with adults and peers and with objects. Stable care was also found to be related to positive longer term development in a recent study by Howes (1988): greater early stability of care predicted better school adjustment in first grade.

Researchers have focused not only on the number of changes children experience in care arrangements, but also on the extent to which children in center care form relationships with individual caregivers. Several studies indicate that children's involvement with particular caregivers in center care is associated with greater security in their behavior. Cummings (1980) found infants and toddlers to be less distressed when transferred from mother to a more familiar, as opposed to a less familiar, caregiver upon arrival at a child care center. In a study by Anderson and colleagues (1981), toddlers in center care who were observed in a laboratory setting with a highly involved (in contrast to a less involved) caregiver more freely explored an unfamiliar room and more often made physical and visual or vocal contact with the caregiver—behaviors suggestive of secure attachment.

Structure and Content of Daily Activities

Researchers have explored two issues concerning daily activities in child care: structure and content. Child care can be viewed as a custodial setting in which physical care is ensured and children's major activity is free play. Alternatively, it can be viewed as a setting in which there are some structured daily activities intended to facilitate social and cognitive development. Does child care with some daily routine differ from unstructured custodial care in terms of the outcome for children? In addition, child care settings that follow a structure or curriculum differ greatly in the particular content of their programs. Is there any indication of differing outcomes associated with differing early childhood curricula?

The contrast of custodial care and some degree of organized learning is well illustrated by the findings of the comprehensive study of child care centers in Bermuda (McCartney, 1984). In that study, the daily amount of free play time in child care centers predicted less advanced language development for children, and the amount of group activity time positively predicted language development. If the director's goal was that the center should simply provide a good, safe place for children to stay, children's language was less developed than that of children in centers in which the director's stated goal was to prepare children for school. Similarly, in the NDCS, when teachers managed children's activities and when children engaged in more structured than open-ended activities, they showed greater gains on cognitive measures from fall to spring (Ruopp et al., 1979). These studies do *not* indicate that free play and unstructured time are inherently negative. Rather, they suggest that a great deal of unstructured time in child care does not contribute to children's cognitive development; some emphasis on organized teaching activities appears to be beneficial to children.

For content, research indicates that a range of quality preschool curricula can facilitate intellectual development, particularly among children in "high-risk" groups. Thus, for example, in a longitudinal study, Royce and colleagues (1983:442) found that "a variety of curricula are equally effective in preparing children for school and that any of the tested curricula is better than no program at all." The Perry Preschool contrast of differing curricular approaches reached a similar conclusion regarding measures of intellectual development (Schweinhart et al., 1986:41): "[D]iverse curriculum models can be *equally* effective in improving children's education."

However, when social development is considered, findings indicate that differing curricula do have differing implications. In particular, the High/Scope Preschool Study (Schweinhart et al., 1986), which randomly assigned children to preschools with different curricula, reported differences according to whether early curricula were structured around teacher-initiated or child-initiated learning activities. This long-term longitudinal study found that the group that had been in a teacher-directed preschool program demonstrated less adequate social adaptation than the groups of children assigned to preschool programs in which children initiated and paced their own learning activities in environments prepared by teachers. While emphasizing the limitations of this study and the need for replication, the authors note that the finding points to the importance not only of the *content* a curriculum attempts to convey, but also of the *process* through which learning occurs. Children's active initiation and pacing of their learning activities may have implications for their social development. Further research on learning processes points also to the need for curricula to allow for individual differences in learning styles and to the importance of learning through interactions (Greenfield and Lave, 1982).

Space and Facilities

The adequacy of space as a qualitative dimension differs for family day care and center care. In family day care, the issue that emerges in the research is whether children are cared for in a space that remains primarily designed for adults or whether adaptations have been made such that the space could be called "child designed." In center care, where space is uniformly child designed, the relevant issues instead are sufficiency and organization of space and equipment.

Howes (1983) found that in family day care the degree to which space was child designed was associated with a number of caregiver behaviors: restrictiveness and responsiveness to children, establishment of a positive emotional climate, and ability to facilitate positive social relations. In considering the results of this study, it is important to note the possibility that caregiver behavior may not differ *because* of differences in space but rather that caregivers who already differ on psychological variables do or do not modify their homes according to children's needs. Howes (1983) raises the important possibility that the need to restrict behavior and monitor safety in an adult-oriented space may have implications for caregiver behavior. However, further work is needed to clarify the causal direction.

In center care, specific aspects of the physical environment appear to be linked to different aspects of children's behavior and development, although, again, issues of causal direction are unresolved. Holloway and Reichhart-Erickson (1988), for example, found that in more spacious child care centers, children spent more time in focused solitary play. In contrast, a child's social problem-solving skills were more influenced by whether the center had a variety of age-appropriate materials and was arranged to accommodate groups of varying sizes. Clarke-Stewart (1987) found that children demonstrated better cognitive and social skills in centers that were more orderly, that had more varied and stimulating materials, and in which space was organized into activity areas.

Summary

Children's development in child care environments is enhanced by the formation of relationships with particular caregivers and by the stability of such relationships over time. Development is supported in settings that caregivers define as learning rather than custodial environments, and where they provide some structured learning. Preliminary findings suggest that children benefit when the learning process involves child-initiated and -paced learning activities rather than teacher-directed learning. Finally, research raises the possibility that more adequate space and physical design in child care settings may be linked with positive caregiver and child behaviors. However, further research is needed to examine the causal direction of these findings.

The dimensions of quality of stability, structure, and space are rarely the subject of state regulations. Caregiver stability is of course not regulatable, although it is clearly important. As we discuss in Chapter 6, as a result of high staff turnover rates, a large proportion of children experience instability rather than stability in their relationships with caregivers. States nearly universally regulate space, defined as square footage per child indoors, for child care centers. However, for a substantial number of states, there is no specification of square footage per child in family day care. Professional child care standards address issues of curriculum and daily routine, but state regulations do not.

Family Day Care:
Additional Dimensions of Quality

In addition to group size, caregiver training, and stability, which pertain to both family day care and center care settings, there are also dimensions of quality that are unique to family day care. Although virtually all child care centers are licensed, a majority of family day care homes are not. Research suggests that the regulatory status of family day care homes is a factor related to caregiver behaviors and child outcomes. Similarly, where most child care centers group children according to age, family day care typically does not. The age mix of children in family day care also appears to have implications for children in this setting.

Studies suggest a pattern of associations between regulatory status in family day care and children's experiences and development. These studies are open to question on the important grounds that different kinds of families may seek regulated and unregulated care, and different kinds of caregivers may or may not pursue licensing. Differences in families and caregivers may underlie the associations that are observed in the research. Clearly, these results need replication and extension through studies that more adequately examine self-selection factors. However, we present the findings because of the possibility that regulatory status and quality of care are linked.

Regulatory status in family day care emerged as an important variable in the NDCHS (Fosburg, 1981). Three family day care groups were considered in this study: sponsored family day care, in which homes are organized into networks; regulated; and unregulated. Unregulated family day care homes showed the lowest levels of caregiver interactions with 1- to 5-year-olds, and sponsored homes the highest. Caregivers in unregulated family day care homes also spent substantially more time uninvolved with children: approximately 26 minutes per hour, in comparison with 18 minutes in sponsored and regulated homes. Observations in sponsored family day care homes revealed more caregiver teaching activities with children, more facilitation of language, and more structured fine-motor and music and dance activities.

Goelman and Pence (1987) similarly found differences by regulatory status for family day care homes in Victoria, Canada: 13 of the 15 family day care homes they rated as high quality were licensed; 2 of 11 low-quality family day care homes were licensed. Children in the low-quality family day care settings scored lower on measures of language development. In addition, they engaged in fewer structured fine- and gross-motor activities, fewer reading and information activities, and fewer art and music activities than children in high-quality family day care.

Center care provides caregivers with opportunities for regular contact with colleagues, sharing of tasks, and the possibility of relief from difficult interactions with children. Family day care does not. The findings in the NDCHS suggest that membership in a network of family day care providers may be beneficial to caregivers, perhaps alleviating a sense of isolation in the working environment. Findings from Rosenthal's (1988) study in Israel also point to the possible importance of caregiver isolation. The frequency of individual supervision that a family day care caregiver received (once a week or less frequently) significantly predicted the quality of caregiver-child interaction. Supportive contacts through a network or through supervision may positively influence the quality of daily experiences for children in family day care.

The limited research into the varying ages of children in individual family day care groups suggests that certain configurations may be more positive for children's development. Rosenthal (1988) found cither a very heterogeneous or a very homogeneous age mix to be detrimental to the quality of interactions. An age range of less than 6 months or of more than 25 months was detrimental. Fosburg (1981) found that the presence of a preschooler in a family day care group was associated with diminished rates of caregiver one-on-one interactions with toddlers. Further research is needed to confirm these patterns and identify age mixes that are optimal.

In summary, existing research raises the possibility that the regulatory status of family day care and quality of care are linked: on average, caregiver behavior appears to be more stimulating in regulated or sponsored family day care, and children's development differs accordingly. Further research is needed on self-selection factors that may affect this pattern of associations. If the findings are borne out in future work, there will be cause for concern about the quality of care children currently receive in family day care in the United States since it is estimated that approximately 60 percent of family day care homes are unregulated. A moderate age range (rather than too broad or narrow) may be closer to optimal in family day care settings, although research is needed to extend and replicate preliminary findings.

Dimensions of Quality That Need Study

There are several further structural features of child care settings that have received minimal research attention and yet may be important to the quality of care. In particular, little is known about the role of overall center size, parent involvement, and sensitivity to children's ethnic, racial, and cultural backgrounds, although some evidence suggests that these factors may be significant.

Although group size within child care centers has been repeatedly studied, the work of Prescott (1970) indicates that overall center size may also be important. Prescott found that in centers with more than 60 children, teachers spent more time in managing behavior and emphasizing rules. In smaller centers, serving 30 to 60 children, teachers were more often rated as sensitive, and children were more often rated as highly interested and enthusiastically involved in activities. Prescott observes that large centers appear to lack a dimension of personalization as childrearing environments. Given the recent shift toward use of child care centers, it is particularly important that additional research attempt to replicate and extend these preliminary findings on center size.

Examination of the professional standards (summarized in Appendix B) helps identify features of quality that are viewed by professionals as important components of child care quality but have not yet been the focus of research: parent involvement and recognition and active appreciation of children's cultures. For example, regarding parent involvement, the National Black Child Development Institute (1987:5) states that "the entire school atmosphere as well as organized activities should reflect respect for and welcome to parents at all times," and the National Association for the Education of Young Children (1984:16) sets as a goal that "parents and other family members are encouraged to be involved in the program."

Parent involvement is a key feature of Head Start programs, but its implications for parents and children have not been carefully evaluated. Slaughter and colleagues (1988) note three distinct patterns of parent involvement through Head Start: participation in children's education, participation in program administration, and participation in skills development programs for parents. Existing research confirms that parents are satisfied with Head Start as a program both for themselves and for their children. Yet no studies have evaluated the differential impact of these three types of parental involvement. Just as Slaughter and colleagues (1988:5) conclude that "Head Start's parental involvement component should be systematically evaluated," we highlight the need to assess the impact of parent involvement in other forms of child care.

Professional standards also stress that curriculum materials should reflect respect for cultural diversity and affirm children's multiple cultures. The Early Childhood Environment Rating Scale (ECERS), for example, gives "cultural awareness evidenced by liberal inclusion of multiracial . . . materials" (Harms and Clifford, 1980:8) as a characteristic of high-quality care. Head Start has played a pioneering role in making multicultural sensitivity an integral part of its program (Slaughter et al., 1988). Indeed, Head Start performance standards require a multicultural approach, and a great deal of work has been done in the context of Head Start to develop and implement multicultural curricula, most recently through the National Head Start Multicultural Task Force (1987). However, as with parent involvement, the research has been sparse. Slaughter and colleagues (1988:8) conclude that "to date the opportunity to use Head Start for the collection of information that would provide a data base on ethnic minority children has not been seized."

The importance of examining the implications for children of a multicultural approach in child care settings is also underscored by developmental research. Findings over a 40-year period have been consistent in indicating that young children in the United States show a Eurocentric bias for racial connotations, attitudes, and preferences, independent of socioeconomic status, race, and sex (Aboud, 1988; Alejandro-Wright, 1985; Clark and Clark, 1939, 1940; Comer, 1989; Goodman, 1964; Phinney and Rotheram, 1988). Linkages between own-group cultural identity and academic competence have been found for minority group children both in the United States (see Chapter 5) and in other countries (e.g., evidence regarding achievement in minority group children in Japan reviewed by Ogbu [1986] and by Spencer et al. [1987]). Future research is needed on approaches in child care settings that affirm children's cultural identities in relation to children's development. Research with older children (Cummins, 1986) suggests that this factor may be particularly important for children's cognitive development.

European research on child care also helps to identify dimensions of quality that have not been explored in research in the United States. One such dimension, that of caregiver autonomy in child care centers, emerged in the work of Tizard and colleagues (1972) regarding residential nurseries in England. Nursery groups in which child care staff had more autonomy (for example, to make decisions about activities, schedules, and menus for children) differed in terms of observed verbal behaviors from nursery groups with low autonomy (rigid daily schedule and decisions made by an administrator rather than by the staff of the individual group). In the high-autonomy groups, staff played and conversed more with children than did staff in low-autonomy groups. Similar findings were reported from a study of day nurseries (child care centers) (Garland and White, 1980). Together, these findings raise the possibility that the organizational structure of child care centers may be a dimension of quality worthy of further study. In U.S.

child care centers, is there variation in degree of caregiver autonomy, and is this linked to other quality measures or to indices of development?

In summary, empirical examinations of quality should be expanded to take account of these additional dimensions of quality that are reflected either in the professional standards or in academic research.

PROFESSIONAL GUIDELINES ON STRUCTURAL ASPECTS OF QUALITY

Although research is helpful in identifying which structural dimensions of quality are important, it is less helpful in clarifying the magnitude of the effects associated with graded improvements in quality (effect sizes) or appropriate limits on such structural dimensions as group size or ratio. In order to identify ranges and limits for specific quality dimensions—for example, at what point does group size exceed acceptable limits, or how many 1-, 2-, or 3-year-olds should a single caregiver be responsible for—it is necessary to turn to program evaluations and professional expertise. These sources provide the basis for four sets of standards for professional practice and two sets of requirements for receipt of federal funding identified by the panel (see Appendix B). For example, the accreditation criteria of the NAEYC were developed following reviews of approximately 50 program evaluation documents, as well as academic research, and by 186 early childhood specialists and the NAEYC membership (Bredekamp, 1986).

The four sets of standards and two sets of requirements for federal funding were developed for a variety of reasons. The accreditation criteria of the NAEYC were developed in 1984 to establish a procedure for center-based programs to engage in a voluntary process of self-evaluation regarding quality, which leads to certification when externally validated. The safeguards of the National Black Child Development Institute (NBCDI) (1987) suggest means of ensuring that programs for early education in public schools are positive learning environments for black children. The ECERS was developed by Harms and Clifford (1980) for research and to help center-based programs engage in a process of self-evaluation regarding quality. The standards developed by the Child Welfare League of America (CWLA) (1984), first published in 1960 and revised in 1984, describe practices considered most desirable for the care of children in center-based programs and in family day care homes. The Head Start performance standards (U.S. Department of Health and Human Services, 1984) were promulgated in 1975 as a condition of the receipt of federal Head Start funding. Finally, the Federal Interagency Day Care Requirements (FIDCR), which were developed in 1968 (U.S. Department of Health, Education, and Welfare, U.S. Office of Economic Opportunity, and U.S. Department of Labor), revised in 1980, and have since been suspended, reflected an effort to standardize the requirements for federally funded child care programs providing comprehensive services to children.

As Appendix B indicates, these sets of standards and requirements provide guidelines for establishing acceptable limits on the structural dimensions of quality. Although the guidelines detailed in the appendix do not always agree precisely, they can be combined to define an acceptable range for each dimension. For example, three professional organizations provide guidelines for maximum ratios and group sizes, though only NAEYC does so for group sizes in the infant and toddler years. For ratios, there is clear agreement across standards that in the first 2 years of life, the staff/child ratio should not exceed 1:4. For older ages, the differences across standards can be used to identify a range within which quality care is possible: for 2-year-olds, the range of acceptable ratios is from 1:3 to 1:6; for 3-year-olds, from 1:5 to 1:10; and for children aged 4 to 5, from 1:7 to 1:10. For group size, professional standards identify the ranges at between 14 and 20 for 3-year-olds, between 16 and 20 for 4-year-olds, and between 16 and 20 for 5-year-olds. The NAEYC-proposed maximum group size in center programs for younger children is 8 for infants and 12 for toddlers.

Four of the organizations provide guidelines for professional qualifications of child care staff. For full teachers in centers, the standards agree on requiring training specific to early childhood education or development. CWLA, NAEYC, and NBCDI standards call for such training as a part of a bachelor's degree or other professional education, whereas the FIDCR specifies only training or demonstrated ability with children. The academic research and professional standards agree, however, that specific training in child development is important for teachers and caregivers of young children.

Beyond the "iron-triangle" dimensions, the professional standards specify that child care programs should provide a daily organization that is both structured and flexible, that curricula should encompass social as well as cognitive components, and that there should be options for children to select and pace their own activities from among several possibilities provided by caregivers (see Appendix B). In addition, professional standards specify the need for a physical environment that is designed for children, orderly, and differentiated. Professional standards also complement the academic research by recommending parent involvement and the affirmation of cultural diversity. Furthermore, the professional standards complement the research by providing specific descriptions of how such dimensions of quality can be addressed in actual practice.

Finally, we note that until quite recently standards of quality specific to family day care programs have been seriously lacking. The professional standards summarized in Appendix B, and the discussion above, pertain almost entirely to center care. However, in June 1988, the National Association for Family Day Care (NAFDC), Washington, D.C., launched a program of accreditation for family day care homes to address this need. Like the NAEYC accreditation program, the NAFDC program involves a process of self-evaluation as well as external validation. It encompasses the dimensions of indoor safety, health, nutrition, indoor and outdoor play environments, interactions, and professional responsibility. To date, there are 36 accredited family day care providers, and 250 providers who have requested applications (Sandra Gellert, NAFDC, personal communication, January 25, 1989). A study guide, now in development, will soon make it possible to add to the professional standards for center day care the perspective from professional practice on dimensions of quality in family day care.

SUMMARY AND CONCLUSIONS

We have noted the need to draw on both academic research and standards for professional practice in order to extract a picture of the components of high-quality care. These sources are most clear regarding the importance of six structural aspects of quality: group size, staff/child ratio, caregiver training, stability of care, daily routine, and the organization of space.

Research shows group size to be a particularly important factor in children's development in child care. Larger groups are associated with less positive interactions and child development. Professional standards provide ranges seen as acceptable for group sizes for children of different ages, with the following as maximums:

to 1 year of age, between 6 and 8 per group;
1- to 2-year-olds, between 6 and 12 per group;
3-year-olds, between 14 and 20 per group;
4- and 5-year-olds, between 16 and 20 per group.

The effect of staff/child ratios appears to be greatest for infants and toddlers. There is a need to examine in future research the differing implications of ratios in groups of different sizes: that is, 1 caregiver for every 4 children may have differing correlates in groups of 4, 8, 12, 16, and 24. Professional standards again provide ranges for acceptable ratios for different age groups:

first 2 years, not higher than 1:4;
2-year-olds, 1:3 to 1:6;
3-year-olds, 1:5 to 1:10;
4- and 5-year-olds, 1:7 to 1:10.

Caregiver training specific to child development, and perhaps also overall years of caregiver education, emerge in the academic research as important to children's experiences and development in child care. There is consensus across professional standards that caregivers should have training specific to child development.

Research indicates that children's development is enhanced by the formation of a relationship with a particular caregiver when several are available and by the stability of that relationship over time. Those professional standards that address this issue identify the need for the assignment of specific caregivers to particular groups of children, and continuity over time in these assignments, in order to foster the development of affectionate relationships between individual caregivers and children.

Research points to the importance of some daily learning activities in child care settings, complementing unstructured time, rather than an environment that is strictly custodial. Learning activities that permit children some choice, initiation of activities, and pacing of activities are also beneficial. Professional standards emphasize the need for a daily organization of activities that is both structured and flexible, that incorporates learning activities that foster both cognitive and social development, and that permit the child choice and self-pacing.

Research suggests that children's experiences in child care are more positive when space is well organized, differentiated, orderly, and, in family day care, designed for children's use. Professional standards concur in identifying the need for a physical setting that is orderly and differentiated, as well as child oriented.

Although we have examined these factors and their influences separately, the overall quality of child care in any one setting is determined by a profile across the multiple quality dimensions. The simultaneous operation of dimensions of quality is clearly portrayed in Grubb's (1987:59-60) description of the "covert curriculum" in high-quality center care:

> The physical space is carefully arranged to provide a variety of activities where children in one area will not interfere with those in another, and where areas for active play and those for quieter activities and privacy are segregated. Activities are carefully paced throughout the day, geared to the rhythms of children coming and going and to different levels of alertness. While most centers devote some time to relatively formal cognitive development, most of the "curriculum" is embedded in games, toys, and different activity centers, and most of it allows children to initiate activities rather than being told what to do on schedule. Teachers circulate constantly, interacting with children, engaging nonparticipating children in activities, and anticipating problems before they develop. . . . The best teachers are in fact warm and loving, but warmth alone is insufficient; an effective teacher . . . understands the developmental stages and thoughts of young children and responds to

them intelligently as well as lovingly. A well-run child care class, bustling with activity, seems to be running itself, but in fact the influence of the teacher is pervasive though covert.

Similarly, Grubb's portrayal of poor-quality care shows the *joint* functioning of inadequate staff/child ratio, poor daily organization, and untrained caregivers (Grubb, 1987:60):

Many children will spend large amounts of time unfocused, drifting among activities in ways that leave them both bored and frazzled. Without constant monitoring some children may become wild, especially if they are bored, and then kicking, throwing and pushing may become dangerous. Under these circumstances untrained teachers . . . may be pushed to the limits of their patience, and then correction becomes harsh and belittling. . . . If the center has cut corners on adult/child ratios—not difficult to do, especially with lax enforcement of licensing—then chaos, the inattention of teachers, the management problems, and the resort to harsh direction and punishment become even more serious.

In conclusion, the combined perspectives of academic research and professional practice together provide a picture of the key features of quality child care. To be sure, as we have noted, there are ways in which this picture needs to be extended. Yet the present state of knowledge is significant, with good agreement between researchers and professionals working with children about features of quality in child care.

State regulations very often fall short of this picture of quality. In some instances these regulations do not appear to be informed by research or professional practice regarding quality. For example, only a minority of states regulates group size for all age groups—and some states have regulations that violate what is known about optimal size—despite evidence that this is an important feature of quality. There are states in which a single caregiver can provide child care for seven infants. Only a minority of states makes any requirement for preservice training for family day care providers. State regulations do not address issues of daily structure or curriculum of child care. In a substantial number of states, there is no space requirement set for family day care homes, either regarding square footage or design of space. Even on a universally recognized aspect of quality such as staff/child ratio, states show major discrepancies in their regulations, with one permitting for 3-year-olds only 6 per caregiver and others as many as 15. Although the evidence points to the importance for children of enduring relationships with caregivers, the United States is experiencing a major problem with staff turnover in child care settings (see Chapter 6).

Our review points to the need for a reevaluation of state child care regulations in light of the available evidence. We also believe steps could be taken to encourage voluntary programs (such as the NAEYC and NAFDC accreditation programs) to improve quality.

REFERENCES

Aboud, F.
  1988   *Children and Prejudice.* New York: Basil Blackwell.
Alejandro-Wright, M.N.
  1985   The child's conception of racial classification: A socio-cognitive developmental model. Pp. 185-200 in M.B. Spencer, G.K. Brookins, and W.R. Allen, eds., *Beginnings. The Social and Affective Development of Black Children.* Hillsdale, N.J.: Erlbaum.
Anderson, C.W., R.J. Nagle, W.A. Roberts, and J.W. Smith
  1981   Attachment to substitute caregivers as a function of center quality and caregiver involvement. *Child Development* 52:53-61.
Belsky, J.
  1984   Two waves of day care research: Developmental effects and conditions of quality. Pp. 1-34 in R.C. Anslie, ed., *The Child and the Day Care Setting.* New York: Praeger.
Berk, L.
  1985   Relationships of educational attainment, child-oriented attitudes, job satisfaction, and career commitment to caregiver behavior toward children. *Child Care Quarterly* 14:103-129.
Bredekamp, S.
  1986   The reliability and validity of the early childhood classroom observation scale for accrediting early childhood programs. *Early Childhood Research Quarterly* 1:103-118.
Carew, J.
  1980   Experience and the development of intelligence in young children at home and in day care. *Monographs of the Society for Research in Child Development* 45(6-7):Serial No. 187.
Child Welfare League of America
  1984   *Standards for Day Care Service* (rev. ed.). New York: Child Welfare League of America.
Clark, K.B., and M.K. Clark
  1939   The development of consciousness of self and the emergence of racial identity in Negro preschool children. *Journal of Social Psychology* 10:591-599.
  1940   Skin color as a factor in racial identification of Negro preschool children. *Journal of Social Psychology* 11:159-169.
Clarke-Stewart, K.A.
  1987   Predicting child development from child care forms and features: The Chicago study. Pp. 21-42 in D.A. Phillips, ed., *Quality in Child Care: What Does Research Tell Us?* Washington, D.C.: National Association for Education of Young Children.
Comer, J.
  1989   Racism and the education of young children. *Teachers College Record* 90:352-362.
Cummings, E.M.
  1980   Caregiver stability and day care. *Developmental Psychology* 16:31-37.
Cummins, J.
  1986   Empowering minority students: A framework for intervention. *Harvard Educational Review* 56:18-36.

Fosburg, S.
 1981 *Family Day Care in the United Sates: National Day Care Home Study, Vol. I, Summary of Findings.* Office of Human Development Services. DHHS Publication No. (OHDS) 80-30282. Washington, D.C.: U.S. Department of Health and Human Services.
Garland, C., and S. White
 1980 *Children and Day Nurseries.* London: Grant McIntyre.
Goelman, H., and A.R. Pence
 1987 Effects of child care, family, and individual characteristics on children's language development: The Victoria Day Care Research Project. Pp. 89-104 in D.A. Phillips, ed., *Quality in Child Care: What Does Research Tell Us?* Washington, D.C.: National Association for the Education of Young Children.
Goodman, M.E.
 1964 *Race Awareness in Young Children.* New York: Crowell-Collier.
Greenfield, P., and J. Lave
 1982 The cognitive aspects of informal education. Pp. 181-207 in D. Wagner and H. Stevenson, eds., *Cultural Perspectives on Child Development.* San Francisco: W.H. Freeman and Co.
Grubb, W.N.
 1987 The Conundrums of Early Childhood and Child Care Programs in California. Unpublished paper. School of Education, University of California, Berkeley.
Harms, T., and R.M. Clifford
 1980 *Early Childhood Environment Rating Scale.* New York: Teachers College Press.
Holloway, S.D., and M. Reichhart-Erickson
 1988 The relationship of day-care quality to children's free play behavior and social problem solving skills. *Early Childhood Research Quarterly* 3:39-54.
Howes, C.
 1983 Caregiver behavior and conditions of caregiving. *Journal of Applied Developmental Psychology* 4:99-107.
 1988 Relations between early child care and schooling. *Developmental Psychology* 24:53-57.
Howes, C., and J. Rubenstein
 1985 Determinants of toddlers' experiences in daycare: Age of entry and quality of setting. *Child Care Quarterly* 14:140-151.
Howes, C., and P. Stewart
 1987 Child's play with adults, toys, and peers: An examination of family and child care influences. *Developmental Psychology* 23:423-430.
Howes, C., C. Rodning, D.C. Galluzzo, and L. Myers
 1988 Attachment and child care: Relationships with mother and caregiver. *Early Childhood Research Quarterly* 3:403-416.
Kontos, S., and R. Fiene
 1987 Child care quality, compliance with regulations, and children's development: The Pennsylvania Study. Pp. 57-80 in D.A. Phillips, ed., *Quality in Child Care: What Does Research Tell Us?* Washington, D.C.: National Association for the Education of Young Children.
McCartney, K.
 1984 Effect of quality of day care environment on children's language development. *Developmental Psychology* 20:244-260.

McCartney, K., S. Scarr, D. Phillips, S. Grajek, and J.C. Schwarz
   1982   Environmental differences among day care centers and their effects on children's development. Pp. 126-151 in E. Zigler and E. Gordon, eds., *Day Care: Scientific and Social Policy Issues*. Boston: Auburn House.

Morgan, G.
   1982   Regulation of early childhood programs in the eighties. Pp. 375-398 in B. Spodek, ed., *Handbook of Research in Early Childhood Education*. New York: Free Press.

National Association for the Education of Young Children
   1984   *Accreditation Criteria and Procedures of the National Academy of Early Childhood Programs*. Washington, D.C.: National Association for the Education of Young Children.

National Black Child Development Institute
   1987   *Safeguards: Guidelines for Establishing Child Development Programs for Four Year Olds in the Public Schools*. Washington, D.C.: The National Black Child Development Institute, Inc.

National Head Start Multicultural Task Force
   1987   Report of First Meeting. December 10-11, 1987. Administration of Children, Youth, and Families, Office of Human Development, U.S. Department of Health and Human Services, Washington, D.C.

Ogbu, J.U.
   1986   Consequences of the American caste system. Pp. 19-56 in U. Neisser, ed., *The School Achievement of Minority Children*. Hillsdale, N.J.: Erlbaum.

Phillips, D.
   1988   Quality in Child Care: Definitions at the A.L. Mailman Family Foundation, Inc. Paper presented at symposium on dimensions of quality in programs for children. White Plains, N.Y., June.

Phinney, J.S., and M.J. Rotheram
   1988   *Children's Ethnic Socialization*. Beverly Hills, Calif.: Sage.

Prescott, E.
   1970   The Large Day Care Center as a Child-Rearing Environment. Unpublished paper, Pacific Oaks College.

Rosenthal, M.K.
   1988   Social Policy and Its Effects on the Daily Experiences of Infants and Toddlers in family day care in Israel. Draft 1988, The Hebrew University, Jerusalem.

Royce, J.M., R.B. Darlington, and H.W. Murray
   1983   Pooled analyses: Findings across studies. Pp. 411-460 in Consortium for Longitudinal Studies, *As the Twig Is Bent . . . Lasting Effects of Preschool Programs*. Hillsdale, N.J.: Erlbaum.

Ruopp, R., J. Travers, F. Glantz, and C. Coelen
   1979   *Children at the Center: Final Results of the National Day Care Study*. Boston: Abt Associates.

Schweinhart, L.J., D.P. Weikart, and M.B. Larner
   1986   Consequences of three preschool curriculum models through age 15. *Early Childhood Research Quarterly* 1:15-45.

Slaughter, D.T., V. Washington, U.J. Oyemade, and R.W. Lindsey
   1988   *Head Start: A Backward and Forward Look*. Social Policy Report, Vol. III, No. 2. Washington Liaison Office and Committee on Child Development and Social Policy. Washington, D.C.: Society for Research in Child Development.

Spencer, M.B., S.R. Kim, and S. Marshall
    1987   Double stratification and psychological risk: Adaptational processes and school
            achievement of black children. *Journal of Negro Education* 56:77-87.
Stith, S.M. and A.J. Davis
    1984   Employed mothers and family day care: A comparative analysis of infant care.
            Child Development 55:1340-1348.
Suwalsky, J.T.D., M. Zaslow, R. Klein, and B. Rabinovich
    1986   Continuity of Substitute Care in Relation to Infant-Mother Attachment. Pa-
            per presented at the convention of the American Psychological Association,
            Washington, D.C., August.
Tizard, B., O. Cooperman, A. Joseph, and J. Tizard
    1972   Environmental effects on longitudinal development: A study of young children
            in long-stay residential nurseries. *Child Development* 43:337-358.
Travers, J., B.D. Goodson, J.D. Singer, and D.B. Connell
    1979   *Final Report of the National Day Care Study: Research Results of the National
            Day Care Study.* Cambridge, Mass.: Abt Associates.
U.S. Department of Health, Education, and Welfare, U.S. Office of Economic Opportunity,
and U.S. Department of Labor
    1968   *Federal Interagency Day Care Requirements.* DHEW Publication No. (OHDS)
            78-31081. Washington, D.C.: U.S. Department of Health, Education, and
            Welfare.
U.S. Department of Health and Human Services
    1984   *Head Start Program Performance Standards.* (Codified at 45 C.F.R. Part 1304.)
            Office of Human Development Services, Administration for Children, Youth and
            Families, Head Start Bureau. Washington, D.C.: U.S. Department of Health
            and Human Services.
Vaughn, B.E., F.L. Gove, and B. Egeland
    1980   The relationship between out-of-home care and the quality of infant-mother
            attachment in an economically disadvantaged population. *Child Development*
            51:1203-1214.

5

Supporting Physical and Psychological Development in Child Care Settings

In Chapters 3 and 4, our discussion of child care and child development traced the evolution of research on child care and identified the key structural dimensions of quality in child care. This chapter takes a more differentiated look at specific aspects of physical and psychological development in the context of child care. Our aim is to identify practices that support both physical and psychological health in child care settings.

We turn first to research on physical health and safety. We ask whether and to what extent participation in child care is associated with risk for infectious diseases, injury, abuse, or neglect; and we point to practices that protect children's health and safety in child care settings. We turn next to the psychological outcomes and examine practices supportive of specific developmental processes in child care. The research on child care is not "developmental" in the sense of yielding a detailed theory or picture of children's changing needs in child care with increasing age (beyond the infancy/postinfancy demarcation). It is developmental, however, in the sense of focusing on particular developmental processes (e.g., peer relations, language development) and asking how these are affected by child care settings. Accordingly, our discussion in this section is organized around developmental processes rather than age groups. In the last part of the chapter we address the needs of two special groups of children: children with developmental disabilities and school-age children. These children's needs differ from those of normally developing infants and preschoolers, and we consider child care practices that are supportive of their development.

PHYSICAL HEALTH AND SAFETY IN CHILD CARE

There is a burgeoning literature on children's physical health and safety in child care. Jarman and Kohlenberg (1988) reviewed more than 200 studies for the panel; they concluded that, despite a bewildering array of methodological obstacles and gaps in the research, the findings on several issues converge and lead to conclusions that have significant implications for policy and practice.

Infectious Diseases

Respiratory Tract Infections

Respiratory tract infections (colds, ear infections, sore throats, laryngitis, croup, epiglottitis, bronchiolitis, bronchitis, pneumonia, and flu) account for the majority of young children's illnesses and absences from school and child care (Denny et al., 1986; Doyle, 1976; Fleming et al., 1987; Strangert, 1976; Wald et al., 1988). The evidence indicates that children in child care tend to experience more of these infections and at a younger age (Denny et al., 1986; Doyle, 1976) than children cared for at home, although some question the strength of the pattern (Haskins and Kotch, 1986). Studies show that children under 3 years of age who are in child care have more episodes of respiratory tract infection than children cared for at home; yet after the age of 3, they appear to have fewer infections of these kinds. Health experts indicate it is likely that these children encounter the common childhood viral pathogens at a younger age, and acquire immunity earlier, than children who first encounter them when entering group settings such as nursery school or kindergarten.

In general, the respiratory tract infections that child care children experience appear to be minor, self-limited, and inevitable. However, findings suggest that frequent early respiratory infections predispose these youngsters to ear infections that are more frequent, persistent, and recurrent (Daly et al., 1988; Fleming et al., 1987; Haskins and Kotch, 1986; Henderson and Giebink, 1986). Such a pattern of early ear infections may have implications for children's language development. Accordingly, there is an urgent need for prospective studies that encompass not only microbial surveillance and measures of illness, but also audiological assessment and measures of language development. Studies of the developmental and family effects of the increased frequency of minor illnesses in infants and young children in child care are also needed.

Diarrheal Disease

The evidence regarding diarrheal disease among children in child care is less consistent than that regarding respiratory illnesses; some but not all studies show these children at increased risk relative to children cared for at home (Bartlett et al., 1985; Dingle et al., 1964; Reeves et al., 1988; Sullivan et al., 1984). Wide variation in risk estimates for diarrhea may partly reflect seasonal and geographic variations in the prevalence of infecting organisms. However, the evidence is consistent in identifying particular child care features that are associated with higher rates of diarrhea. By far the best-established risk factor is the presence of children who are not yet toilet trained (Ekanem et al., 1983). The risk of diarrheal disease is also higher when caregivers both diaper children and prepare food (Lemp et al., 1984). The risk of diarrheal disease can be diminished by limiting group size; separating same age from different age children (Pickering et al., 1981); strictly adhering to the hygienic practice of hand washing after diapering infants and before food preparation (Gehlbach et al., 1973); and excluding from child care and treating those children suspected of having bacterial diarrhea on the basis of blood or mucus in the stool (Weissman et al., 1975).

Meningitis

Meningitis is an example of a formidable disorder of low prevalence that has major consequences for those children who become infected. There is strong agreement across studies that bacterial meningitis (most often caused by *H. influenzae* type b [Hib]) can be transmitted among children and, further, that children attending child care are at increased risk of contracting primary cases of this disease (Cochi et al., 1986; Haskins and Kotch, 1986; Istre et al., 1985; Redmond and Pichichero, 1984). However, there is no agreement across studies as to the extent of the risk to children in child care, once a primary case has occurred: some studies indicate a substantial risk of secondary disease and some do not (Band et al., 1984; Fleming et al., 1985; Ginsburg et al., 1977; Osterholm et al., 1987). The evidence on the household contacts of primary cases more consistently documents increased risk than the evidence for child care contacts of primary cases (Filice et al., 1978; Granoff and Basden, 1980; Ward et al., 1979).

For treatment, Rifampin may reduce the risk of secondary acquisition of Hib meningitis in susceptible youngsters, but recommendations for this therapy vary. The American Academy of Pediatrics recommends such therapy only for household contacts of an index case in households with at least one person 4 years old or younger, whereas the Immunization Practices Advisory Committee of the Centers for Disease Control recommends Rifampin for all contacts in households as well as child care groups with one or more children under 2 years who have been exposed (American Academy of Pediatrics, 1986; Granoff and Basden, 1980). New vaccines currently under development may offer protection for even very young children, thereby further reducing the threat of disease in child care settings (American Academy of Pediatrics, 1986).

Human Immunodeficiency Virus (HIV)

The risk of transmission of HIV infection in a group care setting appears to be extremely low, and to date there is no report of a child or a caregiver becoming seropositive for HIV because of exposure in a child care center or family day care home. Despite the very low risk of transmission of HIV infection in child care settings, however, extremely restrictive guidelines have been promulgated for the exclusion of infected children (American Academy of Pediatrics, 1987; Blackman and Appel, 1987; Centers for Disease Control, 1985). Such guidelines suggest the exclusion of infected children if they are not yet toilet trained, if they place hands or objects in their mouths, if they bite, or if they have oozing skin lesions. The guidelines are reactions to the extreme consequences of infection for a child and family rather than to the extremely limited risk of transmission by body fluids to peers. Retrospective research is clearly needed to evaluate the contacts of children who have been diagnosed with HIV infection to address public fears regarding peer transmission.

Additional areas of concern include compliance with existing infection control recommendations (which reduce the risk to caregivers and to children with AIDS who have not yet been diagnosed) and the development of child care centers to serve children with AIDS.

Viral Hepatitis

Viral hepatitis presents a potentially substantial occupational health problem to child care workers, but a limited problem for child care children (Balistreri, 1988). The limited research concerning viral hepatitis indicates that child care settings that cater to non-toilet-trained children are frequently a source of disease in attendees, adult caregivers, and household contacts. Furthermore, although approximately 75 percent of infected *children* show very mild symptoms, 75 percent of infected *adults* develop a disabling illness lasting from 2 weeks to 2 months (Balistreri, 1988). By far the most significant risk factor associated with an outbreak of viral hepatitis in a child care center is the presence of children under 2 years of age (Hadler et al., 1982).

Fortunately, medical intervention can be highly effective in limiting the transmission of viral hepatitis. Specifically, public health experts recommend that the identification of one or more cases in a child care center should be followed by immunoglobulin prophylaxis for all staff and children in the same room as the index case (Centers for Disease Control, 1981). Although prophylaxis for household members has not been shown to be effective, it is recommended for parents of children who wear diapers in circumstances in which three or more families associated with a child care group show infection. Immunoglobulin prophylaxis can virtually eliminate the spread of viral hepatitis within a child care group.

In addition to the use of immunoglobulin prophylaxis, other practices (hand washing, disinfection of diaper change surfaces and toys, segregation of children by age group) are recommended to curb the spread of any disease that is transmitted via the fecal-oral route, although their efficacy specifically for viral hepatitis has not been demonstrated. There has been some progress in the development of a hepatitis A vaccine for use in humans, but it is not ready for general use (McLean, 1986).

Cytomegalovirus

Although cytomegalovirus (CMV) does not cause symptoms of acute infection in child care children (acute infection is generally asymptomatic), it can cause serious neurological damage to an embryo or fetus in utero if a pregnant woman experiences her first CMV infection during the first half of pregnancy (Conboy et al., 1987; Melish and Hanshaw, 1973; Pass et al., 1980; Stagno et al., 1986). Therefore, there is potential risk to the fetus carried by the mother of an infected child in child care and to that of a pregnant child care worker (Adler, 1988b).

Evidence indicates that CMV is excreted by approximately one-half of the children in centers with 50 or more children. Furthermore, children between 1 and 3 years of age do spread CMV to each other in child care settings. Children bring infections home to their parents and particularly to their mothers. And child care workers are at some risk of acquiring CMV, although less so than parents of child care children (Adler, 1986, 1988b; Pass and Hutto, 1986; Pass et al., 1987). There are as yet no specific measures to control the risks of CMV infection, which remain low for any given pregnancy. CMV transmission in child care settings can be limited by standard hygienic practices because the virus is inactivated by soaps, detergents, and alcohols (Adler, 1988a).

Injury

Data on rates and severity of injuries to children in child care are limited. To date, there are no studies contrasting the incidence of injury among child care children and home-reared children. Nor has there been a prospective study with rigorous measurement procedures. Available information concerning injury among children in child care thus rests on documentation of injury rates within centers and family day care homes.

From the few studies that have examined injuries, it is clear that child care children show similar types of injuries to children reared at home, with the possible exception of bites from other children (Garrard et al., 1988). A majority of injuries in child care settings occur on the playground and particularly on climbing equipment (Aronson, 1983; Elardo et al., 1987; Landman and Landman, 1987). Minor injuries (e.g., abrasions) are common, but they are widespread among young children in general.

The most important conclusion regarding injuries is the need for rigorous prospective studies that contrast children in family day care and center care with home-reared children and document the circumstances associated with injuries.

Abuse and Neglect

There is only one major study of sexual abuse in child care settings. A national survey of sexual abuse in child care (supported by the National Center on Child Abuse and Neglect and the National Institute of Mental Health) indicates that the risk of a child being sexually abused in child care (5.5/10,000 children) is significantly smaller than the risk of sexual abuse by a family member in a child's own home (8.9/10,000 children) (Finkelhor et al., 1988). That study also found that the traditional indicators of quality of care (e.g., group size, ratio) did *not* predict low risk for sexual abuse. Abusers in child care settings rarely had previous histories of arrest for abuse (8 percent did), the majority had some college education, and most had at least 2 years of experience in child care. Sixty percent of the abusers were men; 40 percent were women. Only 35 percent of the abusers were employed in the centers as child care workers.

Similarly, the evidence on physical abuse and neglect is scarce. A study in Kansas, a state with strict supervision and enforcement procedures, indicated reports of abuse and neglect in only 1.4 percent of all child care facilities (which were rapidly followed up by legal intervention) (Schloesser, 1986). By contrast, in North Carolina during 1982-83 (at that time one of the least regulated and supervised states) 16.5 percent of complaints to the Office of Child Care Licensing involved abuse or neglect (Russell and Clifford, 1987). Complaints were filed for 8.6 percent of centers and 2.3

percent of licensed family day care homes. This study indicated problems in the timing, quality, and rate of prosecution following complaints.

There are no overall national figures for rates of physical abuse and neglect in child care. However, state-level data raise the possibility that supervision and enforcement mechanisms, which vary substantially by state, may be a factor associated with actual—or possibly only reported—rates of abuse and neglect.

Exclusion Policy and Child Care for Sick Children

There are substantial differences of opinion among parents, child care staff, and pediatricians about when it is appropriate to exclude a symptomatic child from a child care setting (Landis et al., 1988). Furthermore, decision rules with a goal of limiting or preventing the spread of infection are often not based on sound scientific knowledge concerning transmission, perhaps partly because the period or patterns of contagion and the appearance of symptoms often do *not* correspond closely.

Jarman and Kohlenberg (1988) report that available medical evidence suggests several conclusions:

1. There is no evidence that excluding children with respiratory infection changes the risk of disease for other children in child care or for their caregivers.

2. At present, available evidence does not justify policies that restrict child care attendance for all children with diarrheal disease. Instead, exclusion is potentially valuable only in a small minority of cases, notably those marked by the presence of blood and mucus in the stools.

3. With the exception of children under age 2 (Klein, 1987), there is no evidence to suggest that fever itself merits exclusion from child care as a means of controlling infection (Shapiro et al., 1986). Exclusion in such cases should be based on concerns for the comfort of the child, rather than the spread of infection.

4. In the case of hepatitis A, there is usually considerable spread of virus before the disease is detected. Prompt initiation of immunoglobulin prophylaxis once disease is detected generally eliminates the need for exclusion (Centers for Disease Control, 1981).

5. Exclusion of a child with meningitis occurs automatically as a result of the usual need to hospitalize the ill youngster for appropriate therapy (see discussions of guidelines following identification of an index case, above).

6. The restrictive guidelines for exclusion of children diagnosed with HIV infection reflect the consequences associated with infection rather than the theoretical risk of transmission in child care settings (American Academy of Pediatrics, 1987; Centers for Disease Control, 1985).

When children are ill, employed parents often lack options for their care. Stringent exclusion policies in many child care facilities have provided an impetus for the development of alternative models for child care for sick children. Four models for such care have been identified (Rodgers et al., 1986), though none is widely available: a "get-well room" within a child care center for a mildly ill child; a satellite family day care home to which a sick child is transferred; care in the child's own home by a trained worker from an agency or a caregiver from the child's own center; and an infirmary or independent facility that cares for mildly ill children. Given children's needs for psychological nurturing as well as physical care when they are ill, many professionals prefer care in the child's own home (Chang et al., 1978). However, the feasibility of implementing this model is limited because the financial expense of hiring a trained professional to provide one-on-one care is beyond the means of many families.

Summary and Implications for Practice

Home-reared children and those in child care do not differ significantly in the kinds of diseases or injuries they experience. Differences that do occur are quantitative rather than qualitative. For example, there is a mild to moderate increase in the risk of a number of common infectious diseases for children in child care, but these generally do not entail long-term health consequences. Viral respiratory illnesses appear to be more common among child care children in the first 3 years; there are indications that they have fewer such illnesses in later years. The single longer term consequence of the common infections identified in this review is the possibility that more frequent middle-ear infections in early life may have lasting effects on hearing and language development. Children in child care also contract diarrheal illnesses more frequently than children cared for at home, but these illnesses rarely have any long-term health consequences.

Regarding rare but more serious infectious diseases, group child care does increase the risk for hepatitis A, CMV, and meningitis. There is no evidence of increased risk among child care children of HIV. From the perspective of children's health, it is only Hib disease (meningitis) that is of substantial concern. Children with hepatitis A or CMV are usually minimally symptomatic. Although primary as well as secondary infections with Hib disease are more frequent in child care settings, these account for very small percentages of child-care-related illnesses. Chemoprophylaxis diminishes the risk of secondary infections, and new vaccines may further diminish overall risk.

Finally, there is no evidence to suggest that child care attendance is associated with increased risk of physical injury, sexual abuse, physical abuse, or neglect, although further study of these issues is needed. Thus, despite significant increases in a host of minor infectious diseases, it is apparent from this review that child care attendance poses no major risks to the health status of young children in the United States.

Existing scientific evidence and best professional practice from the fields of pediatrics and public health suggest a number of practices for safeguarding the health and safety of children in child care settings:

- limiting group size;
- separating groups of children according to age;
- strictly adhering to hand-washing practices particularly after diapering and before food preparation;
- regularly cleaning and disinfecting diaper changing surfaces and communal objects and toys;
- excluding children presenting with bloody stool and children younger than age 2 with fever, as well as other selected infectious diseases;
- Rifampin therapy following the identification of an index case of Hib meningitis; and
- immunoglobulin prophylaxis following identification of an index case of viral hepatitis.

There is little documentation of specific measures that can reduce injury, abuse, and neglect among children in child care. Some evidence in the research suggests, however, that instances of abuse and neglect can be diminished by strict supervision, enforcement, and prosecution of reported cases.

PSYCHOLOGICAL DEVELOPMENT IN CHILD CARE

The years when children may be participating in child care are years of rapid transition in several domains of development. At very young ages, children form their first attachment relationships with adults as well as their first friendships with peers. They extract the rules of language from the speech they hear, and they use increasingly complex speech. Children identify themselves as part of a cultural group and, surprisingly early, assess for themselves the way in which their group is seen. From their interactions with the physical and social world, young children are constantly developing their perceptual, reasoning, and problem-solving abilities.

What specific child care practices support these developmental processes? In this section, we examine the existing knowledge of child care features and practices that are related to social development (relationships with adults, relationships with peers, and positive group identity in a multicultural context) and cognitive development (language development and more broadly defined intellectual development).

Relationships With Adults

Research on children's relationships with adults has focused on two processes: the quality of attachment relationships and children's cooperativeness with adults. Although studies examining child care and attachment have traditionally emphasized implications for children's attachment to their mothers, recent evidence suggests the need for a broader perspective. The evidence is as yet limited, but there are indications that children's attachments to their caregivers are also important and, further, that development among children in child care can be best understood through simultaneous consideration of attachments to parents and to caregivers.

Attachment to Mother

As discussed in Chapter 3, the quality of children's attachments to their mothers has been considered a useful index of their overall emotional well-being (Ainsworth, 1985; Bretherton and Waters, 1985; Campos et al., 1983; Sroufe, 1985). Factors influencing that attachment are also assumed to have importance for later development. Individual differences in children's attachments to their mothers have been found to be influenced by the mothers' sensitivity and responsiveness to a child's needs and communicative behavior in its first year and related to the mothers' own emotional well-being and network of support, to the child's personality, and to the socioeconomic stresses experienced by the family (Bretherton and Waters, 1985; Campos et al., 1983; Crockenberg, 1981; Sroufe, 1985). An issue that remains clouded with some uncertainty concerns the nature of the effects of full-time child care during the first year of life on infant-mother attachment. Although research has consistently shown that children of working mothers are attached to their mothers (Clarke-Stewart and Fein, 1983; see also Chapter 3), the question has been raised as to whether the quality of such attachments differs for children in full-time care during their first 12 months.

As we discussed in Chapter 3, current assessments of infants' attachments to their mothers rest on a single laboratory assessment, the "strange situation" that places infants under the stress of separation from their mothers and observes their responses to both the separation and the reunion (Ainsworth et al., 1978). Using this assessment, studies have shown that infants whose mothers work full time in the infants' first year are more likely to show a pattern of "anxious-avoidant" attachment than infants whose mothers do not (Barglow et al., 1987; Belsky, 1988; Belsky and Rovine, 1988; Schwarz, 1983). Children who spent their first year in full-time child care were also found in some studies to be more aggressive and uncooperative, although this finding is not consistent (Barton and Schwarz, 1981;

Haskins, 1985; McCartney et al., 1982; Rubenstein and Howes, 1983; also see below).

Although there is agreement about these research findings, their interpretation remains open. Some researchers argue that these findings indicate that babies whose mothers are absent for most of the day have missed experiences that are essential for the development of social relationships outside the home, but this view has been criticized on several grounds: First, the validity of the laboratory situation as an assessment of the mother-child relationship for children accustomed to full-time child care has not been established. Second, it is not clear whether the observed associations are due to poor quality of care in infancy rather than to care per se, to continuity of poor care beyond infancy, or to differences in the families whose children are in full-time care in infancy from those whose children are not (Clarke-Stewart, 1989). Further stringent monitoring of the implications of early full-time care and a broader based assessment of children's relationships with their mothers are clearly needed before the conflicting interpretations can be assessed.

Attachment to Caregiver

Recent research suggests that there may be important developmental implications of security of attachment not just to mothers but also to caregivers. In addition, secure attachment to a caregiver may function to offset insecure infant-mother attachment (Howes et al., 1988). Positive involvement with a particular caregiver in child care is associated with more exploratory behavior in children (Anderson et al., 1981). Children with secure attachments to a caregiver also appear to spend more time engaged in activities with peers in child care (Howes et al., 1988). Thus, a secure attachment to a caregiver may provide children with a "safe base" from which to explore both the physical and the social worlds.

There are only a few indications from research of the child care circumstances that foster the development of secure attachments to caregivers. Findings indicate that those attachments are more likely to occur in child care settings with fewer children per caregiver, in contexts in which children are less often ignored by caregivers (Howes et al., 1988), and when there is continuity for children in terms of the time they spend with a particular caregiver (Anderson et al., 1981). These findings suggest that the precursors of secure attachment to mother and to a caregiver are similar: interest in, and availability for, interactions with the child.

Cooperation With Adults

As we discussed in Chapter 3, an important finding of the first wave of child care research is a shift in the social orientation of children in child care toward peers and away from adults. In some cases, this shift appears to be accompanied by less cooperation with adults. An important question is whether this pattern occurs for all child care children or whether it is associated with specific features and practices in the child care setting.

There is some evidence to suggest that the overall quality of the child care setting is related to the development of cooperative behaviors. Higher overall center quality among community-based centers is associated, for example, with more positive behavior with adults (Vandell and Powers, 1983) with more child compliance (Howes and Olenick, 1986), and with behavior that is more considerate (McCartney et al., 1985). Children who have attended higher rather than lower quality child care centers at an early age also show differences in their later behavior toward adults. Children with a history of poorer quality early child care have been found to be on average more difficult in preschool settings and more hostile in kindergarten (Howes, 1988a). Clarke-Stewart (1989) notes, however, that a pattern of uncooperative behaviors has also been observed for children from very high quality model intervention programs, like those described by Haskins (1985). As Haskins and others have noted, the focus of such programs to date has been largely on cognitive development, with a lack of emphasis on social skills. Thus, the global assessment of such programs as high quality may need qualifying for particular domains of development.

The implication of these findings is that poor-quality overall care or high-quality care with a lack of emphasis on social skills, may underlie previously observed patterns of uncooperative behavior in child care children. Clarke-Stewart (1989:271) concludes that in child care settings "children do not learn to follow social rules or to resolve social conflicts without resorting to aggression unless special efforts are made by their caregivers." Thus, the feature of child care most important to cooperative behavior in children appears to be "direct training in social skills" by caregivers (Clarke-Stewart, 1989:271). Findings from the National Day Care Study (Ruopp et al., 1979) point also to group size and caregiver training as correlates of child cooperativeness. These features of group care may underlie the frequency with which a caregiver is free to, or motivated to, engage in social skills training.

Relationships With Peers

At one time researchers believed that interest in peer interactions and the formation of dyadic relationships with peers did not occur until children reached age 3. More recent studies indicate, however, that interactions with peers and stable peer friendships begin in the first years of life (Hay, 1985). Early peer interactions follow a developmental sequence, from simple social interest and mutual responsiveness in infancy, through complementary and reciprocal interaction and the sharing of meaning in toddlerhood, to the social organization of peer groups in the preschool years (Howes, 1987).

Relationships with peers appear to be important for both contemporaneous and longer term development. Thus, for example, Clarke-Stewart and Fein (1983), in their comprehensive review of early childhood programs, suggest that greater social competence (e.g., self-confidence, sociability, independence, cooperativeness, perceptiveness regarding social roles) in children who have attended early childhood programs is in part related to their greater experience with peers. Hartup (1983:167), summarizing the evidence on the longer term implications of relations with age-mates, concluded:

> Poor peer relations are embedded in the life histories of individuals who are "at risk" for emotional and behavioral disturbance. . . . There is every reason to conclude that poor peer relations are centrally involved in the etiology of a variety of emotional and social maladjustments.

Some of the factors that foster positive relations with peers among day care children—and, conversely, those that foster antisocial behaviors—have been identified. According to Howes (1987:157), "a large body of literature reported that children with secure attachment relationships with their mothers are more socially competent in their relationships with peers. . . ." New evidence complements these consistent findings in pointing to secure attachment to child care providers as a further, and perhaps ever more important, factor in fostering positive engagement with peers among child care children (Howes et al., 1988). Researchers widely hypothesize that secure attachments provide the basis for young children to have positive expectations for responsiveness and positive interactions with peers (e.g., Howes, 1987), although another perspective suggests that positive and complex relations with adults and peers emerge as parallel developmental accomplishments, rather than as one set of relations growing out of the other (Hay, 1985).

The complexity of peer interactions also appears to be strongly influenced by the stability of the peer group (Howes, 1987, 1988b). Very young children transferred to a new school or preschool class often show signs of disruption, such as sleeplessness and increased aggression (Field et al., 1984). Young children moved to a new child care group without friends are less socially skilled than those whose contacts are with a high proportion of established friends (Howes, 1988b). Thus "parents and teachers may need to be more sensitive to the issue of maintaining friendships" (Howes, 1988b:67).

It is reasonable to infer from the existing evidence that caregiver guidance can also enhance children's peer relations. Research indicates that children's social competence, as manifested in such behaviors as sharing and taking the perspective of another, can be improved through demonstration, guided activity, deliberate encouragement of interpersonal problem solving, and desirable behaviors by adults (Clarke-Stewart and Fein, 1983). Finally, Howes (1987) notes that moderate-sized groups simultaneously permit a choice of partners and protect children from overstimulation, which in turn promotes positive peer relations. In summary, the child care practices that foster the development of positive peer relations appear to be circumstances permitting secure attachment to caregivers, peer group stability, guidance by adults in interactions with peers, and moderate group size.

This picture can be completed by asking if antisocial peer behaviors, identified as a concern in the first wave of child care research, are also related to particular child care features? Uncooperative behavior with adults, like problematic peer behavior, has been found to be related to overall center quality (Vandell et al., 1988), though with the same qualifications noted above regarding cognitively oriented model intervention programs. Within the context of community-based care, larger group size (Holloway and Reichhart-Erickson, 1988; Ruopp et al., 1979), fewer opportunities for children to interact with caregivers, less adequate space, and less adequate educational materials (Holloway and Reichhart-Erickson, 1988) appear to be associated with less positive peer relations. Uncooperativeness with peers, just as with adults, may signal child care circumstances that are disruptive to, rather than supportive of, interpersonal relationships.

Positive Group Identity in a Multicultural Context

Child care experiences can affirm children's cultural identity in the context of a multicultural society. Such affirmation may have significant implications for children's eventual experience in school, which for minority students can represent a "frequently devastating encounter with the values of the broader society" (Holliday, 1985:120).

There are numerous indications that processes of cultural group identification begin quite early and that many young children from minority groups form negative views of their cultural group (Aboud, 1988; Comer, 1989). In one recent study, for example, 80 percent of black middle-class preschoolers showed preferences that valued whites and devalued blacks, despite positive self-concepts (Spencer, 1985). Such dissonance between personal and group evaluations is common among black American children irrespective of age, stage of cognitive development, or geographic region

(Spencer, 1985, 1986, 1988). The role that child care can play in such a pattern is underscored by findings indicating that when parents engage in "proactive" teaching about African-American history and contemporary racial history, in anticipation of children encountering discrimination, the children's academic performance is better. Furthermore, children with positive group identity show greater resilience to psychological stress (Spencer, 1988).

Research points to several ways in which child care can play a role in fostering positive group identity in minority group students. First, child care programs can incorporate information about the cultural groups of children represented in the care group, and positive portrayals of group members, in educational programs and materials. Cummins (1986:25) notes that "considerable research data suggest that, for dominated minorities, the extent to which students' language and culture are incorporated in the school program constitutes a significant predictor of academic success." Well-articulated and detailed curricula have been developed that indicate how such an educational orientation can be carried out: for example, Williams and DeGaetano (1985) on the Alerta program; Arenas (1980) on the Bilingual/Multicultural Curriculum Development Effort; National Head Start Multicultural Task Force (1987); and Phillips (1989).

Second, it is important to build on rather than negate the diverse learning and interaction styles of children (and parents) from minority cultures (Fillmore and Britsch, 1988) and thus to foster an early sense of efficacy rather than helplessness in school. As one example, research has been carried out on understanding and incorporating differing learning styles in the framework of the Kamehameha Early Education Program in Hawaii (Au and Jordan, 1981). As described by Cummins (1986:25): "When reading instruction was changed to permit students to collaborate in discussing and interpreting texts," consistent with discourse patterns among siblings and peers encouraged by Hawaiian culture, "dramatic improvements were found in both reading and verbal intellectual abilities."

Research on early intervention programs extends this concept to the culturally rooted interaction styles of parents as well as of children. Slaughter (1983:68), for example, found that a discussion-group intervention program for lower income black mothers and their young children had "broad, extensive effects on dyads" on personality, attitude, and behavior measures, whereas an intervention focusing on toy demonstration, and modeling of interactive play behaviors, had more "situation-specific effects." In discussing these findings, Slaughter notes that the discussion-group intervention appeared more compatible with cultural values of reliance on extended family. The discussion group was consonant with, and may have substituted for, the functioning of this type of support.

Finally, child care can facilitate the development of minority group children through establishing a pattern of parent-teacher collaboration rather than excluding parents from their children's care and early education settings. Membership in a minority group often carries with it parental expectation of limited access to educational resources and environments. Parent participation develops a "sense of efficacy that communicates itself to children, with positive academic consequences" (Cummins, 1986:26).

Much of the evidence on the effectiveness of parent-teacher collaboration comes from studies with older children (Cummins, 1986). Yet such a collaborative approach is important to children's well-being and development in child care settings from the earliest ages. Examples provided by child care workers concerning infants and toddlers include strong cultural preferences for sleeping positions and whether or not children of one gender should be permitted to enact roles of the other gender, or dress in clothing of the other gender, in fantasy play (Sale, 1986). Respecting the cultural patterns and childrearing values of families with children in child care can be vital to children's positive adaptation.

Language Development

The language development among children in child care reflects both the amount and the kind of speech that is directed to them. Verbal interactions with caregivers rather than with peers appear to be important. Fine-grained examination of language development of children in child care centers suggests that the amount of speech that caregivers direct toward children is an important developmental predictor. McCartney (1984), for example, found that the total number of "functional utterances" by center caregivers predicted several measures of children's language development. And although child-initiated conversations with caregivers positively predicted language development, children's initiations of conversations with peers was a negative predictor.

Several studies go beyond quantity to identify particular types of verbal interactions in child care that foster language development. A key feature appears to be the combination of joint caregiver-child focus on an activity or object and the exchange of information. Carew (1980), for example, notes the importance in both caregiver-child and mother-child interaction of such activities as labeling objects, describing activities, and providing definitions. Similarly, McCartney (1984:252) found that children in child care "seem to profit from experiences in which they are given information and requested to give information . . . Conversely, children seem to be hampered by experiences in which their behavior is controlled."

From these and other findings from the educational research literature (e.g., Brown et al., 1984; Wood, 1988; Wood et al., 1980), it might be expected that child care features that permit caregivers to engage more often in informational exchanges with children, and less often in the sheer management of behavior, would foster children's language development in these settings. In reviewing the relevant evidence, Goelman (1986) identified group size and the age mix of children as conditions that support these interchanges. Smaller groups appear to make it easier for caregivers to engage in joint focus and information exchanges with children. Similarly, in family day care settings, a mixed-age (rather than same-age) group is associated with more frequent (though shorter) verbal exchanges between caregivers and children. Goelman and Pence (1987) suggest yet another significant factor for children's understanding of, and use of language—caregiver training.

These findings have implications for practice. In child care, caregivers' speech involving information exchange promotes language development. Particular child care features that may make opportunities for such caregiver-child interaction more feasible include smaller group size, more extensive caregiver training, and possibly a broader age range of children in family day care groups.

Cognitive Development

Beyond language development, what does research indicate about child care features that more broadly foster cognitive development? As discussed in Chapter 3, existing research shows no indication that child care participation has detrimental effects on intellectual development, provided that the care is of good quality. Further, a range of early childhood cognitive enrichment programs for high-risk groups have been shown to prevent or slow declines on measures of intellectual development characteristic of such groups. These findings are based not only on the widely used IQ assessments, but also on a range of other measures of cognitive growth, including assessments of problem solving; reasoning; perceptual, spatial, and conceptual development; perspective taking; exploratory behavior; and creativity (Clarke-Stewart and Fein, 1983).

As we discussed in Chapter 4, children's cognitive achievement reflects the amount of direct stimulation and teaching provided by caregivers (Clarke-Stewart and Fein, 1983). Stimulating caregiver behavior, in turn, is enhanced by smaller group size and by caregiver training. In addition, child care programs that incorporate some organized educational activities, rather than serving a solely custodial function, have children who show greater cognitive development. The evidence suggests that child-initiated and -paced learning at early ages is more important than teacher-directed learning.

As we noted in Chapter 3, findings from intervention programs, including Head Start and a range of cognitive enrichment programs, indicate significant but temporary gains on IQ measures for high-risk groups when interventions terminate with the end of preschool. Although findings indicate that IQ differences are not sustained into early school years, other variables reflecting overall school adjustment (e.g., retention in grade, referral for special instruction) do show lasting effects (Lazar et al., 1982). Furthermore, there are indications that when interventions continue into the early school years rather than end prior to school entry, there are implications for academic performance in the school years (Horacek et al., 1987).

The extent of exposure to early intervention, and enrollment in a program that focuses on both child and family are factors in terms of cognitive development (Bryant and Ramey, 1986), but variation in educational methods and practices in such projects do not relate systematically to intellectual development. Thus, "there may be multiple paths to intellectual competence" (Bryant and Ramey, 1987:74). Although particular curricular emphases may not have differential effects on global measures such as IQ, future research will need to study whether there are differential effects in terms of specific cognitive skills. A detailed analysis of cognitive development in relation to curricular emphases is especially needed.

In summary, studies of the variation in quality in community-based child care point to stimulating caregiver behaviors as particularly important for children's cognitive development. Such behaviors are more likely in the context of smaller groups, in settings with some educational content, and with better trained caregivers. Studies of cognitive enrichment programs underscore the importance of the amount of time children spend in the program and the need to serve children as well as parents.

The Balance of Emphasis in
Children's Psychological Development

There has been a tendency in the United States to conceive of high-quality child care, and particularly intervention programs for high-risk children, solely in terms of cognitive stimulation. But researchers in the area of early intervention are now sounding a cautionary note. They are suggesting that cognitive stimulation in children's programs be combined with attention to social development.

Haskins (1985:702), for example, voiced concern that the intellectual advantages associated with cognitive stimulation programs were sometimes "purchased at the price of deficits in social behavior," when children in a cognitive enrichment program showed elevated rates of aggression in elementary school. Similarly, as discussed in Chapter 4, researchers tracking participants in the High/Scope preschool curriculum study concluded that the manner in which a cognitive stimulation program was carried out had implications for children's social adaptation: Programs that provided children with options for initiating their learning, rather than more passively following teacher-directed instruction, were associated with better social adjustment over a period of years (Schweinhart et al., 1986).

In contrast with the American experience with cognitive enrichment through child care, which suggests that there are social implications of cognitive programs, the Japanese preschool experience suggests that emphasis on social behaviors in preschool settings may have positive implications for cognitive development. In Japanese preschools, small groups are formed and assigned group projects, and the groups are composed so that children's individual qualities will complement one another. Group roles are rotated so that each child gains experience in being a group leader as well as a follower. Children learn to subordinate individual goals to those of the group, and they develop identification with their group and loyalty to it. As a result, children demonstrate relatively high levels of self-regulation by the time they enter grade school, so that they are able to settle down to classroom regimens and learn well even though they have had much less early training in letters and numbers (Lewis, 1984).

Our intent here is not to suggest that the educational approach of a culturally more homogeneous society such as Japan, in which there is a great deal of consensus (among educators and between parents and educators) regarding educational goals and processes, could or should be transplanted to the U.S. multicultural and highly individualistic society.[1] Rather, the contrast underlines the fact that classroom structure can be designed to place more or less emphasis on teaching children to be effective members of groups. And whether this emphasis is present or not has consequences for children's subsequent social and cognitive development.

As we noted at the beginning of Chapter 3, social and cognitive development do not always occur in unison. Yet development in one domain has implications for development in another. Both the U.S. and the Japanese experiences underscore the need to consider the implications of program emphases for both cognitive and socioemotional development, and indeed to include an explicit focus on both developmental processes. Professional standards emphasize the importance of maintaining a balance (see Appendix B). This view is echoed in the goals established jointly by parents and child care staff in one high-quality center (UCLA Child Care Services, 1989).

---

[1] It is interesting to note, however, that there are cross-cultural similarities in the academic performance of minority-group children in Japan and the United States (Ogbu, 1986; Spencer et al., 1987).

Summary and Implications for Practice

The development of children in child care is fostered by secure attachments to parents as well as caregivers. Research findings suggest that problems regarding cooperativeness with adults and with peers among children are frequently related to poor-quality care or care that focuses exclusively on cognitive development. Furthermore, cooperative relations with adults and peers can be fostered by caregiver behavior aimed directly at training in social skills. Child care also can provide an important opportunity to affirm children's cultural group identity, by incorporating materials affirming children's cultural groups into program curricula, by promoting parent-caregiver collaboration, and by building on rather than negating culturally based patterns of learning and interaction.

Children's language development in child care settings is fostered through frequent verbal interactions with caregiving adults that involve informational content and shared focus. Other aspects of cognitive development are supported by some (though not excessive focus on) organized learning that permits children to initiate and pace their own learning activities. For children from disadvantaged families, intensive exposure to a well-planned child care intervention project, particularly one that serves both child and family, can have important positive implications for intellectual development and later school and social adaptation.

Child care programs need to balance their emphasis on socioemotional and cognitive development, and they need to recognize that efforts to foster development in one domain may well have implications for the other.

CHILDREN WITH DISABILITIES AND SCHOOL-AGE CHILDREN

Children With Disabilities

During the past two decades, the nation's child care systems have faced the growing needs of a new group: children with developmental disabilities. In promulgating the Education for All Handicapped Children Act (P.L. 94-142), the U.S. Department of Education estimated that 12 percent of school-age children have handicapping conditions (Fine and Swift, 1986). At younger ages, estimates of the incidence of disabilities—developmental, neurological, behavioral, or physical vulnerabilities—vary substantially (Hauser-Cram et al., 1988): for example, for children between birth and 3 years, estimates range from 3 percent to 26 percent (Hauser-Cram et al., 1988). Despite this variation, it is clear that a nontrivial proportion of preschool children have potentially handicapping conditions.

There are no national data available regarding the number of children with developmental disabilities presently enrolled in child care (Klein and

Sheehan, 1987). However, state-level data suggest that, as in the general population, a substantial proportion of mothers of young children with disabilities are employed and use child care, often to complement early intervention programs that do not correspond to parents' hours of employment (Rule et al., 1985). For example, a statewide New Mexico survey of early intervention programs for infants and preschoolers with disabilities found that 46 percent of program parents were employed outside the home and that 40 percent used child care of varying types (Klein and Sheehan, 1987). The average use of child care among families using early intervention programs was 26 hours per week (beyond the hours of early intervention).

For parents of children with developmental disabilities, child care is essential to their continued employment, which may be particularly important given the additional financial burdens these families bear. It is also possible that child care is used by families when special programs do not exist to serve children with disabilities (Rule et al., 1985) and as a respite from the stress to parents caring full time for a child with special needs.[2]

Until the early 1970s, the majority of young children with developmental disabilities faced institutionalization or placement in highly segregated child care programs. Subsequently, federal legislation has had a major impact on the integration of children with potentially handicapping conditions into regular child care and educational settings with their normally developing peers. As we discuss in Chapter 6, the Education for All Handicapped Children Act (P.L. 94-142) and the Education of the Handicapped Amendments (P.L. 99-457) substantially altered the way children with handicapping conditions are served. The latter act may have a specific impact on the use of child care by families of young children with disabilities through its Individualized Family Service Plan component (see Chapter 7).

Development of Children With Developmental Disabilities

Research on mainstreaming and integrating[3] children with special needs into preschool settings with their normally developing peers indicates a number of potential benefits to both groups. Guralnick (1978), for example, notes that integration at the preschool level can prevent some of the deleterious effects documented to be associated with segregated

---

[2] See Dyson and Fewell (1986) for a summary of the evidence regarding stress in parents of children with disabilities.

[3] In mainstreaming, children with disabilities spend most of their time in a normal setting with support from special education staff. In an integrated setting, children spend the majority of time in a special education setting, with selected activities (e.g., free play, lunch, music) in a normal setting (Fredericks et al., 1978).

programs for children with disabilities, most notably labeling and isolation. He further indicates that in integrated preschool groups, teachers can see the progress made by children with disabilities within a more complete developmental framework, and the social, play, and language environment available for observational learning is richer.

In addition to the research on mainstreaming and integrating children with disabilities into model programs (e.g., Guralnick, 1976, 1978; Ispa, 1981), there is a small but growing body of research on the participation of these children in community-based child care programs (e.g., Fredericks et al., 1978; Jones and Meisels, 1987; Klein and Sheehan, 1987; Rule et al., 1985; Smith and Greenberg, 1981). In both sets of studies there is a recurring finding that children with disabilities can indeed benefit from participation in settings with their normally developing peers, particularly in social development, but such benefits occur only if there is appropriate staff training and careful programming. For example, Snyder and colleagues (1977:264) note:

> integrated settings do not necessarily result in increased cross group imitation and social interaction between handicapped and nonhandicapped children. Apparently, teaching procedures designed to foster these effects are needed if retarded and other handicapped children are to benefit optimally from integrated preschool programming.

There are some indications of negative effects when children with special needs have been introduced with no special teacher training or programming. Smith and Greenberg (1981) found that without planning and teacher training in the child care setting, children with handicapping conditions showed fewer significant developmental gains over an academic year than their counterparts who remained in a special education setting. With teacher training or special curriculum, children with handicapping conditions in integrated preschool settings show positive changes in social behaviors, and, to some extent, in language behaviors that generalize to situations beyond the training or treatment context. For example, Guralnick (1976, 1978) found that normally developing peers could be trained to model, prompt, and reinforce social and language behaviors in children with disabilities. Such peer instruction was found to be effective regarding social play, reduction of social withdrawal and self-directed behavior, and language usage. Fredericks and colleagues (1978) trained caregiving staff to facilitate the social and language skills of children with disabilities, reinforcing children with special needs as well as their normally developing peers, and found a substantial increase in the quality of play in the children with disabilities. Similarly, Devoney and colleagues (1974) found a noticeable increase in cooperative play when teachers intervened to structure group play between preschool children with and without handicapping conditions.

Thus, while there are potential benefits of integrating children with special needs into child care settings, there are potential negative effects as well if children with disabilities are introduced with no special additional caregiver training or instructional program. Staff training and curriculum have been identified as the key components of integrated child care settings.

Teacher Training   Model projects described by Rule and colleagues (1985) and Klein and Sheehan (1987) for training child care providers to work with children with disabilities show a great deal of agreement in approach. Both reports note that few child care providers have been trained to serve children with special needs and that teacher attitude is an important ingredient in successful integration.

In a program described by Rule and colleagues (1985), child care providers were prepared for the mainstream experience through a workshop involving an introduction to "exceptionalities," the development of an individualized educational program, and use of positive discipline techniques. Caregivers visited special education settings serving children with disabilities. They then received training in educational techniques through informal discussion and demonstration and gradually assumed instruction while receiving supportive feedback in the classroom. A special education coordinator provided ongoing consultation to the child care teachers. This description is essentially in agreement with Klein and Sheehan's (1987) proposal of a special education and early childhood consultation model. It is important to note, however, that Klein and Sheehan also suggest that the other children in child care should be prepared for the introduction of a child with special needs. They should be acquainted with the special needs of the child and with any special equipment and procedures to be used with the child. In sum, both projects underscore the need to go beyond single workshops, to move training into the classroom, to tailor training to individual children's needs, and to provide ongoing support and consultation.

Techniques to Foster Social Development   Research emphasizes that child care, when used to complement special education programs, should have as its primary goal social rather than cognitive development. Programs should stress the social integration of children with disabilities, particularly the development of cooperative play skills and interactive language behavior. Two basic strategies have been described for fostering positive interactions among preschool children with and without disabilities: the use of trained peers (Guralnick, 1976, 1978) and direct modeling and reinforcement by caregiving staff (Fredericks et al., 1978). Both approaches involve modeling, prompting, and reinforcement of appropriate behaviors. Both the peer model and the caregiver reinforcement techniques have been documented to be effective in increasing interactive social behaviors in children with special needs.

Summary and Implications for Practice

The social development of children with developmental disabilities can be fostered by exposure to the language and interactive environment of an integrated child care setting. Yet developmental benefits occur only when child care staff receive initial and ongoing training in the care of particular children with special needs, and techniques are used to encourage social interaction among children with and without disabilities. Research shows possible deleterious effects to children with disabilities of simply introducing them into child care settings without necessary staff training and appropriate programming.

School-Age Children

The need for child care does not end with children's entry into school. The amount of awake time that school-age children spend out of school exceeds the amount of time they spend in school each year, given hours before and after school and vacations. The limited evidence on after-school child care indicates that there is a problem with the amount of care currently available; that the needs of school-age children in child care differ from those of younger children; and that the quality of care is significant for developmental outcomes for school-age as well as preschool-age children.

Estimates of the number of school-age children in self-care (for out-of-school-hours) vary markedly, though all estimates place the number in the millions. According to Fink (1986), the range in estimates of latchkey children from 2 million to 15 million is a reflection of self-report issues (parental reluctance to categorize their children as in self-care) and definition issues (How long must children be in self-care per day? Can a sibling be present?). Fink suggests that detailed studies in localities may yield more reliable estimates. In one such study, Vandell and Corasaniti (1988) found that 23 percent of the third graders attending seven elementary schools in a Dallas suburban school district returned home from school to a setting without adult supervision.

Developmental Implications of Self-Care

Just as estimates of latchkey children vary, so do reports of the implications of self-care. Studies by Rodman and colleagues (1985) and Steinberg (1986) found no differences between latchkey and adult-care children on measures of self-esteem, adjustment, and susceptibility to negative peer pressure. Similarly, a study by Vandell and Corasaniti (1988) found no differences between mother-care and latchkey third graders on grades, standardized test scores, conduct in school, and self-reporting of competence.

In contrast, a study of nearly 5,000 eighth graders in Los Angeles and San Diego (Richardson et al., 1989) found self-care to be a significant risk factor for substance use (alcohol, cigarettes, and marijuana). The relationship between self-care and substance use held for students "in dual-parent as well as single-parent households, those in high income as well as low income groups, those who get good grades as well as those who do not, and those who are active in sports, as well as those who are not . . ." (Richardson et al., 1989:563-564). The researchers note that although substance use is consistently associated with self-care in this sample, there is nevertheless "a large proportion of those in self-care not using these substances" (p. 564). Accordingly, it is important to identify those factors that might be protective among children in self-care, as well as those factors most closely linked with substance use and other high-risk behaviors. Analyses carried out by Richardson and colleagues point to three possible mediating factors: risk-taking behaviors, having friends who smoke, and being offered cigarettes. The researchers speculate that "the self-care situation causes young adolescents to perceive themselves as more autonomous, more mature, and more able to make decisions that may not be approved by adults. This increasing autonomy may be manifested by increasing susceptibility to the influence of their peers" (p. 564).

Work by Long and Long (1983), focusing on a younger sample and on subjective feelings rather than substance use, also points to problems for children in self-care. Studying first- to third-grade latchkey children in a sample of black parochial schoolchildren, Long and Long found problems of loneliness, fear, and stress in these children. This work, however, involved limited documentation of sample characteristics and research procedures.

As noted by Vandell and Corasaniti (1988) as well as Seligson (1988), the implications for children of self-care may vary by whether this arrangement was a necessity (i.e., no other care available or affordable) or chosen particularly for more competent or responsible children; how much time children are in self-care each day and over years; the restrictions placed on children's behavior while in self-care (i.e., to be at home alone or to be with peers); and the character of the surrounding neighborhood. Contradictory results concerning latchkey children may well be clarified by ongoing longitudinal research that takes contextual factors into account (e.g., the work in progress by D. Belle, Boston University).

The sheer number of school-age children in self-care strongly implies a need for child care beyond school hours that is not currently being met.

Little is known about what kind of care is needed for children in this age range; there are very few studies on which to base conclusions. Two recent studies, however, are helpful in portraying high-quality and poor-quality after-school care.

Howes and colleagues (1987) describe a model after-school program for kindergarten children. Between 30 and 40 children were cared for after a morning kindergarten program by a highly trained staff with a good teacher/child ratio (a credentialed kindergarten teacher, two assistant teachers with B.A. degrees, and an aide). The program showed the key features of continuity and complementarity with the morning program. Continuity was provided by keeping children in the same physical setting and having teachers in the morning and after-school programs meet regularly to discuss children's progress and needs. Morning activities were continued and expanded on in the afternoon program: for example, the morning social studies curriculum was reinforced in afternoon walks in the community and other informal activities. Complementarity was manifested in program emphases: the morning program involved prescribed activities that stress preacademic skills development, and the afternoon program involved greater flexibility. In the afternoon program, the children decided whether or not to participate in planned activities, and opportunities were available for youngsters to initiate activities of their choosing, including sensory motor and art activities. Teachers in the afternoon program were observed to be more nurturing and responsive toward children than teachers in the more structured morning program.

In contrast, Vandell and Corasaniti (1988) describe after-school care for third graders in a suburban school district in Dallas, Texas, that did not provide continuity as to setting. Children were transported after school to child care centers. These centers organized children in large groups with limited numbers of caregivers who had minimal special training. Age-appropriate activities were limited and did not relate to curricular activities in their academic classrooms.

Children in these two studies differed on at least one measure of social development. Howes and colleagues (1987) found that the children in the high-quality after-school program received more peer nominations as friends than did children from kindergartens not in the program. Vandell and Corasaniti reported that children who attended the child care centers after school received more negative peer nominations than mother-care children. They also had lower school grades and standard test scores than either mother-care or latchkey children. The two studies differed on many factors beyond quality of after-school care, including the age groups studied and possible differences in self-selection factors for participation in the high- and low-quality programs. Yet the possibility exists that "to the extent that an organized after-school program offers a high quality experience of age appropriate activities . . . one would expect very different outcomes to be associated with it" (Vandell and Corasaniti, 1988:18).

Summary and Implications for Practice

At present, there are few studies of child outcomes related to variations in after-school care. The picture that emerges from the limited data base is that school-age children benefit from communication between teachers or caregivers in different settings and from an after-school program that complements structured school programs through activity options and flexibility, the possibility of more sensory motor activity, and caregiver behavior that is somewhat warmer and more personally responsive in style than that of the regular classroom teacher. Studies are needed to replicate initial findings and extend them to community-based rather than model programs and to varying age and socioeconomic groups. Research examining a variety of approaches to closeness of supervision in comparison with child autonomy, and the nature of activities in after-school programs, would also be helpful.

CONCLUSIONS

As in the previous chapters, our review of the evidence points to gaps and flaws, but existing research findings also suggest several firm conclusions.

The evidence on physical health and safety points to quantitative but not qualitative differences in the health status of children reared at home by parents and those who spend time in child care settings. Our assessment of the magnitude of these differences leads us to conclude that child care attendance does not involve a major risk to the health status of young children. At the same time, we call for continued empirical research, particularly on the developmental implications of middle-ear infections among children in child care and on practices to diminish the risk of bacterial meningitis among these youngsters.

The organization of the settings and the guidance provided by caregivers can foster positive social and cognitive development among children in child care. Thus, for example, positive relations among peers and cooperative behavior with adults are more likely to occur when children receive guidance in social relations from caregivers. Similarly, language development in child care can be fostered by particular kinds of verbal interactions between children and caregivers, namely, those that involve shared focus and informational content. Child care settings also present unique opportunities to enhance particular aspects of social and cognitive development. For example, they can serve as a context for the affirmation of children's cultural, racial, or ethnic group identity.

The social development of children with developmental disabilities can be enhanced by participation in an integrated child care environment. However, benefits occur only when staff receive both initial and ongoing training and there is appropriate programming.

Many children of employed parents are in self-care, and there is some evidence of problems among children in self-care after school. Determining the need for after-school care and those features of after-school child care that are important to the development of school-age children should become a priority. The limited evidence available indicates that high-quality after-school programs involve communication between teachers and after-school caregivers and after-school activities that complement the regular school curriculum.

Child care settings were traditionally viewed as environments that, by comparison with children's own homes, were deficient as contexts for development. This and the previous two chapters present a different picture. Family day care and center care can be environments that effectively support children's health and development. They can also provide some unique opportunities for enhancing development (e.g., for peer interactions, cognitive interventions, cultural affirmation). Yet existing evidence from research and professional practice forces us to face an important caveat: child care supports healthy physical and psychological development only when it is of high quality.

REFERENCES

Aboud, F.
  1988   *Children and Prejudice.* New York: Basil Blackwell.
Adler, S.P.
  1986   Molecular epidemiology of cytomegalovirus: Evidence for viral transmission to parents from children infected at a day care center. *Pediatric Infectious Disease Journal* 5:315-318.
  1988a   Molecular epidemiology of cytomegalovirus: Viral transmission among children attending a day care center, their parents, and caretakers. *Journal of Pediatrics* 112:366-372.
  1988b   Cytomegalovirus transmission among children in day care, their mothers, and caretakers. *Pediatric Infectious Disease Journal* 7:279-85.
Ainsworth, M.D.S.
  1985   Patterns of infant-mother attachments: Antecedents and effects on development. *Bulletin of the New York Academy of Medicine* 61:771-791.
Ainsworth, M.D.S., M. Blehar, E. Waters, and S. Wall
  1978   *Patterns of Attachment: Observations in the Strange Situation and at Home.* Hillsdale, N.J.: Erlbaum.
American Academy of Pediatrics
  1986   *Report of the Committee on Infectious Diseases.* Georges Peter, ed., 20th ed. Elk Grove Village, Ill.: American Academy of Pediatrics.
  1987   Health guidelines for the attendance in day-care and foster-care settings of children infected with human immunodeficiency virus. *Pediatrics* 79:466-471.

Anderson, C.W., R.J. Nagle, W.A. Roberts, and J.W. Smith
  1981   Attachment to substitute caregivers as a function of center quality and caregiver
          involvement. *Child Development* 52:53-61.
Arenas, S.
  1980   Innovations in bilingual/multi-cultural curriculum development. *Children Today*
          9(3):17-21.
Aronson, S.
  1983   Injuries in child care. *Young Children* 17:19-21.
Au, K.H., and C. Jordan
  1981   Teaching reading to Hawaiian children: Finding a culturally appropriate solution.
          Pp. 139-152 in H. Trueba, G.P. Guthrie, and K.H. Au, eds., *Culture and the
          Bilingual Classroom: Studies in Classroom Ethnography*. Rowley, Mass.: Newbury
          House.
Balistreri, W.F.
  1988   Viral hepatitis. In S.L. Kaplan, ed., New Topics in Pediatric Infectious Disease.
          Pediatric Clinics of North America 35(3):637-639.
Band, J.D., D.W. Fraser, and G. Ajello
  1984   Prevention of *Haemophilus influenzae* type b disease. *JAMA* 251:2381-2386.
Barglow, P., B.E. Vaughn, and N. Molitor
  1987   Effects of maternal absence due to employment on the quality of infant-mother
          attachment in a low-risk sample. *Child Development* 58:945-954.
Bartlett, A.V., M. Moore, G.W. Gary, K.M. Starko, J.J. Erben, and B.A. Meredith
  1985   Diarrheal illness among infants and toddlers in day care centers: 1. Epidemiology
          and pathogens. *Journal of Pediatrics* 107:495-502.
Barton, M., and J. Schwarz
  1981   Day Care in the Middle Class: Effects in Elementary School. Paper presented
          at meeting of the American Psychological Association, Los Angeles.
Belsky, J.
  1988   The "effects" of infant daycare reconsidered. *Early Childhood Research Quarterly*
          3:235-272.
Belsky, J., and M. Rovine
  1988   Nonmaternal care in the first year of life and infant-parent attachment security.
          Child Development 59:157-167.
Blackman, J.A., and B.R. Appel
  1987   Epidemiologic and legal considerations in the exclusion of children with acquired
          immunodeficiency syndrome, cytomegalovirus and herpes simplex virus infection
          from group care. *Pediatric Infectious Disease Journal* 6:1011-1015.
Bretherton, I., and I. Waters
  1985   Growing points of attachment theory and research. *Monographs of the Society
          for Research in Child Development* 50(1-2):Serial No. 209.
Brown, G., A. Anderson, R. Shillcock, and G. Yule
  1984   *Teaching Talk. Strategies for Production and Assessment*. Cambridge, England:
          Cambridge University Press.
Bryant, D.M., and C.T. Ramey
  1986   An analysis of the effectiveness of early intervention programs for high-risk
          children. Pp. 33-78 in M. Guralnick and C. Bennett, eds., *Effectiveness of Early
          Intervention*. New York: Academic Press.
Campos, J.J., K.C. Barrett, M.E. Lamb, H.H. Goldsmith, and C. Stenberg
  1983   Socioemotional development. In P.H. Mussen, ed., *Handbook of Child Psychology,
          Vol. III*. New York: Wiley.

Carew, J.
  1980   Experience and the development of intelligence in young children at home
         and in day care. *Monographs of the Society for Research in Child Development*
         45(6-7):Serial No. 187.
Centers for Disease Control
  1981   Immune globulins for protection against viral hepatitis. *MMWR* 30:423-428,
         433-435.
  1985   Education and foster care of children infected with human T-lymphotropic virus
         type III/lymphadenopathy-associated virus infections. *MMWR* 34:517-521.
Chang A., P. Armstrong, and G. Kelso
  1978   Management of Day Care Children During Episodes of Illness: Parent Attitudes
         to a Sick Child Care Center. School of Public Health, University of California,
         Berkeley.
Clarke-Stewart, K.A.
  1989   Infant day care: Maligned or malignant? *American Psychologist* 44:266-274.
Clarke-Stewart, K.A., and G.G. Fein
  1983   Early childhood programs. Pp. 917-999 in P.H. Mussen, ed., *Handbook of Child
         Psychology, Vol. II.* New York: Wiley.
Cochi, S.L., D.W. Fleming, A.W. Hightower, K. Limpakarnjanarat, R.R. Facklam, J.D.
Smith, R.K. Sikes, and C.V. Broom
  1986   Primary invasive *H. influenzae* type b disease: A population-based assessment
         of risk factors. *Journal of Pediatrics* 108:887-896.
Comer, J.
  1989   Racism and the education of young children. *Teachers College Record* 90:352-362.
Conboy, T.J., R.F. Pass, S. Stagno, C.A. Alford, G.J. Myers, W.J. Britt, F.P. McCollister,
M.N. Summers, C.E. McFarland, and T.J. Boll
  1987   Early clinical manifestations and intellectual outcome in children with symp-
         tomatic congenital cytomegalovirus. *Journal of Pediatrics* 111:343-348.
Crockenberg, S.
  1981   Infant irritability, mother responsiveness, and social support influences on the
         security of infant-mother attachment. *Child Development* 52:857-865.
Cummins, J.
  1986   Empowering minority students: A framework for intervention. *Harvard Educa-
         tional Review* 56:18-36.
Daly, K., G.S. Giebink, C.T. Le, B. Lindgren, P.B. Batalden, R.S. Anderson, and J.N. Russ
  1988   Determining risk for chronic otitis media with effusion. *Pediatric Infectious
         Disease Journal* 7(7):471-475.
Denny, F., A. Collier, and F. Henderson
  1986   Acute respiratory infections in day care. *Reviews of Infectious Diseases* 8:527-532.
Devoney, C., M.J. Guralnick, and H. Rubin
  1974   Integrating handicapped and nonhandicapped preschool children: Effects on
         social play. *Childhood Education* 50:360-364.
Dingle, J.H., G.F. Badger, and W.S. Jordan
  1964   *Illness in the Home.* Cleveland, Ohio: Press of Western Reserve University.
Doyle, A.B.
  1976   Incidence of illness in early group and family day care. *Pediatrics* 58:607-613.
Dyson, L., and R.R. Fewell
  1986   Stress and adaptation in parents of young handicapped and nonhandicapped
         children: A comparative study. *Journal of the Division of Early Childhood*
         10:25-35.

Ekanem, E.E., H.L. DuPont, L.K. Pickering, B.J. Selwyn, and C.M. Hawkins
    1983   Transmission dynamics of enteric bacteria in day care centers. *American Journal of Epidemiology* 118:562-572.
Elardo, R., H.C. Solomons, and B.C. Snider
    1987   An analysis of accidents at a day care center. *American Journal of Orthopsychiatry* 57(1):60-65.
Field, T., N. Vega-Lahr, and S. Jagadish
    1984   Separation stress of nursery school infants and toddlers graduating to new classes. *Infant Behavior and Development* 7:277-284.
Filice, G.A., J.S. Andrews, M.P. Hudgins, and D.W. Fraser
    1978   Spread of *Haemophilus influenzae*: Secondary illness in household contacts of patients with *H. influenzae* meningitis. *American Journal of Diseases of Children* 132:757-759.
Fillmore, L.W., and S. Britsch
    1988   Early Education for Children From Linguistic and Cultural Minority Families. Paper prepared for the Early Education Task Force of the National Association of State Boards of Education, Alexandria, Va. June.
Fine, M.A., and C.F. Swift
    1986   Young handicapped children: Their prevalence and experiences with early intervention services. *Journal of the Division for Early Childhood* 10:73-83.
Fink, D.B.
    1986   Latch-Key Children and School-Age Child Care: A Background Briefing. Paper prepared for the Appalachian Educational Laboratory School-Age Child Care Project, Center for Research for Women, Wellesley College.
Finkelhor, D., L.M. Williams, N. Burns, et al.
    1988   Sexual Abuse in Day Care: A National Study. Executive Summary. Family Research Laboratory, University of New Hampshire.
Fleming, D.W., M.D. Leibenhaut, D. Albanes, S.L. Cochi, A.W. Hightower, S. Makintubee, S.D. Helgerson, and C.V. Broome
    1985   Secondary *Haemophilus influenzae* type b in day care facilities: risk factors and prevention. *JAMA* 254:509-514.
Fleming, D.W., S.L. Cochi, A.W. Hightower, and C.V. Broome
    1987   Childhood upper respiratory tract infections: To what degree is incidence affected by day care attendance? *Pediatrics* 79(1):55-60.
Fredericks, H.D.B., V. Baldwin, D. Grove, W. Moore, C. Riggs, and B. Lyons
    1978   Integrating the moderately and severely handicapped preschool child into a normal day care setting. Pp. 191-206 in M.J. Guralnick, ed., *Early Intervention of Handicapped and Nonhandicapped Children*. Baltimore, Md.: University Park Press.
Garrard, J., N. Leland, and D.K. Smith
    1988   Epidemiology of human bites to children in a day-care center. *American Journal of Diseases of Children* 142:643-650.
Gehlbach, S.H., J.N. MacCormack, B.M. Drake, and W.V. Thompson
    1973   Spread of disease by fecal-oral route in day nurseries. *Health Service Reports* 88:320-322.
Ginsburg, C.M., G.H. McCracken Jr., S. Rae, and J.C. Parke, Jr.
    1977   *Haemophilus influenzae* type b: incidence in a day care center. *JAMA* 238:604-607.

Goelman, H.
  1986   The language environments of family day care. Pp. 153-179 in S. Kilmer, ed., *Advances in Day Care and Early Education, Vol. IV.* Greenwich, Conn.: JAI Press.
Goelman, H., and A.R. Pence
  1987   Some aspects of the relationship between family structure and child language in three types of day care. Pp. 129-146 in D. Peters and S. Kontos, eds., *Annual Advances in Applied Developmental Psychology, Vol. II.* Norwood, N.J.: Ablex Publishing Corp.
Granoff, D.M., and M. Basden
  1980   *Haemophilus influenzae* infections in Fresno County, California: A prospective study of the effects of age, race, and contact with a case on incidence of disease. *Journal of Infectious Diseases* 141:40-46.
Guralnick, M.J.
  1976   The value of integrating handicapped and nonhandicapped preschool children. *American Journal of Orthopsychiatry* 46:236-245.
  1978   Integrated preschools as educational and therapeutic environments: Concepts, design, and analysis. Pp. 115-145 in M.J. Guralnick, ed., *Early Intervention and the Integration of Handicapped and Nonhandicapped Children.* Baltimore, Md.: University Park Press.
Hadler, S.C., J.J. Erben, D.P. Francis, H.M. Webster, and J.E. Maynard
  1982   Risk factors for hepatitis in day care centers. *Journal of Infectious Diseases* 145:255-261.
Hartup, W.W.
  1983   Peer relations. Pp. 103-196 in P.H. Mussen, ed., *Handbook of Child Psychology, Volume IV,* 4th ed. New York: Wiley.
Haskins, R.
  1985   Public school aggression among children with varying day-care experience. *Child Development* 56:689-703.
Haskins, R., and J. Kotch
  1986   Day care and illness: Evidence, costs, and public policy. *Pediatrics* 77(supp.):951-982.
Hauser-Cram, P., C.C. Upshur, M.W. Krauss, and J.P. Shonkoff
  1988   Implications of Public Law 99-457 for early intervention services for infants and toddlers with disabilities. *Social Policy Report of the Society for Research in Child Development* 3(3).
Hay, D.
  1985   Learning to form relationships in infancy: Parallel attainments with parents and peers. *Developmental Review* 5:122-161.
Henderson, F.W., and G.S. Giebink
  1986   Otitis media among children in day care: Epidemiology and pathogenesis. *Reviews of Infectious Diseases* 8(4):533-538.
Holliday, B.G.
  1985   Toward a model of teacher-child transactional processes affecting black children's academic achievement. Pp. 117-130 in M.B. Spencer, G.K. Brookins, and W.R. Allen, eds., *Beginnings: The Social and Affective Development of Black Children.* Hillsdale, N.J.: Erlbaum.
Holloway, S.D., and M. Reichhart-Erickson
  1988   The relationship of day-care quality to children's free play behavior and social problem solving skills. *Early Childhood Research Quarterly* 3:39-54.

Horacek, H.J., C.T. Ramey, F.A. Campbell, K.P. Hoffmann, and R.H. Fletcher
  1987   Predicting school failure and assessing early intervention with high-risk children. *Journal of the American Academy of Child and Adolescent Psychiatry* 26:758-763.
Howes, C.
  1987   Social competency with peers: Contributions from child care. *Early Childhood Research Quarterly* 2:155-167.
  1988a   Can Age of Entry and the Quality of Infant Child Care Predict Behaviors in Kindergarten? Paper presented at the International Conference of Infant Studies, Washington, D.C., April.
  1988b   Peer interaction of young children. *Monographs of the Society for Research in Child Development*. 53(1):Serial No. 217.
Howes, C., and M. Olenick
  1986   Family and child influences on toddlers' compliance. *Child Development* 57:202-216.
Howes, C., M. Olenick, and T. Der-Kiureghian
  1987   After-school child care in an elementary school: Social development and continuity and complementarity of programs. *The Elementary School Journal* (September):93-103.
Howes, C., C. Rodning, D.C. Galluzzo, and L. Myers
  1988   Attachment and child care: Relationships with mother and caregiver. *Early Childhood Research Quarterly* 3:403-416.
Ispa, J.
  1981   Social interactions among teachers, handicapped children, and nonhandicapped children in a mainstreamed preschool. *Journal of Applied Developmental Psychology* 1:231-250.
Istre, G.R., J.S. Conner, C.V. Broome, A. Hightower, and R.S. Hopkins
  1985   Risk factors for primary invasive *Haemophilus influenzae* disease: Increased risk from day care attendance and school-aged household members. *Journal of Pediatrics* 106:190-195.
Jarman, F.C., and T.M. Kohlenberg
  1988   Health and Safety Implications of Day Care. Paper prepared for the Panel on Child Care Policy, Committee on Child Development Research and Public Policy, Commission on Behavioral and Social Sciences and Education, National Research Council, Washington, D.C.
Jones, S.N., and S.J. Meisels
  1987   Training family day care providers to work with special needs children. *Topics in Early Childhood Special Education* 7:1-12.
Klein, J.O.
  1987   The febrile child and occult bacteremia. *New England Journal of Medicine* 317:1219-1220.
Klein, N., and R. Sheehan
  1987   Staff development: A key issue in meeting the needs of young handicapped children in day care settings. *Topics in Early Childhood Special Education* 7:13-27.
Landis, S.E., J.L. Earp, and M. Sharp
  1988   Day-care center exclusion of sick children: Comparison of opinions of day-care staff, working mothers, and pediatricians. *Pediatrics* 81(5):662-667.
Landman, P.F., and G.B. Landman
  1987   Accidental injuries in children in day-care centers. *American Journal of Diseases of Children* 141:292-293.

Lazar, I., R.B. Darlington, H. Murray, J. Royce, and A. Snipper
    1982   Lasting effects of early education: A report of the Consortium for Longitudinal Studies. *Monographs of the Society for Research in Child Development* 47(2-3):Serial No. 195.
Lemp, G.F., W.E. Woodward, and L.K. Pickering, P.S. Sullivan, and H.L. DuPont
    1984   The relationship of staff to the incidence of diarrhea in day care centers. *American Journal of Epidemiology* 120:750-758.
Lewis, C.C.
    1984   Cooperation and control in Japanese nursery schools. *Comparative Education Review* 28:69-84.
Long, T.J., and L. Long
    1983   *The Handbook for Latchkey Children and Their Parents.* New York: Arbor House.
McCartney, K.
    1984   Effect of quality of day care environment on children's language development. *Developmental Psychology* 20:244-260.
McCartney, K., S. Scarr, D. Phillips, S. Grajek, and J.C. Schwarz
    1982   Environmental differences among day care centers and their effects on children's development. Pp. 126-151 in E. Zigler and E. Gordon, eds., *Day Care: Scientific and Social Policy Issues.* Boston: Auburn House.
McCartney, K., S. Scarr, D. Phillips, and S. Grajek
    1985   Day care as intervention: Comparisons of varying quality programs. *Journal of Applied Developmental Psychology* 6:247-260.
McLean, A.A.
    1986   Development of vaccines against hepatitis A and hepatitis B. *Reviews of Infectious Diseases* 8(4):591-598.
Melish, M.E., and J.B. Hanshaw
    1973   Congenital cytomegalovirus infections. *American Journal of Diseases of Children* 126:190-194.
National Head Start Multicultural Task Force
    1987   *Report for First Meeting.* December 10-11. Administration for Children, Youth, and Families. Washington, D.C.: U.S. Department of Health and Human Services.
Ogbu, J.U.
    1986   Consequences of the American caste system. Pp. 19-56 in U. Neisser, ed., *The School Achievement of Minority Children.* Hillsdale, N.J.: Erlbaum.
Osterholm, M.T., L.M. Pierson, K.E. White, T.A. Libby, J.N. Kuritsky, and J.G. McCullough
    1987   The risk of subsequent transmission of *Haemophilus influenzae* type b disease among children in day care. *New England Journal of Medicine* 316:1-5.
Pass, R.F., and C. Hutto
    1986   Group day care and cytomegaloviral infections of mothers and children. *Reviews of Infectious Diseases* 8(4):599-605.
Pass, R.F., S. Stagno, A.J. Myers, and C.A. Alford
    1980   Outcome of symptomatic congenital cytomegalovirus infection: Results of long-term longitudinal follow-up. *Pediatrics* 66:758-762.
Pass, R.F., E.A. Little, S. Stagno, W.J. Britt, and C.A. Alford
    1987   Young children as a probable source of maternal and congenital cytomegalovirus infection. *New England Journal of Medicine* 316:1366-1370.
Phillips, C.
    1989   *Anti-Bias Curriculum.* Washington, D.C.: National Association for the Education of Young Children.

Pickering, L.K., D.G. Evans, H.L. Dupont, J.J. Vottet III, and D.J. Evans, Jr.
   1981   Diarrhea caused by Shigella, Rotavirus, and Giardia in day care centers: Prospective study. *Journal of Pediatrics* 99:51-56.

Redmond, S.R., and M.E. Pichichero
   1984   *Haemophilus influenzae* type b disease: Epidemiologic study with special reference to day care centers. *JAMA* 252:2581-2583.

Reeves, R.R., A.L. Morrow, A.L. Bartlett, and L.K. Pickering
   1988   A Case Control Study of Acute Diarrhea in Children in a Health Maintenance Organization (HMO): Risk Estimates Associated with Non Breast Feeding and Day Care. Paper presented at Society for Pediatric Research annual scientific meeting, Washington D.C.

Richardson, J.L., K. Dwyer, K. McGuigan, W.B. Hansen, C. Dent, C.A. Johnson, S.Y. Sussman, B. Brannon, and B. Flay
   1989   Substance use among eighth-grade students who take care of themselves after school. *Pediatrics* 84:556-566.

Rodgers, F.S., G. Morgan, and B.C. Fredericks
   1986   Caring for the ill child in day care. *Journal of School Health* 56(4):131-133.

Rodman, H., D.J. Pratto, and R.S. Nelson
   1985   Child care arrangement and children's functioning: A comparison of self-care and adult-care children. *Developmental Psychology* 21:413-418.

Rubenstein, J.L., and C. Howes
   1983   Social-emotional development of toddlers in day care: The role of peers and individual differences. In S. Kilmer, ed., *Early Education and Day Care, Vol. 3*. Greenwich, Conn.: JAI Press.

Rule, S., J. Killoran, J. Stowitschek, M. Innocenti, and S. Striefel
   1985   Training and support for mainstreaming day care staff. *Early Child Development and Care* 20:99-113.

Ruopp, R., J. Travers, F. Glantz, and C. Coelen
   1979   *Children at the Center: Final Results of the National Day Care Study*. Boston: Abt Associates.

Russell, S.D., and R.M. Clifford
   1987   Child abuse and neglect in North Carolina day care programs. *Child Welfare* 67(2):149-163.

Sale, J.S.S.
   1986   Promoting creativity and independence in young children: A challenge for teachers and parents. Speech delivered at the Centennial Celebration of Japanese Christian Kindergartens, Kanazawa, Japan. Available from UCLA Child Care Services, Los Angeles, Calif.

Schloesser, P.T.
   1986   Children in day care: A public health challenge. *Public Health Currents* 26(5):21-24.

Schwarz, J.C.
   1983   Infant Day Care: Effects at 2, 4, and 8 Years. Paper presented at the meeting of the Society for Research in Child Development, Detroit.

Schweinhart, L.J., D.P. Weikart, and M.B. Larner
   1986   Consequences of three preschool curriculum models through age 15. *Early Childhood Research Quarterly* 1:15-45.

Seligson, M.
   1988   Paper prepared for Workshop on the Developmental Implications of Child Care, Panel on Child Care Policy, Committee on Child Development Research and

Public Policy, Commission on Behavioral and Social Sciences and Education, National Research Council, Washington, D.C.

Shapiro, E.D., J. Kuritsy, and J. Potter
1986   Policies for the exclusion of ill children from group day care: An unresolved dilemma. *Review of Infectious Diseases* 8(4):622-625.

Slaughter, D.T.
1983   Early intervention and its effects on maternal and child development. *Monographs of the Society for Research in Child Development* 48(4):Serial No. 202.

Smith, C., and M. Greenberg
1981   Step by step integration of handicapped preschool children in a day care center for nonhandicapped children. *Journal of the Division for Early Childhood* 2:96-101.

Snyder, L., T. Apolloni, and T.P. Cooke
1977   Integrated settings at the early childhood level: The role of nonretarded peers. *Exceptional Children* 43:262-266.

Spencer, M.B.
1985   Black children's race awareness, racial attitudes, and self-concept: A reinterpretation. *Journal of Child Psychology and Psychiatry* 25:433-441.
1986   Black children's ethnic identity formation: Risk and resilience of castelike minorities. Pp. 103-116 in J.S. Phinney and M.J. Rotheram, eds., *Children's Ethnic Socialization: Pluralism and Development*. Beverly Hills, Calif.: Sage.
1988   Cognition, Identity, and Social Development as Correlates of African American Children's Academic Skills. Invited lecture sponsored by the Center for Afroamerican and African Studies, University of Michigan, Ann Arbor, March.

Spencer, M.B., S.R. Kim, and S. Marshall
1987   Double stratification and psychological risk: Adaptational processes and school achievement of black children. *Journal of Negro Education* 56:77-87.

Sroufe, L.A.
1985   Attachment classification from the perspective of infant caregiver relationships. *Child Development* 56:1-14.

Stagno, S., R.F. Pass, G. Cloud, W.J. Britt, R.E. Henderson, P.D. Walton, D.A. Veren, F. Page, and C.A. Alford
1986   Primary cytomegalovirus infection in pregnancy. Incidence, transmission to fetus, and clinical outcome. *JAMA* 256:1904-1908.

Steinberg, L.
1986   Latchkey children and susceptibility to peer pressure: An ecological analysis. *Developmental Psychology* 22:433-439.

Strangert, K.
1976   Respiratory illness in preschool children with different forms of day care. *Pediatrics* 57(2):191-196.

Sullivan, P., W.E. Woodward, L.K. Pickering, and H.L. Dupont
1984   Longitudinal study of diarrheal disease in day care centers. *American Journal of Public Health* 74:987-991.

UCLA Child Care Services
1989   *UCLA Child Care Services Philosophy Statement*. Los Angeles, Calif.: UCLA Child Care Services.

Vandell, D.L., and M.A. Corasaniti
1988   The relation between third graders' after-school care and social, academic, and emotional functioning. *Child Development* 59:868-875.

Vandell, D.L., and C.P. Powers
   1983   Day care quality and children's free play activities. *American Journal of Orthopsychiatry* 53:493-500.
Vandell, D.L., V.K. Henderson, and K.S. Wilson
   1988   A longitudinal study of children with day-care experiences of varying quality. *Child Development* 59:1286-1292.
Wald, E.R., B. Dashefsky, C. Byers, N. Guerra, and F. Taylor
   1988   Frequency and severity of infections in day care. *Journal of Pediatrics* 112:540-546.
Ward, J.I., D.W. Fraser, L.J. Baraff, and B.D. Plikaytis
   1979   *Haemophilus influenzae* meningitis: A national study of secondary spread in household contacts. *New England Journal of Medicine* 301:122-126.
Weissman, J.B., E.J. Gangorosa, A. Schmerler, R.L. Marier, and J.N. Lewis
   1975   Shigellosis in day care centers. *Lancet* i(7898):88-90.
Williams, L.R., and Y. DeGaetano
   1985   *Alerta: A Multicultural Bilingual Approach to Teaching Young Children.* Menlo Park, Calif.: Addison-Wesley.
Wood, D.
   1988   *How Children Think and Learn.* Oxford: Basil Blackwell.
Wood, D., L. McMahon, and Y. Cranston
   1980   *Working With Under Fives.* London: Grant McIntyre.

III

The Current System

6

Child Care Services

Although many working parents continue to care for their children themselves or to rely on relatives, nannies, and babysitters to provide care at home, many others have turned to caregivers in settings outside the home. These include day care centers, operated on a for-profit or a not-for-profit basis; family day care homes and group homes; public and private nursery schools, prekindergartens, and kindergartens operated as part-day or full-day school programs; before- and after-school programs; and Head Start programs.

There have been striking changes among these care arrangements in the past three decades; see Figure 6-1. Although data on the supply of child care services are largely inadequate because of the broad range of providers and auspices and the lack of systematic collection of information at the national or state level, there is evidence that the supply of out-of-home services has increased substantially since the 1970s (Kahn and Kamerman, 1987).

The most striking characteristic of the existing system of out-of-home child care is its diversity. Like other social services, child care services have not developed within any designed framework of regulations, policy, or legislation. States vary in their commitment to developing, funding, and regulating care, and this variation increases at the community level. The resulting "patchwork quilt" is an amalgam of individual and institutional child care providers (Siegal and Lawrence, 1984); the individual programs do not perceive themselves as interrelated or as sharing a common set of goals.

The need for some coordination and regulation of child care services has been widely recognized for some time, and the debate over which jurisdiction should regulate, what should be regulated, to what extent, with

147

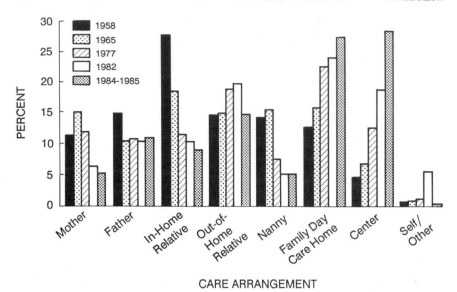

CARE ARRANGEMENT

FIGURE 6-1   Child care arrangements for children, under age 5 of full-time employed mothers, 1958-1985. Source: Data from Bureau of the Census (1987); Lueck et al. (1982); O'Connell and Rogers (1983).

what exceptions, and with what types of enforcement and sanctions is an old one. After more than a decade of legislative and regulatory battles at the national level, the Federal Interagency Day Care Requirements were eliminated in 1982, and states are now responsible for the regulation of child care services. Since the early 1980s, the debate at the state and local levels has focused on ways to improve consumer knowledge and standards for protection as well as government monitoring and enforcement. In general, regulations have gradually become more stringent during the past decade and a half, although states vary dramatically in their specific provisions (see Appendix A). Moreover, within this context, different types of programs are governed by different regulatory authorities, and some providers are exempt because of the auspices under which they operate or the number of children they serve.

   In this chapter we review what is known about the delivery and regulation of child care services and some barriers to effective services. In Chapter 4 we discussed the role of regulation as it affects the quality of care that is provided by different types of programs and arrangements; in this chapter we consider the ways in which regulation and the regulatory environment affect the delivery of child care services. It is important to note at the outset, however, that our knowledge is limited. Information concerning the supply of child care services is not systematically reported, and few programs have been rigorously evaluated. As a result, information about program effects must be cumulated from the growing body of small-scale child care studies that provide some insights into how various delivery approaches work, for whom, under what circumstances, at what costs, and with what intended and unintended consequences, but that generally lack comparability in their design and methods.

CHILD CARE SERVICES

Care by Relatives

Many parents provide care for their own children by working split shifts or other flexible arrangements. A total of 3.7 million children under age 15 whose mothers are in the labor force are cared for exclusively by their parents (Bureau of the Census, 1987). Grandparents, siblings, and other extended family members continue to be important sources of care, especially for infants and toddlers, and to supplement school and school-based programs: approximately 3.1 million children under age 15 are cared for by relatives in their own homes or in the relative's home (Bureau of the Census, 1987). Together, these 4.8 million children constitute more than 20 percent of all children under age 15 who receive supplemental care. But relative care is declining for all children because many grandmothers and aunts who once were available to serve as caregivers are now employed (Bruno, 1987). As discussed in Chapter 2, parents who work evening or night shifts and those who work part time appear to be more likely to rely on relatives to care for their children than those who work regular day shifts, especially if they work full time. In two-parent families, the caregiver is often the father. The direction of the relationship between shift work and the use of relative care is not known, however: it is unclear if families who choose to rely on relatives (including fathers) as caregivers choose to work evening and night shifts or, if having chosen or having been assigned to irregular shifts, they must rely on relatives in the absence of other types of care (Presser, 1986).

Child care provided by parents and other relatives is unregulated whether it occurs in the child's own home or in the relative's home. Only when an adult cares for a related child along with other children in a child care center or a regulated family day care home are these services subject to state or local government monitoring and enforcement. Data concerning the incidence of relative care come from the Current Population Surveys (CPS), the Survey of Income and Program Participation (SIPP), the National Survey of Family Growth (NSFG), and the youth cohort of the National Longitudinal Survey. These sources provide information concerning trends in reliance on relative care, but they do not provide information about the relatives who serve as caregivers, for example, whether they provide care for other children, including their own, in addition to the relative child. Nor is there any information about their qualifications or the amount, if anything, they are paid for their services. There is also no reliable information on their longevity as caregivers.

Nannies and In-Home Babysitters

There is similarly little systematic information on nannies, babysitters, and other unrelated caregivers who care for children in the child's own homes. Data from the NSFG suggest that approximately 1 million children were cared for in this way in 1982; 1985 SIPP data showed that approximately 687,000 (2.6 percent) of children under age 15 who received supplemental care were cared for in their own homes by an unrelated adult. If these data are comparable, there has been a decline of approximately 31 percent in the use of in-home care in just 3 years. Because so little is known about this form of care, it is difficult to speculate about reasons for the decline. It may reflect in part the growth in out-of-home care alternatives. In addition, as Hofferth and Phillips (1987) point out, recent migrants have often served in this role. As immigration patterns and laws have changed, and as women who have been in this country for some time accumulate labor market experience, their likelihood of becoming child care providers in someone else's home will probably continue to decline. Like relative care, in-home care provided by nannies, babysitters, and other unrelated caregivers is unregulated.

Nanny placement agencies, which have sprung up in recent years in many large metropolitan cities across the country, provide some anecdotal information on women who serve as in-home caregivers. Many are young, in their late teens and early 20s, from small communities in the Midwest and far West who want to have the experience of living and working in a large city. Some are black women living in urban centers. Others are immigrant women from Central America, the Pacific Islands, and the Caribbean, newly arrived in this country and often illegal aliens. A few are Europeans on short-term visas who have come as a part of an *au pair* or living-abroad program. Some have professional training and experience; many do not. Some live on their own; many live in the homes of their employers. Many in-home caregivers combine child care responsibilities with some housekeeping duties. Although salaries vary dramatically, recent information from Washington, D.C., suggests that the range is $150 to $350 per week, depending on hours of work, specific duties, and benefits (Granat, 1988).

Family Day Care

Although there are no reliable data on the number of family day care homes or the number of children in those homes, this form of care clearly represents a significant portion of the supply of child care services in the United States in the late 1980s. Since many family day care providers operate in the underground economy, however, precise estimates of their numbers and the number of children they serve are illusive. In the 1977-1978 Family Day Care Home Study, the U.S. Department of Health and Human Services estimated that 1.8 million unregulated providers and 115,000 licensed or regulated providers were caring for 5 million children and that approximately 23 percent of these children were of school age (Fosburg, 1981). Adams (1982) reported that a 1982 telephone survey of all states and territories found 137,865 licensed, registered, or certified family day care homes. A 1988 survey of the states and Washington, D.C., undertaken as a part this panel's study, showed 198,257 licensed family day care homes nationwide (see Figure 6-2). Estimates of unregulated care cited in congressional testimony and elsewhere range from 60 to 90 percent of the total supply, suggesting that there may now be between 496,000 and 1,983,000 such homes in the United States.

Estimates of the number of children cared for in family day care homes are similarly wide. The Family Day Care Home Study reported an average of 3.5 children per home (excluding the caregiver's own children), with a range of 2 to 6 children per home (Fosburg, 1981). Average enrollments varied according to the regulatory status of the home: sponsored homes (those in a network, which may or may not be regulated) averaged 4.3 children; regulated homes averaged 4.0 children, and unregulated homes averaged 2.8 children. Using the average of 3.7 children per home suggests that there may be as few as 1.8 million or as many as 7.3 million children, including school-age children, in family day care. Using an average of 3.5 children per house, Kahn and Kamerman (1987) point out that the total 5.0 million estimate that is widely quoted could be correct. However, Kahn and Kamerman (1987), using NSFG data, estimate 5.1 million children in family day care.

An increasing number of states treat large family day care homes or group homes as a separate category for regulatory purposes. Typically these providers serve between 7 and 12 children (although some include larger groups). The number of large family day care or group homes appears to be expanding rapidly, from 2,371 in 1985 to 5,373 in 1988, according to survey data collected by the panel.

Data from the CPS and the NSFG show that the highest rate of use of family day care is for very young children (Hofferth and Phillips, 1987). In 1982, approximately 10 percent of children in family day care homes

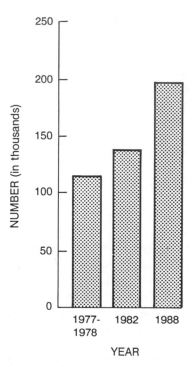

FIGURE 6-2   Regulated family day care homes, 1977-1978, 1982, 1988.   Source: Data from Adams (1982); Fosburg (1981); unpublished panel survey.

were infants, 26 percent were toddlers, 27 percent were preschoolers, and about 36 percent were of school age (unpublished tabulations from the 1982 NSFG). Although these measures are rough, they suggest that the percentage of toddlers in family day care has declined somewhat since 1977 and the percentage of school-age children receiving care before and after school hours and on school holidays has increased (Fosburg, 1981; Hofferth and Phillips, 1987).

Family day care is not a monolithic service. It differs greatly from provider to provider and from community to community. In general, however, family day care providers fall into one of three broad categories (Fosburg, 1981). The first is young white mothers in their late 20s and 30s with their own young children at home. Many of these women left the paid labor force when they became mothers, and they provide care to other children as a means of supplementing their family income while at home. Although their income is still low by general standards, these women have relatively higher incomes than those in the other groups. Many of them resume employment outside their homes when their own children are of school age or when they no longer require care.

The second group comprises women in their 40s and 50s who care for at least one related child, often a grandchild. Like the younger women in the first category, they often decide to take on the care of other unrelated children as a means of earning some money while they are staying home with their relative's child. It is not uncommon for them to close down their family day care services when the related child no longer requires care. Many black or Hispanic caregivers fall into this group.

The last group includes women in their 30s to 50s who care only for unrelated children. They may have begun providing child care when they were caring for their own young children and then developed their services into a business and a career. These providers are more likely to have had some professional training in child development and child care, and they are more likely to be regulated and sponsored than are providers in the first two groups. They also tend to stay in the family day care market for more sustained periods of time than the others. Overall, however, three-quarters of family day care providers describe this as a permanent role (Fosburg, 1981).

Family day care is distinguished by small group size (typically 6 or fewer children) and generally mixed-age groups (including school-age youngsters during before- and after-school hours), although some providers care only for infants and toddlers or only for preschoolers. Despite variation in the ages of children in their charge, however, family day care providers are unlikely to care for children whose race or ethnicity is different than their own. The National Day Care Home Study found that 80 percent of children in family day care are the same race and ethnicity as the caregiver (Fosburg, 1981).

Consumer surveys indicate that among parents who prefer family day care, it is the intimacy of a small group and a home environment as well as a sense of shared values with the caregiver that are important (Leibowitz et al., 1988). Parents frequently live in close proximity to their family day care providers and, especially black or Hispanic parents, are of similar economic backgrounds (Waite et al., 1988). Several researchers emphasize the close relationships that often develop between providers and children and between providers and parents. These adult relationships are frequently more informal and social than between parents and caregivers in other settings, and they are thought to enhance communications and interactions that can positively affect the child.

In 1988, 27 states required some form of licensing for family day care providers depending on the numbers of children in their care. Twenty-three states did not have any formal licensing requirements, although 13 required or offered voluntary registration, and 6 states had an approval or a certification procedure for providers seeking to receive federal funds (Blank and Wilkins, 1985; Morgan, 1987; unpublished data from panel survey). Some states exempted homes serving fewer than four children. Despite the existence of licensing requirements and registration or certification provisions, few family day care providers appear to operate under them. Fosburg (1981) found that in three cities in states with regulations, 94 percent of providers were operating informally and independently; another 3 percent were independent and licensed or registered, meeting state regulations (and federal standards governing the Child Care Food Program); and another 3 percent were regulated and a part of a family day care network, under the auspices of a sponsoring agency. In a recent study of the Child Care Food Program, Glantz and colleagues (1988) estimated that approximately 70 percent of family day care providers are unlicensed.

Despite recent efforts in many states to register family day care providers (as opposed to licensing them) and to bring them into organized systems, there is consensus that the vast majority are still unregistered and unregulated (Kahn and Kamerman, 1987). The reasons are not clearly understood. Undoubtedly, some providers regard themselves as temporarily caring for the children of relatives and neighbors while raising their own children, and they may be unaware of the requirements or may regard the licensing process as too complex and costly to negotiate. Others may regard licensing as an intrusion, especially if they have no interest in seeking government subsidies. Still others may be hoping to avoid the tax liabilities or lost welfare benefits and transfers that would result from having to report their income (Kahn and Kamerman, 1987; Morgan, 1980). The primary incentives for becoming licensed or registered appear to be public subsidies, such as the Child Care Food Program and funds for serving children in low-income families, referrals from resource and referral agencies and public social service agencies, as well as the ability to obtain liability insurance. Providers who see their activities as a business or a career are frequently more eager to gain the visibility that licensing and registration may bring.

Kahn and Kamerman (1987) report that 94 percent of family day care is carried out through "largely invisible and unprotected" cash transactions; generally, reliable cost data are lacking. Fosburg (1981) found early in the 1980s that sponsored and regulated care was more expensive than unregulated care; see Table 6-1. In more recent estimates of the costs of family day care in selected cities, Work/Family Directions, Inc., found a wide range within and across 15 cities; see Table 6-2. On the whole, family day care is slightly less expensive than center care, and unregulated family day care is least expensive of all. Kahn and Kamerman (1987) note that independent, unregulated providers rely solely on market fees and

TABLE 6-1 Average Weekly Fee per Child by Type of
Family Day Care Home and Race of Provider

Race of Provider	Type of Care Sponsored	Regulated	Unregulated
White	$31.80	$23.68	$19.70
Black	24.68	21.61	16.57
Hispanic	24.49	21.42	16.54
Average	6.36	22.65	17.80

Source: Data from Fosburg (1981:96).

TABLE 6-2 Weekly Child Care Rates for Family Day Care in 15 Cities,
August 1987

City	Infants	Toddlers	Preschool-Age Children
Atlanta, Ga.	$35-150	$45-70	$45-70
Boston, Mass.	150	95-125	80-105
Chicago, Ill.	60-100	65-85	50-80
Cleveland, Ohio	25-100	25-100	25-100
Denver, Colo.	60-100	455-95	55-95
Greenville, S.C.	35-60	35-60	35-60
Los Angeles, Calif.	44-88	44-88	38-84
Miami, Fla.	25-75	25-65	20-65
Minneapolis, Minn.	70-90	60-75	50-65
New Orleans, La.	30-45	30-45	30-45
New York, N.Y.	35-150	35-150	35-150
Oklahoma City, Okla.	35-60	40-80	40-65
Raleigh, N.C.	25-125	25-85	25-85
Seattle, Wash.	46-58	69	69
Washington, D.C.	35-125	35-125	35-100

Source: Unpublished data from Work/Family Directions, Inc.

therefore both charge and earn somewhat less than sponsored and regulated
providers. Those that are a part of a network or are agency sponsored are
more likely to have their services partially or completely subsidized by
public funds, including the Child Care Food Program. Indeed, the cost
differences between sponsored or regulated family day care and center care
are generally modest. As a result, these caregivers are more likely to earn
somewhat higher wages (Kahn and Kamerman, 1987).

Advocates of licensing and registration argue that bringing family day care providers into the regulated system would improve the quality of care and professionalize these services. Anecdotal horror stories of children receiving inadequate care in unsafe, unregulated family day care homes are prevalent, although there are no reliable data on such care. When registration was first proposed, it was hoped that it would facilitate entry into the market and provide continuing in-service support to providers, in contrast to licensing procedures which had often screened out many caregivers on the grounds that they are offering substandard services. Although the development of registration programs has been uneven and haphazard, many observers believe that such programs are expanding the visible supply of child care and helping to improve the quality of care for children and the working conditions of caregivers (Norris Class, University of Southern California, personal communication, Apr. 4, 1988; Kahn and Kamerman, 1987; Morgan, 1980). Other efforts to improve the quality of care in family day care homes—including grading systems, municipal coordinating agencies, and advisory councils—have been proposed and implemented in some localities, but there are no studies of the effects and effectiveness of these initiatives.

Center Care

Child care centers serving children from infancy through school age have been established in most communities across the country. The types of programs and the auspices under which they operate range dramatically. Not-for-profit centers are run by local government agencies, community institutions, and employers. Some are freestanding; while others are located in the facilities of their sponsoring organizations, including churches, schools, hospitals, social service agencies, and places of employment. For-profit centers, operated by large national corporations and independent providers, are typically found in freestanding facilities.

Child care centers trace their roots to the day nurseries of the late nineteenth century, but with the entry of mothers into the labor force and the early childhood education developments of the 1960s and 1970s, child care and child development programs have been joined. Child care centers typically serve both purposes, and the difference between child care centers and nursery schools is often blurred. In many communities, the difference between high-quality child care and early childhood education programs is only the difference between the sponsoring agencies or the auspices under which they operate.

In 1971 Caldwell described day care as a "timid giant growing bolder," and in the late 1980s the giant was still growing. Although estimates vary, data from the National Day Care Study reported approximately 34,000 licensed centers nationwide in 1976 (Coelen et al., 1979); a 1986 survey of state licensing offices by the National Association for the Education of Young Children showed a total of 62,989 child care centers with a capacity of approximately 2.1 million children (Hofferth and Phillips, 1987; National Association for the Education of Young Children, 1986). The former number represents a 234 percent increase in the number of centers between the mid-1970s and the mid-1980s. The panel's own survey of state licensing offices in 1988 indicates a further modest increase, to approximately 64,078 licensed centers nationwide with a capacity of 2,568,000. This increase in the number of licensed centers and their capacity is consistent with the 50 percent growth in the use of center-based care between 1980 and 1985 by children under age 5 with full-time employed mothers (Hofferth and Phillips, 1987). It is important to note, however, that even though a center is licensed, it may not be currently in operation. Data from state licensing agencies are not always up to date, and there is evidence that providers enter and leave the market with some frequency. Estimates of the total supply of licensed child care, therefore, may be somewhat inflated.

Characteristics of center care programs differ from provider to provider, for curricular programs and materials, configuration of facilities, and caregiver characteristics. State regulations provide minimum thresholds for staff/child ratios, group size, caregiver qualifications, and physical space requirements. They may also specify program content requirements, although these are rarely, if ever, enforced. Performance standards established by several professional organizations provide guidelines for safeguarding children's health and safety and for optimizing developmental outcomes, but the extent to which they are followed is unknown. Within the range represented by regulations and standards, the specific characteristics of center-based care vary substantially.

An important distinguishing feature of center care, in comparison with family day care, is that children are generally grouped according to age and developmental stage. Although centers vary in the developmental range of children in a group, they typically include a spread of 6 to 9 months; in contrast, family day care settings may have children whose ages range from infancy through school age in the same space with the same caregiver. Although centers group children more homogeneously by age, they frequently include children that are racially and ethnically more diverse than in family day care homes, especially if they receive federal subsidies for serving children in low-income families or are located in urban settings (Coelen et al., 1979).

Child Care Workers

Among the most critical characteristics of child care is the caregiver. The number of child care workers has grown by an astounding 90 percent since 1977 and by approximately 43 percent since 1982. The vast majority of these new caregivers are working in centers (National Association for the Education of Young Children, 1985). Among child care workers, there are notable differences between those in center-based programs and those in family day care. According to the National Day Care Study, in 1977, center care providers had an average of 14 to 15 years of formal education, and 29 percent had 16 or more years of education—twice the percentage among all employed females in the United States at that time. Fifty-four percent of caregivers had some post-secondary education, and only 10 percent had not completed high school (Coelen et al., 1979). In contrast, family day care providers had an average of 11.3 years of formal education. Although the majority had completed high school (57 percent), only about 30 percent had received some post-secondary education (Fosburg, 1981; National Association for the Education of Young Children, 1985).

Caregiver training in early childhood development has been correlated with positive outcomes for children in care (see Chapter 4). Yet there is no national educational requirement for child care providers. State regulations are not consistent in their requirements for caregiver training; in fact, 23 states do not require preservice training for teachers in child care centers (Morgan, 1987). States that require training recognize a variety of methods for meeting the standard, including receipt of the Child Development Associate (CDA) credential, coursework in institutions of higher learning, and preservice training provided by community organizations. The CDA credential that recognizes the competency of caregivers working with children is awarded by the Council for Early Childhood Professional Recognition, a subsidiary of the National Association for the Education of Young Children. Since 1975, more than 30,000 caregivers have been awarded the credential; just over 4,000 caregivers were certified in 1989 alone (Carol Phillips, Council for Early Childhood Professional Recognition, personal communication, Jan. 8, 1990). No analogous data are available on the training of caregivers through colleges or community organizations.

Despite their higher levels of education, child care workers in centers command very low salaries. In 1987 more than half of child care workers earned less than $5.00 per hour. Low salaries have contributed to high turnover rates among child care workers. The National Association for the Education of Young Children (1985) and the Child Care Staffing Study (Whitebook et al., 1989) estimate that, between 1980 and 1990, 40 to 42 percent of child care workers will have left their jobs annually, many to seek employment in other fields. These rates are more than double the average replacement rate of 19.4 percent for all occupations. Low pay, lack of benefits, and stressful working conditions are the major reasons child care providers leave their jobs in such high numbers (National Association for the Education of Young Children, 1985; Phillips and Whitebook, 1986; Whitebook et al., 1989). Teachers and teaching assistants who earn $4.00 per hour or less left their jobs at twice the rate of those who earned more than $6.00 per hour (Whitebook et al., 1989).

For-Profit and Not-for-Profit Centers

In 1977 the National Day Care Study estimated that approximately 41 percent of child care centers were operated on a for-profit basis, either by national corporations or by independent providers (Coelen et al., 1979). As we discuss in more detail in Chapter 7, efforts by the federal government during the 1980s to "privatize" social services, including child care, has shifted public funding away from direct subsidies to public centers toward subsidies to consumers (parents). Some observers conclude that the availability of consumer subsidies has fueled the growth in proprietary (for-profit) care since the mid-1970s (Kahn and Kamerman, 1987). Others contend that the decline in direct subsidies to providers has limited the ability of not-for-profit providers to cover the costs of their services and that they have, therefore, not expanded as rapidly. Regardless of the causal relationship, most of the growth in center-based child care over the past decade and a half appears to have been among for-profit providers. Although reliable estimates of the number of for-profit centers are unavailable, the growth of one form of proprietary care—national corporations—supports this observation. Kinder Care, the largest national chain, had 510 centers in 1980 and 1,100 centers in 1988. And Children's World Learning Centers, a recent merger of Children's World and Daybridge Learning Centers, had 485 centers in operation in 1988. This growth reflects both internal expansion and the acquisition of other chain and independent operations. Funded by eager investors and meeting the growing child care needs of middle-class suburban families, the national chains are expected to continue to grow into the early 1990s, although at a somewhat slower pace than during the past decade (unpublished 1988 market research by Merrill Lynch; *Business Week*, July 10, 1989).

Independent centers are by far the most numerous type of for-profit providers (Kagan and Glennon, 1982). They are also the most diverse in terms of their facilities, programs, and staff. To date little research has focused on them, and data concerning their growth over the past decade and a half are unavailable. Independent centers often are managed by a husband-and-wife team, and they are distinguishable from not-for-profit centers in the same communities only by their legal designation. According to Kagan and Glennon (1982), independent centers were especially hard hit by inflation and minimum wage requirements in the early 1980s. As a result, many faced bankruptcy, or sold their businesses to a chain, or converted to not-for-profit status. Those that maintained their independence continually face the need to raise fees in order to cover costs, often more than the increases by corporate chains and not-for-profit centers. In so doing, they risk losing clients for whom even marginally higher fees cause care to be unaffordable. In contrast, the large for-profit chains can take advantage of economies of scale in bulk purchasing and central production in order to reduce operating costs. They can also afford to operate one center at a loss for a period of time if they have sufficient revenues from other centers.

Although the quality of care varies dramatically across all types of services (see Chapter 4), many child development experts and social welfare advocates have been skeptical of for-profit providers. Many of these critics have worried that in the absence of national regulations, for-profit child care would sacrifice the needs of children and caregivers in the interest of generating profits for shareholders. In response, proprietary operators maintain that efficient managerial skills make their centers profitable without any reduction in the quality of care (Kagan and Glennon, 1982). The Child Care Staffing Study (Whitebook et al., 1989), however, concluded that profit status was a strong predictor of quality of care. Not-for-profit centers were found to provide better quality care than for-profit centers regardless of whether either kind received government funds (Whitebook et al., 1989).

There are some significant differences between for-profit and not-for-profit centers that should be noted. First, the percentage of a center's annual operating budget that is spent on staff wages clearly varies by the profit status of the center (although there may be some differences between independent and corporate proprietary providers). Kagan and Glennon (1982) report that for-profit centers consistently spend 10 percent less of their budgets on wages—63 percent, compared with 73 percent spent by not-for-profit centers. Data from the recent Child Care Staffing Study show an overall decline and an even greater discrepancy—an average of 45 percent for for-profit centers and 64 percent for not-for-profit centers (Whitebook et al., 1989). Data from the National Day Care Study showed that average weekly salaries (in the mid-1970s) ranged from $89 to $124 in for-profit centers and from $94 to $160 in not-for-profit centers. Whether or not a center received some federal subsidy for serving low-income children was not a decisive factor in the difference (Coelen et al., 1979). More recent data suggest that this gap still exists. However, large national chains may be somewhat distinct from independent centers in this regard. Data provided by Children's World Learning Centers indicate that although many aides are at the low end of the salary scale, earning $3.50 to $5.50 per hour, senior teachers are paid wages comparable to the high end of the scale for not-for-profits, $4.50 to $7.50 per hour. Salary ranges, however, vary locally. In addition, many of the large corporate providers offer benefits that include child care tuition for caregivers' children, educational benefits for workers themselves, and health and pension benefits. Overall, salaries and benefits are less generous on the whole among independent for-profit providers.

Most for-profit child care centers have grown up in suburban areas, largely because their prime market is middle-class families with young children; very few are in rural or inner-city areas. Although both government-sponsored and privately funded not-for-profit centers often receive outside donations to help cover their operating costs, for-profit centers rely almost entirely on parent fees for their support. They are not likely to receive volunteer staff or donated space and equipment, which is common among not-for-profits (especially those that are church sponsored). As a result, most for-profit centers serve families with median incomes that are above the national average. Although some states have made Social Service Block Grant (SSBG) Program funds available to for-profit as well as not-for-profit centers to subsidize the care of low-income children, many proprietary providers are reluctant to accept children if the reimbursement rates do not cover their full costs of providing care or if additional fees can not be collected from parents. As a result, in general, the population of children in for-profit centers is likely to be more homogeneous than that in not-for-profit centers.

Personnel costs account for the bulk of the operating costs of child care centers. The National Day Care Study reported that the average monthly resource cost per full-time equivalent child (in 1977) was about $161; the range was from $80 to $310 per month, with about two-thirds of center expenditures for personnel (Travers and Ruopp, 1978). Costs are not necessarily affected significantly by group size, but the staff/child ratio and the caregivers' level of education and length of experience do affect costs.

For-profit centers typically have fewer staff per child than not-for-profit centers, although they follow state regulations (Coelen et al., 1979; Kagan and Glennon, 1982). There are a relatively larger number of for-profit centers located in southern states, perhaps because those states have less stringent regulations concerning staff/child ratios. Georgia, for example, requires only one staff member for every seven infants; while Massachusetts requires one for every three infants, and Georgia has significantly more proprietary centers than does Massachusetts. It should be noted, however, that among the national chains providing very high-quality (and high-priced) care, staff/child ratios often equal those found in not-for-profit centers. As a consequence of higher staff/child ratios, federally funded, not-for-profit

TABLE 6-3 Weekly Rates for Center-Based Child Care in 15 Cities, August 1987

City	Infants	Toddlers	Preschool-Age Children
Atlanta, Ga.	$120	$30-75	$30-75
Boston, Mass.	125-148	90-146	39-110
Chicago, Ill.	85-125	75-90	50-85
Cleveland, Ohio	42-105	30-78	20-78
Denver, Colo.	60-110	55-95	50-100
Greenville, S.C.	35-80	35-80	35-75
Los Angeles, Calif.	58-134	58-134	40-81
Miami, Fla.	45-93	35-83	35-83
Minneapolis, Minn.	100-150	80-100	70-90
New Orleans, La.	45-65	45-50	40-50
New York, N.Y.	45-190	60-150	60-150
Oklahoma City, Okla.	50-80	45-65	40-65
Raleigh, N.C.	35-100	25-85	25-85
Seattle, Wash.	115-150	81	69
Washington, D.C.	52-135	52-135	52-110

Source: Data from Work/Family Directions, Inc.

centers typically have higher per capita operating costs. But when ratios and wage rates are held constant, there are no significant differences in per child costs between federally funded and parent-fee centers (Travers and Ruopp, 1978).

Fees charged for care vary widely within and across all types of care and geographic regions; see Table 6.3. In some areas (e.g., Seattle), family day care is considerably less expensive than center-based care for infants and toddlers. However, in other areas (e.g., Boston and Denver), family day care may be similar in price for infant and toddler care. Although regulations such as those for staff/child ratios affect the cost of providing care, there seems to be no direct correlation between staff/child ratios and the fees charged to parents: for example, the fees for center-based care for infants in Atlanta and Boston are similar even though required staff/child ratios are 1:7 and 1:3, respectively. The price of care declines as the age of the child increases, largely because the ratio of caregivers to children decreases. However, very little is known about the relative effects of regulations and other factors such as teacher qualifications, local labor market conditions, and local cost of living, on center care fees. No research has been conducted to study how programs establish their fees.

Employer-Provided Care

There is growing involvement of employers in providing on- or near-site child care for their employees' children. Most are operated by outside providers contracted to manage a facility on behalf of the employer. Most of the providers are not-for-profit organizations, although, increasingly, national corporate chains are contracting with employers, including government employers, to provide child care services for employees' children (Dana Friedman, The Conference Board, personal communication, Dec. 9, 1988). The number of on- or near-site child care centers, whether employer-owned and -operated, contracted, joint with unions, or as a consortium of several employers, has clearly grown in the past 10 years. A 1978 employer survey reported 105 centers, and a 1988 report found approximately 600 hospitals, 200 corporations, and 100 public agencies providing on-site care (Friedman, 1988). The Bureau of Labor Statistics (1988) found that about 1 percent or less of private establishments surveyed (that were not in business to provide child care services) sponsored centers. Few of these establishments were in manufacturing industries, approximately two-thirds were service industries, and one-third were government (federal, state, or local). Hospitals, medical-related facilities, hotels, and government agencies are the most likely employers to provide on-site child care. Employers that provide centers report that they are "satisfied," and the centers contribute to several employer goals, including improved productivity, less absenteeism and turnover, and lower recruitment costs (Burud et al., 1984).

Although the current trend is new, it is not unprecedented. Employers provided work-site care during the Civil War and both world wars. During World War II, 2,500 centers were established to increase the number of women employees.

Public-sector unions have been particularly successful at negotiating for day care centers. The federal government, as an employer, continues to establish work-site centers; the Internal Revenue Service recently announced plans to open 10 new centers, and the U.S. Department of Defense has opened a center at the Pentagon in Washington, D.C. The most extensive public-sector initiative, however, is in New York State, where 30 centers serving over 2,000 children have been established through collective bargaining. The state provides for start-up costs, space, utilities, and maintenance. After start-up, the centers are expected to be self-supporting (U.S. Department of Labor, 1988). In the 48 programs cited by the U.S. Department of Labor and the Service Employees International Union, work-site child care is the most frequent child care support negotiated by both public-sector (59 percent) and private-sector (37 percent) unions.

It seems unlikely, however, that work-site centers will become a major source of care for young children. Employers report that establishing a center is an expensive and unfamiliar undertaking. Quality control and potential liability are concerns, as are siting and transportation problems (Bureau of National Affairs, 1984). Firms also report concern about the perceptions or reality of an expensive benefit applicable to relatively few employees and the uncertainty of employee use. For example, one employer reported that, even with a subsidy, the fees charged at a high-quality center were beyond the reach of single mothers on the support staff who were the primary target beneficiaries (Kamerman and Kahn, 1987). Therefore, on-site child care is sometimes regarded as a recruitment and retention mechanism for women in professional and managerial jobs.

There is also some evidence that employees prefer care close to home: they may not want to commute with children, especially on public transportation, or the on-site care might not be the type of preferred care. Kamerman and Kahn (1987) provide several examples of work-site centers—corporate centers (AT&T), union centers (Amalgamated Clothing and Textile Workers Union), and employer consortium (Northside Child Development Center in Minneapolis)—that were unsuccessful because they were underused by employees. Yet in 1989 contract negotiations, AT&T and its union highlighted the importance of child care as an employee benefit.

School-Based Programs

Increasingly over the past several years, public schools have expanded their role in early childhood education and child care. In 1988 more than half of the states mandated the provision of kindergarten programs for 5-year-olds; even among states where kindergartens are still optional, most local districts have been providing programs (Whaley, 1985; data from panel survey). Most states require school attendance in first grade at age 6 or 7, and kindergarten attendance is discretionary. In 1986 approximately 95 percent of 5-year-olds were enrolled in public or private kindergarten programs (Pendleton, 1986). In fact, many school systems across the country are moving to change from part-day programs to full-day programs.

As kindergarten programs have become virtually universal, many states and local school systems have begun to offer prekindergarten programs for 4-year-olds. In 1987 24 states were funding such programs, and several others were considering them (Marx and Seligson, 1988). In all but three cases, they were administered by the state's department of education; in New Jersey, Alaska, and Washington, they were operated by other state agencies. According to estimates provided by the Public School Early Childhood Study (Marx and Seligson, 1988), 130,452 children received services in 1987, with Texas alone serving nearly 49,000 children. Most state laws governing school programs for 4-year-olds permit but do not mandate attendance. A few states provide funds in the state-aid formula pattern followed for kindergarten, but most set specific limits on the amount that local districts have to spend for these programs (Kahn and Kamerman, 1987).

Local school districts also operate and fund prekindergarten programs. More than 8 percent of the early childhood programs catalogued in the District Survey of the Public School Early Childhood Study were locally funded (Mitchell, 1988). Unlike state-funded programs, those programs rely on a combination of local funds and parent fees. When states fund programs for 4-year-olds, the programs are almost always targeted to children at risk of educational failure, and priority is given to low-income children. Most locally funded programs, in contrast, do not use income as an eligibility criterion; nevertheless, to date, most state and local prekindergarten initiatives have been compensatory in their orientation (Mitchell, 1988).

School-based prekindergarten programs range from those that use kindergarten facilities, staffing ratios, and schedules to others that attempt to approximate the Head Start model. Marx and Seligson (1988) report that to some extent the growth of public school programs has resulted in increased competition with Head Start programs for staff and space. Most public schools that have prekindergarten classes offer part-day programs, although in a few cases states have contracted with agencies outside the schools to coordinate child care services to offer full-day coverage for working parents. However, Marx and Seligson (1988) indicate that although many of these programs serve children's educational needs well, most do not completely fulfill working parents' or children's full-day child care needs.

Most programs are exempt from state licensing requirements relating to health, nutrition, group size, teacher qualification, and physical space. Staff/child ratios and group size vary somewhat from state to state; in general, however, programs have limited their class size to 20 children and maintain a ratio of 1 staff member for every 10 children (Gnezda and Robinson, 1986). The lack of regulatory restriction has facilitated the expansion of school-based prekindergarten programs. In New York City, Project Giant Step supports programs for 4-year-olds and provides funding both to public schools and to the social service system; the schools have been able to move more quickly to establish programs and enroll students, partly because the schools do not have to contend with the lengthy and complicated licensing process required of social service programs (Kagan, 1988). In many cases, the schools do not meet the licensing requirements imposed on child care provided by social service agencies. Public schools also have the added advantage of available, suitable space.

The staff of public school programs is also different from that of center-based programs. Typically, school-based programs employ certified teachers, whose qualifications are the same as those for teachers in the elementary grades (Gnezda and Robinson, 1986; Marx and Seligson, 1988; Mitchell, 1988). Some states and local districts also require that caregivers have training in early child development and early childhood education. An important implication of the higher education levels of teachers in prekindergarten school programs is that the teachers command higher salaries than do those in center-based programs. In 1984 the median income of a prekindergarten or kindergarten teacher in the public schools was $15,648; for caregivers in organized child care programs operated under social services auspices it was $9,204 (National Association for the Education of Young Children, 1985). This earnings differential has been a source of tension. As school-based prekindergarten programs have expanded, many of the best-qualified caregivers in child care centers have moved to the public schools because of higher salaries and benefits. And some observers project that this issue will become more salient as both the educational system and the social service system seek to further expand their programs, so they will be competing for an insufficient pool of highly qualified staff.

The expansion of public school programs for 4-year-olds has fueled the long-standing controversy between advocates of child care and early childhood education. Those who favor school-based programs argue that the schools have an established and stable funding base, as well as access to school building space, transportation systems, and other ancillary services, and are trusted institutions in most communities. Consequently, early childhood programs in school settings could provide a universal integrating experience to help overcome the two-tiered system that has developed in the present child care system—in which poor children are served in means-tested day care programs while middle- and upper-class children attend proprietary or private nursery programs (Kahn and Kamerman, 1987; Kagan, 1988). On the other side, child care advocates argue that many inner-city schools are doing so badly at educating poor and minority children that making such schools responsible for very young children would only cause the failure to begin earlier. They cite the lack of regulations, insensitivity of traditional elementary teachers, resistance to parent involvement, and overly rigid academic programming as factors that make schools inappropriate settings for preschool-age children (Kagan, 1988; Kahn and Kamerman, 1987). In addition, because many public school programs do not operate all day, they are not responsive to the child care needs of working parents.

The expansion of school-based programs for 4-year-olds, and increasingly for 3-year-olds, has implications for organized child care programs and vice versa. During the 1970s and early 1980s, seeing a need for out-of-home programs for young children, small private providers and large national chains invested heavily and created a significant child care resource at a time when the public schools showed no interest in becoming involved. A substantial shift of prekindergarten care to the public schools could threaten these businesses. Indeed, for-profit as well as not-for-profit centers "need" to serve preschoolers in order to serve infants and toddlers at reasonable weekly rates. In short, to remove preschoolers from these settings would probably create a funding crisis for infant and toddler care. Given the limits on the numbers of infants who can be served in a single center under some state regulations, it would be economically infeasible to operate a center without a supply of preschoolers in the census in many jurisdictions (Kahn and Kamerman, 1987). In light of this economic reality, it is likely that the existing amalgam of public and private, for-profit and not-for-profit child care programs will not easily or quietly relinquish the 3- and 4-year-old market to the public schools.

Head Start

Established in the mid-1960s, Head Start continues as the only federally funded comprehensive early childhood program for low-income preschool children. Over more than 20 years it has managed to sustain the strong support of the Congress and of Republican and Democratic administrations, despite significant cuts in most other education and social service programs. Approximately 1,300 local programs across the country serve children between the ages of 3 and 5, with primary emphasis on 3- and 4-year-olds. The stated goal of Head Start is to provide economically disadvantaged children with an early socialization and education experience that will prepare them to begin elementary school on an equal footing with their more economically advantaged peers.

Head Start is a comprehensive services program that includes four major components: education, health, social services, and parent involvement. The program was not established as a child care service, and the fact that it operates as a part-day program at most sites limits its ability to meet the child care needs of many low-income working parents or the developmental needs of many children who would benefit from a structured full-day program. Currently, about 20 percent of local Head Start programs operate full day in order to combine high-quality compensatory education, social, medical, and nutrition services, as well as parent education, with more traditional child care services and schedules. Yet program officials are quick to distinguish Head Start from child care programs, and there is some disagreement within and outside of the federal government about whether to include Head Start funding in a tally of federal expenditures for child care.

To be eligible for Head Start, children must live in families below the poverty line or have disabilities; only about 10 percent of Head Start participants are nonpoor. Matching roughly the poverty distribution in the United States, approximately 42 percent of Head Start participants are black, 20 percent are Hispanic, 4 percent are American Indian, and 34 percent are white. Ten percent of the children have disabilities. The program serves about 450,000 children, which is less than 20 percent of the income-eligible 3- to 5-year-olds across the country, and that proportion has remained stable since its establishment (unpublished data from the Administration for Children, Youth, and Families, U.S. Department of Health and Human Services).

From its inception, Head Start has involved parents. The Head Start performance standards require that parents have an opportunity to be involved as decision makers and as classroom participants. Many are involved as paid staff and as volunteer aides to the programs. A 1982-1983 study found that 29 percent of Head Start staff nationally were parents of children in the program (McKey et al., 1985). Head Start staff run parent education programs and conduct home visits to strengthen the links between families and the program. In the future, however, the increasing labor force participation of mothers may reduce parents' ability to be active program participants. Increasingly, full-time working parents may find it difficult to volunteer in the classroom or to attend parent education groups.

In addition to the comprehensiveness of its program, several characteristics distinguish Head Start from other preschool education programs, particularly those provided by public schools. Most important among these are licensing and staffing. Head Start programs and child care programs are licensed by the same state-level department—usually human services, welfare, or community development (Goodman and Brady, 1988). Requirements for physical facilities are usually quite strict and may be a barrier to the establishment of programs. In contrast, school programs have no licensing standards. For staff, the reverse is often the case: states require less education for personnel in child care centers and Head Start programs than they do for teacher certification. This difference has in some cases been a barrier to Head Start programs' receiving state supplemental funds or working with local education agencies to provide preschool programs (Goodman and Brady, 1988). Many Head Start teachers have the relevant coursework and experience necessary for working with children, including a child development associate credential, but lack the formal college education and public school teaching credential required to teach in a school-based program. Goodman and Brady (1988) report that even though Head Start teachers have appropriate credentials, the fact that the program is licensed by state welfare departments creates image problems in the public school community.

Head Start is one of the few 1964 antipoverty programs to have survived through the 1980s. Two significant factors have undoubtedly contributed to its success. First, Head Start has always been a demonstration program, not an entitlement program: that is, the program is not automatically available to all eligible children. The federal government provides direct grants to local agencies, including churches, community action agencies, public and private not-for-profit organizations, and education agencies. Regardless of the local sponsoring agency, Head Start programs can be located in public school facilities. Approximately 20 percent of local programs are administered by local school districts and located in local public school buildings. Grubb (1987) reports that there is little evidence to suggest that programs run by education agencies differ markedly from those operated by other agencies. Clearly articulated national performance standards provide program structure, but with enough flexibility to take advantage of the strengths and resources of local communities.

Second, in addition to federal funding, several states have laws that provide funds for the expansion or enhancement of Head Start programs or other preschool programs. Eight states support only Head Start, whereas 25 states and the District of Columbia support only school districts or school districts and other nonprofit agencies, including those that sponsor Head Start programs. Two states, Connecticut and Massachusetts, specify that the program funds be used for increasing the salaries of Head Start staff. In other states, the funds have been used either to enlarge the population served or to extend the program to full day. A major issue for states that have sought to use the funds to extend services is that Head Start income eligibility requirements exclude many at-risk preschool children and their families who would benefit from the comprehensive services but do not meet the poverty criterion. In Rhode Island, for example, legislative priority has been given to children of working parents who are poor but not income eligible for Head Start and do not have enough money to purchase needed services themselves. Rhode Island Head Start directors expanded services to this population by adding a new eligibility category—the working poor—whose incomes exceed the federal income guidelines of $11,650 for a family of four. This step has extended services to 500 children in that state who would otherwise not have qualified (Goodman et al., 1988).

A potential disadvantage of state Head Start–only programs is that Head Start staffs are not encouraged to form coalitions with other child care and early childhood education systems to achieve parity in services, credentials, and wages. Moreover, this approach does not foster coordination between Head Start and state education agencies, adding to existing concerns that Head Start is isolated from other child care and early childhood programs and that it is insulated from the space, funding, and staffing

stresses that affect others. Goodman and Brady (1988) urge that state legislation require that Head Start programs coordinate with state and local
education agencies as a condition of funding.

Programs for Children With Disabilities

Federal funds are available to support a variety of child care services for
children with disabilities. The Education for All Handicapped Children Act
(P.L. 94-142) and the Education for the Handicapped Act Amendments of
1986 (P.L. 99-457) provide funds for the education of children with special
needs under the direction of the public schools. Chapter I of the Elementary
and Secondary Education Act (P.L. 89-313) provides funds for the public
school education of disabled children who are in need of compensatory
services because of economic disadvantage. SSBGs provide funds to the
states to be used in part to reimburse child care costs for disabled children in
low-income families. And Head Start reserves a proportion of its enrollment
for disadvantaged children with disabilities. To coordinate these separate
programs, the Administration for Children, Youth, and Families in the
U.S. Department of Health and Human Services and the Office of Special
Education and Rehabilitative Services in the U.S. Department of Education
signed an interagency agreement in 1978 to promote collaboration between
the social service system and the public schools in serving very young
children with disabilities. The result was a national network of resource
access projects mandated to work with state education agencies to establish
effective local mechanisms for collaboration between local public schools
and Head Start programs. By 1988 this initiative had produced a total
of 39 interagency agreements at the state level. Goodman and Brady
(1988) conclude that this activity has improved formal and informal working
relationships between Head Start programs and the schools. They also
conclude that these interagency efforts to serve children with disabilities
have significantly enhanced Head Start's visibility as a service provider
and in many cases have paved the way for Head Start participation in
state-funded preschool activities.

Care for School-Age Children

In the mid-1980s concern that a large number of children of working
parents might be in self-care during the afternoons, between the closing
of elementary schools and the time parents are home from work, led
to widespread discussion of latchkey children. Although estimates of the
actual number of children of working parents who are unsupervised when
school is not in session vary widely, concern about the issue has led to

numerous proposals and programs to provide organized before- and after-school care for school-age children. Current programs are both publicly and privately provided, through the schools, child care centers, and community agencies. Although there are no reliable national data on the supply of such programs, many observers conclude that there is still a shortage (U.S. Department of Labor, 1988).

By 1988 12 states had legislated some form of funding for school-age child care initiatives, and the federal government was providing modest support through a dependent-care block grant. Programs differ greatly and are administered by a diverse group of providers, including public and private schools, child care centers, youth centers, and family day care providers. According to Michelle Seligson of the School-Age Child Care Project at Wellesley College (personal communication, May 23, 1988), the services provided by these organizations have grown significantly in the past several years: approximately 50 percent of YMCAs now operate after-school programs 5 days per week, twice the number reported 5 years ago. It is estimated that the Boys Clubs of America, Campfire, Inc., and other youth organizations run more than 250 programs. In a National Council of Churches survey of churches that reported providing child care services, at least 30 percent indicated that they also provide after-school care. Approximately 300 independent schools—about half of all independent elementary and middle schools—now have extended-day programs. And, increasingly, large for-profit providers are introducing before- and after-school programs in their centers.

Public schools are beginning to supplement these efforts in many communities. A recent survey conducted by the National Association of Elementary School Principals found that 22 percent of principals think school-age child care programs are important, compared with only 8 percent in 1980 (National Association of Elementary School Principals, 1988). Some states that fund school-age child care programs restrict those funds to school-based and -administered programs. However, the use of school facilities has been a significant issue in many communities considering extended-day programs. Both the teachers' unions, which restrict the work hours of teachers and the use of nonunion staff in classrooms, and the custodians' unions, which have opposed use of the facilities by other groups during off-school hours, have presented barriers (Gannett, 1985). As a result, school-based, extended-day programs have not been developed in many communities. Community centers, churches, and youth-serving social service agencies have more often been the auspice of service, creating a need for transportation between schools and after-school programs.

Many not-for-profit and proprietary providers of child care have also begun to offer after-school programs and to escort children or transport them by vans from school to the centers. Kinder Care and Children's

World Learning Centers, for example, offer school-age programs in all their centers. And Kinder Care reports that it serves 20,000 children in a summer program called Club Mates (Michelle Seligson, Wellesley College, personal communication, May 23, 1988). For 6- to 8-year-olds, many of these programs offer interesting and stimulating activities. For older elementary school children, however, center-based models may not be appropriate. Children between the ages of 9 and 12 clearly need some monitoring and need to know that responsible adults are available to them if needed, but many do not need or want the close supervision that is required for younger children. For those who prefer "down time" after school rather than another 2 hours of organized classroom activity, for those who need more physical and athletic outlets for their energies at the end of the school day, and for those who want a quiet place to do homework, a child care center with its classroom confinement and large groups of children of mixed ages is frequently unappealing.

Family day care is the second most popular out-of-home after-school arrangement for school-age children. Approximately 24 percent of school-age children are cared for in family day care homes, compared with 7 percent who attend child care centers after school (Bureau of the Census, 1987). These arrangements may owe their popularity to the flexibility of the provider. The provider may allow children to play outside, within earshot, or to check in on a regular basis if they leave the vicinity. This may make for a more satisfying experience for children who, as they get older, desire more autonomy (Seligson, 1989).

Another issue in the provision of before- and after-school care is the availability of funds to pay for staff, facilities, and transportation (if needed). Because even publicly funded programs are typically not fully subsidized, parent fees are necessary to cover the costs of services. Available data suggest that these fees range from $10 to $60 per week depending on the funding arrangements. Michelle Seligson reports that programs in the South and Midwest are lower in cost than those in the Northeast and far West because of variations in staff salaries in the regions. Public school programs are able to reduce the costs of providing care if they do not hire a separate program administrator and if programs are not charged for space, utilities, and janitorial services. Currently, school-based after-school programs are largely funded by parent fees—about 65 percent—and for many low-income families the fees may be unaffordable (National Association of Elementary School Principals, 1988). In 1986 the Children's Defense Fund found that only two of the states that had initiated legislation on school-age child care had directed the funds to serve children in low-income families (Blank and Wilkins, 1986).

PROGRAMS TO SUPPORT
THE DELIVERY OF CHILD CARE SERVICES

Resource and Referral Services

Responding to the diversity and decentralization of child care services, child care resource and referral programs have been a major development of the 1980s. Their purpose is to assist parents in understanding the choices of child care arrangements available to them, to give support and information to providers, and to collect and report data concerning the supply and demand for child care that can be used for planning community, state, and national resources. Motivated by a desire to improve the child care system in their communities, these programs developed as grassroots organizations representing the perspectives of parents, providers, and community groups. They have grown rapidly over the past several years with support from the states, community groups, and a few large employers.

Despite a diversity of origins, resource and referral programs across the country have emerged with a similar orientation and typically provide a set of services designed to reach their separate and yet overlapping constituencies: (1) information and referral, (2) technical assistance and training, and (3) advocacy and community education (Siegal and Lawrence, 1984). Beyond this core set, programs provide a range of other services that are responsive to local needs and circumstances. In Massachusetts and California, for example, they also administer vendor-voucher programs. In these states and others, some resource and referral programs administer the Child Care Food Program, organize family day care networks, operate hot lines (or "warm lines") to provide information to parents on children's health and behavior, operate programs to stimulate interactions between school-age children and senior citizens, and provide market information and assistance to prospective child care providers. Programs are usually staffed by former center and family day care providers, child development specialists, and family counseling and parent education experts. Depending on levels of public subsidy, most agencies charge fees to consumers. Some use sliding scales so that low-income users pay less, and parents who are eligible for public subsidy are not charged for services. Some agencies also offer different levels of service and vary their fees accordingly.

California, Massachusetts, and New York now provide statewide resource and referral services. Many cities have also developed systems of resource and referral services. More recently, the private sector has also recognized the effectiveness of these initiatives. Some corporations contract with service programs and pay client fees for their employees. IBM, for example, provides a national service for its employees by contracting with existing local services or creating programs. To help potential service programs handle their employee load, IBM provided computer systems and developed software programs. Other companies were ahead of IBM in contracting with local programs, but IBM launched the first large national program. Subsequently, several other corporations have modeled their own initiatives on that of IBM. Kahn and Kamerman (1987) report that in some instances local resource and referral agencies are providing company clients with special services and quality assurance, as well as assigned staff and telephone lines. Employers have also recognized the role of resource and referral services in the development of child care services. For example, the Bank of America and several other private and public employers funded resource and referral services in the San Francisco area to recruit and train family day care providers.

Resource and referral services represent a significant innovation to enhance the effectiveness of the child care delivery system and to assist parents in choosing child care arrangements. Although there have been no national studies to evaluate the impact of these programs, there is a lot of anecdotal information at the local level on their effectiveness in linking consumers and providers; developing a cooperative relationship with community agencies and private organizations serving children and their families; recruiting new providers; and providing information, training, and technical assistance to providers. They have also served public education and information functions at a time when both the supply of and the demand for child care services have grown rapidly, and when the policies, programs, and regulations governing child care have been changing just as rapidly. As child care services continue to expand, resource and referral services will undoubtedly play a central role. Nevertheless, as advocates and observers readily acknowledge, they are not a panacea. They cannot solve many of the problems that plague child care in the United States, including the quality of staffing, equitable salaries, the types of services available, and the levels of public subsidy (Kahn and Kamerman, 1987; Morgan, 1982; Siegal and Lawrence, 1984).

Provider Networks

Another innovation of the 1980s was the growth of family day care networks. The National Day Care Home Study estimated in 1978 that approximately 30,000 caregivers serving at least 120,000 children were operating as a part of a "network of homes under the sponsorship of a local administrative agency" (Fosburg, 1981). In 1986 approximately 85,000 family day care homes participating in the Child Care Food Program were affiliated with 800 sponsoring institutions (Glantz et al., 1988). And of course, there may be others that do not participate in the federal food program of the U.S. Department of Agriculture.

Networks developed initially as a result of state or local requirements governing federal subsidies (under Social Security) for the care of children from low-income families. Because funding was linked to state licensing requirements, the formation of networks enabled government agencies to deal efficiently with individual family day care providers. Payments, audits, inspections, and referrals could be handled routinely for a number of providers through one central administrative organization, usually child care agencies that were also operating centers. As participation in the Family Day Care Food Program has expanded since the mid-1970s, this source of federal subsidy has also created incentives for family day care providers to become a part of a network. In some instances, networks guarantee a number of places for children from low-income families, certify providers' eligibility and guarantee that they meet specified standards of care, and manage vacancy control, bookkeeping, and reimbursements. A recent study of the Child Care Food Program reports that participation by family day care providers has increased dramatically: in 1980 there were 18,000 homes participating in the program; in 1986 there were approximately 85,000 (Glantz et al., 1988). Most of the increase is attributable to the increase in the number of sponsoring networks or systems.

Networks may include as few as 10 homes or as many as 1,000; the vast majority have about 50 (Glantz et al., 1988). Over time the role of many provider networks has expanded to include other services, such as training and referral services to providers, toy lending libraries, shared activities, drop-in centers for providers, and emergency back-up caregivers. To cover the costs of these services, many networks collect parent fees in addition to modest state and local funding. On average, sponsors visit homes eight times per year, and these visits combine monitoring with training and technical assistance to providers (Glantz et al., 1988).

Sponsors' administrative costs per home decline as the number of homes in the network increases. The estimated monthly administrative cost per home is $77 for sponsors with no more than 50 homes, $49 for sponsors with 51 to 200 homes, and $46 for sponsors with more than 200 homes (Glantz et al., 1988).

Many observers hope that provider networks, like resource and referral services, can help to bring family day care providers into the regulated system and provide support and services to improve the professionalism of these providers and the quality of their services. Although the financial incentives and available technical support will undoubtedly make it attractive for some family day care providers to join a network, others see a significant disadvantage in outside supervision of private in-home services.

Vendor-Voucher Programs

Another innovative strategy for expanding parental choice in arranging child care, providing subsidies for the care of children from low-income families, and providing support for providers is vendor-voucher programs. In some cases these programs are supported by public funds alone; in others, they are packaged with philanthropic contributions or supplements from employers. These programs provide "vouchers" to parents to purchase approved child care.

In vendor-voucher programs financed with public funds, parents select a child care provider (center or family day care home) and pay an income-tested fee (unless they are eligible for full subsidy). The agency administering the vendor-voucher program pays a weekly supplement at an agreed upon rate after the child's attendance is verified. Providers must be licensed or registered (or be in the process of qualifying) to be eligible to receive voucher payments. Depending on the particular provisions of the program, performance standards used to determine eligibility may or may not be more stringent than those imposed by the state for child care licensing. In some cases, they are used as a leverage for providing technical assistance and monitoring (Kahn and Kamerman, 1987).

Vendor-voucher programs have emerged in several states and communities, the largest being California's alternative payments program. Some have been developed specifically as vendor-voucher programs; others have grown out of ongoing community-based child care initiatives. An important result of all of these programs has been a considerable increase in the use of family day care in jurisdictions in which most public child care funds have been directed to centers. To some extent, this trend undoubtedly reflects parental preferences concerning the care of infants and toddlers, an inadequate supply of center care for very young children, and lower fees for family day care (Kahn and Kamerman, 1987).

Another outcome of these programs has been an increase in the number of centers serving low-income and publicly subsidized clients. Previously, "purchase of service" contracts limited participating centers to confined geographic areas, generally in the inner cities; vouchers have expanded the type and location of centers that participate. Program officials report that providers sometimes include proprietary centers as well as specialized nursery schools. And in some communities after-school programs are also included in the vendor-voucher system (Ruth Freis, Resources for Family Development, personal communication, Feb. 9, 1988). A decided benefit of these programs is that they have enabled some low-income families to purchase services outside their own segregated inner-city neighborhoods (Kahn and Kamerman, 1987).

Some employers provide child care benefits through vender-voucher programs. Employers may negotiate reduced rates for their employees at a local child care center. Most often the vendor programs are negotiated with large for-profit chains that have multiple locations. Employers usually negotiate a fee reduction of approximately 10 percent, and they guarantee a certain number of places for the provider. In some of the programs reported by Friedman (1985), the employer contributed an additional 10 percent, reducing employee costs by 20 percent. This type of program requires that employees use the selected type of care. The large chains are likely to be more expensive than alternative forms of care and thus may be of primary benefit to the higher paid professional workers. As of 1984, Friedman (1985) reported that Kinder Care had 75 companies participating in the industry program. At LaPetite Academy, 155 companies worked with "employer care" discounts program, and at Children's World, 17 employers were participating in the career care program.

Many observers conclude that vendor-voucher programs are an attractive way to administer public funding to support child care. In accord with the general movement in the early 1980s to provide more direct support to consumers (parents) than to suppliers (providers), vouchers give parents the ability to choose the types of child care they want for their children, relatively unconstrained by government intervention. As Kahn and Kamerman (1987) point out, part of the attractiveness of such an approach derives from the facts that the child care market is very diverse and that there is no universal system of care.

To date, there have been no major evaluations of vendor-voucher initiatives, so definitive evidence of their effects on the quality of care and the efficiency of administering public subsidies is lacking. However, Grubb (1988) points out that vendor-voucher mechanisms in California have been enthusiastically supported by fiscal conservatives seeking to reduce the costs of care. They argue that the use of vouchers causes the market to operate more efficiently because it puts providers in competition with one another and therefore drives down the wages of child care workers (but see below). To the extent that this "efficiency" fosters high turnover and instability, it is likely to have negative effects on the quality of care and on child outcomes (as discussed in Chapter 4).

Kahn and Kamerman (1987) report that those who administer vendor-voucher programs are enthusiastic and believe that they can operate successfully, both because they enhance parents' choices and because they offer a simple mechanism for channeling resources. It is up to the providers to make services attractive and desirable to consumers. There is, however, significant opposition to these programs, from several sources. Some economists worry that vouchers will necessarily raise the price of child care for all consumers, because they will increase the demand (Grubb, 1988).

Many traditional child welfare advocates believe that trained case workers may be better able to choose appropriate care settings than parents. They frequently oppose vouchers on the grounds that parents may not make well-informed decisions that are in the best interests of their children, especially if the children are too young to communicate about their experiences in child care. Opposition also comes from providers who are accustomed to purchase-of-service contracts that guaranteed them fees for an agreed upon number of children (Kahn and Kamerman, 1987). To address these latter concerns, California administers its vendor-voucher program through its resource and referral services. Parents receive information on the care alternatives available to them and counseling on how to assess their choices. Centers and family day care homes receive referrals if they are listed as eligible providers.

BARRIERS TO THE DELIVERY OF SERVICES

Staffing

There is perhaps no issue more essential to the future of child care in the United States than staffing. As child care research demonstrates, the quality of caregivers and the interaction between caregivers and children are major determinants of the developmental effects of supplemental care. There is growing recognition of the importance of early childhood staff and the factors that threaten the quality and stability of the current and future labor pool, including salaries and wages, working conditions, training, and professionalism.

As we have discussed above, although the salaries of child care workers vary among programs and settings, they are low in comparison with salaries in other occupations that require similar levels of education and work experience (Hartmann and Pearce, 1989; National Association for the Education of Young Children, 1985). In fact, census data and information from salary surveys confirm that, overall, child care workers earn wages below the poverty level (Phillips and Whitebook, 1986; Whitebook et al., 1989). Estimates of the hourly earnings of child care workers depend on the categories of workers that are included. In 1988 the Child Care Staffing Study (Whitebook et al., 1989) reported that the average hourly wage for child care workers was $5.35, which is an annual income of $9,363 for full-time employment. Because many of these caregivers are unmarried heads of household, it is worth noting that in 1988 the federal poverty level (for a family of three) was $9,431 (Bureau of the Census, as cited in Whitebook et al., 1989). Most child care workers do not receive yearly cost-of-living or merit increases, and they receive only minimal benefits. Only 40 percent receive health coverage. Moreover, despite gains in overall formal education and experience, child care workers were paid even less in 1988 than in 1977. Wages, adjusted for inflation, fell 27 percent for child care teachers and 20 percent for teaching assistants (Whitebook et al., 1989). Although salary figures reflect some geographic variation, Hartmann and Pearce (1989) report that more than 40 percent of full-time child care workers in 1987 earned less than $5.00 per hour. Part-time workers fared even worse, with just over 60 percent of the teachers and virtually all of the child care workers earning wages of $5.00 an hour or less.

Longer job tenure—that is, experience—is not substantially rewarded for child care workers. Hourly wages of workers with 4 or more years of experience average $3.45 per hour, only slightly more than the average of those with 3 years or less on the job, $3.19 per hour (Hartmann and Pearce, 1989). There is also little wage increase for educational achievement: child care workers who are college graduates received only $3.73 per hour; high school graduates received $3.02 per hour.

Data concerning the income of family day care providers are more difficult to obtain. The National Day Care Home Study reported that the net weekly incomes of family day care providers in 1978 ranged from $50 to $62. No national updates of this information are available, but Kahn and Kamerman (1987) indicate that local surveys in 1984 found little relative improvement. A recent study of the Child Care Food Program found that among licensed family day care providers participating in the program, the household incomes of workers varied from less than $9,000 to more than $20,000 per year and that the proportion from child care work was inversely related to the total. Approximately 77 percent of workers who reported household incomes of less than $15,000 derived 100 percent of their income from their child care work (Glantz et al., 1988). Kahn and Kamerman (1987) conclude that most family day care providers are earning less than the minimum wage in caring for the children of other low-income earners. And even the lack of taxation on these wages does not make the weekly or annual net incomes competitive with low-paying jobs covered by minimum wage laws.

Researchers, administrators, and child care workers point to low pay, poor benefits, and lack of opportunities for promotion as explanations for high turnover rates among child care workers in centers and Head Start programs (Hartmann and Pearce, 1988; National Association for the Education of Young Children, 1985; Phillips and Whitebook, 1986; Whitebook et al., 1989; Zinsser, 1986). Using a variety of data, Hartmann and Pearce (1988) found that, between 1983 and 1986, child care workers' salaries failed to keep pace with rising prices. In addition, one-third to one-half of caregivers in social service and private educational settings did not have any health insurance coverage provided by their employers, even if they worked full time. And many did not receive paid time off for holidays and vacations. Turnover rates have been found to be as high as 41 percent annually in some localities and among some types of providers (Whitebook et al., 1989). In conducting the National Child Care Staffing Study, Deborah Phillips (University of Virginia, personal communication, May 23, 1988) reports that it was not uncommon to find that, in the one week between the time interviews were scheduled and researchers arrived at the centers, staff had left. Although it has often been assumed that child care workers are more motivated by their love and concern for young children than by their concern about remuneration, low pay and poor benefits are clearly factors that drive many qualified staff from these jobs (Hostetler, 1984; Pettygrove et al., 1984). Data from several studies confirm that as salaries rise, turnover rates decrease (Goodman et al., 1988; Pettygrove et al., 1984; Zinsser, 1986). In Massachusetts, for example, Head Start programs were allocated approximately $359.67 per child for staff raises, and the state established suggested hourly minimum wages for many Head Start positions. A recent study examining the impact of state supplemental funding found that the grants had increased staff wages and benefits, as well as job satisfaction. Moreover, the findings suggested that the grants have had a positive effect on staff recruitment and retention (Goodman et al., 1988).

Interviews with Head Start teachers who are leaving their jobs, as well as with those who are still working in child care centers, confirm that many leave for higher paying jobs in public schools or in other fields, including jobs that require much less formal education and specialized training (Goodman et al., 1988). As we noted above, there is some concern that public schools will drain the pool of qualified staff from child care services as they increase their role in the provision of early childhood education and child care programs. Alternatively, competition for a limited pool of staff may put pressure on child care providers to reach some parity with schools in staff salaries and benefits, but that will not occur without effects on the cost of care and the fees that are charged to parents.

Some of the differences in the salaries of early childhood staff reflect differences in their levels of education. As we discussed above, most teachers in public school prekindergartens have college degrees (Marx and Seligson, 1988). Although some Head Start teachers also have bachelor's degrees, many do not (Goodman and Brady, 1988). Head Start is governed by the state licensing requirements for child care programs, and although many states require specialized training and experience, none requires a bachelor's degree. Recent national data suggest that 57 percent of teachers and assistants in licensed child care centers have high school diplomas, and many have credentials through the CDA program; only a minority hold college degrees (National Association for the Education of Young Children, 1985; Whitebook et al., 1989). And family day care providers on average have even fewer years of formal education; many have not even graduated from high school (Fosburg, 1981).

The institutional auspices of child care workers may have more to do with income levels than their education. Salaries in education, although low, have traditionally been higher than salaries for social services positions, even when levels of education are comparable. Child care workers employed by schools consistently earn more than those in nonschool settings. In addition, working in the public sector pays better than working in the private sector. Not-for-profit centers pay teachers and assistants more on average than do for-profit centers, with chain for-profit centers having the lowest average wage, $4.10 per hour. For-profit centers also provide fewer benefits, such as health coverage, retirement, and sick leave. As a consequence, for-profit centers have significantly higher turnover rates, up to 74 percent annually in some national chains (Whitebook et al., 1989). Education does not account for the differences in earnings between early childhood staff and individuals in other occupations. Because child care has traditionally been a woman's responsibility and an unpaid home function, Hartmann and Pearce (1989) and Whitebook and colleagues (1989) in the Child Care Staffing Study concluded that salary differences between child care workers and other occupations requiring comparable levels of education and training are attributable to gender discrimination and to the low value placed on child care as paid work in U.S. society.

The lack of professional stature accorded to early childhood staff is partly a problem of societal perception and partly a problem of the perception of many child care workers themselves. Low salaries have undoubtedly contributed. Unfortunately, a prevailing view from outside and within is that if a child care worker really enjoys the work, the money should not be important (Goodman et al., 1988). Moreover, many child care workers have had a tenuous attachment to their careers. Many women regard child care as an interim activity, between the end of their schooling and the time that they get married and start their own families, or during the period when their own children are very young, or while they are serving as the primary caregiver for a grandchild or other relative. Explicit or implicit attitudes that child care is a temporary means of earning some "extra money" have militated against many workers seeking professional credentialing through the CDA program or some other early childhood education program or in seeking in-service training. Many observers also believe that professional training may be one key to improving the quality of early childhood staff (Almy, 1982).

One path to greater professionalism is unionization. Unions are common among public school teachers (who do receive higher salaries and better benefits), but there has been only modest movement to date to unionize workers in child care centers. Yet unionization is not an unlikely direction. Although many early childhood experts express concerns about the effects of unions on the nature of the intimate relationships between staff, parents, and children in child care (Almy, 1982), working in unionized settings is associated with improved working conditions and reduced turnover, as is working in the public sector (Hartmann and Pearce, 1989). Child care workers in the public sector earned over $1.00 more per hour than those in the private sector. Employees who were union members earned an average of $5.21 more per hour than their nonunion counterparts. The increase in salary is due to both union membership and setting (Hartmann and Pearce, 1989).

Regulations

As we have discussed, regulation of child care services is the province of the states. Although states vary dramatically in the stringency of their requirements, with a few exceptions there has been a general gradual trend toward tighter regulations since the mid-1970s. However, different types of programs are governed by different regulatory authorities, and some providers are exempted because of the auspices under which they operate or the number of children they serve. In addition, enforcement systems have not grown proportionately to the growth in out-of-home child care services. As a result, very real questions have been raised about the effectiveness of regulation as a means of ensuring the quality of care in child care centers and in family day care homes, even in jurisdictions in which such care is regulated. Since the early 1980s, discussion of regulation has increasingly included consideration of alternatives to regulation, especially for family day care homes.

Some child care advocates who urge stringent regulation of child care services have opposed low standards and lax enforcement because of the pernicious effects of poor-quality care. They cite cases of child abuse and fundamental health and safety violations in unregulated or laxly regulated environments. In response, opponents of state regulation have argued that government interference in the private decisions of families is neither a benefit to parents nor necessarily a protection to children; that "excessive" regulation increases the cost of care and provides disincentives for many providers to become a part of the licensed system; and that, in the absence of effective enforcement, regulation does not ensure that consumers receive high-quality care.

The existence of regulations does not guarantee their adequate and fair enforcement, and programs are rarely closely monitored. Most centers receive an annual announced visit (Morgan, 1987). The personnel who conduct these visits are often overburdened and poorly trained. Although there has been a rapid increase in the number of licensed programs, there has not been an analogous increase in licensing staff. In addition, licensing personnel are under great pressure to interpret a myriad of regulations that may have been drafted to allow flexibility but in fact create confusion. Individual regulations may use such words as "adequate" or "sufficient" very differently and, therefore, subject similar programs to very different standards.

A major question that remains largely unanswered is the effect of regulations on the supply of child care services. Do stringent regulations drive some providers out of the market or discourage others from entering? Do they significantly raise the costs of care, and if so, who bears these additional costs? Do they affect the quality of care that is provided? There is no shortage of opinion on these matters, but there is little convincing evidence. Many observers conclude that the elimination of the Federal Interagency Day Care Requirements in 1981 led some large commercial chains to expand their operations in the southern states where there is less stringent regulation of child care. Low standards, particularly as they apply to staff qualifications and to staff/child ratios, allow providers to reduce staff costs and enhance profitability. At the same time, however, relatively lower real estate costs in the South have meant lower capital expenditures for providers developing facilities. Hence, it is difficult to determine the extent to which regulation has actually affected the supply of center care.

Critics of state licensing and registration requirements insist that they increase the costs of providing services, "driving providers underground and limiting the number of children who can benefit" (Lehrman and Pace, 1985:1). This has been a special concern with regard to family day care homes. Although there are no definitive data that show that providers have closed—or closed and then reopened as unlicensed facilities—data from state licensing offices indicate that in states with more stringent regulations and registration requirements, there are relatively fewer licensed family day care providers and fewer licensed spaces for children (data from panel survey).

Twenty-seven states require some form of licensing or registration for family day care providers, depending on the number of children in the home; 13 states require or offer voluntary registration, again depending on the number of children in the home; 4 states combine these two mechanisms; and 6 states have an approval or certification procedure if a provider receives federal funds (Morgan, 1987; data from panel survey). As Kahn and Kamerman (1987) indicate, most child care experts agree that for the most part this licensing or registration does not constitute an accountability or monitoring system. Some experts worry that this lack of accountability may be a problem; others believe there is no way to effectively regulate all family day care.

The registration and certification systems may provide positive incentives for some family day care providers to come into the regulated system, by offering referrals, training and technical assistance, and help in obtaining federal subsidies, especially through the Child Care Food Program. Evidence concerning the growth of family day care networks suggests that this incentive may be operating in many states, even those with stringent regulatory policies. And advocates from many points on the political spectrum have supported such incentive (rather than punishment) approaches to promoting the adoption of performance standards in family day care homes. To date, there has been no analysis of the effects of registration or certification on the quality of child care services or on developmental outcomes among children in family day care. The National Day Care Home Study in the late 1970s did show that regulation and sponsorship were associated with many of the characteristics that are desirable in family day care settings (Fosburg, 1981).

Building and Zoning Restrictions

In many communities, restrictions on local land use, building, and zoning have become barriers to the development of child care programs and facilities—centers as well as family day care homes—whether operated on a for-profit or not-for-profit basis.[1] Local ordinances that affect child care services include zoning and land use laws, building codes, and deed restrictions. The use of these types of provisions to restrict the location and operation of child care services has two different origins. In many communities, concerns about the effects of child care facilities on the character of neighborhoods, noise levels, property values, traffic, and the like have led citizens' groups to invoke such provisions as a means of discouraging or opposing the establishment of centers and family day care homes. Those provisions have also been invoked by child care activists to try to ensure the basic health and safety of children in out-of-home care, using restrictive local building and land use provisions as means of compensation for lax state licensing and enforcement. In states with lenient regulations on group size and staff/child ratios, for example, proponents of regulation have used local zoning and building restrictions to create barriers to the establishment of programs that are of poor quality in other dimensions. Although there are no national data available, experience suggests that local restrictions have in many cases limited the development of licensed child care services.

---

[1] The information in this section comes largely from the Child Care Advocacy Center in San Francisco (Abby Cohen, personal communication, May 23, 1988).

Zoning and land use laws have been used to exclude child care services, especially family day care homes, from residential neighborhoods, where ironically they are by definition intended to operate in many states. Opposition has been greatest toward large family day care or group homes, which serve as many as 12 to 15 children. Some communities have invoked occupation ordinances, which limit the use of space (especially outdoor space), restrict hiring home employees for child care purposes (other than to care only for the occupant's children), or prohibit operating any kind of business in the home. In addition, by establishing impossible conditions (e.g., requiring 10-foot masonry walls around the residential property, costly use permits, conditional use permit hearings), child care services are excluded de facto whether or not local ordinances explicitly prohibit operations.

Building codes have similarly been used to restrict child care services in commercial spaces and residential areas. Specific requirements concerning the configuration of indoor and outdoor space, building permits, and the use of materials have stymied many commercial developers willing to establish child care centers in new office complexes and proprietary providers building their own new facilities (Claudia Ostrander, Maryland National Bank, personal communication, May 23, 1988). They have also affected family day care providers who adapt residential spaces for child care. It is not uncommon for building codes and fire codes to be contradictory, which creates impossible problems for providers and takes months or even years to resolve through administrative and judicial processes.

In addition to local public ordinances that limit use and set conditions concerning the configuration of space, deed restrictions have been adopted in many developments, condominiums, and cooperative properties. These private agreements limit the rights of property owners to acquire, own, use, or dispose of their property, and, increasingly, they are being used in suburban condominium and townhouse developments to exclude family day care providers. Even if providers become licensed, homeowners' associations can force them to close down.

One way to overcome such barriers is through state preemption laws. Approximately 10 states have passed legislation prohibiting local zoning officials and private homeowners' agreements from excluding family day care. In most cases, these laws specify that family day care is a permitted residential use requiring no further approval. Preemption laws have helped to alleviate, and in some cases overrule, local building and zoning restrictions, but they also present problems. For example, because there are no uniform definitions of family day care from state to state and even from locality to locality, questions often arise as to whether the service in question is a family day care home or a group home and, therefore, which provisions do or do not apply. In addition, in suspending deed restrictions, preemption laws may affect the ability of commercial developers and homeowners' associations to obtain liability insurance for common areas.

Local ordinances vary, and even within the same community they may be inconsistently applied. The enforcement of building and zoning restrictions has had a disproportionate impact on providers in low-income neighborhoods. Public housing frequently restricts its use for business purposes. Lacking the resources to meet building and fire provisions, providers may either shut down or operate illegally, thus limiting the supply of licensed child care in communities where it is needed.

Liability Insurance

In the early 1980s, economic hardship in the insurance industry coupled with wide media attention to several cases of alleged sexual abuse in child care centers led many insurance companies, fearful of their potential liability, to significantly increase premium rates to providers or to discontinue coverage for child care operators. A national survey of centers and licensed family day care homes in 1985 revealed that more than two-thirds of providers had experienced policy cancellations, nonrenewals, reductions in coverage, or large rate increases. Rate increases averaged approximately 300 percent (Strickland and Neugebauer, 1985). These results were corroborated by several state-level surveys (Phillips and Zigler, 1987).

Although there is disagreement about whether claims records justified these actions, by the mid-1980s child care was regarded as a high-risk business by insurance actuaries (U.S. House of Representatives, 1985). In congressional hearings, insurance industry representatives cited inadequate regulation and monitoring as a fundamental concern and indicated that companies that continued to write policies during this period applied their own "loss" standards (Phillips and Zigler, 1987; U.S. House of Representatives, 1985). These standards varied by company but in most cases were more stringent than applicable state licensing standards on matters of staff/child ratios, employee screening, and staff supervision (Phillips, 1986).

Over the past few years, as the financial health of the insurance industry has improved and as publicity about sensational cases of alleged child abuse has subsided, some companies have resumed writing liability coverage for child care providers, particularly for centers. Premiums vary on the basis of a number of factors, including building structure, program size, and perceived safety factors. Together with the National Association for the Education of Young Children (NAEYC), for example, Cigna has begun to offer coverage to centers that meet NAEYC credentialing criteria. In 1988 approximately 3,500 centers nationwide were covered by this policy, which provides package coverage for the building and its contents, liability, worker's compensation, and transportation liability. (Plans are currently under way to develop a similar program for family day care homes.) Independent insurance brokers report that in 1986, the first year that the program was in operation, it was so profitable that Cigna paid a 7.1 percent dividend back to the insured; in 1987 Cigna paid back a 23.4 percent dividend (William Ashton, Forest T. Jones & Co., personal communication, May 23, 1988).

An important policy issue, however, is the extent to which the high costs or unavailability of liability insurance may have forced providers to shut down or to operate without coverage. Unfortunately, there are no definitive data on this issue. In 1988 24 states required insurance coverage for child care centers and 7 required coverage for family day care homes (unpublished data from panel survey). Therefore, it seems likely that if the liability insurance crisis of the mid-1980s had an impact, it was more likely to have been felt by child care centers than family day care homes. There is a widespread perception that many family day care providers operate with no special coverage other than a regular homeowner's policy (if that). Strickland and Neugebauer (1985) concluded that very few centers or family day care homes shut down as a direct result of actions by the insurance industry. Moreover, the success of programs such as that offered through NAEYC may help to alleviate the problem of obtaining insurance for centers and family day care homes that meet set performance standards.

Coordination and Planning

As we have described throughout this chapter, the child care system in the United States is characterized by diversity—by different types of programs, providers, and institutional auspices that represent different professional and economic interests. In the absence of a strong national child care policy, child care services have grown haphazardly, in response to an array of perceived needs at the community level, with partial and fragmented leadership from the states and the federal government. Child care providers and advocates speak with many voices and inevitably represent a range of interests and perspectives that are as likely to be competing as coordinating.

As a result, planning and coordination are unusual at every level. Because the federal government reduced its role in the provision, financing, and regulation of child care during the 1980s, there has been no focal point, either in Congress or in the executive branch, for child care issues. Child care and early childhood education are reasonably the concerns of numerous committees in both houses of Congress, and hearings on pending legislation have been held over the past 2 years by nearly all of them. Within the executive branch, no single agency or department has responsibility for establishing policy, setting priorities, or facilitating coordination on child care issues.

With a couple of exceptions, the same has been true of the states. Although many have passed legislation for funding early childhood programs through the schools, licensing and registering centers and family day care homes, subsidizing care for children from low-income families and those with special needs, and developing resource and referral services, few have effectively developed mechanisms for planning and coordination among these separate initiatives. The two notable exceptions are Massachusetts and California. In Massachusetts, the Office of Human Resources works across departments and provides a focal point for the range of state programs and initiatives. On the basis of a 1983 planning report by the Department of Social Services and a 1984 report by the Governor's Day Care Partnership, a statewide advisory group was established, the state-level administrative capacity was upgraded, and priorities were established for future policy and program development. Among those priorities were a significant increase in child care funding through the social service system, a commitment to statewide resource and referral coverage, a pilot grant program to assist school districts in establishing programs for 3- and 4-year-olds, a corporate child care program to assist employers, and a voucher program (Commonwealth of Massachusetts, 1985; Massachusetts Department of Social Services, 1983; Catherine Dunham, Massachusetts Governor's Office, personal communication, Nov. 3, 1987).

In many ways, California served as the model for actions in Massachusetts. California has the highest state budget for child care services and the longest history of involvement and leadership on child care. The Governor's Advisory Committee on Child Development Programs has lobbied effectively for funding, advocated specific policies, and kept child care issues visible in the state. In addition to its strong support for the development of school-based programs, resource and referral services, vouchers for subsidizing care for low-income families, and a self-insurance program (administered through the Department of Education), the state has provided support and incentives for planning and coordination at the local level. These efforts have effectively involved corporations, and in turn, their resources have been mobilized in a systematic way to join local government in increasing and improving the child care supply. In the San Francisco Bay area, Bank of America raised over $2 million from local corporations and helped establish a "supply development" project for six pilot sites. The state's well-developed system of resource and referral services has provided the administrative core for assessing supply and demand at the local level and for facilitating the coordination of resources at the municipal and county level. As a result, child care has become a municipal political issue in many California communities (Kahn and Kamerman, 1987).

At the local level, there are other scattered models of efforts to effectively link public and private resources and to coordinate the activities of different providers and institutional organizations. In Minneapolis and St. Paul, Minnesota, two strong and effective organizations were formed in the mid-1980s to address the child care issue—the Greater Minneapolis Day Care Association and the Resources for Child Caring. These organizations often collaborate to improve child care services in the twin cities. Minneapolis and St. Paul have long traditions of effective human services delivery and of the public and private sectors working together to address local social service needs. These two organizations have involved schools, social services agencies, family day care networks, parent consumer groups, and local corporations to expand child care and Head Start. Much of their programmatic activity resembles initiatives in California cities and counties, combining community organizing and advocacy with resource and referral and technical assistance to local child care centers and prospective family day care providers. In contrast to the California experience, where local initiatives grew out of a strong state structure, however, the developments in Minneapolis and St. Paul have led the way for new initiatives at the state level.

These initiatives provide a great deal of encouragement that the differences between programs, providers, and institutions can be bridged, but they are by no means the rule in states and communities across the country. Clearly they depend on both political will and the creation of an infrastructure at state and local levels to plan and coordinate, to create networks, to allocate resources, and to cover gaps in the existing array of service delivery components. In the few states and local areas where planning and coordination have occurred, there has been an increase in the supply of child care and a more efficient allocation of funds.

REFERENCES

Adams, D.
    1982   *Summary of Findings: National Survey of Family Day Care Regulation.* Chapel Hill, N.C.: Bush Institute for Child and Family Policy.

Almy, M.
    1982   Day care and early childhood education. In E. Zigler and E. Gordon, eds., *Day Care Scientific and Social Policy.* Boston, Mass.: Auburn House.

Blank, H., and A. Wilkins
    1985   *Child Care: Whose Priority? A State Child Care Fact Book.* Washington, D.C.: Children's Defense Fund.

    1986   *State Child Care Fact Book 1986.* Washington D.C.: Children's Defense Fund.

Bruno, R.
    1987   *After School Care of School Age Children. December 1984.* Current Population Reports, Series P-23, No. 149, Bureau of the Census. Washington D.C.: U.S. Department of Commerce.

Bureau of the Census
    1987   *Who's Minding the Kids?* Current Population Reports, Series P-70, No. 9.
            Washington, D.C.: U.S. Department of Commerce.
Bureau of Labor Statistics
    1988   BLS reports on employer child care practices. *News* (January). Washington,
            D.C.: U.S. Department of Labor.
Bureau of National Affairs
    1984   *Employers and Child Care: Development of a New Employee Benefit.* Washington,
            D.C.: Bureau of National Affairs.
Burud, S., P. Aschbacher, and J. McCroskey
    1984   *Employer Supported Child Care: Investing in Human Resources.* Boston, Mass.:
            Auburn House.
Caldwell, B.
    1971   A timid grant grows bolder. *Saturday Review* 54(February 20):47-49, 65-66.
Coelen, C., F. Glantz, and D. Calore
    1979   *Day Care Centers in the U.S.: A National Profile, 1976-1977.* Cambridge, Mass.:
            Abt Associates.
Commonwealth of Massachusetts
    1985   *Final Report of the Governor's Day Care Partnership Project.* Boston, Mass.:
            Executive Department.
Fosburg, S.
    1981   *Family Day Care in the United States. Summary of Findings.* DHHS Publ. No.
            80-30282. Washington D.C.: U.S. Department of Health and Human Resources.
Friedman, D.
    1985   *Corporate Financial Assistance for Child Care.* Research Bulletin No. 177. New
            York: The Conference Board.
    1988   Estimates from the Conference Board and Other Monitors of Employer Sup-
            ported Child Care. Unpublished memo. The Conference Board, New York.
Gannett, E.
    1985   State Initiatives on School Age Child Care. Unpublished paper. School Age
            Child Care Project, Wellesley, Mass.
Glantz, F., J. Layzer, and M. Battaglia
    1988   *Study of the Child Care Food Program. Final Report.* Cambridge, Mass.: Abt
            Associates.
Gnezda, T., and S. Robinson
    1986   State approaches to early childhood education. *State Legislature Report* 11(14).
            Denver, Colo.: National Conference of State Legislatures.
Goodman, I., and J. Brady
    1988   *The Challenge of Coordination: Head Start's Relationship to State-Funded
            Preschool Initiatives.* Newton, Mass.: Education Development Center, Inc.
Goodman, I., J. Brady, and B. Desch
    1988   *A Commitment to Quality: The Impact of State Supplemental Funds on Mas-
            sachusetts Head Start.* Newton, Mass.: Education Development Center, Inc.
Granat, D.
    1988   Are you my mommy? *Washingtonian* 24(1):164-201.
Grubb, W.N.
    1987   *Young Children Face the States: Issues and Options for Early Childhood Programs.*
            New Brunswick, N.J.: Center for Policy Research in Education.
    1988   Choices for Children: Policy Options for State Provision of Early Childhood
            Programs. Paper prepared for the Education Commission of the States. School
            of Education, Stanford University.

Hartmann, H., and D. Pearce
  1988   *Wages and Salaries of Child Care Workers. The Economic and Social Realities.*
          Washington, D.C.: Institute for Women's Policy Research.
  1989   *High Skill and Low Pay. The Economics of Child Care Work.* Washington, D.C.:
          Institute for Women's Policy Research.
Hofferth, S., and D. Phillips
  1987   Child care in the United States, 1970-1995. *Journal of Marriage and the Family*
          49:559-571.
Hostetler, L.
  1984   The nanny trap: Child care work today. *Young Children* (January):76-79.
Kagan, S.
  1988   Current reforms in early childhood education: Are we addressing the issues?
          Young Children 43(2):27-32.
Kagan, S., and T. Glennon
  1982   Considering proprietary child care. In E. Zigler and E. Gordon, eds., *Day Care
          Scientific and Social Policy Issues*. Boston, Mass.: Auburn House.
Kahn, A., and S. Kamerman
  1987   *Child Care: Facing the Hard Choices.* Dover, Mass.: Auburn House.
Kamerman, S.B., and A. Kahn
  1987   *The Unresponsive Workforce: Employers and a Changing Labor Force.* New York:
          Columbia University Press.
Lehrman, K., and J. Pace
  1985   *Day Care Regulation Serving Children or Bureaucrats.* Cato Institute Policy
          Analysis No. 59. Washington, D.C.: Cato Institute.
Leibowitz, A., L. Waite, and C. Witsberger
  1988   Child care for preschoolers: Differences by child's age. *Demography* 25(2):205-
          220.
Leuck, M., A. Orr, and M. O'Connell
  1982   *Trends in Child Care Arrangements of Working Mothers.* Current Population
          Reports, Series P-23, No. 117, Bureau of the Census. Washington, D.C.: U.S.
          Department of Commerce.
Marx, F., and M. Seligson
  1988   *The Public School Early Childhood Study: The State Survey.* New York: Bank
          Street College of Education.
Massachusetts Department of Social Services
  1983   *A Comprehensive Child Day Care Delivery System: A Working Plan.* Boston:
          Massachusetts Department of Social Services.
McKey, R., L. Condell, H. Ganson, B. Barrett, C. McConkey, and M. Plantz
  1985   *The Impact of Head Start on Children, Families, and Communities*. Prepared
          for the Head Start Bureau, Administration for Children, Youth, and Families.
          DHHS Publ. No. (OHDS) 85-31193. Washington, D.C.: U.S. Department of
          Health and Human Services.
Mitchell, A.
  1988   *The Public School Early Education Study: The District Survey.* New York: Bank
          Street College of Education.
Morgan, G.
  1980   Can quality family day care be achieved through regulation? Pp. 77-102 in S.
          Kilmer, ed., *Advances in Early Education and Day Care*. Greenwich, Conn.: JAI
          Press, Inc.
  1982   Demystifying Day Care Delivery Systems. Unpublished paper. Work/Family
          Directions, Inc., Watertown, Mass.

1987   *The National State of Child Care Regulation, 1986.* Watertown, Mass.: Work/
        Family Directions, Inc..

National Association for the Education of Young Children
    1985   *In Whose Hands? A Demographic Fact Sheet on Child Care Providers.* Washington,
            D.C.: National Association for the Education of Young Children.
    1986   *The Child Care Boom: Growth in Licensed Child Care from 1977 to 1985.*
            Washington, D.C.: National Association for the Education of Young Children.

National Association of Elementary School Principals
    1988   NAESP's child care survey. *Principal* 67(5):31.

O'Connell, M., and C. Rogers
    1983   *Child Care Arrangements of Working Mothers: June 1982.* Current Population
            Reports, Series P-23, No. 129, Bureau of the Census. Washington, D.C.: U.S.
            Department of Commerce.

Pendleton, A.
    1986   *Preschool Enrollment: Trends and Implications.* Office of Educational Research
            and Improvement. Washington, D.C.: U.S. Department of Education.

Pettygrove, W., M. Whitebook, and R. Weir
    1984   Beyond babysitting: Changing the treatment and image of child caregivers.
            Young Children (July):14-21.

Phillips, D.
    1986   Testimony. In *Child Care: The Emerging Insurance Crisis.* Hearings before the
            Select Committee on Children, Youth, and Families, U.S. House of Representa-
            tives, 99th Congress, 1st Session. Washington, D.C.: U.S. Government Printing
            Office.

Phillips, D., and M. Whitebook
    1986   Who are child care workers? The search for answers. *Young Children* (May):14-
            20.

Phillips, D., and E. Zigler
    1987   The checkered history of federal care regulation. Pp. 3-42 in E. Rothkopf,
            ed., *The Review of Research in Education 14.* Washington, D.C.: American
            Education Research Association.

Presser, H.
    1986   Shift work among American women and child care. *Journal of Marriage and the
            Family* 48:551-563.

Seligson, M.
    1989   *Models of School-Age Child Care: A Review of Current Research on Implications
            for Women and Their Children.* Wellesley, Mass. Wellesley College Center for
            Research on Women.

Siegal, P., and M. Lawrence
    1984   Information referral and resource centers. In J.T. Greenman and R.W. Fuqua,
            eds., *Making Day Care Better.* New York: Teachers College Press.

Strickland, J., and R. Neugebauer
    1985   Yes, we have no insurance. *Child Care Information Exchange* (July):26-30.

Travers, J., and R. Ruopp
    1978   *National Day Care Study. Preliminary Findings and Their Implications.* Cambridge,
            Mass.: Abt Associates.

U.S. Department of Labor
    1988   *Childcare: A Workforce Issue.* Report of the Secretary's Task Force. Washington,
            D.C.: U.S. Department of Labor.

U.S. House of Representatives
  1985   Child Care: The Emerging Insurance Crisis. Hearings before the Select Committee on Children, Youth, and Families, 99th Congress, 1st Session. Washington, D.C.: U.S. Government Printing Office.
Waite, L., A. Leibowitz, and C. Witsberger
  1988   What Parents Pay For: Child Care and Child Care Costs. Unpublished paper. Rand Corporation, Santa Monica, Calif.
Whaley, M.
  1985   *The Status of Kindergarten: A Survey of the States*. Springfield: Illinois State Board of Education.
Whitebook, M., D. Phillips, and C. Howes
  1989   *Who Cares? Child Care Teachers and the Quality of Care in America*. Executive Summary, National Child Care Staffing Study. Oakland, Calif.: Child Care Employee Project.
Zinsser, C.
  1986   *A Study of New York Day Care Worker Salaries and Benefits*. New York: Center for Public Advocacy Research.

7

Child Care Policies and Programs

Previous chapters have documented trends in family structure, women's labor force participation, and types of child care (Chapter 2) and the range of child care services (Chapter 6). In this chapter, we focus on public and private child care policies and programs, emphasizing their costs and the groups they serve. We begin with an overview of child care expenditures and federal, state, and local government policies and private initiatives. We then detail specific policies that provide subsidies for parents, subsidies for service providers, and subsidies to strengthen the child care infrastructure.

CHILD CARE EXPENDITURES AND POLICIES

Conceptual problems and the lack of adequate data make it very difficult to estimate with any precision the total amount and types of resources spent on child care in the United States. It is possible, however, to piece together a general picture from various sources of information.

Parents have increased the inflation-adjusted amount they spend directly on child care at least fourfold over the past 20 to 25 years, from less than $3 billion in the early 1960s to approximately $12 billion in 1989 (in constant dollars). This large increase undoubtedly reflects the growing labor force participation of mothers with young children and the rising need and willingness of parents to depend more on paid child care. However, not all of this increase reflects a greater financial burden on parents. A significant share of it was underwritten by public policies at the federal (and, to a much lesser extent, the state) level. As shown in Table 7-1, subsidies for parental child care expenditures, provided through the personal income tax system (e.g., the child care tax credit) currently amount to more than $4.1 billion. This is an increase from only a few hundred million dollars (in

1989 dollars) in the mid-1960s. Subtracting these federal subsidies from the $12 billion total, we estimate that out-of-pocket expenditures by parents are about $8 billion annually.

In addition to these so-called tax expenditures, governments at all levels spend money on child care by subsidizing providers who deliver these services, by supporting programs such as Head Start and preschool education, and by supporting the development of a child care infrastructure, including staff training and resource and referral networks. The amount allocated to these activities is more difficult to estimate, but probably currently amounts to almost $2.6 billion at the federal level and at least another $1 billion at the state and local levels (see Table 7-1). Finally, in recent years, employers, unions, churches, and various charitable organizations have increasingly provided and subsidized child care services. No reliable national data exist on the magnitude of these activities, but local data suggest that the dollar value is somewhat less than $1 billion. Although significantly less than the level of public contribution, this private support is clearly important to programs and parents.

In total, approximately $15-$17 billion is currently spent on an annual basis on child care in the United States, either directly by governments or by parents or other private sources. This amount is expected to increase three fold by 1995 to $48 billion (Institute for American Values, 1989). Even this increase, however, is believed by many observers to represent only a small fraction of what might be required to adequately care for all children in the United States in the future. To understand this point it is useful to consider what the monetary costs would be if every child under age 6 was in full-time paid care that met the standards of quality detailed in Chapter 4 and if every child aged 6 to 14 was in paid care during nonschool hours. At an estimated cost of $4,000 per preschool-age child and $2,000 per school-age child (see Chapter 8), the total would be approximately $126 billion. Although it is unlikely that the United States would ever have a fully monetized child care system or that every child would be in paid care, this calculation provides a vivid illustration that monetary expenditures from whatever source—parents, employers, government, and other private sources—cover only a portion of the economic costs for child care. A parent or other relative who stays at home to care for a child does not provide "free child care" even though these services are unpaid to the degree that they do not involve a monetary exchange.

Federal Policy

There is no single system of federal support for paid child care. Rather, there is a fragmented array of consumer, provider, and infrastructure policies and programs that have developed over the past 40 years. Stephan

TABLE 7-1 Federal Subsidies for Child Care

Subsidy	Fiscal 1988 Estimated (in millions)	Fiscal 1980
Consumer Subsidies[a]		
Dependent care tax credit	$3,920	$ 956
Dependent care assistance plan	65	--
AFDC disregard	44	60
Food Stamp disregard	50	36
Housing disregard	18	--
Support for education	66	1
Total	$4,163	$1,053
Provider Subsidies		
Social services block grant[b]	$ 591	$ 600
Child Care Food Program (including Special Milk Program)	584	216
Head Start	1,200	736
Special education and rehabilitative programs	219	39
Work-welfare programs	19	--
School-age programs	3	--
Provider tax incentives	3	--
Total	$2,619	$1,591
Infrastructure Subsidies		
Human Services Reauthorization Act resource and referral	$2	--
Child Development Associates Program	1	--
Total	$3	--
Total	$6,785	$2,644

NOTE: Data on federal subsidies for child care are imprecise. These figures are based on Besharov and Tramontozzi (1988), Kahn and Kamerman (1987), Robins (1988), and U.S. Department of Labor (1988); they do not include expenses for child care provided to government or military personnel.

[a]These consumer subsidies do not include general income support programs: personal tax exemptions, Aid to Families with Dependent Children (AFDC), and the earned income tax credit.
[b]Figures are averages from sources.

and Schillmoeller (1987) identify 22 child care programs, and the U.S. Department of Labor (1988) details 31 programs in 11 federal agencies (with some disagreement among scholars and government agencies concerning which federal programs should be included in an accounting of child care expenditures). These initiatives include an array of targeted activities and subsidies, including Head Start, the provision of food to children from low-income families who are cared for in approved settings, and tax credits to assist employed parents offset a portion of the costs of child care as work-related expenses. During the past decade, the policy debate has shifted from whether the federal government should play a role in the provision and financing of child care to what its role should be in light of current budget constraints (Besharov and Tramontozzi, 1988; Robins, 1988; Stephan and Schillmoeller, 1987; U.S. Department of Labor, 1988).

As shown in Table 7.1, we estimate that the total amount of federal support for child care in fiscal 1988 was $6.8 billion. The amount of assistance has been increasing. Besharov and Tramontozzi (1988) found that federal child care assistance rose from $1 billion in fiscal 1972 to $6.2 billion in 1987, reflecting a real increase (after inflation) of 127 percent. They project a further 24 percent rise by 1989, to approximately $8 billion.

The mix of consumer, provider, and infrastructure subsidies provided by the federal government for child care, and thus the mix of beneficiaries, has changed substantially over the past two decades. In 1972, 80 percent of federal child care dollars were targeted at low-income families through provider subsidies. In 1980, low-income families benefited from 50 percent of federal expenditures, primarily through the Social Services Block Grant (SSBG) program and Head Start. By 1986 these programs accounted for only between 26 and 30 percent of the total: funding for Head Start and the Child Care Food Program had increased, whereas child care support for recipients of welfare and job training programs had declined. From the limited data available, it appears that SSBG funding also declined during the 1980s (Besharov and Tramontozzi, 1988; Kamerman and Kahn, 1987; Robins, 1988).

In contrast, by the early 1980s direct consumer subsidies, which primarily benefit middle- and upper-income families, had become the predominant form of federal support for child care, and they have greatly increased since then; see Figure 7-1. In particular, the child care tax credit, which accounted for about one-third of total federal expenditures at the beginning of this decade, now accounts for nearly two-thirds. Infrastructure subsidies, which generally benefit all income groups, are a very small but growing area of federal expenditures. In sum, despite the increasing number of poor children, federal child care resources no longer primarily benefit low-income families; instead, they increasingly benefit middle-class families in which the mother is employed outside the home.

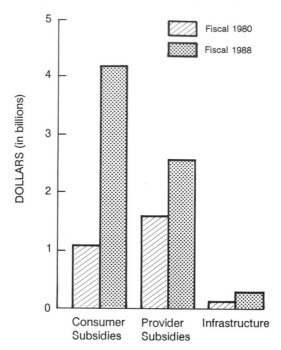

FIGURE 7-1   Federal subsidies for child care, 1980 and 1988.

State and Local Policies

The total amount of financial support for child care is much more modest at the state level than at the federal level, but state governments also provide an array of consumer, provider, and infrastructure subsidies. Unlike the federal government, however, the states establish and enforce regulations for out-of-home child care (discussed in Chapters 4 and 6).

In addition, state governments are responsible for administering many of the federal and state programs. They administer welfare programs, manage reimbursement systems, provide job training for caregivers, and provide services to children with disabilities. City and county governments are often designated as the agencies responsible for implementing these child care programs and policies. Responsibilities for child care at state and local levels fall within the jurisdiction of several departments and public agencies, adding to the complexity of the system.

Although states and local governments play a key role in child care, very little information is available about their revenues or expenditures. From the panel's state survey, we estimate state subsidies at approximately $500 million annually. It appears that some states have significantly increased expenditures in recent years, whereas in other states they have decreased

(Kahn and Kamerman, 1987). Only 12 states in our survey provided data on total state spending for child care. Of the total $390 million reported, 72 percent was spent in California, which has the most extensive child care system in the country, spending more total dollars and more dollars per child than other state (Grubb, 1988; Mitchell, 1988). California provides approximately $315 million in direct funds for a wide variety of child care programs, nine times as much as the next most generous state, Massachusetts. Other states provide considerably less funding, and most of that is limited to part-day preschool programs.

Private Initiatives

The private sector includes charitable organizations, not-for-profit and for-profit child care providers, employers, and unions. Although the total amount of resources involved are small and difficult to quantify relative to governmental efforts, these groups have responded to the demand for child care in a variety of ways that are often influenced by public policies. Charitable organizations—for example, churches and the United Way—have contributed primarily by developing child care centers directly and by making monetary and in-kind contributions to existing service providers (such as child care centers in church basements). A 1979 study estimated that approximately 6 percent of child care center budgets came from in-kind donations of space, materials, volunteer time, and so on, usually to not-for-profit programs (Coelen et al., 1979). These programs are often targeted for low- and middle-income families, with combinations of funding from sliding-scale fees, public subsidies for children in low-income families, and some tax benefits. It is likely that the number of church basements and volunteer hours may be reaching their practical limits; further expansion of private support for child care is likely to be limited.

The private sector also includes for-profit child care centers, and it has expanded in recent years. As described in Chapter 6, several large chains and thousands of independent centers have developed into a multimillion dollar business over the past decade. Large chains tend to target their programs to meet the needs of middle- and upper middle-income, two-earner families; thousands of "mom-and-pop" operations reach lower income families. Merrill Lynch estimates that publicly held for-profit child care corporations account for about 5 percent of center care providers and places (unpublished 1988 market data on publicly held corporations that provide child care services).

Finally, employers and unions are active and growing participants in the child care market. In response to the need to attract and retain a productive work force, which is increasingly comprised of women with young children; to union negotiations on behalf of these women employees;

and to tax incentives, a growing number of employers are developing a variety of supports for working parents. The primary child care support programs include on-site child care centers, benefit plans such as flexible spending accounts, financial assistance for purchasing child care services in the market, resource and referral programs, flexible schedules, and parental leaves. The most rapidly growing form of employer support is dependent-care assistance programs, in which employers establish benefit plans that allow employees to reduce their taxable income by using a fixed portion (up to $5,000) for child care expenses. This benefit costs the employer little or nothing other than administrative expenses; it is financed by federal and state tax expenditures (i.e., by forgone tax receipts). Many private- and public-sector employers have established a range of informal maternity and disability leave policies through contract and labor law (Piccirillo, 1988).

These programs are available primarily to employees working in large companies, for federal and state governments, and to employers with special scheduling needs, such as workers in the military and hospitals. Although the number of employers with such programs appears to be increasing, even the most optimistic accounts suggest that only 11 percent of the nation's firms with 10 or more employees provide some specific benefits or services to workers to assist with their child care arrangements (Bureau of Labor Statistics, 1988). Infant care leave rarely exceeds 4 months, is generally unpaid, and may not include job guarantees or continued health insurance.

In addition to direct benefits and services, there are other employment-related child care policies that may ease work-family strains (e.g., flexible schedules, counseling, parenting seminars) or that may enable parents themselves to care for children (e.g., part-time work, job sharing, working at home). The number of employers offering these types of policies has been increasing, and currently about three-fifths of firms with 10 or more employees provide such assistance (Bureau of Labor Statistics, 1988). There are no data available on the costs associated with these programs. Largely untouched by direct and indirect policies and programs are parents, particularly mothers, working at low wages for small employers, the domain where job growth has been the greatest in the past several years and is expected to be greatest during the 1990s.

Surveys suggest that the primary reason employers invest in child care is to address problems of recruitment, productivity, absenteeism, turnover, morale, and public relations (Friedman, 1985; Galinsky, 1988). Employers have generally opposed government mandates of any particular programs or benefits (Meyer, 1989; Shaine, 1987).

Unions are less likely to see child care as a recruitment or productivity issue for their growing number of women members. Although some unions increasingly negotiate child care supports in local union contracts, they are more often strong advocates of national child care legislation and mandated parental leave. Public-sector unions have been particularly active (Joyce Long, American Federation of State, County, and Municipal Employees, personal communication, June 8, 1988; Peggy Connerton, Service Employees International Union, personal communication, May 5, 1988). Employers and unions in both the public and the private sectors provide important and growing sources of support, responsive to diverse parental needs. The 1989 agreement between AT&T and its union (see Chapter 6) represents a significant step toward joint support for child care.

CONSUMER SUBSIDIES: SUPPORT FOR PARENTS

Programs and policies offering direct support to parents to subsidize their child care expenses take several forms, most linked to employment and earnings. The largest of these are the federal tax subsidies provided through the dependent care tax credit (DCTC) and employer-based dependent care assistance plans (DCAPs). Other forms of support are provided through voucher plans, the welfare-related income disregard programs, and parental leave policies. In this section we also discuss the major forms of more general federal income supports that are not tied to parents' employment and paid child care expenses—personal income tax exemptions, the earned income tax credit, and the Aid to Families with Dependent Children (AFDC) program. These programs affect families with children, and proposals for their change are often related in part to child care concerns.

Employment-Related Support

Dependent Care Tax Credit

The federal child care tax credit permits parents with taxable earnings to deduct a portion of their child care expenses for children under age 13 (until 1989, under age 15) from their federal income taxes. Credits for documented child care expenses are available to families in which a single parent or both parents are employed. Transportation costs are not covered. If parents use child care that is provided for seven or more children, the providers must meet state licensing requirements. Payments to relatives qualify only if these individuals are employed by an organization or are self-employed and Social Security tax is withheld. Relatives who are caregivers cannot also be declared as dependents for tax deduction purposes (Burud et al., 1984; Friedman, 1985; Marr, 1988).

The credit treats child care as an allowable employment-related expense. By providing only partial support, however, it also recognizes that child care costs are, to some extent, optional personal expenses. In 1976 child care tax benefits were changed from a deduction to a credit in order to provide more support to middle-income rather than upper-income families and were made more progressive by providing a higher proportionate subsidy to lower and moderate-income groups. Currently, the credit is 30 percent of allowable expenses—to a maximum of $2,400 for one dependent and $4,800 for two or more dependents—for families earning $10,000 or less; it decreases to a minimum of 20 percent for families earning $28,000 or more. Nearly half of all families with working mothers now claim the credit; an estimated half of families claiming the credit have incomes of more than $25,000 per year. Because the credit is nonrefundable, working poor people who have no tax liability do not benefit (Marr, 1988; Nelson and Warring, 1982; Robins, 1988).

In 1985 approximately $3.1 billion in child care credits was claimed, with an average credit of $372 (Besharov and Tramontozzi, 1988). Use of the credit had increased dramatically, from claims on 2.7 million tax returns in 1976 to 8.4 million tax returns in 1985 (Robins, 1988). The percentage of returns claiming the credit rose from 3.9 percent to 9.8 percent of taxpayers in those years, in part in response to the 1983 change in the tax law enabling families to use the 1040 short form to claim the credit. The most dramatic increase, however, came in the percentage of families with working mothers that claimed the credit. The number rose from 18 percent in 1976 to 44 percent in 1986. In fact, most of the dollar increase in child care subsidies through the tax credit came from more people claiming the credit rather than from larger subsidies per family. Adjusting for inflation, the average credit per family increased by only 12 percent during that 10-year period. In 1988 the estimated total claimed was $3.9 billion.

Currently, 29 states that tax income also provide dependent care tax credits or deductions, and only 6 of these states limit eligibility for the credit or deduction on the basis of income. Although state policies generally provide much more modest tax relief than the federal credit, some are designed to benefit low-income families. In Minnesota, for example, taxpayers are entitled to as much as $720 per dependent, up to $1,440 total. The credit is available as a refundable cash payment to families that have no tax liability. In Alaska, which has no income tax, families with dependent-care expenses may file a return to obtain a small allowance of up to $115 per dependent, or $230 total (Issensee and Campbell, 1987).

Employer-Based Dependent Care Assistance Plans

In the Economic Recovery Act of 1981, dependent care was made a nontaxable benefit: employers can provide this benefit to employees with children under age 15 by establishing a DCAP under section 129 of the

Internal Revenue Code.[1] These plans allow employees to specify anticipated expenses up to $5,000 per year and to exclude this amount from their gross taxable income. Preschool and kindergarten programs that charge tuition are eligible. Designated amounts not used in a given year are forfeited by the employee. The plan must not provide "excessive" benefits to higher income employees, particularly shareholders, directors, and officers. The provider cannot be an employee's own child under age 19 or any person for whom the employee or spouse can take a personal exemption (Burud et al., 1984; Friedman, 1985; U.S. Department of Labor, 1988).

The benefit can be offered either under a comprehensive "cafeteria benefit plan" or as a freestanding flexible spending account. Under cafeteria plans, there are usually a core set of benefits—such as health and life insurance, vacation, and retirement—as well as an optional set of benefits, such as nonreimbursed medical or legal expenses, from which employees can choose according to their needs and preferences. Dependent care can be offered as an optional nontaxable benefit if the plan meets IRS requirements.

Flexible spending accounts (FSAs) are separate accounts added to an existing benefits package, almost always funded through salary reduction plans, with a $5,000 maximum. Employers can, but rarely do, provide an additional contribution up to the $5,000 limit. Employees pay for child care out of pretax dollars at no expense (other than administrative) to the employer. In fact, an employer may save money since unemployment and Social Security taxes do not have to be paid on that portion of the salary allocated for child care. The Bureau of National Affairs (1984) reports that FSAs are now one of the most popular types of employer benefits and that they are expected to grow rapidly in the coming several years, but there are no available estimates of their current or projected cost to the federal government.

In 1985 the Conference Board estimated that 500 medium-sized companies and large corporations offered dependent care as a part of their benefit plans (Kamerman and Kahn, 1987). A more recent survey of more than 2,000 large and small employers found that 19 percent of the respondents offered flexible benefit programs; of those, almost three-quarters had flexible programs that offered a dependent-care reimbursement option (The Wyatt Company, 1988). The estimated loss of tax revenues for dependent care was $30 million in fiscal 1987 and $65 million in 1988. Because rapid expansion is expected, the Office of Management and Budget projected a large increase in this revenue loss, perhaps totaling $150 million in 1989 (in Besharov and Tramontozzi, 1988).

---

[1] The Family Support Act of 1988 (commonly referred to as the Welfare Reform Act), lowered the age limit for eligible dependents to 13 as of 1989 (Bureau of National Affairs, 1988).

FSAs are regressive in their distribution because the subsidy is worth more to families in higher tax brackets. For example, a $5,000 FSA is worth approximately $750 to a family in the 15 percent tax bracket, but $1,400 to a family in the 28 percent tax bracket. This regressive effect is compounded by the fact that many low-income families, particularly single women with young children, are less likely to work for large firms and are therefore less likely to receive this benefit (Bureau of National Affairs, 1988; Robins, 1988).

Friedman (1985) reports that most companies interviewed in one survey hoped to reduce benefit costs, especially for health premiums, and to improve recruitment and retention by offering cafeteria programs. They found that 1.5 to 6 percent of employees use dependent-care options in cafeteria benefit plans. These rates, however, can be deceptive. At Proctor and Gamble, for example, approximately 5 percent of the employees chose dependent-care assistance, but that represents 25 percent of the employees with children. Utilization rates for FSAs ranged from a low of 2 percent of Mellon Bank employees, to 6 percent at Pepsico, to 8.7 percent at the Chemical Bank. The Wyatt Company (1988) found that 7 percent of eligible employees participated in the dependent-care reimbursement plans. An average of slightly over $2,000 per employee was contributed to such accounts in 1988.

Although a relatively small number of companies provide dependent-care programs, they represent a relatively large increase in employer assistance for child care. The Bureau of Labor Statistics (1988) reports that 3 percent of the establishments in its recent survey were providing some form of financial assistance specifically for child care. These services were more likely, although not exclusively, to be offered by establishments with 250 or more employees and a high percentage of female employees (e.g., those in finance, insurance, and real estate). They were more likely to be found in service industries (3.5%) than in manufacturing industries (1.9%) or government (2.9%).

Voucher Programs: Employer and Public

As discussed in Chapter 6, voucher programs are designed to expanded parental choice, but with more constraints than tax credits or flexible spending accounts. Private employers as well as public agencies offer vouchers, although they are not widely available in either sector; there are no data on the costs of the subsidy.

In the public sector, vouchers are one method of payment under the SSBG program. This program, a form of provider subsidy, primarily contracts directly with providers and reimburses them for services to children in low-income families. A small percentage of payments are made through vouchers to parents. Voucher programs are designed to respond to fluctuations in the demand for subsidized care and can make available to parents a broader range of child care programs than the direct provision of services can make. Instead of purchasing spaces, the voucher program gives parents a coupon that can be redeemed by any child care service that meets legal requirements, including family day care. The provider is then reimbursed for the value of the coupon.

In the private sector, voucher programs are one of the most expensive, and least offered, forms of employer financial assistance for child care. In providing a voucher, employers make a financial contribution, unlike the salary reduction plans, which are generally financed by tax expenditures at no direct cost to the employer. Voucher payments may be administered through the employee, directly with a provider, or through community agencies. Employer voucher programs may or may not be linked to family income. Polaroid, for example, limits its voucher program to low-wage employees, based on a perception that care is available but not affordable for these families. Polaroid defines the program as a service rather than a benefit because of its restricted access (Friedman, 1985).

Welfare Income Disregard

Several welfare programs enable poor parents to deduct some child care expenses when calculating their benefits. The AFDC disregard, for example, is a consumer child care subsidy for low-income families. Under this program, families may set aside up to $175 of income per month for child care for children 2 years and older and $200 a month for children under 2 years (previously $160 a month); this income will be disregarded when benefits are computed. The total cost of the AFDC child care disregard was estimated at between $40 and $44 million in 1987 (Besharov and Tramontozzi, 1988; U.S. Department of Labor, 1988). Besharov and Tramontozzi calculated the $44 million figure based on an average monthly caseload of 3.5 million families, of which about 1 percent (33,000 families) make use of the option, which averages $1,152 per recipient per year.[2] Similar disregard programs exist for food stamps ($50 million) and housing programs ($18 million). Funding for the AFDC disregard program has declined during the past 8 years, whereas it has increased slightly for the other programs.

---

[2]The majority of low-income families rely on unpaid family members for child care (Isaacs, 1988).

Education and Training Programs

Several welfare programs are designed to reduce welfare dependency by providing money, primarily to states, to help AFDC recipients find and keep jobs. This is part of a larger strategy to train economically disadvantaged and dislocated workers and to use federal funds to subsidize child care services to enable such workers to participate in appropriate programs. The Work Incentive Program (WIN), specifically for welfare recipients, had total costs in 1987 of $126 million, but there are no recent data on the cost of child care under WIN. A 1977 study estimated that 10 percent of the WIN budget was allocated for this purpose, and Besharov and Tramontozzi (1988) therefore estimate the 1988 cost to the federal government at $9 million. The U.S. Department of Labor (1988) did not estimate WIN child care costs, which it jointly supports with the U.S. Department of Health and Human Services.

Under the Job Training Partnership Act (JTPA), the U.S. Department of Labor allocates funds to states or local service delivery areas—on the basis of unemployment rates and the number of economically disadvantaged persons—to provide employment and training services. No more than 15 percent of funds may be spent for supportive services, which can include child care, transportation, and health services. Under JTPA, funds are also available to help displaced workers, farm workers, and youth in the Job Corps program. The U.S. Department of Labor (1988) estimates the total child care expenditures for these work training programs at $9.5 million for 1988.

States use a variety of federal, state, and local funds to pay for child care for participants in work-welfare programs. Thirty-one states have allocated supplemental state funds to pay for child care services under welfare reform initiatives. Combinations of state, AFDC, and WIN funds appear to be the most common approach for funding work-welfare–related child care services (Maximus, Inc., 1988).

Two programs are designed to help low-income students. The U.S. Department of Education provides grants to states to provide child care for participants in local vocational education programs. Funds are specifically set aside for single parents and homemakers and individuals participating in programs to reduce gender stereotypes. The estimated costs for child care are $1 to $1.5 million annually, of a total program budget of $800 million. Also under the U.S. Department of Education, the Pell Grant Program provides need-based grants for postsecondary education for students from low-income families. As of 1988, child care is defined as an attendance cost, with an allowance of up to $1,000 per student per year. The estimated cost of child care benefits provided by this program in 1988 was $65 million (U.S. Department of Labor, 1988).

Parental Leave

Thus far, we have described policies and programs that subsidize parents' purchase of out-of-home care for their children. Other policies and programs, however, facilitate parents' staying at home to care for their children themselves. Parental leave is the general term used for a range of policies, primarily maternity leave and infant care leave, that enable parents to take time off from their jobs for pregnancy and childbirth or to care for infants or sick children.

Maternity Leave

The United States—unlike most other industrialized countries and many developing countries—does not have a national policy encouraging or mandating that working parents be given time off from their jobs (with or without pay, benefits, or job guarantees) to give birth, to care for infants, or to care for sick children. Current federal and state policies, as interpreted through the courts, address only pregnancy-related leaves through two different approaches: equal treatment and special treatment.

Federal policy addresses childbirth and infant care under the equal treatment approach. Pregnancy, childbirth, and recovery from childbirth are treated like any other temporary physical disability that prevents an employee from performing his or her job. This policy is embodied in the Pregnancy Discrimination Act of 1978, amending the Civil Rights Act of 1964, which expands the definition of sex discrimination to prohibit employment discrimination based on pregnancy and pregnancy-related conditions. The act's primary purpose is to ensure that pregnancy be treated as other medical disabilities with similar employment effects. Thus, employers are not required to have a disability plan, but if they do have one they are required to treat pregnancy and childbirth as they would any other short-term disability.

According to the Bureau of Labor Statistics (1986), 93 percent of all employees in medium-sized and large firms have some form of short-term disability coverage. Professional and administrative employees generally have different types of leaves, however, and part-time workers are less likely to have coverage than full-time workers. Five states and one territory have temporary disability laws that now include pregnancy as part of the short-term disability program: California, Hawaii, New Jersey, New York, Rhode Island, and Puerto Rico. These states and Puerto Rico have expanded medical coverage to include some variation of wage protection (usually partial) during disability leave and some form of employment guarantees. In New Jersey, for example, an employee who has worked at least 20 weeks and earned at least $4,300 for the year (or $76 each week during that year) is eligible for a maximum of 26 weeks of leave and up to $200 per week, which is approximately 53 percent of the statewide average weekly wage. The fund, administered by the state treasurer, is financed through employer and employee contributions of 0.5 percent of an individual's earnings, not to exceed $53.50 a year (Kean, 1988).

In contrast to the equal treatment approach, the special treatment model has roots in the much older tradition of protective labor laws, dating from the early 1900s, designed to protect women and their maternal status. Under this model, maternity, pregnancy, childbirth, and infant care (to the extent that it encompasses breast feeding) are viewed as unique to women and meriting special treatment to accommodate and protect those who are employed (Piccirillo, 1988). In 1987, the Supreme Court upheld a California law providing job security for up to 4 months for women "disabled" by pregnancy, but this protection was not extended to other disabilities (*California Federal Savings and Loan* v. *Guerra*, No. 85-494). The court concluded that special treatment is necessary for women to have equal employment opportunity. Montana, Connecticut, Massachusetts, and California have implemented maternity leave laws, and more than 20 states are now considering leave or disability statutes.

Infant Care Leave

Current laws address the physical disability aspects of pregnancy, but there is no federal law allowing or mandating parental leave to enable mothers or fathers to care for newborn or newly adopted infants. According to one study (National Association of Working Women, 1988), 21 states have some form of parental leave policy, but most existing parental leave practices have been established in the private sector. Contract and labor laws have been used to establish a wide range of pregnancy disability and infant care leaves (Piccirillo, 1988). Employers and unions offer a wide range of benefit packages combining maternity leave, vacation days, sick leave, and personal leave to care for infants. Unions in the public sector have been particularly active to secure infant care leaves for mothers and fathers, whereas very large companies have led the way in establishing maternity and parental leave policies in the private sector. Under at least five recent cases or settlements, fathers have secured the same right to take leave benefits for child care as those offered to mothers (Pleck, 1988).

Availability of Parental Leave

There are no national data measuring the extent or coverage of parental leave policies or the costs of such policies. During the past few years, however, there have been several independent studies to determine the current range and costs of policies. Although each study has methodological and conceptual limitations, taken together they form a rough picture of maternity and infant care leave policy in the United States (for reviews see Kahn and Kamerman, 1987; Trzcinski, 1988a,b; Zigler and Frank, 1988).

In the private sector, among those employers who provide parental leave, the average is 2 to 3 months, but this varies from a minimum pregnancy disability leave of a few weeks to up to 1 year of unpaid leave for personal reasons (Bureau of National Affairs, 1983; Catalyst, 1986; Kamerman and Kahn, 1983; Minnesota House of Representatives, 1987; National Federation of Independent Businesses, 1985; U.S. Chamber of Commerce, 1985). Smaller companies have a variety of flexible schedule arrangements, but paid leaves, either partial or full, are found almost exclusively among large companies. A Columbia University study, for example, found that 47 percent of the respondents with more than 500 employees had some form of paid maternity leave, but only 37 percent of those with between 50 and 500 employees and 10 percent of those with fewer than 100 employees had such policies (Kamerman and Kahn, 1983; Trzcinski, 1988a). These differences are important since almost half of all employed women work in companies with fewer than 100 employees.

Large and medium-sized firms tend to provide some paid disability leave for pregnancy and childbirth, either through disability insurance (usually available to production employees) or through paid sick leave (usually available to managerial, professional, and clerical employees). A substantial majority of employees in small, medium-sized, or large firms have no leave available to care for infants (Kahn and Kamerman, 1987; Trzcinski, 1988a,b). When leave is available, women remain the primary beneficiaries. Pleck (1988) reports that unpaid leaves for fathers, although becoming more common, are still rare. In a Catalyst (1986) study of 384 companies, 37 percent reported offering unpaid leaves to fathers, but only 9 companies reported that a father had actually taken advantage of the leave option.

Federal employees may use annual or sick leave for pregnancy and postpartum recovery at the discretion of supervisors. In the military, there is considerable variation among services and locations, and supervisors have a great deal of discretion. At a minimum, military women are eligible for some prenatal leave and convalescent leave after childbirth, based on a physician's determination (Makuen, 1988).

In a survey of states, Makuen (1988) found that employees in 27 states had benefit protection with paid leave and 23 had some form of job protection. Extended leave was at the discretion of supervisors. Liberal state policies, including paternity leave, were attributed, in large part, to unionization (Makuen, 1988; Pleck, 1988). In New York, for example, the collective bargaining agreement entitles either parent to infant care leave for 7 months on a mandatory basis and 2 years on a discretionary basis (Makuen, 1988).

As noted above, there are data on the utilization and costs of these policies. For the federal government, Makuen (1988:200) found that because parental leave policies were part of the fringe benefit package "there [are] no reliable data on financing, percentage of employees taking leave, percentage of leave takers returning or average length of leave time." Of 36 states responding to a state survey, most reported that 90 percent of leave takers returned to work full time within 1 year, with 5 percent returning part time and 5 percent not returning at all. Louisiana reported 70 percent returning, the lowest in the survey. The average length of time taken ranged from 6 weeks (Utah) to 26 weeks (Vermont and Ohio). The state of Washington estimated that a 6-month leave without pay cost the state $1,002 per person (Makuen, 1988).

According to the New Jersey Department of Labor, for 1 year (July 1983 to June 1984), 17 percent of 19,652 temporary disability claims paid by the state were pregnancy related. The average amount paid was $1,367, and the average number of days claimed was 70.9. Over half of the women under 35 years of age who filed for a benefit claimed pregnancy. The average disability claim across all categories, however, was lower for women ($14,937) than for men ($15,348) (Kean, 1988). Kean further reports that 31 percent of the women filing temporary disability claims earned between $10,000 and $15,000 per year, and only 3 percent earned $25,000 or more. He claims that the wage replacement (i.e., benefit) "fosters the economic survival of the low and middle income women who wish to bear children" (Kean, 1988:336).

In a survey of 80 firms in two metropolitan labor markets—Detroit, Michigan, and Charleston, South Carolina—the General Accounting Office (GAO) found that only about one in three workers who took pregnancy leave was actually replaced, and employers reported no significant loss of output. Eighty-four percent of women taking leave returned in 10 weeks, and few women took any unpaid leave. The National Association of Working Women (1988) argues that small businesses in states with parental leave policies had a larger growth rate than in states without leaves: between 1976 and 1986, employment in firms with fewer than 20 employees grew by 32 percent in the seven states with parental leave policies and by 22 percent in the seven states without leave policies. The extent to which a causal relationship exists between state parental leave policies and the growth of small businesses is unknown. Clearly, many other factors, including local economic conditions, play a significant part in that growth.

Using Current Population Survey data for 1979 and 1983, Trzcinski (1988b) found that for women of childbearing age, maternity statutes had a negative effect on wages and the probability of health insurance, pension coverage, and tenure on the job. These effects were more likely among women employed in small firms. In states with temporary disability plans for women of childbearing age, however, wages and the probability of health insurance and pension coverage were higher than for women in other states. Years of tenure on the current job were significantly higher for women in states with disability policies than for women in other states, and tenure was found to be positively related to increased wages, pension, and health insurance coverage.

Using data from the Panel Study on Income Dynamics, Spalter-Roth and Hartmann (1988) estimate that childbirth and adoption cost American women $31 billion annually in lost earnings. The loss is greater for black women, who experience more unemployment when there are no leave and benefit provisions in their jobs. The researchers conclude that women who report having no leave benefits other than vacation are in worse economic condition both before and after birth than women with some form of leave; they estimate that women without leave annually lose $607 million in income and benefits in comparison with women with leave. Spalter-Roth and Hartmann (1988) found that taxpayers pay an additional $108 million in public assistance for these women.

General Income Support

Personal Tax Exemption

Since the 1940s families have been able to claim a personal exemption for each of their children (and other household dependent relatives), thereby reducing their taxable income. In 1948 three-quarters of the median family income of $3,486 was exempt from federal tax because of the personal exemption (and the standard deduction). At that time this amount bore some reasonable resemblance to the minimum cost of supporting a child. By the mid-1980s, the median family income had increased from $3,486 to $29,184. According to the Joint Committee on Taxation, less than one-third of median family income was then exempt from taxation (Hewlett et al., 1986).

The current personal exemption of $2,000 saves approximately $300 in federal taxes per child for the majority of all families who are in the 15 percent federal tax bracket if their income is sufficiently high to have such taxes to offset; $550 to $600 per child is saved for families in the 28 percent and 33 percent tax brackets. Personal exemptions may also provide some additional tax relief at the state level, but they are of far less significance since state income tax rates (where they exist) are much lower than federal rates and state personal exemptions are also lower.

Although the value of the personal exemption is declining (as income levels rise over time), it still remains a major support to families with children, resulting in a revenue loss of approximately $20 billion per year in federal dollars (Robin Barnes, Urban Institute, personal communication, Aug. 3, 1988). The personal exemption is administratively simple and provides modest support to taxpaying families without the stigma of explicit income eligibility requirements. However, it is of little or no assistance to families whose income is insufficient for them to incur a significant personal income tax liability.

Earned Income Tax Credit

In contrast to the personal income tax exemption, the earned income tax credit (EITC) provides support to low-income families that have any wage earnings. This refundable tax credit was created to roughly offset the burden of Social Security payroll taxes for low-income people with dependent children, married or single, regardless of whether they incur child care expenses. Families with low earnings gain tax credits for each dollar that they earn. Under current law, families with earnings below $6,200 per year receive a credit of 14 cents for each $1 they earn, up to a maximum credit of $868. Those with incomes between $6,200 and $9,840 receive flat credits of $868 if their earnings are sufficient. For those with incomes over $9,840, the credit is reduced by 10 cents for each additional dollar, so that it phases out if family income is more than $18,709. The credit is first applied as an offset to a family's federal income taxes. However, if the credit exceeds a family's total income tax liability, the difference is refundable and is paid by check from the government (Marr, 1988). The most recent annual cost to the federal government of the EITC was estimated at $6 billion (Ellwood, 1988).

Aid to Families With Dependent Children

AFDC is a major component of U.S. welfare policy. It is state administered but funded jointly by the federal and state governments. Established in the 1935 Social Security Act, it originally was intended to enable mothers who were single as a result of divorce, separation, out-of-wedlock birth, or widowhood to stay home with their children. In 1950 the law was amended to provide benefits to the parent as well as the child (Garfinkel and McLanahan, 1986). The law enables low-income single women with young children to stay at home to care for their children. The cost of AFDC benefits in 1950 was $1.7 billion; today the program transfers approximately $16 billion to more than 3 million poor families with dependent children each year.

The philosophy behind the welfare program has been to reflect and enforce community values. In the 1950s, the standard was for women to be at home with young children. However, the Family Support Act, passed in October 1988, reflects the changing trends in women's labor force participation: since the majority of women with young children in the 1980s are now in the paid labor force, the new law requires low-income women with young children to work or to be in an education or training program in order to receive benefits.

This new approach has more immediate implications for child care than did the previous AFDC program. States are required to develop a job opportunity and basic skills (JOBS) program to provide welfare recipients with the education, training, or employment experience they need to become economically self-sufficient. Women with children aged 3 years or older (at state option, age 1 year or older) must participate at least 20 hours a week. They are then guaranteed child care, transportation, and other support for up to 12 months. States can reimburse child care costs up to the market rate. At a minimum, they must pay the actual cost of care or the dollar amount of the current child care income disregard ($175 per month for children over 2 and $200 per month for children under 2). The act requires states to provide extended child care benefits for the first year a recipient is employed and out of the welfare program. States may provide care directly or use vouchers, provider contracts, or sliding-fee scales to subsidize existing providers. Under the new law, adult mothers with no children under the age of 3 and all adolescent parents, regardless of the ages of their children, are required to participate in order to receive AFDC support. States must assess the availability of child care and inform parents of what is available, and they must extend help at parents' requests.

The 1988 legislation could result in a dramatic increase in the demand for child care, especially for 3- and 4-year-olds and possibly for 1- and 2-year-olds as well. The Congressional Budget Office (CBO) (1989) projects the cost of the child care provisions at $410 million annually by 1993. The federal share would be 55 percent ($200 million) and the state share 45 percent. On the basis of current studies of the use of paid child care and current costs, CBO estimates that 68 percent of the eligible children under age 6 (210,000 children) and 16 percent of children aged 6 to 14 (80,000 children) will participate in the program. The CBO concludes, however, that the costs will vary by state, and the actual costs will depend on the behavior of state agencies and families that receive welfare as well as the mix of existing child care programs.

PROVIDER SUBSIDIES: SUPPORT FOR CAREGIVERS

Provider (supply) subsidies offer financial resources to the individuals and organizations that provide care for children, rather than to consumers (parents). The goal of provider subsidies is to stimulate the supply of specific types of care or to control and improve the quality of the care offered. Provider subsidies, which have been funded through general tax revenues and tax expenditures, are generally more targeted than consumer subsidies. In particular, they have been an important source of child care support for children in low-income families and for meeting specific categorical needs of low-income parents. For example, Head Start addresses social and educational deficiencies among disadvantaged children, and the Child Care Food Program (CCFP) addresses health and nutrition concerns for children in low-income families. Provider subsidies are also used to increase the supply of care for children with disabilities, for school-based programs, and for employer-supported child care programs.

As shown in Table 7.1, subsidies for Head Start and the CCFP have increased during the past 10 years. Modest gains have also been shown for school-based and employer-based programs and programs for handicapped children. Funding has actually declined for more general care programs under the SSBG and employment- and training-related programs.

Social Services Block Grant Program

The SSBG program provides subsidies for programs serving low-income and troubled families. The federal government provides funds to the states in the form of block grants, which each state then allocates among its social service programs, including services to the elderly, child protective services, and foster care, as well as child care. States determine eligibility; family day care homes are, in most cases, not eligible for SSBG subsidies. In 1987 more than $2.7 billion was allocated to the states, and 45 states used a portion of their SSBG funds plus some of their own revenues to provide child care assistance (Blank et al., 1987).

Information on the allocation of SSBG funds to child care is generally lacking since states do not keep separate records on the federal and state allocations. A U.S. Department of Health and Human Services survey estimated the combined state and federal spending at $1.1 billion per year. Besharov and Tramontozzi (1988) estimated the annual federal cost of child care at $726 million or 27 percent of total SSBG spending. The U.S. Department of Labor (1988) estimated the expenditures at $660 million in 1988. Kahn and Kamerman (1987), however, show a decline in SSBG child care spending from $600 million in 1980 to $387 million in 1986, because of a one-fifth reduction in SSBG appropriations in 1987. Given the lack of federal or state data on SSBG spending, we are unable to resolve this difference of opinion concerning trends in child care expenditures; we therefore use an average of these estimates, $591 million, for accounting purposes. It is clear, however, that SSBG funding for child care has declined in real (inflation-adjusted) terms even under the most generous assumptions.

To gauge the benefit of the program it would be helpful to know how many children receive care that is subsidized by SSBG funds. However, there is no standardized federal reporting system: some states record the number of child care slots; others record the number of children served. Although it is impossible to estimate the number of children receiving SSBG-subsidized care, a 1981 U.S. Department of Health and Human Services survey found 11,000 centers and 29,000 homes funded in full or in part by SSBG (Stephan and Schillmoeller, 1987). In light of estimated decreases in SSBG during the 1980s, it is unlikely that as many programs are still funded to the extent that they were in 1981.

The traditional method of subsidizing child care is through purchase-of-service contracts: state or local governments contract with child care centers to provide services to children from low-income families. The contract usually specifies the number of spaces to be subsidized and the reimbursement rate. This system offers permanence to working clients with stable child care needs, but cannot respond to fluctuations in the demand for subsidized care. Spaces can be paid for without being used or long waiting lists for subsidized care can exist with no mechanism for expanding the pool of available care.

Child Care Food Program

The CCFP provides food subsidies for children in low-income families. The U.S. Department of Agriculture (USDA) distributes funds to provide nutritious meals to children enrolled in child care centers and family day care homes. Over 1 million economically disadvantaged children were served daily in 1986 (Stephan and Schillmoeller, 1987). In fiscal 1987, total program costs were approximately $550 million (unpublished USDA data); $250 million was distributed to child care centers, $225 million was distributed to family day care homes, and the remaining funds were used for administrative costs by the sponsors and for commodity costs. The estimated expenditure for 1988 is $580 million. According to the U.S. Department of Labor, an additional $4 million is provided by the Special Milk Program; however, the Congressional Budget Office has a substantially lower estimate for this related subsidy (in Besharov and Tramontozzi, 1988).

As we discussed in Chapter 6, child care centers can operate in the program either independently or under the auspices of a sponsoring organization, which accepts administrative and financial responsibility for the program; family day care homes must participate under a sponsoring organization. Tax-exempt organizations are eligible for the program as are those private for-profit centers that receive compensation under SSBG for at least 25 percent of the children in care. All programs receiving funds through the CCFP must be licensed or approved. There is no apparent pattern to the distribution of funds between centers and family day care homes. In some states (e.g., New York and Florida) substantially more monies are distributed to center-based programs; in other states (e.g., Minnesota and North Dakota) the lion's share of USDA funding is received by family day care homes.

Head Start

Head Start is a direct program subsidy addressing compensatory educational needs of children in families below the federal government's poverty guidelines. As discussed in Chapter 6, it was created to provide a quality early childhood education program to children in low-income families in order to help break the cycle of poverty. The program provides educational, social, medical, and nutritional services to preschool children in low-income families, usually between the ages of 3 and 5. Most programs operate part day, although some have been extended to full day. Head Start requires parental involvement and is not intended to meet the child care needs of working parents.

Although Head Start is a federally funded child development program, it is locally administered by education agencies, community action agencies, and public and private not-for-profit organizations. In recent years, funding for the program has increased modestly. In fiscal 1989 somewhat more than $1 billion was distributed directly to Head Start grantees, and the program served approximately 450,000 children; this number represented less than 20 percent of the total number of eligible children. Head Start funds are allocated to states on the basis of a formula that takes into account their fiscal 1981 allocations and the proportion of all poor children and of children in families receiving AFDC who are residing in each state. The funds are distributed in the form of competitive grants to local Head Start agencies, with local grantees providing an amount equal to 20 percent of the federal share.

In addition to the federal funds available to local programs to provide Head Start services, nine states have passed legislation providing funds for the expansion or enhancement of Head Start programs. Two states, Connecticut and Massachusetts, specify that these funds be used to increase staff salaries. In Massachusetts, Head Start programs were allocated $359.67 per child and strongly encouraged to use the funds to improve staff salaries.

To reinforce this intent, the state established suggested hourly minimums for many Head Start positions on the grant application (Goodman et al., 1988:104).

Children With Disabilities

Federal funds are available to support a variety of child care services for children with disabling conditions: the Education for the Handicapped Act (P.L. 94-142 and its amendment, P.L. 99-457) provides funds for the education of children with disabilities under the direction of the public schools; Chapter I of the Elementary and Secondary Education Act (P.L. 89-313) provides funds for the education of children with disabilities in state schools or institutions.

The 1986 amendments to the Education of the Handicapped Act (P.L. 99-457) included services to children under the age of 3 and was less specific in its definition of eligible handicapping conditions than the general act. Therefore, states must now determine the population to be served, the delivery system for screening and provision of services, and the mechanisms for coordination of services. The definition of disability directly affects services and costs (Graham and Scott, 1988). In some states there is growing pressure from advocacy groups to include children who are at risk of developmental delay and disability as well as those with physical and mental handicaps. During the 1985-1986 school year, over 4.32 million students, approximately 11 percent of the total public school population, received services under P.L. 94-142; during the 1986-1987 school year, 265,814 children aged 3 to 5 were served under its amendment (U.S. Department of Education, Office of Special Education and Rehabilitative Services, unpublished data).

As noted above, states also receive Chapter I funds (P.L. 89-313) for the education of institutionalized children with disabilities. These funds flow from the federal government to the states for services to children in state schools or institutions. In 1988, 29,693 children with disabilities under the age of 3 and 48,462 children aged 3 to 5 received services under this program. Besharov and Tramontozzi (1988) report that the U.S. Department of Education provided states with $178 million in 1987 through this program for 3- to 5-year-old children and estimate that $219 million was provided for 1988.

Both Chapter I and P.L. 99-457 are designed to provide education services to children with disabilities, but the legislation recognizes that some children require more than educational services to be successful in school. The original Education of the Handicapped Act (P.L. 94-142) provides funds for related services, such as transportation and other support services necessary to enable students to take advantage of the benefit from the educational program. The amendments (P.L. 99-457) also reflect concern about the poor coordination across programs serving very young children with disabilities (Hauser-Cram et al., 1988). To address this concern, a primary intent of the law is to make federal funds available for the establishment of a coordinated state-level service system. It also involves the coordination of services for individual families through the individualized family service plan (IFSP). An IFSP involves the identification and the inclusion of family strengths and needs (Hauser-Cram et al., 1988). This component of the law has potential implications for the provision of child care to young children with disabilities, in that parents may identify child care as a necessary service to complement early intervention. Carole Brown (Office of Special Education Programs, U.S. Department of Education, personal communication, Feb. 21, 1989) confirms that child care could fall within the framework of services under an IFSP, although a monograph describing IFSP best practices (Johnson and McGonigel, 1989) does not discuss child care extensively.

The U.S. Department of Education's acknowledgment of the needs for child care for children with disabilities is more directly expressed in a "priority" (#84024), which appeared in the *Federal Register* on January 26, 1989. This priority called for multidisciplinary training of child care personnel to meet the needs of children with disabilities in early education settings.

Federal legislation and administrative actions reflect an emphasis on placing children with disabilities in the least restrictive care and education settings possible and enhancing them to take advantage of free public education. Although most states have yet to implement the IFSP component of P.L. 99-457, it is possible that many will interpret the law to include child care services as a complement to early intervention programs.

Public Schools

As discussed in Chapter 6, public schools have a long history of involvement in early childhood education programs. They provided nursery school classes during the Great Depression (under the Work Programs Administration) and day care centers during World War II (under the Lanham Act). More recently, compensatory programs for children from low-income families, including Head Start, have operated in public schools. Since the mid-1970s, a growing number of states and local school systems have expanded their elementary schools to include prekindergarten programs for 3- and 4-year-olds, as well as before- and after-school programs for older children.

According to a recent survey by Marx and Seligson (1988), 23 states and the District of Columbia provide funds for pilot or statewide prekindergarten programs; half serve only 4-year-olds and half serve 3- to 5-year-olds. Two-thirds of all public prekindergarten programs are targeted to children from low-income families or those with other special needs that put them at risk of later academic failure. A majority are half-day programs; just over one-quarter are full-day programs. Levels of funding and the numbers of children served vary dramatically from state to state. In fiscal 88, for example, funding ranged from $197,000 in Alaska, serving 45 children, to $46.2 million in Texas, serving 54,493 children.

The number of before- and after-school programs operated in or by the public schools is unknown because most are operated by local schools or school systems and the data are not reported. However, 12 states legislated some form of state funding for school-age child care; one state (Ohio) restricts school-age child care funding to public schools; all other states permit the schools to contract with community organizations (Marx and Seligson, 1988). School-age child care programs may also use funds provided by the USDA for the school breakfast program to reimburse the cost of children's meals.

The federal government also provides funding to states for the planning, development, establishment, expansion, and improvement of school-age child care services. Under the Human Services Reauthorization Act, in 1986, a total of $4,785,000 was distributed to states and territories under this act. The federal share of the state grant ranged from $50,000 to $445,289 on the basis of state population. Sixty percent of these funds were to be used for school-age child care services. Thus, the federal share of funding for school-age child care was approximately $3 million. The act requires that the federal share of any project supported under this program shall not exceed 75 percent, thereby requiring a minimum 25 percent match from state or local funds.

Tax Incentives for Providers

There are several mechanisms by which providers indirectly receive support for child care services. Under Internal Revenue Code §502(C)(9), Voluntary Employees Beneficiary Associations (VEBAs) can provide for payment for life, health, and accident insurance or other benefits to employees and their dependents. VEBA funds can be used to offer grants to child care centers that serve employees' children and for which employees have financial responsibility for the child care program. Typically, unions have negotiated these programs for child care support (Burud et al., 1984; Friedman, 1985).

Employers can make contributions to qualified tax-exempt organizations, such as child care centers or information and referral agencies, and deduct them as charitable contributions. The contributions cannot be tied to reduced fees or reserved admissions for employee children. Employers can also deduct child care business expenses, if they are intended to reduce absenteeism and turnover. If an employer establishes a child care center, the capital costs are eligible for depreciation under the Accelerated Cost Recovery System, Internal Revenue Code §168. Under section 501(K) of the Internal Revenue Code, not-for-profit child care centers can receive deductible contributions, and they have been exempt from taxation since 1984. The U.S. Department of Labor (1988) estimates the annual federal revenue loss at approximately $3 million.

Several states provide other tax benefits to employers. In Connecticut, a 50 percent tax credit is offered to businesses that subsidize part or all of their employees' child care costs, and there is a tax credit up to 40 percent of the costs incurred by employers who provide financial or technical support to begin child care services for their employees. Rhode Island provides a tax credit of up to 30 percent for employers who provide property, in lieu of cash, for child care (Virginia Department for Children, 1988). Additional tax benefits to not-for-profit centers are also available in some states. In Arizona, for example, child care providers can take advantage of tax deductions for purchase, construction, renovation, or equipment costs over 5 years. In Connecticut, low-interest loans, payable over 5 years, are available to not-for-profit child care providers. Similarly, Massachusetts has a set-aside program to assist child care providers with extraordinary insurance and rent costs (Gnezda, 1987).

As discussed in Chapter 6, employer- and union-sponsored child care programs have been increasing during the past 10 years (Friedman, 1988; U.S. Department of Labor, 1988). However, there are no data on how much money employers currently spend on providing child care services, whether on site or in consortium centers or through contracted centers, union operated, or discounted slot programs. Nor are there data on how many employers receive tax benefits or the amount of these tax benefits. There is some sense, however, that the amount of employer tax benefits is small, and in fact the number of employers supporting the direct provision of child care is known to be small.

There are no studies on the relationship of these tax incentives to employers' decisions; Douglas Besharov (American Enterprise Institute for Policy Research, personal communication, 1989) suggests that although tax incentives may be helpful to a company or union, they appear to be a minor part of public policy discussion. Our review of the existing research on employer initiatives suggests that issues of cost and tax liability are generally secondary considerations in an employer's decision of whether to provide child care benefits. Of more immediate concern are the economic health of the company, the degree to which child care provision can solve management problems, the needs of the employee population, the availability of child care in the community, and the general attitude of corporate decision makers toward family issues in general, and child care in particular. Accordingly, it appears that tax credits or deductions may affect decisions about how to structure child care benefits only after employers have decided to provide some type of support.

SUBSIDIES TO STRENGTHEN THE INFRASTRUCTURE

Governments, employers, and unions have also created policies and programs to enhance and expand the existing paid child care system, particularly the development of resource and referral services. Smaller efforts have been made in the areas of caregiver training, regulations, and service coordination.

In addition to allocating funds for training Head Start personnel, the federal government provides $1.2 million through Title VI of the Human Services Reauthorization Act (P.L. 99-425) for the training and credentialing of approximately 2,700 early childhood caregivers through the Child Development Associate (CDA) program. Scholarships are available to CDA candidates who are employed in family day care homes or privately and publicly funded child care centers and have incomes below the poverty line (Whitebook et al., 1986). State and local governments and community organizations have also allocated funds for training caregivers but no data are available on expenditures for this purpose.

In addition to funds for training of caregivers, several state and local governments provide funds for salary initiatives. For example, Massachusetts provides supplemental funds to child care programs that contract with the state and Head Start programs, through a grant process. Using a different strategy, Minnesota links funds to salaries: to receive a higher rate of reimbursement, programs must show that they pay 110 percent of the county average rate for child care workers (Whitebook et al., 1986). To date, public monies to supplement caregiver salaries have only been available to caregivers in programs that provide child care services for children who receive public subsidies.

Recognition of the need for coordination among programs at the state and local levels is not new. For example, as discussed in Chapter 6, the USDA Child Care Food Program serves as a focal point for organizing independent family day care homes. In 1968 the U.S. Department of Health, Education, and Welfare (HEW) initiated the Community Coordinated Child Care (4-C) program. Some of these 4-C agencies still exist, notably in communities in Madison, Wisconsin, and in central Florida. Recently, several states have begun to organize statewide efforts to coordinate child care services. In March 1983, Thomas Kean, then governor of New

Jersey, created the Governor's Committee on Children's Services Planning. In a similar effort, Lamar Alexander, when governor of Tennessee, appointed the Governor's Task Force on Child Care to recommend ways to encourage the development of child care for children of working parents. Maryland and several other states have launched similar initiatives. Recommendations from these groups are now under consideration by the states.

Under the Human Services Reauthorization Act of 1984 (P.L. 98-558), the federal government provided grant funds for the planning, development, establishment, expansion, and improvement of dependent-care resource and referral services and school-age child care services. Of the total $4.8 million allocation, 40 percent was earmarked for independent resource and referral activities. Therefore, federal monies allocated to the states for resource and referral are estimated at $2 million for 1988. The act required that the federal share of any project not exceed 75 percent, thus requiring 25 percent in state or local funds. Few data are available on expenditures and effectiveness of the grant funds.

In 29 states, resource and referral agencies operate without state financing or coordination; 14 states and the District of Columbia assist in the funding of resource and referral agencies. This assistance may be in the form of start-up grants (Iowa), contracts with resource and referral agencies for services to state employees (Vermont), matching-fund grants (Oregon), or operating funds (the District of Columbia, Maine, Maryland, Minnesota, New Jersey, New Mexico, New York, Pennsylvania, and Rhode Island). Three states—California, Massachusetts, and Michigan—fund resource and referral services and provide funds for coordination among the referral services in the state (U.S. Department of Labor, 1988).

One of the fastest growing models of employer and union support for child care is resource and referral services. The Bureau of Labor Statistics (1988) reports that 5.1 percent of establishments provide this service. In a survey by the U.S. Department of Labor and the Service Employees International Union of a small sample of unions, 14 percent of public-sector unions and 32 percent of private-sector unions reported negotiating resource and referral services. According to Kahn and Kamerman (1987), such services are considered an inexpensive and simple yet helpful and highly visible way for employers and unions to address the child care needs of employers.

Galinsky (1988) makes an important distinction between resource and referral and information and referral programs. Resource and referral programs provide both counseling to help employees make child care decisions and money (or other resources) to help increase the quantity or quality of the child care available in the community. The California initiative (discussed in Chapter 6) is an example of several private corporations' joining with the state and federal governments to help raise both the quantity and the quality of care. The combined funding for this program is now approximately $2 million annually.

SUMMARY

The major federal policy response to the dramatically increasing number of young children with employed mothers in recent years has been a substantial increase in consumer subsidies, largely benefiting middle- and upper-income families, in the form of tax expenditures to offset the cost of employment-related paid child care (i.e., the dependent care tax credit and the dependent care assistance plans). The primary federal response to the needs of economically disadvantaged children over the same time period has been a much more modest increase in provider subsidies, especially through Head Start and the Child Care Food Program, both of which support children whether or not their mothers are employed. The most recent new federal initiative related to child care is the Family Support Act, which requires poor women with young children to participate in training or employment and provides support for child care.

States and localities, as well as businesses and unions, have also become more active in the child care arena in a variety of ways. However, their resource commitment remains quite small, both absolutely and relative to that of the federal government. Parental leave remains at the discretion of employers, whereas most states and localities are just beginning to address infrastructure needs and preschool compensatory care.

REFERENCES

Besharov, D., and P. Tramontozzi
    1988   *The Costs of Federal Child Care Assistance.* Washington, D.C.: American Enterprise Institute for Policy Research.
Blank, H., A. Wilkins, and M. Crawley
    1987   *State Child Care Fact Book 1987.* Washington, D.C.: Children's Defense Fund.
Bureau of Labor Statistics
    1986   *Employee Benefits in Medium and Large Firms 1985.* Bulletin 2262 (July). Washington, D.C.: U.S. Department of Labor.
    1988   BLS reports on employer child care practices. *News* (Jan. 15). Washington, D.C.: U.S. Department of Labor.
Bureau of National Affairs
    1983   *Policies on Leave From Work.* Washington, D.C.: Bureau of National Affairs.
    1984   *Employers and Child Care: Development of a New Employee Benefit.* Washington, D.C.: Bureau of National Affairs.
    1988   Employers' dependent care programs slanted to fund welfare reform. *Tax Management Weekly Report* (Nov. 14):1446-1447. Washington, D.C.: Bureau of National Affairs.
Burud, S.L., P. Aschbacher, and J. McCroskey
    1984   *Employer Supported Child Care: Investing in Human Resources.* Boston, Mass.: Auburn House.

Catalyst
   1986   *Report on a National Study of Parental Leaves.* New York: Catalyst.
Coelen, C., F. Glantz, and D. Calore
   1979   *Day Care Centers in the U.S.: A National Profile 1976-1977.* Cambridge, Mass.:
        Abt Associates.
Congressional Budget Office
   1989   *Work and Welfare: The Family Support Act of 1988.* Washington, D.C.: U.S.
        Government Printing Office.
Ellwood, D.
   1988   *Poor Support Poverty in the American Family.* New York: Basic Books.
Friedman, D.
   1985   *Corporate Financial Assistance for Child Care.* Research Bulletin No. 177. New
        York: The Conference Board.
   1988   Estimates from the Conference Board and other national monitors of employer
        supported child care. Unpublished memorandum. The Conference Board, New
        York.
Galinsky, E.
   1988   Child Care and Productivity. Paper prepared for the Child Care Action
        Campaign. Bank Street College of Education, New York.
Garfinkel, I., and S. McLanahan
   1986   *Single Mothers and Their Children: A New American Dilemma.* Washington,
        D.C.: The Urban Institute Press.
Gnezda, T.
   1987   State fiscal policies for child care and early childhood education. *State Legislature*
        Report, Vol. 12, No. 7. Denver, Colo.: National Conference of State Legisla-
        tures.
Goodman, I., J. Brady, and B. Duech
   1988   *A Committment to Quality: The Impact of State Supplemental Funds on Mas-*
        sachusetts Head Start. Newton, Mass.: Education Development Center, Inc.
Graham, M., and K. Scott
   1988   The Fiscal Impact of Definitions of High Risk for Education of Infants and
        Toddlers. Unpublished paper. University of Miami.
Grubb, N.
   1988   Choices for Children: Policy Options for State Provision of Early Childhood
        Programs. Paper prepared for the Education Commission of the States, Wash-
        ington, D.C.
Hauser-Cram, P., C.C. Upshur, M.W. Krauss, and J.P. Shonkoff
   1988   Implications of P.L. 99-457 for early intervention services for infants and
        toddlers with disabilities. *Social Policy Report of the Society for Research in Child*
        Development 3(3).
Hewlett, S., A. Ilchman, and J. Sweeney, eds.
   1986   *Family and Work. Bridging the Gap.* Cambridge, Mass.: Ballinger Publishing
        Company.
Institute for American Values
   1989   Everything money can buy: An economic analysis of child care. *Family Affairs*
        2(1, Spring).
Isaacs, J.
   1988   *Estimating the Costs of Transitional Child Care.* Paper presented at the Na-
        tional Association for Welfare Research and Statistics, 28th annual workshop,
        Baltimore, Md., July 28.
Issensee, L., and N. Campbell
   1987   *Dependent Care Tax Provisions in the States: An Opportunity for Reform.* Wash-
        ington, D.C.: National Women's Law Center.

Johnson, B.H., and M.J. McGonigel, eds.
　1989　*Guidelines and Recommended Practices for the Individualized Family Service Plan.* Washington, D.C.: Association for the Care of Children's Health.
Kahn, A.J., and S.B. Kamerman
　1987　*Child Care: Facing the Hard Choices.* Dover, Mass.: Auburn House.
Kamerman, S.B., and A.J. Kahn
　1983　*Maternity Policies and Working Women.* New York: Columbia University Press.
　1987　*The Unresponsive Workplace: Employers and a Changing Labor Force.* New York: Columbia University Press.
Kean, T.
　1988　The state's role in the implementation of infant care leave. Pp. 333-340 in E. Zigler and M. Frank, eds., *The National Parental Leave Crisis: Toward a National Policy.* New Haven, Conn.: Yale University Press.
Makuen, K.
　1988　Public servants, private parents: Parental leave policies in the public sector. Pp. 195-210 in E. Zigler and M. Frank, eds., *The Parental Leave Crisis: Toward a National Policy.* New Haven, Conn.: Yale University Press.
Marr, M.
　1988　*The Child Care Crisis: Are Tax Credits the Answer? An Analysis of Seven Child Care Tax Credit Bills.* Washington, D.C.: Citizens for Tax Justice.
Marx, F., and M. Seligson
　1988　*The Public School Early Childhood Study: The State Survey.* New York: Bank Street College of Education.
Maximus, Inc.
　1988　*An Evaluability Assessment of Child Care Options for Work–Welfare Programs.* Prepared for Assistant Secretary for Planning and Education, Office of Social Services Policy, U.S Department of Health and Human Services. Falls Church, Va.: Maximus.
Meyer, J.
　1989　*Mandated Benefits for Employees: A Policy Analyses.* Washington, D.C.: National Chamber Foundation.
Minnesota House of Representatives
　1987　*Maternity Leave Policies: A Research Report.* St. Paul: Minnesota House of Representatives Research Department.
Mitchell, A.
　1988　*The Public School Early Childhood Study: The District Survey.* New York: Bank Street College of Education.
National Association of Working Women
　1988　*New Work Force Policies and the Small Business Sector: Is Parental Leave Good for Small Business?* Cleveland, Ohio: National Association of Working Women.
National Federation of Independent Businesses
　1985　*Small Business Employee Benefits.* Washington, D.C.: National Federation of Independent Businesses.
Nelson, J.R., and W.E. Warring
　1982　The child care tax credit deduction. Pp. 206-265 in C.D. Hayes, ed., *Making Policies for Children: A Study of the Federal Process.* Committee on Child Development Research and Public Policy, Commission on Behavioral and Social Sciences and Education, National Research Council. Washington, D.C.: National Academy Press.
Piccirillo, M.
　1988　The legal background of parental leave policy and its implications. Pp. 293-314 in E. Zigler, ed., *The Parental Leave Crisis.* New Haven, Conn.: Yale University Press.

Pleck, J.
    1988   Fathers and infant care leave. Pp. 177-191 in E. Zigler and M. Frank, eds., *The Parental Leave Crisis: Toward a National Policy.* New Haven, Conn.: Yale University Press.

Robins, P.
    1988   Federal support for child care: Current policies and a proposed new system. *Focus* 11(2):1-9.

Shaine, F.
    1987   Statement on S. 249, the Parental and Medical Leave Act of 1987, before the Subcommittee on Children, Drugs, and Alcoholism of the Senate Subcommittee on Labor and Human Resources. U.S. Chamber of Commerce, Washington, D.C.

Spalter-Roth, R., and H. Hartmann
    1988   *Unnecessary Losses: Costs to Americans of the Lack of Family and Medical Leave.* Washington, D.C.: Institute for Women's Policy Research.

Stephan, S., and S. Schillmoeller
    1987   *Child Day Care: Selected Federal Programs.* Division of Education and Public Welfare, Congressional Research Service, Library of Congress. Washington, D.C.: U.S. Government Printing Office.

Trzcinski, E.
    1988a   Incidence and Determinants of Maternity Leave Coverage. Unpublished paper. Department of Consumer Economics and Housing, Cornell University.
    1988b   Wage and Employment Effects of Mandated Leave Policies. Unpublished paper. Department of Consumer Economics and Housing, Cornell University.

U.S. Chamber of Commerce
    1985   *Employee Benefits 1985.* Washington, D.C.: U.S. Chamber of Commerce.

U.S. Department of Labor
    1988   *Child Care: A Workforce Issue.* Report of the Secretary's Task Force. Washington, D.C.: U.S. Department of Labor.

Virginia Department for Children
    1988   *Report of the Governor's Corporate Advisory Commission on Employers' Initiatives for Child Day Care.* Richmond: Virginia Department for Children.

Whitebook, M., C. Pemberton, J. Lombardi, E. Galinsky, D. Bellam, and B. Fillinger
    1986   *Raising Salaries: Strategies That Work.* Berkeley, Calif.: The Child Care Employee Project.

The Wyatt Company
    1988   *A Survey of Health and Welfare Plans Covering Salaried Employees of U.S. Employers.* Washington, D.C.: The Wyatt Company.

Zigler, E., and M. Frank, eds.
    1988   *The Parental Leave Crisis: Toward a National Policy.* New Haven, Conn.: Yale University Press.

8

The Child Care Market and
Alternative Policies

In response to a dramatic increase in the demand for out-of-home child care services in the past decade and a half, a diverse array of organized programs and informal arrangements has emerged, and a variety of public policies have been implemented to improve the child care system and its efficiency. In previous chapters we described the delivery and regulation of services and the mix of public policies that support and supplement the child care "market." By market we refer to the interaction of demand for child care (the number of parents who purchase or want to purchase care) and the supply of child care (the amount of child care available); both are influenced by government intervention (policies) in the market. Although the concept of an economic market is foreign to most early childhood professionals, concern about the inadequacy of many existing programs and arrangements, about shortages of services for selected children and families, and about the costs of care—in short, issues of supply and demand—are familiar. In this chapter we review what is known about how well the child care market currently meets the needs of parents and children, and we explore several policy alternatives that have been proposed to improve it. Before we do so, however, some general observations are needed about the evidence that is available on these topics.

Understanding of the child care market is at an early stage. In some respects the market fails to meet several of the economic conditions that characterize an efficiently operating market: lack of information available to consumers (parents); high transaction costs associated with changing child care arrangements; and resistance to profit maximization by some providers (not raising prices as demand increases). In addition, there are the costs or benefits of a program that are not (or cannot be) reflected in the price paid by individual consumers, "externalities." For example, the benefit to society as a whole of better education for 4-year-olds is not accounted for in the price of a preschool enrichment program. It is also possible that there are several child care markets, rather than one. Distinguishing among various geographic markets or different product (program types) markets, or both, might explain some of the observed supply and demand phenomena, but such analyses have not been done. As a consequence, standard economic tools for measuring supply and demand and the related costs and benefits must be applied with caution.

Assessing current practices and considering alternatives is also complicated by the dynamic and diverse nature of the child care market. It is one in which providers are a mixture of private for-profit firms, national chains as well as independent operators; private not-for-profit organizations, such as neighborhood churches; public programs, such as Head Start; and individual family day care operators. It is a market in which funds come from the federal, state, and local governments, community groups, philanthropic organizations, employers, and parents. It in fact consists of many segmented, localized markets with little coordination and enormous turnover among providers and changing needs among consumers. It is also a rapidly expanding market and one in which many parents have difficulty obtaining adequate information about how to locate and arrange services that will meet their needs.

The difficulties of analyzing the child care market are further compounded by the relative inadequacy of data on the current supply of, and demand for, child care services and by the lack of sophisticated analyses of the likely consequences of alternative policies. In short, although understanding of the issues in this chapter has advanced substantially in recent years, it is still at a fairly rudimentary stage, due to the underdeveloped nature of the relevant analytic base. Nevertheless, a number of conclusions can be drawn by assembling the often fragmented, existing information, although many of these conclusions are highly qualified.

A common perception about paid child care—among parents, providers, and politicians—is that there is a major, perhaps even severe, shortage of supply. However, there are three dimensions, often not clearly distinguished, to this perceived shortage. One dimension relates to the sufficiency of the number of places for the children of parents who wish to purchase care of the prevailing quality at market-determined prices: we refer to this dimension as availability. This kind of shortage may arise because demand is temporarily increasing faster than supply or because particular kinds of care are not available in certain locations. It is most vividly evident in the long waiting lists of many programs, as well as the high ratios of applicants to places in many private nurseries and preschools. The second dimension is affordability: Are the available places offered at prices that parents who need or want out-of-home child care can afford to pay? The third dimension is quality: Regardless of the number of places or their affordability, what is the quality of care offered?

AVAILABILITY OF CHILD CARE

Although it might seem simple to count the number of child care places available, it is not. Many exist in unlicensed, unregulated centers and homes, and, as we discussed in Chapter 6, there is no national system to collect standardized data on the supply of child care services. It is also difficult to discuss availability without also considering the cost and quality of services.

What is known about the availability of child care? The predominant form of nonparental care for all children 12 years old and under remains relatives, the majority of whom are not paid or are paid very little for their services. However, reliance upon care by relatives has been rapidly diminishing in recent years. In 1965 nearly two-thirds of nonparental care for children aged 5 or younger was provided by relatives; in 1985 about one-half was provided by relatives (Bureau of the Census, 1987). Currently, the proportion is thought to be about 40 percent, and, as more and more women enter and remain in the labor force, the share is likely to decline even further. Nevertheless, relative care remains the least expensive form of nonparental care and an important resource for low-income families, who rely on immediate and extended-family members more than do middle-income families (McGroder, 1988). And indeed, one study suggests that on one isolated objective indicator of quality—caregiver/child ratio—care by relatives is superior, on average, to care by nonrelatives (Waite et al., 1988).

Only 18 percent of children under age 5 are in group or center care, most of which is licensed and, therefore, potentially countable from administrative data. About 32 percent are in family day care homes, approximately 60 to 90 percent of which are thought to be unregulated. And 11 percent of children under age 5 are cared for by nonrelatives in the child's own home. The supply of family day care and in-home babysitting is very difficult to measure. The existing data, however, suggest that the availability of nonrelative care differs according to children's ages and their special needs—particularly needs related to economic disadvantage and disabilities.

Infants and Toddlers

The most common (and some argue the preferred) form of nonrelative care for children under age 3 is a family day care home, in which a provider looks after other people's children in her own home. For employed mothers during 1984-1985, 23 percent of infants (ages birth to 12 months) and 27 percent of toddlers (ages 12 to 36 months) were cared for in the home of an unrelated caregiver (Bureau of the Census, 1987); only 14 percent of infants and 17 percent of toddlers were in child care centers. Center care for infants and toddlers is increasing but at what rate is not known. Thus, the predominant form of out-of-home care for infants and toddlers is family day care. Most family day care homes appear to operate in an underground market (see Chapter 6) in which prices are relatively low and caregivers do not pay taxes on their income from child care, although many parents who use this type of care currently receive a tax credit.

In the panel's 1988 survey, state licensing offices reported 198,257 licensed family day care homes. If 10 to 30 percent of homes are licensed, as many observers suggest, there may be as many as 1.2 million family day care homes in the United States. How does this presumed supply relate to the demand for places? Hofferth and Phillips (1987) estimate that the number of licensed homes increased by about one-third between 1977 and 1986. But during the same period mothers of infants and toddlers entered the labor force at a much faster pace. The percentage of mothers with children under age 3 who were employed or looking for work rose from 32.6 in 1975 to 52.7 in 1988, an almost 62 percent increase (Bureau of Labor Statistics, 1988). Moreover, the absolute number of young mothers rose considerably during this period, as the large baby-boom cohort reached the prime childbearing ages. Although each new family day care home presumably can care for more than one child, the increase in places in family day care homes does not appear to have matched the increase in the number of infants and toddlers of employed mothers.

Looked at another way, the *number* of young children with mothers in the labor force has increased dramatically. For example, the number of infants with mothers in the labor force nearly doubled from 977,000 in 1975 to 1,796,000 in 1985 (Hofferth and Phillips, 1987), and in March 1988 there were 3.1 million children under age 2 with mothers in the paid labor force (data from Current Population Survey). This increase in the number of employed mothers of infants and toddlers has also reduced the pool of potential providers of home care. Direct evidence of a shortage of infant care was provided by a recent survey of the child care market in three low-income urban areas, which found relatively little center-based care available to infants and no excess capacity of infant care either in family day care homes or in centers (Kisker et al., 1989). Staff in resource and referral agencies consistently report that the highest demand is for places for infants and toddlers and that requests are more difficult to fill for them than for older children (Patricia Siegal, California Child Care Resource Referral Network, personal communication, May 23, 1988). In a number of surveys, employed parents with infants have been more likely than parents of older children to report difficulties in finding their current arrangements (see Galinsky [1988] for a summary). According to Grubb (1988), several recent commission and task force reports in California suggest that availability is more of a problem for parents of infants than for parents of toddlers and preschoolers. Thus, although aggregate national data do not exist, other evidence suggests that, in general, the supply of child care places for infants and toddlers has failed to keep pace with the demand.

Preschoolers

The rate of increase in the number of preschool children (ages 3 to 5) with working mothers was smaller than that for younger children: from 3,872,000 in 1975 to 4,984,000 in 1985, a 28 percent increase (Bureau of Labor Statistics, 1988). Almost all 5-year-olds are enrolled in a school program, although fewer than half are in full-day programs (Kahn and Kamerman, 1987). Among 3- and 4-year-olds, the predominant form of nonrelative care is some type of group care, for example, nursery school, prekindergarten, or a child care center. The number of licensed child care centers alone almost doubled over a 12-year period: from approximately 34,000 in 1976 (Coelen et al., 1979) to 64,879 in 1988 (panel survey). Although all licensed centers are not operating at full capacity, the number of available licensed center care places increased from approximately 1 million to 2.1 million during that period (Haskins, 1988).

Of course, it is possible that the number of places for preschoolers still is inadequate, despite the rapid growth of centers and the existence of part-day programs and family day care homes. Not all licensed centers operate full-day or full-year programs. Evidence suggests that many children are on waiting lists for places at child care centers, but caution must be exercised in interpreting this finding as an indication that child care is unavailable. These queues might be for ones in desirable locations or for ones that provide special opportunities for parents and children, such as especially gifted teachers or cost subsidies. If so, queues would not necessarily indicate an absolute lack of availability. Also, waiting lists tend not to be routinely updated and therefore may contain names of children who have since been placed in other care.

A recent survey in three cities found that child care centers were operating at 92 percent of their capacity, but it also found significant (50 percent) unutilized capacity in family day care for preschool and school-age children (Kisker et al., 1989). An important question is whether the unutilized capacity is accessible to parents in need of care now (or in the future). If it is not accessible due to a lack of information or inconvenient location, the increased demand for care for preschoolers that will undoubtedly be prompted by implementation of the 1988 Family Support Act (FSA; see Chapter 6) could result in more obvious shortages.

Other indirect evidence suggests that availability is less of a problem for preschoolers than for toddlers and, especially, for infants. After a comprehensive examination of national data on the availability of child care, Kahn and Kamerman (1987:14) concluded:

> Parents continue to complain about shortages, and most requests for help in finding care are for this age group [infants and toddlers]. The supply of services for 3- to 5-year-olds appears to be quantitatively adequate. However, much of what is available is still only part-day, as parents seek full-day care and as many preschool programs, both full- and part-day, are more expensive than most parents can afford.

In sum, the evidence of a shortage of child care places at prevailing prices for preschoolers is currently not persuasive, although availability undoubtedly varies by geographic region.

School-Age Children

Family day care homes are the dominant form of paid care for older children of working mothers. It is used most often by mothers who work full time and primarily for children 6 to 8 years old (Cain and Hofferth, 1987). As detailed in Chapter 6, the number of before- and after-school programs is growing, both in public schools and in other community agencies and organizations, but the number of children who need such care appears to far exceed the available program places. Although it is very difficult to compare the supply and demand for school-age child care because of limited data, there is a serious concern about the large and growing number of children who are without adult supervision during nonschool hours.

The Bureau of the Census (1987) reports that approximately 2.1 million elementary school and junior high school students are latchkey children. The U.S. Department of Labor (1988) concludes that this may well be the largest shortage in child care, and Hofferth (1988:564) suggests that as the current group of preschool children ages, there may be "a growing population of school-aged children who are unsupervised when they are not in school." Although school-age children who go unsupervised during non-school hours are not a new phenomenon, their growing numbers coupled with increasing incidence of drug use, youth violence, and other problem behaviors have made the care for these children a special concern.

Children With Special Needs

Child care providers, teachers, social workers, special educators, parents, and policy makers all believe there is a shortage of child care services for children with special needs. Two types of special needs merit special attention: children from economically disadvantaged families and children with disabilities. Currently, there are no systematic data on the demand for or the supply of child care services for children with special needs; however, there are several indicators that a shortage exists.

Economically Disadvantaged Children

An estimated 25 percent of children under the age of 5 are living in poverty (Bureau of the Census, 1988). In terms of chid care and development, these children and their parents have special problems. As discussed in Chapters 3 and 4, poor children have been shown to benefit from compensatory education programs (such as Head Start, Chapter I school-based programs for 4-year-olds, and child care services funded by the Social Services Block Grant [SSBG] program) and from programs that address nutritional and health needs (e.g., Head Start immunizations and U.S. Department of Agriculture food and nutrition programs). As these programs suggest, children from economically disadvantaged families are the target of several public intervention programs (see Chapters 6 and 7). But many poor children are not served by these programs. Head Start, for example, serves fewer than 20 percent of the income-eligible population of 3- and 4-year olds despite increased funding since 1980. In 1981 it was estimated that SSBG programs served only 13 percent of the eligible children; since then the number of eligible children has grown, but funding has not (Reismon et al., 1988).

In one study, low-income women were more likely than others to report that they would work if affordable child care were available. The new welfare reform legislation acknowledges a shortage of child care for low-income families by specifically requiring that child care services be made available so that mothers with young children can participate in job training or seek employment. Implementation of the FSA may significantly increase the amount of care for economically disadvantaged children.

The parents of these children also have special needs, some of which are not addressed by the current programs. For example, Head Start helps poor parents develop parenting skills, but it is primarily a part-day child development program, and it does not provide child care for parents working full-time. Yet 22 percent of all children aged 3 to 5 who live in poverty have mothers who work full time (Bureau of the Census, 1988). Low-wage jobs, geographic location, irregular work schedules, and transportation needs constrain many low-income parents in finding child care.

Public child care funding for low-income families varies dramatically by state. California and Massachusetts have made major commitments to low-income child care, but other states have not. For example, Blank and colleagues (1987) found that half of all the counties in Kentucky provide no child care assistance for low-income families. In New York City, publicly funded child care is available for only 20 percent of the eligible children (Blank et al., 1987).

Although there has been rapid growth in for-profit child care, particularly by large corporate chains, few of these programs serve children in low-income families. Restrictions under the SSBG program make it difficult for these providers to cover their costs in many states, and therefore there is little economic incentive for new centers or family day care homes to open in rural areas or inner cities where there are large concentrations of low-wage jobs and poor families.

Hours of service may also be an important issue affecting the availability of care for children from low-income families. In a study of employed mothers with children under 6 who receive support from Aid to Families with Dependent Children (AFDC), Sonnenstein and Wolf (1988) found that one-third required care after 5:30 p.m. and one-fifth required care after 8:30 p.m; 70 percent of that care was provided by relatives. As noted in Chapter 6, it is not known if these women work late hours because that is when inexpensive or free child care is available or if these are the only work hours available and they must use relatives because other types of care are in short supply (at any price) during these hours.

Children With Disabilities

There are very few data on the availability of care for children with handicapping conditions. Under national criteria specified in the Education for the Handicapped Act (P.L. 94-142), it is estimated that 1 to 2 percent of all infants will be born with some disabling condition (Scott, 1988). Depending on the definition of disability and high risk, the numbers and costs of caring for those children vary tremendously. However, it appears that both the number of children and the need for out-of-home care has been increasing faster than the supply of such care. Public policies to deinstitutionalize children with disabilities and require that they be integrated into programs with the least restrictive environments have exacerbated the need for specialized programs and caregivers. There are more children being diagnosed with serious emotional problems, and advances in modern medicine have lowered the death rate of high-risk infants. As more of these children live longer at home, the diagnostic, therapeutic, and medical costs of their care have increased. These increased costs may in turn necessitate more mothers seeking employment.

It is not known whether parents of children with disabilities choose to provide full-time care themselves rather than seek employment and out-of-home care or whether adequate services are simply not available. Under amendments to the Education for the Handicapped Act (P.L. 99-457), decisions concerning whether or not to serve infants and toddlers are left to the discretion of the states. In Florida, for example, only a few districts serve 3- to 5-year-olds or those up to 2 years old; for the younger group, only visually impaired and hearing-impaired children are served. Scott (1988) concludes that, in Dade County, only 199 places are available annually for an estimated 265 to 530 handicapped infants and toddlers potentially in need of child care.

When services for children with disabilities are available, they are used. Head Start requires its local programs to reserve 10 percent of their places for children with disabilities, and approximately 65,000 children with professionally diagnosed handicaps are now served by Head Start. In a small exploratory study, Fink (1988) found that a lack of child care programs for school-age children with disabilities resulted in employment problems for parents, especially for single parents. Evidence suggests that there may be a shortage of care for disabled children and that this shortage may be greatest for infants and toddlers, school-age children, and children from low-income families.

In sum, for all children under age 6, the evidence suggests that, the younger the child, the more serious the availability problem. Finding a place seems to be most difficult for the parents of infants, somewhat less difficult for the parents of toddlers, and least difficult for parents of preschoolers. Finding places for school-age children and those with disabilities also appears to be difficult. All of these availability problems are compounded for children from economically disadvantaged families. If the places that are available are not affordable to most parents, they are not really available.

AFFORDABILITY OF CHILD CARE

Not all employed mothers pay cash for child care. In a sample of young employed parents using child care in 1985, 77 percent paid for care for their youngest child under 5; 57 percent paid for care for their youngest child over 5 (Hofferth, 1988). The U.S. Department of Labor (1988) estimates that families who do pay for services, spend more than $11 billion per year: approximately $8.6 billion by married couples with both parents working and $2.5 billion by single working mothers. There are two significant aspects of the affordability issue: the absolute amount spent for care and the proportion of total income spent for care.

Amount Spent

For families whose youngest child was under 5 and who paid for at least 30 hours of child care per week in 1985, the amount spent was approximately $35 per child per week (Hofferth, 1988). On an annualized basis, this totals $1,820, considerably less than the $3,000 estimate frequently cited (Clifford and Russell, 1989; Haskins, 1988). However, the $1,800 figure may be low for several reasons. It is an average that includes care that is less than a full day; it averages the costs of center care, family day care, and relative care; and it does not adjust for large regional variations. In addition, the population used in the survey is from the National Longitudinal Survey of Youth (NLSY): parents in this survey are generally younger—aged 20 to 27—than the majority of parents who purchase child care services. Older parents, who usually have higher incomes, typically spend more on care.

Analysis of data from the Survey of Income and Program Participation (SIPP) found that 27 percent of the women surveyed paid more than $50 per week per child (Bureau of the Census, 1987). Kisker and colleagues (1989) report the median total expenditure for those paying for care was $50 per week. These estimates reflect the amount parents report spending: they do not reflect the actual costs to the provider or the fees they charge, since many parents benefit from public subsidies that reduce the amount they pay for child care.

The differences in the amount paid for care reported in the NLSY are informative. In direct outlays, the least expensive type of care was that provided by relatives, about $30 per week; family day care homes and center or nursery care, about $37; and a babysitter in the home (the most expensive form of care), $42. On an hourly basis, relative care was also the least expensive, at about $1.14 per hour, and babysitter care was the most expensive at about $1.60 per hour. Family day care homes were $1.17 per hour, and center and nursery school care was about $1.40 per hour. For a 40-hour week, 52 weeks per year, the fees paid ranged from $2,280 for family care to $3,200 for babysitter care. Despite the increased use of out-of-home care, weekly expenditures for child care appear to have risen only modestly in recent years (Hofferth, 1987).

Not unexpectedly, Hofferth (1987) and Brush (1987) both found that the number of children in a family and the mother's employment status were the most significant predictors of how much parents paid for care. Mothers employed full time obviously paid more than mothers employed part time because they purchased more hours of care. In addition, mothers living in metropolitan areas, those with higher educations, those who are white, and those living in families with higher earnings were all likely to pay more money than others for child care.

Proportion of Income

Among all families paying for care for children under age 5, the cost averages about 10 percent of family income (Grubb, 1988; Hofferth, 1988). This represents a substantial expense, comparable to the share of income most families spend on food. Among low- and moderate-income families, however, the burden of child care expenses is much heavier. Data from the 1985 NLSY showed that child care expenses were 30 to 50 percent of the family incomes of those earning under $5,000 per year; 15 to 20 percent for those earning $5,000 to $9,999; 10 to 15 percent for those earning $10,000 to $14,999; 5 to 10 percent for those earning $15,000 to $49,999; and under 5 percent for those with incomes of more than $50,000 (Hofferth, 1988).

For a single parent who earns the minimum wage and pays a caregiver $30 per week for one child, the data suggest that that family is spending 22 percent of its gross income on child care. Hofferth (1988) finds that, overall, poor families paid an average of 23 percent of their incomes on child care; nonpoor families paid only 9 percent. Although low-income employed families do receive some subsidized care and although they tend to use the least expensive form of out-of-home care, their relative expenditures are vastly larger than those of higher income families.

The potential burden of out-of-home child care on low-income households is even greater when children are infants or if they have disabilities. One study has found that infant care costs run, on average, one-third higher than the costs of care for preschoolers (Grubb, 1988). Head Start estimates the additional cost of serving a child with disabilities (compared with a child without disabilities) at $1,000 per child per year (Brush, 1988). Additional staff (a major cost component) and services required for children with disabilities account for this difference.

Hofferth (1988) also found that single-parent families tend to pay a larger proportion of their incomes on child care than do two-parent families, in part because they have lower earnings and less flexibility to reduce their expenses—for example, by working different shifts. As indicated in Chapter 2, shift work is surprisingly common among two-parent, two-earner families (Presser, 1988). One study found that in one-third of all such families with children under 6 in which both parents worked full time, one parent worked other than a regular day shift (Presser and Cain, 1983).

Although out-of-home child care expenses absorb 20 percent or more of the gross income of working poor families who use it, these costs are not borne by a large proportion of all poor households, since the proportion of the poor who work full time all year and use out-of-home care is small. Paradoxically, this fact suggests that the burden of out-of-home care is even more important than the data suggest: it implies that child care costs may discourage work altogether for some parents.

In response to a hypothetical question about whether they would work if affordable child care were available, 26 percent of nonworking mothers with preschoolers said they would seek employment if child care were available at a "reasonable cost." This response was more prevalent among women from low-income families, unmarried women, black women, and women who had not finished high school (O'Connell and Rogers, 1983). Blau and Robins (1986) found that low-income women who faced higher child care costs were actually less likely to enter the work force than those who faced lower costs. Moreover, employed women were also more likely to leave paid employment if they faced higher child care costs than were those who had lower costs. This evidence suggests that the cost of care is a significant constraint on employment for some women, particularly for those with low incomes.

An important unresolved question is whether out-of-home child care costs are most appropriately considered in relation to total family income or to the wages (or potential wages) of the spouse earning less in a two-adult household. This conceptual issue is of particular importance when considering middle-income couples. Although they may spend up to 10 percent of their total income on child care, that amount typically represents 25 percent of the wife's income (or potential income) (Waite et al., 1988). If the prevailing view is that the costs of child care should be borne by women's earnings net of taxes, then out-of-home child care costs can be a disincentive to employment for many women in middle-income households as well as for those in low-income households.

Determining the "appropriate" share of a family's budget to be devoted to child care is not a scientific matter. It entails value judgments that only individual families can make in light of their needs and preferences and other budget constraints. Confronted with the same income and child care costs, one family might choose eagerly to make the expenditure to allow both parents' careers to progress, another family might bear the expense reluctantly out of real or perceived financial necessity, and another might happily or unhappily decide that one parent should withdraw from the labor force. But when the costs of child care and the average share of income actually going to child care are as substantial as they are for many low-income working families, there is no choice possible. Many people would consider this situation a serious problem—although just how serious depends on the strength of their views about the benefits of out-of-home child care and of working parent(s). Overall, we conclude that the lack of affordable child care is a major public concern for low- and even many moderate-income families. It is especially significant for single parents, for young families with infants, and for families with children with disabilities.

QUALITY OF CHILD CARE

Although employed parents pay a substantial proportion of their incomes for child care, it is not clear how many are purchasing services of adequate, let alone, high-quality, care. As Chapters 3 and 4 detailed, academic research and best professional practice provide the bases for establishing broad parameters of the quality of child care services. They suggest ranges for group size, staff/child ratios, and other characteristics of child care settings that constitute a minimum threshold for safe and developmentally sound care. In light of that knowledge our assessment raises important concerns regarding the quality of care many children are receiving.

As discussed in Chapter 6, the wages and benefits of child care workers are very low. The Child Care Staffing Study (Whitebook et al., 1989) estimates that full-time teachers and aides earn, on average, less than $10,000 annually. No current comparable figures exist for family day care providers, but the evidence suggests that their wages are even lower, although there may be some nonmonetary compensations, such as not paying taxes or caring for their own children at the same time. Fuchs (1988) found that child care workers earn only about two-thirds as much per hour as other women with comparable levels of education. And Hartmann and Pearce (1989) and Whitebook and colleagues (1989) found that workers with more education are not consistently paid higher wages than those with less education. Turnover among child care workers is extremely high. According to U.S. Department of Labor statistics, the annual turnover rate is 42 percent for workers in group programs and 59 percent for those who work in other people's homes (Eck, 1984). These rates are twice the average for all employed persons; they are comparable to the rates for gas station attendants. Consistency of care is an important component of quality (see Chapter 4). High staff turnover, undoubtedly fueled by low wages, makes it difficult to provide consistent and, therefore, adequate care.

Staff/child ratios are also important to quality, yet many states' regulations governing center care do not require staff/child ratios that reflect what scientific knowledge and best practice indicate is appropriate for infants and toddlers. Raising wages, especially for caregivers with more education, has been shown to increase the quality and stability of staff. But raising wages is expensive, since staff salaries constitute between 60 and 85 percent of the operating budgets of centers and nearly 90 percent of the budgets of family day care providers (Coelen et al., 1979; Fosburg, 1981; Lombardi, 1988).

The magnitude of the increases in cost necessary to improve the quality of out-of-home child care was best demonstrated by Clifford and Russell

(1989). These researchers estimated the cost per child of care in four hypothetical center care settings that offer full-day care and include infants. Model 1 was an "ideal" center that met the accreditation standards set by the National Association for the Education of Young Children (see Appendix B). Salaries were relatively high—$20,000 per year for teachers and $10,000 to $14,000 for assistant teachers—although still lower than the average salary of elementary school teachers (Grubb, 1988). Staff/child ratios were relatively low—for example, 1:4 for infants, 1:8 for 3-year-olds, and 1:12 for school-age children. Modest amounts were budgeted for staff development ($125 per staff member per year), parental involvement ($10 per child per year), and so forth. These costs are similar to those of a full-day Head Start program (Brush, 1988). Model 2 retained the higher standards and salaries for teachers, staff development, and parental involvement, but increased the staff/child ratios—for example, 1:6 for infants, 1:12 for 3-year-olds, and 1:20 for school-age children. Model 3 retained the staff/child ratios of Model 1, but decreased the funds for salaries ($12,000 per year for teachers and $8,320 to $10,000 for assistant teachers), staff development ($50 per staff member per year), and parental involvement ($5 per child per year). Model 4 included both the lower salaries of Model 3 and the higher staff/child ratios of Model 2.

Clifford and Russell (1989) maintain that Model 4 typifies existing programs. Their estimate of the cost per child per year for Model 4 is $2,937, an amount at the high end of the $1,800 to $3,000 average cost discussed above. Raising the standards for staff/child ratios but keeping salaries low—Model 3—raises the estimated cost by 27 percent, to $3,743 per child. Raising salaries but maintaining the higher staff/child ratios—Model 2—raises the cost relative to Model 4 by 37 percent, to $4,030 per child. The ideal center of Model 1 raises the cost by 79 percent, to $5,267 per child.

Even the highest standard (Model 1) pays teachers only $20,000 and allots just one staff member for every four infants. But raising all centers to this standard would require a massive increase in fees charged to parents, in government subsidies, or both. Even instituting the more modest improvements in quality of Models 2 and 3 would place the cost of child care beyond the reach of many more parents than are excluded from the market today unless large new subsidies were forthcoming. In family day care homes, increased wages would have an even greater affect since wages account for 90 percent of the cost of care.

Parents, Quality, and Costs

A major issue in the child care debate is who should determine whether a child's care is of adequate quality. If one wishes to subsidize child care expenses and believes that parents should determine the quality of care for their children, one strategy would be to provide subsidies to low- and moderate-income parents, to refrain from regulating the market, and to let parents make their own decisions about how much to pay and what level of quality to purchase. This strategy is consistent with the widely held value that it is parents' right and responsibility to determine what forms of child care and patterns of childrearing are best for their children. However, research provides some contraindications to this approach to public policy.

One recent study examined whether parents pay more for the characteristics of child care that are associated with higher quality—regulatable characteristics such as the caregiver/child ratio, group size, physical facilities, and education of the caregiver (Waite et al., 1988). Analyses of the 1985 NLSY data revealed that parents who purchased better quality care typically did not pay more than other parents. This finding can be interpreted to mean either that better quality care was no more expensive than lesser quality care or that parents did not value the characteristics of quality care as highly as other characteristics (such as location and hours of operation) and therefore were unwilling to pay for them. In fact, better quality care now appears to be subsidized in part by staff, who accept low wages, which in turn leads to high turnover. Part of the reason wages are low may be because parents, even upper income parents, value other factors, including costs, more than characteristics associated with quality in choosing child care arrangements. Studies of parents' search for child care show that surprisingly few parents visit more than one program before deciding where to enroll their children. In one study of parents using proprietary centers, 9 percent of the parents did not even visit the center in which they ultimately enrolled their children (Bradbard et al., 1983). Kisker and colleagues (1989) reported that in three cities only half of parents using out-of-home child care for their preschoolers visited more than one provider before making their selection. For many parents, the overriding considerations in choosing child care arrangements were convenient location, cost, and hours that matched the parents' work schedule. In a study of callers to a resource and referral service, however, 77 percent were found to have visited more than one setting (Bogat and Gensheimer, 1986). Powell and Eisenstadt (1980) found that the parents most interested in using resource and referral services are well-educated single parents, new their residential area and living in neighborhoods with relatively few contacts between neighbors. These parents rely on print as a source of information and tend to engage in a wider search than people who do not use resource and referral services.

These preliminary studies suggest that many parents may not be able to weigh considerations of program quality in comparison with considerations of cost, location, and hours. Furthermore, many parents are not well informed about how to identify high-quality child care and what to look for when visiting programs. Because of the relative newness and decentralized nature of the child care delivery system in the United States, it is often difficult for parents to obtain adequate information. Looking for out-of-home care is a new and unfamiliar task that may be difficult for many parents (Grubb, 1988). Accordingly, the expansion of services that provide better information to parents as well as to providers might improve the quality of care and the match between consumers and providers without significantly affecting affordability.

BENEFITS AND COSTS OF ALTERNATIVE POLICIES

This evaluation of the child care market suggests that the current mix of child care services does not adequately meet today's child care needs. For some children and families, services are not available at any cost; for others, the cost of available care is prohibitive; and for many, the quality of care is less than research suggests is needed to protect children's health and safety and foster their social and cognitive development. Although we have identified numerous local initiatives to begin to address these inadequacies, they are isolated and do not appear to be sufficient to meet identified needs. There is a need for a broad expansion of federal and state support and involvement.

The call for government action is not new, but since 1987 child care has received growing attention. Indeed, more than 100 bills were introduced in the 101st Congress in 1989; the Senate and House each passed a version of the Act for Better Child Care, but they failed to reconcile differences in conference. This movement has been echoed by numerous initiatives at the state and local level (Stephan and Schillmoeller, 1987). For policy makers, the challenge is to define socially desirable and politically feasible child care objectives and to help meet them with policies and programs that divide the costs and the benefits of child care policies in ways that are fair and efficient. In attempting to achieve each goal one must ask several questions: Who will benefit? How much will it cost? Who should pay? Is it the best way to achieve the benefit? Is the benefit worth the cost?

National Objectives and Alternative Policies

The first step in assessing the benefits and costs of alternative policies is to understand the relationship between stated objectives and alternative types of policies. The panel has identified the following range of objectives for child care policy, which affect the supply of and the demand for nonparental as well as parental care:

1. Quality: to improve the quality of out-of-home child care services;
2. Quantity: to increase the availability of child care services, especially care for infants, school-age children, and children with disabilities;
3. Specialized care: to increase the availability of high-quality compensatory care for children from economically disadvantaged and stressed families;
4. Costs: to increase the affordability of high-quality care for children from moderate- and low-income families;
5. Parental choice: to increase parents' choices about employment and the type of child care they use;
6. Parental labor force participation: to increase parents' labor force participation;
7. Labor force stress: to reduce the stress on parents participating in the paid labor force to attain or maintain their economic self-sufficiency.

These objectives are intended to improve the current environment for children and families. Some, however, may be mutually inconsistent, and to achieve all of them within a short time frame would be economically infeasible. Policy makers must make choices based on the costs and benefits of these alternatives.

As described in Chapter 7, there are three general types of policies to consider: support for consumers (parents), support for providers, and support for the infrastructure of the child care system. There are four potential funding mechanisms for this support: general revenues, earmarked revenues, tax expenditures (lost revenues), and mandated programs (which would result in reliance on private funding). There are many variations on these basic types of policies and funding mechanisms; we examine several selected combinations. The behavioral consequences of alternative policies are not well understood and are in need of further research. Evidence from the United States and several European countries, however, suggests that government policies in the child care area will have few undesirable effects, or unintended consequences in birth rates, fertility patterns, divorce rates, and labor force productivity (Bane and Jargowsky, 1988; Cherlin, 1988). Rather, the successful pursuit of policies to improve child care would have generally salutary consequences for children, their parents, and society as a whole.

Although the response to any specific policy cannot be predicted with certainty, responses that might be expected, based on economic models, enable us to make some general predictions about the benefits and the costs of various policy options (Connelly, 1988; Fuchs, 1988; Garfinkel, 1988). In a very simplified way, Table 8.1 presents the key types of policies and their expected effects. For example, the effect of a consumer subsidy, such as a child allowance on quality of out-of-home care is unclear. Parents might use the money to buy higher quality nonparental care. But if the allowance is used to enable parents to stay home or to buy more hours of care at the same quality level, then the policy does not help improve the quality of nonparental child care. In contrast, a provider subsidy for service delivery should help meet five of the objectives. It may limit parental choice, however, since it only benefits those who purchase nonparental care, and even for those parents it limits their choice of types of care.

The costs of selected policies are summarized in Table 8-2. Although limited by the amount of available research, the following discussion reviews the state of knowledge regarding likely benefits and costs of various policy changes and points out the areas of substantial uncertainty that must be considered in decision making.

Consumer Subsidies

Consumer subsidies provide resources to parents, increasing their flexibility in making decisions about whether to provide care themselves or purchase it in the market. Such subsidies may or may not be tied to earnings, employment, or actual use of paid child care. Consumer subsidies do not directly affect the supply or quality of child care. These subsidies assume that parents will make the best choice of care for their children and that the market will respond to changes in the demand for out-of-home care. We consider several different forms of consumer subsidies, the likely consumer and provider responses, and the related benefits and costs.

Child Allowances

Various forms of child allowances are the most generally supportive forms of family policy and are quite common in other Western industrialized countries. Under the most generous policies, financial resources are made available to all parents with children without regard to their income or employment-related child care expenses. The basic rationale for this approach is to support families' ability to rear children and to increase parental options with respect to child care, while remaining neutral with respect to mothers' employment and family structure, neither encouraging nor discouraging dual-earner, single-earner, two-parent, or single-parent family arrangements.

Such an allowance could be funded through general tax revenues. Fuchs (1988) estimates that providing all families an allowance of $2,000 per child under the age of 12 would cost about $83 billion annually. (In contrast, we have conservatively estimated the gross monetary costs of

TABLE 8-1 Child Care Policy Objectives, Selected Policy Alternatives, and Possible Effects

| | Public Policy Alternatives | | | | | | | |
| | Consumer Subsidies | | | Provider Subsidies for Direct Services | Infrastructure Subsidies for: | | | |
General Objectives	Child Allowances	Child Care Tax Credits	Parental Leave		Training and Wages	and Coordination	Planning Regulations and Standards	Resource and Referral Services
Improve the quality of out-of-home care	?	?	0	+	+	?	+	+
Increase the quantity of out-of-home care	?	+	-	+	+	+	-	+
Increase specialized care	?	?	?	+	+	+	-	+
Increase the affordability of out-of-home care	+	+	0	+	?	0	-	0
Increase parental choice	+	+	+	-	0	+	0	+
Increase labor force participation	0	+	#	+	+	0	0	+
Reduce labor force stress	+	0	+	+	0	+	?	+

Key:
+   The policy should help meet the goal.
-   The policy may hinder meeting the goal.
0   The policy should be neutral.
?   The effect of the policy is unclear.
The policy decreases labor force participation in the short run, increases it in the long run.

providing adequate care to all children under the age of 13 at $126 billion [see Chapter 7]—the result of providing $4,000 to families for every child aged newborn to 5 and $2,000 for every child aged 6 to 12.)[1] With such an allowance, parents could more easily afford to provide care themselves or to purchase care of adequate quality at prevailing market rates. The net cost to government of providing child allowances would actually be considerably less than the gross cost since it would presumably replace the current personal income tax exemption for children, as well as several current child care subsidies and general income support programs (e.g., AFDC, the dependent-care tax credit, and the earned income tax credit). Moreover, in most countries that have a child allowance, it is subject to income taxes and, therefore, families in the upper income brackets pay back a portion of the benefit. Just how much less the net cost would be is impossible to say, however, since it would depend on other policy changes. The overall result of a policy of child allowances would be a substantial redistribution of income from adults and families without children to those with children.

An alternative and less ambitious form of child allowances could be achieved by greater reliance on current tax expenditures, through increased personal income tax exemptions or refundable tax credits. The United States currently has a personal tax exemption for dependent children and a refundable tax credit for low-income families with earnings (the earned income tax credit). More general-income support for families with children could be achieved by raising the personal tax exemption for dependent children: this policy would benefit all families who pay significant income taxes, although larger and higher income families would benefit more than smaller and middle-income families. Converting the exemption to a flat credit would result in the same benefit to middle- and higher-income families with the same number of children. A 1986 study (Cherlin, 1988) recommended an increase in the deduction from $2,000 to $5,000. Espenshade and Minarik (1987) estimate that doubling the personal exemption for dependent children from $2,000 to $4,000 would cost about $19 billion per year. One criticism of higher tax exemptions and tax credits is that they provide little benefit to low-income families who have little or no income tax liability; the benefits disproportionately go to upper income families who may not need them as much. One way to change this effect is to make the tax credit refundable: If parents do not owe a tax equal to the amount of the credit, they would receive a check from the government for the amount of the credit. To reduce the costs of making the tax credit

---

[1] This is a conservative estimate because it does not take into account the higher costs of child care for children with special needs, which are difficult to quantify; those costs could potentially add tens of billions of dollars to the estimate.

TABLE 8-2 Estimated Costs of Proposed Policy Alternatives

Policy Alternatives	Annual Costs (billions)	Source
Consumer Subsidies		
Child allowance		
$4,000/child (0-5 yr)	$126.0[a]	Panel on Child Care
$2,000/child (6-13 yr)		Policy
$2,000/child (0-15 yr)	83.0[a]	Fuchs (1988)
$700/child (0-12 yr)	33.0	Barnes (1988)[b]
Doubled personal tax exemption	19.0	Espenshade and Minarik (1987)
Refundable child care tax credit	3.4	Barnes (1988)[b]
Cap on dependent care tax credit	-0.4	Sen. Orrin Hatch and Rep. Nancy Johnson (1988)[c]
Tax credit for low-income families	2.2	President Bush (1989)[c]
Unpaid 10-week parental leave	0.1	General Accounting Office (1988)
Fully paid 6-month parental leave	5.0	Frank (1988)
Provider Subsidies		
Universal child care	126.0[d]	Panel on Child Care Policy
Extending Head Start to full day, full year for existing clientele	2.3	Brush (1988)
Expanding current Head Start to serve all eligible 3- and 4-year-olds	5.7	Brush (1988) and Panel on Child Care Policy
Expanding Head Start to all eligible children, full day, full year	8.7	Brush (1988) and Panel on Child Care Policy
Educational services for 4-year-olds	1.0	Sen. Edward Kennedy (1988)[c]
Expanded services	2.5	Sens. Christopher Dodd and Orrin Hatch (1989)[c]
Infrastructure Subsidies	0.4	

[a]These are gross costs. The net costs would likely be considerably less since offsets would occur from elimination of personal income tax exemptions for children and other federal program costs.
[b]Robin Barnes, The Urban Institute, personal communication, Aug. 3, 1988.
[c]Proposed legislation.
[d]Would not be used by everyone, unless mandated like public schools; these are also gross costs.

refundable to low-income families, some observers have suggested that the tax credits be phased out at higher levels of family income (Robins, 1988).

The costs of a hypothetical refundable child allowance in the form of a $700 tax credit for all children under the age of 15 have been estimated by Robin Barnes (The Urban Institute, personal communication, Aug. 3, 1988): approximately 30 million families would receive an average of $1,100 each, for a total cost of $33 billion annually. Simultaneously eliminating the current personal exemption and the dependent care credit would restore $23 billion to the federal government, resulting in an overall net cost of $10 billion. Raising the level of the credit would obviously increase the cost substantially, but it could be phased out at higher income levels in order to reduce the cost.

A refundable tax credit could also be linked to employment and income, as is the current earned income tax credit. In his fiscal 1990 budget, President Bush proposed a $1,000 refundable per-child tax credit that would go to families with children under the age of 4 and annual earnings of between $8,000 and $20,000. At an estimated eventual annual cost of $2.2 billion, this credit would be refundable and available to all income-eligible families with children, regardless of whether one or both parents worked and regardless of the auspices of child care. This policy would be limited to low-income families, but it is neutral as to mothers' employment and form of child care. It is far less expensive than any policy providing support to all families regardless of income or employment, although, as many observers have noted, $1,000 does not go very far toward the purchase of high-quality child care in most localities. Elements of this approach were incorporated in the Senate and House versions of proposed child care legislation in the 101st Congress.

The benefits of a child allowance differ for different groups. For example, an allowance of $1,000 per child would bring little additional benefit to parents on welfare, because the allowance would tend to substitute for the current welfare benefit. Among working mothers, one would expect a slight decrease in employment, both in the number of mothers who work outside their homes and in the number of hours they work. Some mothers would choose to care for children themselves, thus decreasing slightly the need for nonparental or paid child care. Some employed parents might use the benefit to increase the quality of the child care they purchase. Allowances would clearly benefit single mothers who must work. Low-income families would benefit if the allowance is provided as a direct payment in addition to current welfare benefits or as a refundable tax credit. There is no guarantee, however, that any of the money would be used for children at all.

Clearly, child allowances and tax exemptions or credits that do not vary with parental income are expensive and only modestly redistribute income among income groups, although the redistributive effects depend on what they replace and how they are taxed. Overall, resources would be transferred from individuals and families without dependent children to those with children. Such a change may be responsive to a growing perception that children are an important national resource in which society as a whole should invest. But much of the benefit of tax exemptions or credits as they are currently structured accrues to middle- and upper income families. In a time of large budget deficits, policy makers as well as taxpayers must weigh the importance of a strong symbolic statement in support of all families with children against the needs of many low- and moderate-income families.

Policies that limit eligibility on the basis of income, however, have other drawbacks. Some observers believe that they perpetuate a stigma against support for children. Rather than a national policy in support of all children, beneficiaries are limited to those defined as economically disadvantaged, perhaps regardless of how high the eligibility limit is set. "Means testing" also introduces incentives and disincentives that influence employment behavior. Fuchs (1988:134) provides the following example:

> For instance, suppose a woman is eligible for a $4,000 allowance for her children if she makes only $10,000 per year, but the allowance falls to $2,000 if her income rises to $15,000 per year. Her effective tax on the extra $5,000 of earnings would be about 60 percent, because she loses $2,000 in benefits as well as paying about $1,000 in additional income tax and social security tax. This high marginal tax lowers her incentive to seek a better job or to work harder. Another disadvantage of varying the allowances inversely with income is that it distorts the pronatal effect toward low-income families.

Subsidy for Paid Child Care

The second major form of consumer subsidy is directly linked to nonparental child care expenses related to employment. As we have noted, the current dependent care tax credit subsidizes employed parents who purchase child care services: child care is regarded as a work expense, at least part of which is credited in calculating a family's income tax liability. This approach is a form of tax expenditure. Subsidies available to low-income families participating in AFDC or the Job Training Partnership Act (JTPA) program, which offer work-related income-disregard programs, operate in a similar way.

The current dependent care tax credit and income disregard programs and any expansion of these programs reduce the effective price of child care, thus benefiting employed parents with young children. Lower costs presumably would induce some parents to increase their use of nonparental care, that is, encourage mothers to work; others who are already employed may use the cost savings to purchase higher quality care. There is no direct link between employment-related tax credits and the quality of care, however, unless the availability of the credit is limited to child care services that meet specified standards.

Current tax credit benefits are distributed to an estimated 9 to 12 percent of working families who pay for child care and claim the credit to reduce their income tax liability. The costs are distributed across all other taxpayers. In other words, the estimated $300 to $700 average family benefit to those using the credit is paid for by an average "tax" of $40 to $80 on nonusers. On a much smaller scale, the redistribution of child care resources associated with the low-income disregard programs similarly involves transferring a small amount of resources from a large number of taxpayers to relatively few beneficiaries.

Policies that support increased parental employment entail a number of benefits that accrue to taxpayers in general: higher total income tax receipts; potentially enhanced economic growth due to greater stability in the work force arising from workers' use of more reliable (and generally more costly) child care; and lower income transfer costs due to the greater labor force participation of parents. In addition, there may be long-term secondary effects of higher work-related income of parents and more high-quality child care for children.

The 1988 Family Support Act reflects a growing public consensus that low-income mothers should increase their labor force participation. Yet it also acknowledges that this goal will not be attained unless child care is available and affordable. The work requirements of FSA are likely to increase the demand for out-of-home child care over the coming several years. However, current budget estimates of funds that will be allocated for child care are low. There is considerably less consensus, however, on the goal of maintaining or increasing labor force participation of all mothers, especially those in middle- and upper middle-income families. Critics of the current tax credit argue that it penalizes women who stay at home to care for their children. Several proposals have been put forward to extend the credit to parents who stay home, making it similar to a child allowance and neutral toward women's employment. Such a change would disproportionately benefit affluent families, since they are more likely to have a spouse at home who would receive this additional benefit (see Marr, 1988). However, it would also enable at least some women who are employed to decrease their hours of work or to leave the labor force altogether.

Critics also argue that tax credits unnecessarily benefit middle- and upper income families who have less need for support than low-income families. Other alternatives, what Marr (1988) calls "targeting" bills, attempt to reduce the tax credits for upper income families or increase the credits for low-income families. For example, one proposal would eliminate the current dependent care credit for those making more than $75,000. The congressional Joint Committee on Taxation estimates a savings of about $375 million a year—one-tenth of the cost of the current credit. This relatively small savings would be achieved by penalizing working women in families with two middle or high incomes. Many critics argue that if this change were implemented, a tax credit that was intended to enhance women's opportunities to seek employment outside their homes would become another antipoverty policy. Another proposal would make the current credit refundable up to $400 per child under 6 years of age and cap the refund at the level of the household's Social Security payroll tax liability. Such a policy would provide benefits to about 20 percent more households than benefit from the current dependent care tax credit, at a cost about 25 percent higher than the current credit.

Unlike child allowances, child care tax credits guarantee that the benefit is spent on (nonparental) child care. They also provide benefits to a wide range of working parents while supporting parental flexibility in the choice of care. They do not directly influence quality, however, and may present a cash flow problem for low-income families who must pay for care on a weekly basis but wait until the end of the tax year for reimbursement. A system of child allowances or refundable tax credits would more directly address the needs of low-income families. None of these forms of support, however, directly address the issue of quality. The amounts of the subsidies per family are modest in relation to the amounts families actually pay for child care and, therefore, they may have only marginal effects on the affordability of care for low-income families.

Parental Leave

A third form of consumer subsidy, intended to provide working parents with more choice and to reduce the stress of work-family conflicts, is parental leave. Proposed policies range from unpaid leave of a few weeks, which guarantees job security and extended medical coverage, to the generous paid leave policies characteristic of many European countries. Current proposals for unpaid parental leave mandate government policies, but the costs would be paid by employers and employees, not by taxpayers.

Arguments in support of parental leave policies relate to the developmental needs of children and parents, women's equity in the work force, and the labor force efficiency. Proponents argue that parental leave policies will result in better parenting and childrearing practices by giving parents more time to establish relationships with their infants and reducing the inevitable stress that accompanies combined work-family roles after the birth of a baby (Zigler and Frank, 1988). Parental leave policies increase parental choice about whether to work outside the home or to work at home caring for a young child.

Extended paid leaves are expected to increase the number of parents, primarily mothers of infants, who would temporarily leave their jobs and care for their children themselves, thus easing the demand for infant care services. Paid leave, however, could be expected to have a much stronger impact than unpaid leave on reducing the demand for infant care since unpaid leave is not a real option for many low- and moderate-income mothers or fathers. At the same time, paid leaves can be expected to promote equal opportunity for women workers by increasing their attachment to the labor force and their seniority in their jobs. These outcomes, in turn, would lead to greater promotion opportunities and higher relative expected wage rates (higher than if women left the work force completely, but lower than if they did not have or take any parental leave). Higher family income may have secondary effects on the type and quality of child care that parents purchase.

The primary beneficiaries of parental leave policies are working parents of very young children. Proposed benefits include extended job security, continued health insurance coverage, and, under some proposals, wage replacement income. Parents who use parental leave purchase less out-of-home child care during the period when they are on leave, which helps offset their wage loss. Job guarantees also prevent some women from having to participate in a welfare program. The parents who use and benefit from parental leave also pay some costs, however. They experience an immediate loss of income if leaves are unpaid or paid at an average rate that is lower than their employment earnings; they may also receive lower wage rates in the future because of less work experience. In other words, future earnings may be lower than if parents had not taken time off.

Unlike the other subsidies discussed so far, parental leave policies may affect the behavior of employers. Proponents of such policies argue that they promote greater attachment of workers to their employer and, thereby, increase the stability of the work force and may induce associated efficiencies in the workplace. Critics argue that such policies encourage an increase in the incidence of employee leaves, thereby imposing significant direct costs and productivity losses on employers because of the need to hire temporary workers. The net result, they argue, may be increased consumer costs, lower overall wages to compensate for higher nonwage labor costs, or discrimination against women of childbearing age.

Cost estimates for different types of parental leave vary enormously depending on the length of the leave, whether or not it is paid, and the number and type of benefits that are maintained during the leave time. It is very difficult to estimate the costs, because employers are already providing many types of leave (see Chapter 7) and because there are no reliable data on who would use various kinds of leave and how employers would compensate for the workers on leave. For the unpaid leave version of the proposed Family and Medical Leave Act, however, the General Accounting Office (GAO) used several national surveys and carried out its own survey of 80 firms in two metropolitan labor markets to estimate its costs and effects (General Accounting Office, 1987). The GAO estimated the cost to firms with 35 or more employees of a 10-week unpaid leave to care for a new baby to be $102 million annually. Approximately 931,000 parents would be covered. In recent testimony, GAO officials estimated a 30 percent increase in costs for health insurance, increased births, and expanded employment (General Accounting Office, 1989). They further found that employers were more likely to reallocate work than hire replacement workers for those on leave. In general, they did not conclude that reallocating or replacing workers would result in a significant loss of output or higher costs.

Frank (1988) provides rough estimates for a range of paid parental leave options. Based on labor force, age, and birthrate data, these estimates range (in 1983 dollars) from a low of $1.25 billion annually for 3 months' leave with 50 percent earnings replacement to slightly more than $5 billion for 6 months' leave with 100 percent earnings replacement. This estimate does not take into account what employers are currently providing, but few offer paid leave for any extended period of time. Spalter-Roth and Hartmann (1988) also point out that not having parental leave has a cost to women workers and to society. They also estimate an annual loss of $607 million in wages and time for women who leave the work force. They also estimate an additional $108 million cost to taxpayers in increased public assistance for women no longer able to support themselves, having quit their jobs to care for their infants.

Under current proposals for unpaid leave, the costs of continued health insurance benefits, administration, and the need to reallocate work or for temporary employees to fill vacancies are borne by the employer. Fuchs (1988), however, argues that "employer-provided benefits" is a misleading term, that the costs of proposals that rely solely on employer mandates are likely to result partly in higher prices for goods and services and partly in lower wages. They would have little effect on profits unless foreign competition prevented higher prices and resistance to wage reductions required increased investment. Because the utilization of infant child care services is not equal among workers across industries, the effects would be uneven. In apparel manufacturing, for example, mothers of young children constitute 15 percent of the work force, but in firms manufacturing durable goods they account for only 4 percent and in mining and construction less than 2 percent. The costs weigh more heavily on consumers of certain products and on employees in certain industries (Fuchs, 1988). In another approach, researchers at the Yale Bush Center (Zigler and Frank, 1988) recommend 3 months of paid leave at 75 percent of salary to be supported through an insurance fund with employee and employer contributions, similar to the New Jersey disability plan (see Chapter 7). Overall, it appears that the costs to employers of current unpaid leave proposals are modest. Expanding leave to cover small employers, longer leaves, or wage replacement, however, would necessitate considering various cost-sharing alternatives.

Provider Subsidies

Provider subsidies directly affect the ability of and the incentives for individuals to enter the child care business as well as the level, quality, and price of the services they offer. In contrast to consumer subsidies, which are directed primarily at increasing the affordability of child care and increasing parental choice, provider subsidies have more targeted objectives to increase the supply of care for special categories of children and families, and to improve the quality of available services. Head Start, for example, is designed primarily to help poor children prepare for school, and the Child Care Food Program is designed to promote better nutrition among poor children who are in child care. Provider subsidies direct resources to specified groups and increase public control over the characteristics of care that is offered, but they also limit parents' flexibility in choosing programs and arrangements.

Universal Child Care

Universal child care is the provider-subsidy equivalent of the full-scale child allowance. Child care would be available to every family, in a manner similar to the public school system, with some minimum level of quality guaranteed. Since high-quality child care costs, on average, between $3,000 and $5,000 per child, the gross cost of universal child care would be similar to a child allowance of the same amount available to all children regardless of income and employment status. However, unlike child allowances, not every family would make use of a universally available service. Many parents would continue to care for their own children or make private arrangements. In addition, the estimated gross costs would be reduced by savings from eliminating some current programs. The cost of providing universal child care could be met through sliding fees to parents and some combination of federal, state, and local funding.

A child allowance gives maximum support to parental choice, whereas universal child care limits choice and emphasizes quality, availability, and affordability. It would also encourage women's labor force participation as a means of economic self-sufficiency and reduce the stigma of programs for poor children. Such a policy would provide maximum support for worker stability and increase the available supply of labor for employers. Research suggests that comprehensive early childhood programs can have short-term as well as long-term benefits to children, families, and society (see Chapter 4). They can also be designed for facilities in neighborhoods where they are most needed.

Another alternative is to consider only school-age children. The problem of care for school-age children would be reduced if the school day were extended to more accurately match the typical work day and if vacation and summer holidays were similarly cut back; of course, teacher hours and salary costs would rise. As for universal child care proposals, the money would be used to provide care directly.

Services for Children in Low-Income Families

Several alternative policies have been proposed to improve services for children in low-income families. One option is to extend the current Head Start program to make it a full-day, full-year program. This would enable parents to work full time, if they don't already, or it would enable them to place their children in high-quality care throughout the day rather than having to coordinate arrangements that may differ in significant respects. Brush (1988) estimates that the added cost of extending Head Start to a full-day, full-year program would be 1.5 times the current expenditures or about $2.3 billion annually.

Another option is to make Head Start available to all income-eligible children. Currently, the program serves fewer than 20 percent of the income-eligible 3- and 4-year-olds. How many children would attend Head Start if it were universally available is not known, but there is considerable evidence that the current low participation rate reflects, in part, the fact that there are not enough spaces available to meet parental demand for the program. If Head Start were available to all income-eligible children, we estimate that it would cost $5.7 billion as a part-time program and $8.7 billion as a full-time program. There are estimates of how much this cost would be offset (e.g., by increased long-term work-force productivity, reduced welfare expenditures) for the parents of Head Start children. Such long-term effects are hard to assess, but for the Perry Preschool Project, begun in 1962, it is estimated that for every $5,800 spent on comprehensive child development services per child, there was a long-term savings of $28,000 (in constant 1981 dollars discounted at 3 percent annually) (Weikart, 1989). Whether or not these savings would be realized on a national scale is not known, but they give some indication of the long-term benefits of high-quality care for young children.

A variation of the proposal to expand Head Start is to expand an array of public prekindergarten programs for 4-year-olds. As discussed in Chapter 6, a number of states have launched such initiatives, and federal legislation to provide added subsidies is also pending. For example, one proposed federal bill would authorize $1 billion a year for a full-day school program, building on the Head Start and state compensatory education programs already in place. The program would be voluntary, with a funding formula based on the number of children in the state (or community) aged newborn to 5 years who live in families below the poverty line, the number who live in single-parent families, and the number in families with both parents in the labor force. This formula reflects a commitment to serve poor children from families with no employed parents as well as children from low-income working families. Similar specific programs could also be designed for school-age children and children with disabilities.

A third and more comprehensive approach was presented in a major bipartisan child care initiative—the Act for Better Child Care (ABC). Initially introduced in the 100th Congress, it would target approximately 75 percent of a $2.5 billion budget to subsidize child care programs for families at or below 115 percent of a state's median income. A 20 percent state match would be required. The legislation proposed a block grant approach, combined with income targeting and direct provider grants to increase the supply of child care. The bill also contained provisions for some consumer subsidies, such as sliding-fee scales and vouchers. Quality guidelines were mandated, and states were required to coordinate child care resources and services. Despite significant negotiation and compromise, the bill failed to pass in the first session of the 101st Congress; it is expected to be reconsidered in the second (1990) session.

We believe that provider subsidies for services to low-income families and other categories of children who are underserved in the current market would probably raise the quantity and overall quality of care. Parental choice, however, would be less than if the same sums were provided through direct consumer subsidies. Increased self-sufficiency through increased maternal employment should also result in reduced welfare costs, although gains would be small if proposed expenditures are small.

For all of the proposed provider subsidies, the most likely source of federal funding would be general revenues, with the financial burden spread across all taxpayers, although Watts and Donovan (1988) propose using projected surpluses from the Social Security trust fund. However, these funds are already being used to offset the general fund deficit, so that any use to pay for child care would be equivalent to using general revenues and would increase the current budget deficit. Direct services could also be funded through the public schools by using the local tax base, although it can be argued that federal funding is essential since fiscal capacity varies considerably across communities.

Infrastructure Subsidies

A third type of subsidy supports the infrastructure of the child care system. Such policies do not provide financial benefits directly to families, nor do they finance the direct provision of services to children. Rather, they address the more general questions of quality and efficiency through increased training and wages for caregivers, expanded planning and coordination, improved standards and regulations, and extended resource and referral services. Related infrastructure supports include liability insurance pools and provider networks. By themselves, such policies may be less expensive than consumer or provider subsidies. Many of the increased costs are borne by providers and consumers (unless other subsidies are also available). Since there is currently no federal child care policy, and most initiatives are undertaken at the state and local levels, there are no accurate data from which to project the costs of investments in the child care infrastructure. They would, however, directly affect the cost and quality tradeoffs discussed earlier: they may improve quality and efficiency, but increase costs and reduce availability if implemented in the absence of additional subsidies.

The primary goals of caregiver training and wage subsidies are to encourage individuals to become child care workers, to increase their skills, to increase their tenure, and, therefore, to improve the quality of child care that is provided in a variety of programs and settings. Although child care workers in centers generally have some formal child development training, a high proportion of workers in family day care homes have limited formal education and little or no formal child care training (Coelen et al., 1979; Fosburg, 1981; Kisker and Strain, 1988). Increasing the supply of trained providers is likely to increase the wages of child care workers and, hence, increase the cost and affordability of care.

Implementing a comprehensive policy for training child care workers would involve initial as well as recurring costs. There are a substantial number of current providers who would benefit from basic training in child care, as would new child care workers. A less intensive program of in-service training would benefit all workers in centers, schools, and family day care homes on an ongoing basis. Increased wages, however, are a significant and continuing cost (Clifford and Russell, 1989).

Only a few states have explored the possibility of providing subsidies directly earmarked to increase the wages of child care workers (see Chapter

7). Massachusetts, for example, allocated supplemental funds to Head Start programs for salary enhancement through a grant program. To reinforce the intent that supplemental funds be used to increase staff salaries, the state established suggested hourly minimum rates for several positions. Initial findings of a study of the impact of this allocation reports reduced staff turnover and an increased ability to recruit qualified staff (Goodman et al., 1988), but the full impact of wage subsidies on the quality, availability, and affordability of care is unknown. Increasing staff salaries through wage subsidies in one segment of the child care market is likely to create competition for qualified staff, which may result in higher wages and higher fees for parents in programs not receiving wage subsidies. Programs unable to charge higher fees and therefore to provide higher wages may have to hire less qualified staff.

The goal of subsidies for service planning and coordination is to improve the efficiency of the child care market. Planning and coordination efforts at the local and state levels focus on identifying needs and available program resources, coordinating programs, and allocating funding across myriad departments and jurisdictions. These planning efforts may bring together the public and private sectors in an effort to increase the supply of services, enhance the provision of resource and referral services, and more efficiently allocate funds (see Chapter 6).

Infrastructure support for the development of standards and the improvement and enforcement of regulations is intended to increase the quality of care children receive. As detailed in Chapters 3 and 4, many current state regulations fail to reflect what research and best professional practice suggest is necessary to protect children's health and safety and to enhance their social, emotional, and cognitive development. Efforts to establish federal child care regulations have a long and beleaguered history; efforts to encourage states to adopt more stringent regulations have been limited. Although there is convincing evidence that increasing the stringency of regulations and their enforcement improves the quality of care, there is widespread disagreement about whether national standards or regulations are feasible, whether the federal government can or should enforce child care regulations, how the states could be induced to adopt and implement more stringent regulations, and whether it is possible to effectively regulate family day care homes as well as child care centers.

If agreement could be reached on national standards of quality for child care and the federal government then endorsed such standards for states to use as the basis for their regulations, the likely effect would be to reduce poor-quality care by establishing a minimum threshold for services. It would also raise the costs of care. To encourage states to act, the federal government would have to link any existing or new child care subsidies to states' incorporation of the specified standards in their regulatory system.

However, as several observers have noted, unless sufficient public funds are available both to help providers meet new regulations and to assist low-income families in purchasing care, the unfortunate side effect of more stringent regulations is likely to be a reduced supply of affordable child care services.

Regulations that establish recommended levels for staff/child ratios, group size, and physical facilities could as much as double the current average costs of care and of caregiver training, putting them on a par with high-quality Head Start (Brush, 1988). More stringent regulations will tend to discourage unlicensed providers from entering the regulated market and might encourage some currently licensed providers to go underground. One analysis reported by the Heritage Foundation (1988) found that regulations in the proposed House version of the ABC bill in the 100th Congress would result in the closing of roughly 20 percent of current child care centers, primarily those in the private sector, and would replace them with publicly funded child care centers. An alternative interpretation, however, is that the centers would raise their fees rather than close. If increased costs are not offset by public subsidies, many parents would be unable or unwilling to pay the increased costs of purchasing care, thus reducing their flexibility of choice and, perhaps, leading them to place their children in lower quality care.

The administrative costs of regulations vary with the extent of enforcement activity. Critics of stronger regulations point to the difficulties of widely varying parental views about what constitutes quality care and the inadequacy of current enforcement efforts. They also note that it is extremely difficult to effectively enforce services provided in family day care homes. An alternative approach has been to link standards for quality to the provision of technical assistance, resource and referral services, and provider subsidies for family day care providers (e.g., the Child Care Food Program benefits and Work Incentive Program [WIN] child care subsidies). If the financial incentives are substantial enough, and technical support is available, there is evidence that providers are willing to comply with applicable standards, thereby improving the quality of the services they offer (see Chapter 6).

Regulations and standards are similar to parental leave in that they can be mandated but are not necessarily funded by the government. If national guidelines were mandated without funding, the costs of meeting them would be borne by providers, who would presumably pass them along to consumers. Enforcement costs, however, would be borne by the government, that is, taxpayers.

Resource and referral services can complement regulations and serve as an alternative mechanism to increase the quality of care by offering consumer education to parents and technical assistance and training to providers. Parents generally have limited knowledge of the child care options available to them, and they choose largely on the basis of convenience or recommendations from friends (Kisker and Strain, 1988; Liebowitz et al., 1988). Educating parents about the factors that affect quality and providing information on available programs will enhance their ability to make informed decisions to select high-quality programs. Some proponents of resource and referral services claim that they will encourage parents to become effective monitors and so fill the gap between appropriate standards and enforcement of regulations.

Resource and referral services can provide critically needed support and assistance to family day care providers, who tend to work in isolation, to lack efficient mechanisms for filling staff vacancies, and to have limited access to training and technical assistance (Kisker and Strain, 1988). The costs of establishing and maintaining resource and referral services are relatively low in comparison with the costs of other mechanisms to enhance the quality of care. In addition to improving the quality of care through consumer education and provider training and assistance, resource and referral services are a source of valuable information about the supply of and demand for services that is essential for state and local planning and coordination.

Although there are insufficient data to estimate the costs of specific programs, there are general estimates associated with various proposals to strengthen the child care infrastructure. For example, in the ABC proposal (cosponsored by Senators Christopher Dodd and Orrin Hatch in the 101st Congress), approximately 22 percent of the originally proposed $2.5 billion authorization was earmarked for investments in infrastructure, including state-level planning and coordination.

CONCLUSIONS

In the 1950s most child care was provided free and "off the books" by at-home mothers and relatives; since then it has increasingly been replaced by paid nonrelative care. During the 1950s and 1960s, a great deal was written about the economic value of the services that women were performing in the home. Now the great expense of replacing the quality and quantity of those services is becoming apparent. There is also increasing recognition that even in the 1950s child care was not free; it was paid for by women in lost wages and by society in lost tax revenues. There is now much greater public awareness and discussion of the current child care market and alternative public policy responses to the perceived child care problem.

Discussion about shortages must include three linked but distinct concerns: availability, affordability, and quality. The number of places available is probably of most serious concern for children aged 0-2, for children from low-income and, especially, single-parent families, and for children with disabilities. But availability alone is of little import unless the places available are affordable and of adequate quality. Most parents are paying a nontrivial proportion of their family income for care. But the burden is much heavier for low- and moderate-income parents, among whom the share of income for child care may approach the share of income for housing. And this burden is magnified for single parents, for parents of infants, and for parents of children with disabilities. Improving the quality of child care will inevitably raise the cost. Increasing wages to levels that would reduce the extremely high rate of staff turnover and implementing standards that would reduce the number of children per caregiver now allowed by some states would be very expensive. It is hard to see how low- and moderate-income families would be able to afford high-quality care without substantially more assistance from government or employers.

This evidence demonstrates the very difficult tradeoffs in the child care market, among availability, affordability, and quality. Improving staff/child ratios is expensive, and raising staff salaries is even more expensive. Yet current salary levels and staff/child ratios are generally not adequate for the kind of child care that research and best professional practice suggests is safe and developmentally sound. Thus, intervention in the market—such as stricter licensing and regulation—may be desirable from the standpoint of improving quality, but it would be likely to aggravate the problem of affordability, and it might reduce availability.

How should the United States find the optimal balance of cost and quality? One way is to ensure that parents have adequate resources, and allow each family to make its own decisions. Most American parents want to retain a high degree of independence from government in choosing employment and child care, and the panel agrees that parental choice should be a key feature of public policy. Current policies do in fact provide some subsidies for most families, and this approach could be expanded through tax credits and child allowances.

It is possible, however, that sometimes the choices parents make for the care of their children do not meet the criteria necessary to achieve a safe, healthy, and developmentally sound environment. For example, should parents have the choice of placing an infant in a child care center in which one worker cares for six or more infants at a time (as eleven states allow), even though it is known that such staff/child ratios are not good for children? The U.S. government already supports low-income families in improving the intellectual and social development of their children and strengthens parenting skills through programs such as Head Start. Indeed, one of the common political rationales for expanded child care programs is to improve the health and life chances of children at risk by building on the positive results of Head Start. The government also intervenes in family choices—to their and the larger society's benefit—through the public school system. It is not a large step to argue for more intervention in the child care market, at least on behalf of the youngest children, regardless of family income, with particular emphasis on those whose needs are greatest.

Because of the limited research available, this panel cannot fully explore the many policy alternatives available to address the child care needs we have identified. On the basis of our review of the available research and our evaluation of the current system and selected policy alternatives, however, we can make specific recommendations for research and policy.

REFERENCES

Bane, M.J., and P. Jargowsky
    1988   Links between government policy and family structure: What matters and what doesn't. In A. Cherlin, ed., *The Changing American Family and Public Policy*. Washington, D.C.: The Urban Institute Press.
Blank, H., A. Wilkins, and M. Crawley
    1987   *State Child Care Fact Book 1987*. Washington, D.C.: Children's Defense Fund.
Blau, D.M., and P.K. Robins
    1986   Fertility, Employment and Child Care Costs: A Dynamic Analysis. Paper presented at the annual meeting of the Population Association of America, San Francisco.
Bogat, G.A., and L. Gensheimer
    1986   Discrepancies between the attitudes and actions of parents choosing day care. *Child Care Quarterly* 15(3):159-169.
Bradbard, M., R. Endsley, and C. Readdick
    1983   How and why parents select profit-making day care programs: A study of two southeastern college communities. *Child Care Quarterly* 12(2):160-169.
Brush, L.
    1987   Usage of Different Kinds of Child Care: An Analysis of the SIPP Data Base. Paper prepared for the Social Services Policy Division, Planning and Evaluation, U.S. Department of Health and Human Services, Washington, D.C.
    1988   Projecting the Costs of Full Day Child Care from the Costs of Head Start. Paper prepared for the Panel on Child Care Policy, Committee on Child Development Research and Public Policy, Commission on Behavioral and Social Sciences and Education, National Research Council, Washington, D.C.
Bureau of the Census
    1987   *Who's Minding the Kids?* Current Population Reports, Series P-70, No. 9. Washington, D.C.: U.S. Department of Commerce.
    1988   *Poverty in the United States 1986*. Current Population Reports, Series P-60, No. 160. Washington, D.C.: U.S. Department of Commerce.
Bureau of Labor Statistics
    1988   Marital and Family Characteristics of the Labor Force: March. Unpublished data.
Cain, V., and S. Hofferth
    1987   Parental Choice of Self Care for School Age Children. Paper presented at annual meeting of the Population Association of America, Chicago.

Cherlin, A., ed.
1988   *The Changing American Family and Public Policy*. Washington, D.C.: The Urban Institute Press.
Clifford, R., and S. Russell
1989   Financing programs for preschool-aged children. *Theory into Practice*. 28(1, Winter):19-27.
Coelen, C., F. Glantz, and D. Calore
1979   *Day Care Centers in the U.S. A National Profile 1976-1977*. Cambridge, Mass.: Abt Associates.
Connelly, R.
1988   Utilizing Market Child Care: An Economic Framework for Considering the Policy Issues. Paper prepared for the Panel on Child Care Policy, Committee on Child Development Research and Public Policy, Commission on Behavioral and Social Sciences and Education, National Research Council, Washington, D.C. Department of Economics, University of Vermont.
Eck, A.
1984   New occupational separation data improve estimates of job replacement needs. *Monthly Labor Review* 107(3):3-10.
Espenshade, T., and J. Minarik
1987   Demographic implications of the 1986 U.S. tax reform. *Population and Development Review* 13:115-127.
Fink, D.
1988   A Quick Fight All the Way: A Report on the Need for Child Care Among Parents of School-Age Children with Handicapping Conditions. Working paper No. 178. Wellesley, Mass.: Wellesley College Center for Research on Women.
Fosburg, S.
1981   *Family Day Care in the United States. Summary of Findings*. Cambridge, Mass.: Abt Associates.
Frank, M.
1988   Costs, financing, and implementation mechanisms of parental leave policies. Pp. 315-325 in E. Zigler and M. Frank, eds., *The Parental Leave Crisis: Toward a National Policy*. New Haven, Conn.: Yale University Press.
Fuchs, V.
1988   *Women's Quest for Economic Equality*. Cambridge, Mass.: Harvard University Press.
Galinsky, E.
1988   The Impact of Child Care Problems on Parents on the Job and at Home. Paper presented at the Child Care Action Campaign Conference, Wingspread, Racine, Wisc. Bank Street College of Education, New York.
Garfinkel, I.
1988   The Potential of Child Care to Reduce Poverty and Welfare Dependence. Unpublished paper. Institute for Research on Poverty, University of Wisconsin.
General Accounting Office
1987   *Parental Leave: Estimated Costs of H.R. 925, The Family and Medical Leave Act of 1987*. Washington, D.C.: U.S. Government Printing Office.
1988   *Parental Leave: Estimated Cost of Revised Parental and Medical Leave Act*. Washington, D.C.: U.S. Government Printing Office.
1989   *GAO's Cost Estimate of the Family and Medical Leave Act of 1989 (H.R. 770)*. Washington D.C.: U.S. Government Printing Office.

Goodman, I., J. Brady, and B. Desch
   1988   *A Committment to Quality: The Impact of State Supplemental Funds on Massachusetts Head Start.* Newton, Mass.: Education Development Center, Inc.
Graham, M., and K. Scott
   1988   The Fiscal Impact of Definitions of High Risk for Education of Infants and Toddlers. Unpublished paper, University of Miami.
Grubb, W.N.
   1988   Choices for Children: Policy Options for State Provision of Early Childhood Programs. Unpublished paper. School of Education, University of California, Berkeley.
Hartmann, H., and D. Pearce
   1989   *High Skill and Low Pay. The Economics of Child Care Work.* Washington, D.C.: Institute for Women's Policy Research.
Haskins, R.
   1988   What day care crisis? *AEI Journal on Government and Society Regulation* 2:13-21.
Heritage Foundation
   1988   The "ABC" child care bill: An attempt to bureaucratize motherhood. *Issue Bulletin* No. 145, October 6. Washington, D.C.: Heritage Foundation.
Hofferth, S.
   1987   Child Care in the U.S. Statement before the Select Committee on Children, Youth, and Families, July 1. The Urban Institute, Washington, D.C.
   1988   The Current Child Care Debate in Context. Paper prepared for the 1987 annual meeting of the American Sociological Association (revised). The Urban Institute, Washington, D.C.
Hofferth, S., and D. Phillips
   1987   Child care in the United States, 1970-1995. *Journal of Marriage and the Family* 49(3):559-571.
Kahn, A., and S.B. Kamerman
   1987   *Child Care: Facing the Hard Choices.* Dover, Mass.: Auburn House.
Kisker, E., and M. Strain
   1988   Child Care Markets: A Brief Look at the Markets for Child Care in Camden and Newark, New Jersey. Notes for presentation at annual meeting of the Association for Public Policy Analysis and Management. Mathematica Policy Research, Inc., Princeton, N.J.
Kisker, E.E., R. Maynard, A. Gordon, and M. Shain
   1989   *The Child Care Challenge: What Parents Need and What Is Available in Three Metropolitan Areas.* Princeton, N.J.: Mathematica Policy Research.
Leibowitz, A., L. Waite, and C. Witsberger
   1988   Child care for preschoolers: Differences by child's age. *Demography* 25(2):205-220.
Lombardi, J.
   1988   Child Care Workers. The Hidden Subsidy in the Child Care Delivery System. Paper prepared for the Panel on Child Care Policy, Committee on Child Development Research and Public Policy, Commission on Behavioral and Social Sciences and Education, National Research Council, Washington, D.C. Child Care Employee Project, Alexandria, Va.
Marr, M.
   1988   *The Child Care Crisis: Are Tax Credits the Answer? An Analysis of Seven Child Care Tax Credit Bills.* Washington, D.C.: Citizens for Tax Justice.

McGroder, S.M.
    1988   A Synthesis of Research on Child Care Institution Patterns. Paper prepared for the Panel on Child Care Policy. Office of the Assistant Secretary for Planning and Evaluation, U.S. Department of Health and Human Services.

O'Connell, M., and C.C. Rogers
    1983   *Child Care Arrangements of Working Mothers: June 1982.* U.S. Bureau of the Census, Current Population Reports, Series P-23, No. 129. Washington, D.C.: U.S. Department of Commerce.

Powell, D., and J. Eisenstadt
    1980   *Finding Child Care: A Study of Parents' Search Processes.* Detroit, Mich.: The Merrill-Palmer Institute.

Presser, H.
    1988   Shift work and child care among dual earner American parents. *Journal of Marriage and the Family* 50:133-148.

Presser, H., and W. Baldwin
    1980   Child care use and constraints in the United States. In A. Horberg, ed., *Women and the World of Work.* New York: Plenum Press.

Presser, H.B., and V.S. Cain
    1983   Shift work among dual-earner couples with children. *Science* 219:876-879.

Reismon, B., A. Moore, and K. Fitzgerald
    1988   *Child Care: The Bottom Line—An Economic and Child Care Policy Paper.* New York: The Child Care Action Campaign.

Robins, P.
    1988   Federal support for child care: Current policies and a proposed new system. *Focus* 11(2):1-9.

Scott, K.G.
    1988   The Fiscal Impact of Definitions of High Risk for Education of Infants and Toddlers. Unpublished paper. University of Miami.

Sonnenstein, F.L., and D.A. Wolf
    1988   Caring for the Children of Welfare Mothers. Paper presented at the annual meeting of the Population Association of America, New Orleans, April 21-23.

Spalter-Roth, R., and H. Hartmann
    1988   *Unnecessary Losses: Costs to Americans of the Lack of Family and Medical Leave.* Washington, D.C.: Institute for Women's Policy Research.

Stephan, S., and S. Schillmoeller
    1987   *Child Day Care: Selected Federal Programs.* Congressional Research Service, Library of Congress, Division of Education and Public Welfare. Washington, D.C.: U.S. Government Printing Office.

U.S. Department of Labor
    1988   *Child Care: A Workforce Issue.* Report of the Secretary's Task Force. Washington, D.C.: U.S. Department of Labor.

Waite, L., A. Leibowitz, and C. Witsberger
    1988   What Parents Pay for: Child Care and Child Care Costs. Unpublished paper. Rand Corporation, Santa Monica, Calif.

Watts, H., and S. Donovan
    1988   What Can Child Care Do for Human Capital? Paper presented at the Child Care Action Campaign, Wingspread, Racine, Wisc. Department of Economics, Columbia University.

Weikart, D.P.
    1989   *Quality Preschool Programs: A Long-Term Social Investment.* Occasional Paper 5. New York: The Ford Foundation.

Whitebook, M., D. Phillips, and C. Howes
   1989   *Who Cares? Child Care Teachers and the Quality of Care in America.* Executive
           Summary, National Child Care Staffing Study. Oakland, Calif.: Child Care
           Employee Project.
Zigler, E., and M. Frank, eds.
   1988   *The Parental Leave Crisis: Toward a National Policy.* New Haven, Conn.: Yale
           University Press.

IV

Future Directions

9

Recommendations for
Data Collection and Research

The panel has reviewed a broad array of data sets, academic research studies, and program evaluations for their contribution to understanding issues related to child care policy. In previous chapters we have summarized what is known about the consequences of supplemental care for children's health and development, described existing child care services and related public policies and programs, and analyzed the adequacy of existing services, policies, and programs to meet current and increasing needs for out-of-home child care and the effects of alternative proposals to meet those needs. Although researchers have made significant advances in knowledge about child care in recent years, we have repeatedly noted that many questions remain unanswered, and those questions suggest priorities for future data collection and research. Many of the panel's recommendations reiterate and expand on the work of previous panels and study groups of the Committee on Child Development Research and Public Policy (see Committee on Child Development Research and Public Policy, 1981; Hayes, 1987; Hayes and Kamerman, 1983; and Kamerman and Hayes, 1982).

Essential to framing an agenda for research is an underlying concept of the possible applications of increased knowledge. What do concerned policy makers, program administrators, advocates, employers, and parents need to know? How would particular information make a difference for public or private efforts to develop responses to parents' growing needs for out-of-home child care? The relationship between empirical study, scientific theory, and policy and program development is interactive and continuously evolving. Advances in one domain inevitably influence new initiatives in others. Implicit in the research questions that have emerged in previous chapters is the need to link data collection, analyses of the developmental consequences of different forms of child care, and studies of program costs and effects to underlying theoretical constructs, for example, theories of child development, theories of social structure and adaptation, and theories of human ecology.

What is the meaning of mothers' employment and child care in the context of parents' and children's psychosocial, cognitive, and physical development? How do mothers' employment and child care relate to race, family structure, and socioeconomic status? What do they mean in different cultural communities and neighborhood environments? And what do they mean in terms of national productivity, public welfare, and public costs? In light of such questions, data needs can be specified, measures can be derived, hypotheses concerning the relationships among relevant variables can be tested, and programmatic approaches can be developed with some logical connection between often distinct and unrelated activities. Within this framework, the rest of this chapter presents the panel's recommendations for data collection, research on child care and child development, and policy and program analysis.

DATA COLLECTION

The panel recommends that data systems that monitor parents' employment and use of child care, as well as indicators of children's health and well-being, be maintained and strengthened. Such data are essential for understanding trends and correlates of employment, their effects on child and family well-being, the demand for and supply of child care services, and the availability and affordability of child care as a basis for policy and program development.

Data concerning levels and variations in parents' employment, income, family structure, and the availability, use, and costs of child care services of different types were the basis for much of the panel's deliberations. In addition, the panel relied on data concerning the health and well-being of children and their adaptations to the social and economic changes in U.S. society over the past decade and a half. Such data will continue to be essential for future research and analysis of child care issues. Relevant information is available from several sources, including large-scale surveys, federal and state administrative reporting systems, and service providers. Each of these sources has particular strengths and weaknesses, and individual data sets vary in their underlying purposes and special emphases as well as their specific characteristics (e.g., definitions, sampling, data collection intervals). Thus, the panel concludes that a multidimensional strategy for data collection is essential.

Several general issues are relevant to the collection of information in large-scale data sets that affect their usefulness in studies of child care.

First, in many cases the definitions of key concepts (such as types of child care programs or arrangements) are not uniform across data sets, making it difficult for researchers studying particular phenomena or relationships to use or compare information from different sources. Within individual data sets, standardized information is often unavailable in sufficient detail to support the desired analyses: for example, data on the age of children in licensed child care facilities; data on children's gender, race, and ethnicity; or data on parent's work patterns and sources of income.

Second, there are no national data on the supply of child care and early childhood education programs. Information concerning the availability of different types of child care programs and arrangements and their regulation and financing is not available from any central source. And although states collect some of these data, they are not centrally available even at the state level: for example, although state licensing agencies collect data on the number of licensed child care facilities and their capacities, they do not keep information on early childhood programs operated by schools or Head Start.

Third, data necessary to match supply of and demand for child care of different types, within a relevant range of costs and within and across relevant geographic units, is currently unavailable. Efforts to compare the demand for services to the available supply are stymied by the unavailability and inconsistency of data at the local, county, state, or national level.

Finally, some important information on employment, attitudes about work and child care, and indicators of child health and well-being are not collected on a routine basis. Consequently, researchers and policy analysts cannot track changes over time that may have significant implications for the development and implementation of policies and programs.

Our discussion of priorities for data collection is organized according to the types of relevant data sources: large-scale surveys, national and state reporting systems, and special surveys.

Large-Scale Surveys

The major large-scale surveys that provide cross-sectional information on parental employment and child care include general population surveys, surveys of income and program participation, and youth surveys, many of which have had long-standing federal support. The panel endorses the protection and maintenance of these data sets and highlights several specific ways in which their usefulness in studies of parental employment and child care could be enhanced.

General Population Surveys

General population surveys contain a broad array of descriptive information on characteristics of a population. Because they provide lengthy time series, they permit analyses of population trends, such as employment, over time. Because of their very large sample sizes, they support analyses of small population subgroups that are difficult to study using other data sources. Two of the most relevant U.S. general population surveys for the study of child care issues are the decennial census and the Current Population Survey (CPS).

The decennial census provides the largest sample and most complete information on general characteristics of the U.S. population of any available data source. In addition to identifying patterns of change in household and family composition, racial and ethnic composition, age composition, geographic distribution, and employment and personal income, it is invaluable for tracing trends and making estimates at the state and local levels. It is especially useful for analyses of small geographic areas, such as towns and neighborhoods, within larger metropolitan areas. Data on employment status, family structure, marital status, and fertility among small populations, such as small ethnic groups and recent immigrants, allow researchers to examine the trends and patterns of diverse population subgroups. Moreover, because of its broad coverage of the population, decennial censuses frequently provide the basis for sampling designs for other data collection efforts.

Unfortunately, however, census data are not detailed in many areas of interest to researchers studying child care. For example, they do not contain information about the type of child care arrangement that a family uses, the costs of care, or the hours care is provided. Nor do they contain separate information on the incomes of husbands and wives when both parents are earners. Although there is a great detail of resistance to further expansion of the census, these data would be extremely useful to child care researchers and policy analysts.

The CPS is the source of monthly estimates of employment and unemployment, including extensive detail on population characteristics. Through the regular addition of supplemental questions, the survey also provides both annual and one-time information on a broad spectrum of subjects, such as family and personal income, poverty, receipt of noncash transfers, annual work experience, school enrollment, and migration. Among the many supplements that have been included periodically on the CPS are questions concerning child care use and attitudes about work and child care. Information about these issues is related to age of child, family structure, and household income. However, these data only cover the child care arrangements for the youngest child under age 6 in a household. Therefore, the data provide a limited view of parents' use of multiple arrangements and especially the packaging of arrangements when their are several children in the family of different ages with different child care needs. In addition, information concerning school enrollment, employment, and child care patterns among very young parents who are not living on their own are not reported separately from those of the head of household. Therefore, it is difficult to determine the need for and the use of child care by this population subgroup. Such data would greatly facilitate analyses of public income transfers and child support to teenage mothers as well as their patterns of labor force participation and their use of child care outside the home.

Survey of Income and Program Participation

The Survey of Income and Program Participation (SIPP) is a major source of information on the demographic and economic circumstances of U.S. individuals and families. It covers a stratified sample of the U.S. civilian noninstitutionalized population. It is a particularly useful tool for understanding the effects of government transfer and service programs. SIPP gathers detailed data on earned, unearned, and asset income, and it measures monthly variations in contributing factors such as household structure, the determinants of program eligibility, and actual program participation. It is a continuous survey in which overlapping panels are added and existing panels are rotated out periodically. In addition to its fixed questions, covered in "topical modules," SIPP also contains variable "topical modules," one of which in 1984-1985 covered child care arrangements. These data have been extremely useful in examining parents' use of alternative child care arrangements as they relate to income and program participation, as well as other demographic factors. This special topical module should be continued in order to allow researchers, policy makers, and program managers to track the dynamics of social change and the effectiveness of public policies and programs designed to address the child care needs of working parents.

National Longitudinal Survey—Youth Cohort

The National Longitudinal Survey—Youth Cohort (NLSY) provides data on social, educational, occupational, and other aspects of the lives of adolescents and young adults. Because the NLSY collects detailed data on the youth experiences of males and females, it permits comparisons of patterns of family formation and parenting in conjunction with education and labor market experiences. A recent supplement to the NLSY, the Mother-Child Assessment, includes detailed information on the health and development of the children of young mothers in the NLSY. These home assessments of children's social, emotional, and cognitive development, as well as information on child care arrangements and other parenting supports and services, will greatly facilitate researchers' ability to link specific child development outcomes to those factors for a nationally representative sample of the U.S. population. We applaud plans to replicate the first wave of the Mother-Child Assessment, which will provide researchers and policy analysts with time patterns of family structure, income, parental employment, and child care arrangements as they relate to children's health and behavior.

National and State Reporting Systems

As we have noted, there are no national data sources on the overall supply of and demand for child care. The demand for services is generally inferred from national survey data. Data on supply are provided by state departments or agencies responsible for the regulation of child care programs and by child care resource and referral agencies. They are also available at the federal level for specific programs such as Head Start and the Child Care Food Program.

State regulatory agencies usually collect data on the programs they regulate, including licensed child care centers and family day care homes. They do not, however, collect data on unregulated facilities, which means that their estimates of the supply of child care are certainly less than the actual supply. For example, in many states, programs that operate only part day, those that are administered by the schools or as a part of the Head Start program, and those that are operated under the auspices of religious organizations are exempt from regulation and therefore not included in states' estimates. In addition, unlicensed family day care homes are not included in state reports of the supply of care.

State regulatory agencies usually can provide detailed information on regulatory requirements and enforcement and on the licensed capacity— distinct from the actual number of children being served—of centers and family day care homes. However, they usually do not collect information on the population served or on program characteristics, such as the profit status of the program or facility, or on financing or program fees. Therefore, it is impossible to determine the extent to which current licensed programs serve children of different ages, from families with different characteristics, and those with special needs. Moreover, it is difficult to trace the flow of public funding from the federal government, from states, and from local revenues to particular child care programs.

Local resource and referral agencies do collect more complete information on child care programs than do state agencies, including information on program characteristics (e.g., profit status, hours of operation, caretaker qualifications) and on the population served. Many resource and referral agencies also collect information on unlicensed and unregulated facilities in jurisdictions in which certain types of facilities and programs are exempt from state regulation or licensing. Because they attempt to match consumers and providers of care, they generally also have data on the demand for particular types of care. However, because resource and referral agencies may or may not be located in any community, their coverage is uneven. The information they collect may provide a relatively complete picture of the supply and demand in a particular community, but the data from all resource and referral agencies do not by any means add up to a complete national picture.

In addition to presenting an incomplete picture of the available programs and the children and families they serve, these three data sources—national and state reports and resource and referral agencies—suffer from noncomparability. For example, there is no common definition across states of what constitutes a child care center, a family day care home, or a group home. In addition, age categories of children specified in state regulations also vary: infants may be defined in one state as newborn to 12 months of age whereas in another they are children up to 22 months. In the absence of common terminology and definitions, it is difficult to accurately estimate the demand for and supply of licensed care (let alone unlicensed care) or to assess the factors that affect supply.

At the national level, uniform information from each Head Start grantee is reported to the Administration for Children, Youth, and Families (ACYF), which compiles it in a computerized data base that is updated annually. These data include a wide range of information on program characteristics and costs, as well as the characteristics of children who are enrolled. The data permit program comparisons by type of sponsoring agency and geographic region, as well as projections of costs and enrollments. Similarly, information collected by the local sponsoring agencies for the Child Care Food Program is reported to the U.S. Department of Agriculture, which compiles it in a computerized data base. Information from the food program is valuable because it presents a partial picture of family day care in addition to center care. Both Head Start and the Child Care Food Program data bases are extremely useful for program planning and evaluation purposes. Unfortunately, they are not matched with other comparable data sets that would facilitate analyses across programs and types of providers of regulated and unregulated care.

The panel concludes that there is a critical need for better and more systematic information on the supply of child care and early childhood education programs and on the characteristics of the children and families that are served by these programs. These data should include information on financing, costs of operation, and fee scales. They should be collected at the state level and reported and compiled at the federal level.

Special Surveys

In addition to data on the supply of child care and early childhood education programs that should be collected regularly at the state level and compiled at the national level, there is an urgent need for special surveys to provide current information on the demand for and supply of child care and the experiences of children in child care. Such data are needed as a basis for decisions by policy makers and program planners who are responsible for responding to changing conditions and needs. Information is also needed on families' child care arrangements, including preschool and before- and after-school programs; how child care affects work patterns and household responsibilities; and how parents make their choices of care for their children. Data on the demand for child care should be matched with information on the supply of programs and arrangements. Detailed information is needed about the national supply of child care options and how they are distributed among families in different social, economic, and cultural circumstances and among different regions of the country and community settings.

The panel applauds a joint initiative by the ACYF within the U.S. Department of Health and Human Services and the National Association for the Education of Young Children to undertake the National Child Care Survey. This survey of a nationally representative sample of 5,400 parents with children under the age of 13 will be conducted in early 1990. It will be complemented by a Profile of Child Care Settings Study, sponsored by the National Center for Education Statistics in the U.S. Department of Education, that will survey directors of child care centers, preschools, and licensed family day care providers. Although unlicensed providers will not be included, these two surveys, taken together, will provide the most comprehensive picture of child care supply and demand yet available.

RESEARCH ON CHILD CARE AND CHILD DEVELOPMENT

The panel recommends the continued support of a broad-based research program on the relationship between child care and child development to enhance understanding of the consequences of children's experience in out-of-home care for their social and cognitive development as well as for their physical health and safety. The results of such studies will have continuing value in the development of policies and programs related to children and families.

Over the past decade and a half, research has added significantly to the knowledge of trends, correlates, and consequences of children's experience in supplemental child care programs and arrangements. These research findings have provided an essential basis for the panel's work. Numerous studies have examined the effects of child care on children's growth and development. As child care research has become more theoretically and methodologically sophisticated, researchers have refined their questions and designs to explore the specific features and characteristics of child care programs and settings that affect psychosocial, physical, and cognitive development and the practices that can safeguard children's health and safety and promote positive outcomes. Despite advances in knowledge about child care and child development, many questions remain unanswered. In some cases, gaps reflect issues that have not been adequately studied because of methodological problems; in other cases, new issues have emerged from the findings to date.

In Chapters 3 through 5, we highlighted a variety of salient research issues and questions. They are presented here under five general headings: dimensions of child care quality; the relationship between child care quality and family characteristics; participation in child care during the first year of life; family day care, care by relatives, and use of multiple forms of care; and health in child care settings. Those chapters also pointed to a need for studies using new research strategies and focusing on emerging questions; these are summarized in the final part of this section.

Dimensions of Child Care Quality

As we discussed in Chapter 4, widespread reliance on global or summary measures of quality in child care research is not simply a function of convenience or simplicity. Rather, it reflects the fact that the individual components of quality have often been found to be intercorrelated. Several researchers have observed that "separation of . . . various dimensions of care quality may be difficult, if not impossible, as they seem to occur naturally in clusters" (Anderson et al., 1981:60) and that "good things" in child care seem to go together (McCartney et al., 1985).

Although research has documented the interrelatedness of structural features of child care that constitute quality, additional work is needed to clarify the implications of those links for child outcomes. If dimensions of quality tend to cluster, then policies or programs may well need to be designed around clusters of features as well as individual features. Such studies will need to consider the assumption that improvements in one quality feature may have implications for others. To give just one example, it may well be that improving staff/child ratios has a meaningful effect on children only if caregivers are well trained or only if groups are of limited size.

On the basis of our review of the existing literature, the panel concludes that studies of the interrelatedness of quality dimensions should include attention to several issues: (1) What is the nature of the correlation among quality variables? Do consistent clusters of variables emerge across studies of different types of child care programs and settings? (2) Does manipulation of one variable (or cluster of variables) have ramifications for others? (3) Does the relatedness of the quality dimensions depend on a program's level of funding or on the philosophy of the program director? For example, do more generously funded centers show higher quality across dimensions? Or does a director with more training or a particular philosophy struggle to maintain quality across dimensions?

Understanding of the dimensions of quality and their implications for development would be improved by the use of research designs involving random assignment or manipulation of quality dimensions. At present, there appear to be two virtually segregated approaches to the study of quality: intervention studies in high-risk populations, which rely heavily on random assignment and manipulation of program features, and naturalistic studies of community-based child care, which are vulnerable on the grounds that they do not isolate characteristics of the children who are served, the characteristics of the programs, or quality variables. A decade after the publication of the National Day Care Study, which set forth the methodological and conceptual basis for using randomization and manipulation in studies of quality dimensions in community-based child care, it is surprising that subsequent research on quality has not complemented the body of naturalistic studies with more experimental ones. Future research should examine the implications of (1) initiating change in particular quality features (e.g., providing training for caregivers, improving the staff/child ratios, disrupting or permitting continuity of peer groups) in a random subset of classrooms; and (2) randomly assigning children to child care settings that vary on key quality dimensions (or clusters). The absence of such approaches is particularly glaring in the study of caregiver training, when it is clearly possible that self-selection factors may influence levels of training and education.

The panel's review suggests that understanding of child care quality needs to be expanded to include dimensions that have not yet received a great deal of attention by researchers and to include consideration of acceptable and unacceptable ranges on the traditional quality variables. Features of quality that may well be linked to development but that have not been adequately studied include size of center (as opposed to size of group); affirmation of children's racial, ethnic, or cultural group identity; parental involvement; stability of the peer group; and, for family day care, the age mix within groups. There is a need for further study of child care curricula, of both the content and the process of learning. The guidelines for group sizes and staff/child ratios at different child ages proposed in professional standards should form the basis of research focusing on ranges on these variables and the extent to which they are associated with developmental outcomes.

Our review of the studies on quality also pointed to a lack of research assessing magnitude of effects: that is, what is the magnitude of improvement on child outcomes for measured improvements in quality? Such data would be extremely important in evaluating the benefits to children of selected quality improvements. Finally, our review points to the need for further study of the longer term implications for children's development of participation in child care of high versus low quality, of quality dimensions that may be uniquely important in the care of children with disabilities, and of variation in the quality of care according to auspice of care.

Links Between the Quality of Child Care and Family Characteristics

In Chapter 4 we summarized the growing body of evidence that the quality of child care and family characteristics are linked, and we noted the "double jeopardy" of children from stressed families being placed in poor-quality child care. Future studies should attempt to clarify the nature of the association between the quality of child care and family characteristics. As a first step, researchers need to ask whether existing studies have captured the full range of family variables that may be related to child care quality. In addition to socioeconomic variables, it now appears that family stress and social support are important. Other variables, such as marital discord, marital status, job characteristics of one or both parents, motivation for parenting, and the quality of parent-child interactions, also merit attention.

Future studies should examine the process by which parents in different circumstances choose child care. Do more stressed families allocate less time to search for child care? Are they less informed about alternative arrangements, about the significance of choosing high-quality care, or about what constitutes high quality? Are they equally knowledgeable but less able to persevere (given such factors as long waiting lists) in obtaining higher quality care? Or are they simply less able to afford care of higher quality?

In this regard, future studies should explore the everyday decision-making process regarding child care. How do parents weigh various dimensions of quality in judging and choosing child care settings for their children? What are the relevant folk beliefs or cultural norms that influence their decisions? For example, how important is it to parents that their children are cared for by kin or others from their own community or social group rather than by strangers? How important is it to them that child care includes moral training, that gender differences are managed in a particular way, or that a particular type of discipline is used? Indeed, parents may want quality arrangements for their children, but their concept of quality may be shaped more by culturally determined folk views of what is important for child development than by scientific research. Cultural beliefs and norms may or may not be related to race and ethnicity; therefore, they need to be studied and understood separately from racial and ethnic differences in child care. In the future, decisions concerning the organization of child care programs and the mix of public child care policies should be much more explicitly linked to the results of research on what parents prefer and what they are really choosing in child care.

The links between family characteristics and child care quality may provide an exemplar of what we have referred to as transactional processes in development: the mutual influence of the child (and family) on the child care environment and of the child care environment on the child (and family). A longitudinal study of this association could explore patterns of mutual influence over time. For example, while the level of family stress may influence choice of child care quality, the choice of child care may also subsequently influence stress within the family and affect the child's development. As noted in Chapter 3, studies are needed not only of the direct effects of child care on children, but also of the indirect effects on children of the influences of child care on parents.

Consistent with our suggestion concerning studies of the relatedness of dimensions of quality, knowledge of the family-quality association would be improved by studies that systematically alter quality variables in a randomly selected set of families that are similar on social, economic, and psychological factors.

Participation in Child Care During the First Year of Life

As discussed in Chapter 3, children who participate in child care for more than 20 hours a week during the first year of life show higher rates of behaviors that are categorized on a frequently used laboratory measure as "anxious avoidant" in their attachment to their mothers (see Chapter 3 for definition and discussion). Although there is agreement on this finding, its bases and its implications are still subjects of heated debate. This debate will only be resolved through rigorous examination of several sets of questions. First, are differences in security of attachment rooted in ongoing features of the mother-child relationship rather than in the timing and amount of exposure to child care? Are there relevant self-selection factors, that is, are mothers who resume employment (early and more than part-time) different from those who do not? Are there differences in their responsiveness to their infants that both antedate choice of care and underlie later differences in security of attachment or other indices of development?

Second, what are the implications for the development of infant-mother attachment (as well as for mothers' commitment to their infants) of child care experiences in the first year of life of families with employed mothers? For example, do variations in mothers' subjective sense of stress, of overload, or of role conflict influence the emergence of mutual attachment or the way in which the child's attachment influences other relationships and behavior?

Can anxious-avoidant attachment be modified? Would such factors as a daily visit to the child care setting (perhaps during lunch time) or counseling parents on structuring evening reunion time to maximize parent-infant interaction time affect the incidence of anxious-avoidant attachment in infants?

How does the assessment of security of attachment relate to other indices of socioemotional development and well-being? Is avoidant attachment in infants indeed associated with less optimal development both contemporaneously and over time? Or is it a reflection of adaptive behavior? Future research needs to move beyond this single measure of emotional functioning and question whether it predicts subsequent development equally well in children with markedly different early experiences. It would be particularly useful to include recognized clinical measures that help distinguish between variations in child functioning within the normal range and disturbed functioning (e.g., assertive versus hostile behavior). Studies need to question and examine the developmental implications of higher rates of anxious-avoidant attachment in infants in child care rather than assume they are negative.

To what extent do findings of anxious-avoidant attachment in infants with a history of full-time child care attendance in the first year reflect the use of poor-quality infant day care rather than the use of infant day care per se? Throughout the earlier chapters of this report, we have questioned whether infant care is of adequate quality given the developmental needs of these very young children and the cost of providing that care. Is there a difference in security of attachment to mothers among infants who have experienced high-quality infant care?

In short, scholars of child development agree on the observed behavior, but they disagree about what it means and whether it necessarily has negative implications for children's future development. Resolving this disagreement should be a high priority for further research because it has significant implications for the role of public policies in establishing standards for the quality of infant care and in the debate about parental leave.

Family Day Care, Care by Relatives, and
Use of Multiple Forms of Care

Most research on the effects of child care has studied children in center care. Yet most of the children in out-of-home care are in family day care. The disproportionate research focus on center care undoubtedly reflects the greater difficulty in finding and gaining research access to family day care homes, particularly those that are unlicensed and unregulated. As a result, less is known about the development of children in this type of child care setting and about the specific features of family day care that risk or support children's development.

Future child care research needs to examine systematically the experiences of children in family day care (especially unlicensed family day care). Studies should go beyond the variables included in studies of center care to examine features unique to family day care. For example, do older and younger children form stable friendships in family day care groups? Do children of certain ages experience problems in mixed-age groups, as some studies suggest? Is family day care associated with greater concordance of values and cultural practices from home to care setting than is the case with center care? If so, what are the implications for children's development?

We note that there are few curricula or other materials to guide family day care providers. Such materials should be developed, tested, and evaluated. Similarly, study is needed of the effective ways to provide training and technical assistance to family day care providers.

Because of the primary research focus on center care, there is also little knowledge about care by relatives. Although a substantial proportion of infants, toddlers, and preschoolers whose mothers are employed are cared for by relatives (including fathers), almost no research in the United States has included examination of the nature or effects of such care. Research on the effects of child care needs to include comparisons of care by relatives (including care by parents in split-shift arrangements) with other forms of care and with care by at-home mothers. Such studies could inform the continuing debate about the appropriateness and desirability of public policies that encourage or discourage care by relatives for children with employed mothers.

As discussed in Chapter 4, there is evidence that children experiencing a sequence of caregivers over time (unstable care) differ in their development from children experiencing more stable care. Do such developmental differences also exist for children who experience multiple caregiving arrangements in the course of a day or week? At present, data suggest that there are families for whom a single child care setting does not suffice. What are the implications for children when they are placed regularly in more than one care setting?

Health in Child Care Settings

Our review of existing research on illness and injury in child care also highlighted directions for future study. Of particular importance are two issues that have not been carefully studied: middle-ear infections among children in group care and their possible implications for language development, and rates and circumstances of injury, abuse, and neglect in child care settings. With regard to both issues, future studies should contrast the experiences of children in different types of care, including care by parents. In addition, with regard to both issues, researchers should employ prospective as well as retrospective research designs. Of significant concern is the possibility that reports by parents, teachers, and physicians of children's past injuries and illnesses are biased by their attitudes about mothers' employment and the lack of availability of emergency services and child care for sick children. Additional research is also needed to evaluate the health and safety implications of peer contacts of children diagnosed with HIV infection.

New Research Strategies and Issues

Throughout our review of the evidence there were indications that knowledge about child care and development would be strengthened by the use of particular research strategies and by addressing issues that have been neglected to date. For example, there is a need for long-term longitudinal research. Such research is needed both to understand the changing needs of children in child care with increasing age (using more developmental demarcations than that between infancy and the remaining preschool years) and to expand knowledge concerning the long-term implications of early child care experiences.

Research is needed on the implications of child care experiences for children of different racial, ethnic, or cultural backgrounds. For example, what are the implications for children in programs that stress multicultural sensitivity, both regarding their own group identity and their attitudes about children of other groups? Does such exposure have implications for later adaptation to school? Are there differences in development according to whether the child care environment is consonant or dissonant with the cultural orientation of the home?

Research is also needed on the implications of child care participation for children's mental health. For example, does child care result in early identification of family and child mental health problems? Is there follow-through on such problems? We pointed to evidence in Chapter 3 that maternal participation in Head Start has implications for mothers' mental health. Are there similar effects in other child care settings or only for those that stress parental involvement? What are the implications of child care participation for children from families stressed by divorce, mental illness of parents, or parental tendencies toward abuse or neglect? In general, what are the implications of participation in child care for the mental health of children as well as parents?

As noted above, there have been few studies that examine the perspectives of parents on child care choice and child care quality. User surveys are needed that ask on what bases parents choose child care. To what extent are parents aware of dimensions of quality? How important are particular dimensions of quality in the choice of a child care setting?

The generalizability of results could be improved through use of nationally representative data sets that include questions regarding child care. It would be valuable to incorporate within national surveys particular questions, using subsamples of the survey. For example, observational data are not readily obtainable in a large representative sample, but such data could be obtained for a small subsample with selected demographic characteristics.

Finally, studies that focus on school-age children are needed. The evidence regarding child care for school-age children is extremely limited. Studies should examine the extent of need for child care in this age range and the implications of self-care for school-age children. And studies should examine the dimensions of quality for child care for school-age children.

RECOMMENDATIONS FOR POLICY AND PROGRAM ANALYSES

The panel recommends that policy and program analyses to measure the costs, effects, and effectiveness of alternative proposals for the provision, financing, and regulation of child care be an essential component of child care research. Federal and state funding agencies, along with private foundations and corporations, should support policy analyses and program evaluations to inform public- and private-sector decision making.

Between the late 1970s, when the National Day Care Study and the National Day Care Home Study were completed, and the late 1980s there was a dearth of national policy studies of child care issues. Throughout this period mothers of very young children entered the labor force in unprecedented numbers, and the need for and supply of out-of-home child care programs and arrangements expanded significantly. Knowledge of the costs and effects of government policies, employer policies and practices, and community services and programs has not kept pace with social change. As a result, there is a sparse base of rigorous scientific knowledge to guide future policy and program development. Accordingly, the panel concludes that greater investment in evaluating the direct and indirect outcomes of existing and proposed policy and program initiatives is urgently needed.

Federal, state, and local government policies play an important role in influencing the nature and extent of social and economic change in society as well as the responses to them. Federal labor and wage policies affect employment and unemployment rates; income tax policies may affect decisions, especially married mothers' decisions, to work; income transfer policies may affect the employment decisions of single as well as married mothers by providing incentives and disincentives to work; and federal policies toward employers, through direct legislation, tax incentives, and regulation, influence the extent and ways in which employers structure their employee policies and benefits (Kamerman and Hayes, 1982).

The federal and state governments have been the major funders of publicly subsidized child care and related services since World War II. The federal government and some states provide direct subsidies through the dependent care tax credit to offset the child care expenses of employed parents. They supplement the funding available to schools for early childhood programs and before- and after-school programs through such means as direct grants for special programs and funding for compensatory education. All states regulate child care services, and some support the development and maintenance of resource and referral agencies and other supportive services. Both the federal and the state governments invest in the training and certification of child care providers, and the federal government also provides some subsidies to employers who develop child care policies and programs for their employees. As we have shown, however, patterns of government funding have shifted over the past decade. Direct support to providers for the provision of child care services, through programs such as the Social Services Block Grant, has declined as more public resources, especially at the federal level, have given way to consumer subsidies through the tax system.

Proponents of both approaches debate the effects of these changes on the quantity and quality of child care services. Except in the most general sense, there is little systematic knowledge of the consequences of these policies for children, parents, employers, or child care providers. For example, these patterns of support have clearly led to the development of a diverse array of child care programs and providers, but what is not known is the extent and ways in which they have altered the behavior of providers and consumers and whether they have improved or decreased the quality of care. As Congress and state legislatures now consider a range of proposals for new child care initiatives, there is little empirical basis for making choices. Accordingly, the panel concludes that studies should be launched to assess the effects of different types of government child care policies. In particular, the panel has identified several sets of questions that merit attention:

- What are the effects of regulation on the supply and mix of child care? Do more restrictive requirements discourage center care providers or family day care providers from entering the market? Do they affect the cost of providing care and the fees that are charged? Do they affect the location of child care facilities and, as a consequence, their accessibility to families living in different areas?

- What are the effects of alternative financing mechanisms on the supply and mix of child care and on the behavior of consumers? Do particular types of financing (e.g., direct provider subsidies, tax benefits to consumers, vouchers) foster or discourage the development of different types of programs provided under different institutional auspices? Do they cause parents to prefer or select one type of care or another?

- How does the growth of public school programs for 3- and 4-year-olds affect the supply and mix of child care services for children of these ages provided under other auspices? Has the growth of school-based programs diminished the demand for center-based or family day care? Has it affected the costs or quality of care provided under other auspices (e.g., through competition for a limited pool of qualified staff)?

- How have various employer policies and programs (e.g., on-site child care, flexible spending programs, child care subsidies, resource and referral services, parental leave) affected staff recruitment and retention in different industries and geographic regions? How has it affected employee productivity and firm profitability?

- What are the effects and effectiveness of policies and programs to improve the qualifications and wages of child care workers? Do investments in education and training lead to increases in the supply and quality of child care workers? What effects do wage subsidies have on the quality of staff and retention rates? What are the effects of alternative interventions to provide preservice and in-service training for family day care providers on the supply of home-based providers and on the quality of care they offer?

- To what extent and in what ways does the availability of affordable high-quality child care influence parents' decisions to work? To what extent and in what ways is the lack of adequate care a barrier to labor force entry or retention? Do the effects differ for mothers (and fathers) in different social, economic, and cultural circumstances, among those in different occupational categories, those of different ages, and those with different educational backgrounds?

The Family Support Act of 1988 offers an important opportunity to examine the direct and indirect effects of a fundamental shift in the U.S. approach to income security policy. The new act requires mothers of preschool-age children to work, attend school, or participate in an employment training program as a condition of receiving welfare support. The act requires the states to provide child care services for children of dependent mothers, and it further requires them to provide "transition" child care services for up to one year after mothers find jobs and become economically self-sufficient. As the states move to implement the provisions of the new law, analyses of the changes and families' adaptations to them could offer valuable insights into many child care issues. The findings from this (or other) natural experiment could provide the basis for formulating more refined hypotheses for subsequent demonstration and experimentation and for future policy.

This chapter outlines a broad agenda for future data collection and research aimed at filling the gaps in the current knowledge basis. Together, such work to expand the existing body of knowledge will significantly strengthen the basis upon which decisions concerning the care of the nation's children are made.

REFERENCES

Anderson, C., R. Nagle, W. Roberts, and J. Smith
   1981   Attachment to substitute caregivers as a function of center quality and caregiver involvement. *Child Development* 52:53-61.
Committee on Child Development Research and Public Policy
   1981   *Services for Children: An Agenda for Research.* Commission on Behavioral and Social Sciences and Education, National Research Council. Washington, D.C.: National Academy Press.
Hayes, C., ed.
   1987   *Risking the Future: Adolescent Sexuality, Pregnancy, and Childbearing.* Panel on Adolescent Pregnancy, Committee on Child Development Research and Public Policy, Commission on Behavioral and Social Sciences and Education, National Research Council. Washington, D.C.: National Academy Press.
Hayes, C., and S. Kamerman
   1983   *Children of Working Parents: Experiences and Outcomes.* Panel on Work, Family, and Community, Committee on Child Development Research and Public Policy, Commission on Behavioral and Social Sciences and Education, National Research Council. Washington, D.C.: National Academy Press.
Kamerman, S., and C. Hayes, eds.
   1982   *Families That Work: Children in a Changing World.* Panel on Work, Family, and Community, Committee on Child Development Research and Public Policy, Commission on Behavioral and Social Sciences and Education, National Research Council. Washington, D.C.: National Academy Press.
McCartney, K., S. Scarr, D. Phillips, and S. Grajek
   1985   Day care as intervention: Comparisons of varying quality programs. *Developmental Psychology* 6:247-260.

10

Conclusions and Recommendations for Policies and Programs

THE CHILD CARE ISSUE

Like many other individual scholars and commissions of experts who have considered child care in recent years, the Panel on Child Care Policy recognizes that the issues are complex and controversial. In the United States, as in other developed countries, the majority of children now have mothers who work outside their homes; as a result, child care now includes an important and growing component of services provided in an array of out-of-home settings. Child care is no longer simply a protective or remedial service for poor children or those from troubled families; it is an everyday arrangement for the majority of children in the United States.

With the dramatic increase in mothers' labor force entry, child care increasingly has become a large and diverse enterprise of public and private, for-profit and not-for-profit services. The revenues of this sector are currently about $16 billion per year and are expected to grow to $48 billion by 1995. As a result of these changes, the terms of the child care policy debate are very different in the late 1980s than they were just a generation ago.

It is now recognized that the significant economic costs of caring for children must be borne by parents, employers, governments, or some combination of these sources. Since a mother who cares for her own child is not paid a wage for doing so, her labor is not counted as productive economic activity in official government statistics. Nevertheless, child care provided in this traditional mode is not free. Families "pay" in the income lost from mothers' absences from the labor force, and the mothers "pay" in the

288

long-term cost of lost employment opportunities and perhaps permanently lower earning potential.

There is general agreement—regardless of one's political philosophy or ideological perspective—that mothers are in the labor force to stay and, thus, that children need to be well cared for in safe and healthy environments. But the agreement ends there. Debate over who should provide care, who should pay for it, and who should regulate it is bitterly waged in the Congress, in state legislatures, in city councils, and in corporate boardrooms. To what extent should parents bear the responsibility and the economic burden? What role should employers play? What role should the federal, state, and local governments play? Moreover, how does the generally recognized need for more and better child care relate to competing social policy priorities, including health care, education, child welfare, housing, and law enforcement?

What public policy ought to be, of course, depends on assessments of the needs and preferences of families in different social, economic, and cultural circumstances, as well as judgments about the costs and benefits of providing and financing child care and the individual and social costs of inadequate or insufficient care. It also depends on consideration of who reaps the benefits and who pays the costs. But rigorous cost-benefit analyses have not been undertaken both because there are insufficient data and because many of the costs and benefits may be inherently unquantifiable: for example, how does one measure the benefit to society of an improved future for a child?

Despite the limitations on economic analyses, research and best professional practice clearly show that the quality of care that children receive has significant implications for their social, emotional, and cognitive development, as well as for their physical health and safety. Yet the United States does not have public policies to ensure that employed parents are able to provide adequate and appropriate care for their children. In the absence of any overall policy, child care services have developed haphazardly: an uncoordinated patchwork of programs, supported by a variety of public and private funding sources, serving some but far from all of the families who need out-of-home care.

The absence of national policies is sometimes linked to the limited knowledge about the costs, effects, and feasibility of alternative policies and programs. Although the relevant body of empirical research has grown over the past decade and a half, knowledge of the effects and effectiveness of formal and informal, public- and private-sector responses to the child care needs of working families has not kept pace with social change. Scientists have learned a great deal about the characteristics of childrearing environments and caregiver interactions that foster healthy development, but there is insufficient evidence to predict the magnitude of effects of alternative policy and program proposals on children's development.

In the previous chapter we made a number of recommendations for future data collection and research aimed at expanding the body of empirical evidence to inform child care policy. We agree with scholars who assert that much more should be known about this and other difficult social policy issues. However, building the knowledge base will take time, and the policy process—and the nation's children—will not wait for scientists to produce complete and flawless data. Policy makers at all levels of government, as well as decision makers in the private sector, face difficult choices about how best to support the health and development of the nation's children and how to enhance the productivity of today's and tomorrow's work force. Accordingly, it is critically important to draw upon existing information, while acknowledging its shortcomings, to inform today's policy and program debates.

FINDINGS AND CONCLUSIONS

1. Existing child care services in the United States are inadequate to meet current and likely future needs of children, parents, and society as a whole. For some families, child care services are simply unavailable; for many others, care may be available, but it is unaffordable or fails to meet basic standards of quality. The general accessibility of high-quality, affordable child care has immediate and long-term implications for the health and well-being of children, parents, and society as a whole. Developmentally appropriate care, provided in safe and healthy environments, has been shown to enhance the well-being of young children. It enables parents who need or want to work outside the home to do so, secure in the knowledge that their children are being well provided for. It can contribute to the economic status of families and enhance parents' own personal and career development. And since today's children are tomorrow's adult citizens and workers, their proper care and nurturance will pay enormous dividends to society as a whole.

2. Of greatest concern is the large number of children who are presently cared for in settings that do not protect their health and safety and do not provide appropriate developmental stimulation. Poor-quality care, more than any single type of program or arrangement, threatens children's development, especially children from poor and minority families. Quality varies within and across programs and arrangements provided under different institutional auspices. High-quality and low-quality care can be found among all types of services, whether they are provided in the child's home or outside it, in schools, child care centers, or family day care homes, in programs operated for profit or those operated not for profit.

3. Irrespective of family income, child care has become a necessity for the majority of American families. Yet specific gaps in current programs and arrangements mean that many children and families lack access to services. Families with infants and toddlers, those with children with disabilities, those with mildly or chronically ill children, those with school-age children, and those in which parents work nontraditional schedules often have particular difficulty arranging appropriate child care services.

4. Arranging quality child care can be difficult, stressful, and time consuming for all families. However, the problems are inevitably compounded for low-income families who lack time, information, and economic resources. For these families, the choices are often more limited, and the consequences of inadequate care are likely to be more severe. Therefore, in addressing specific child care needs, public policies should give priority to those who are economically disadvantaged.

5. The most striking characteristic of existing child care services is their diversity. The current system is an amalgam of providers, programs, and institutional auspices that have little interconnectedness and do not share a sense of common purpose or direction. This diversity is at once a source of strength and a challenge to the development of a more coherent system that meets the needs of all children and all families. On the positive side, the diversity means that parents seeking child care outside their homes have a range of programs and arrangements from which to choose. On the negative side, the diversity means that the costs, availability, and quality of care vary substantially. Preserving parents' choices in the care and rearing of their children is essential; however, it has to be balanced against the need to plan and coordinate services in a way that ensures their quality and accessibility to all families who need them.

6. There is no single policy or program that can address the child care needs of all families and children. The nation will need a comprehensive array of coordinated policies and programs responsive to the needs of families in different social, economic, and cultural circumstances and to children of different ages, stages of development, and with special needs.

7. Responsibility for meeting the nation's child care needs should be widely shared among individuals, families, voluntary organizations, employers, communities, and government at all levels. Americans place a high priority on individuals' values and on the rights of parents to raise their children according to their own beliefs. Therefore, all child care policies should affirm the role and responsibilities of families in childrearing. Governments, community institutions, and employers should support rather than detract from that role.

GOALS OF A CHILD CARE SYSTEM

The panel has identified three overarching policy goals that should guide the future development of the child care system in the United States:

- achieve quality in out-of-home child care services and arrangements;
- improve accessibility to quality child care services for families in different social, economic, and cultural circumstances; and
- enhance the affordability of child care services for low- and moderate-income families.

Achieving all three of these goals is critical to the development of an improved child care system in which all children and families have access to affordable programs and arrangements that meet fundamental standards of quality and parents have increased choice in combining child care and employment. In the absence of fiscal constraints, these goals are not mutually exclusive, nor do they necessarily reflect competing priorities; in the current environment, however, pursuing them simultaneously will inevitably involve some difficult tradeoffs.

In the long run, reaching the goals will be costly. Just how costly is difficult to estimate precisely since it will depend not only on the particular public and private policies and programs that are adopted, but also on how parents respond to them and to other future changes in the economy and society, in their choices regarding childbearing, labor force participation, and child care arrangements. However, it seems clear that far more real resources will have to be devoted to the care of the nation's children, with government at all levels contributing a substantial share, at least for low-income families. Moreover, in the absence of a revolutionary reversal of recent trends in women's labor force participation, the current $16 billion that is the monetized portion of resources devoted to child care will certainly have to grow substantially. Because the well-being of children is critical to the nation's future, we believe that a major investment of financial resources by governments, as well as by employers, community organizations, philanthropists, and parents who are able, is necessary and warranted in the long run.

The panel believes that the long-term goals of quality, accessibility, and affordability should be pursued simultaneously and in a coordinated fashion, with recognition that they will require different types of policy instruments and programmatic approaches. Those instruments and approaches will include subsidies to parents to enhance their choices and ability to pay for the services and arrangements that best meet their needs, as well as parental leave policies that will allow them the choice of caring for their infants themselves. They will include subsidies to provider organizations to improve their facilities and the salaries and qualifications of caregivers and to subsidize the costs of care and special services for children in low-income families and those with special needs. And they will include subsidies to states and communities to establish the infrastructure needed to effectively mobilize public and private resources, administer programs, assist parents and providers, and monitor the quality of care.

Goal 1: Achieve Quality in Out-of-Home Child Care Services and Arrangements

All families, regardless of their social, economic, or cultural background, should be able to place their children in child care settings that meet fundamental standards of quality. Regardless of geographic location or the type of program or arrangement in which children are placed, certain characteristics of the setting, the caregiver, and the program are important indicators of the quality of care that is being provided. Although a specific definition of quality is somewhat elusive, the existing body of scientific research and best professional practice indicate that there are clearly identifiable features of child care that are associated with quality. Some of these are regulatable: that is, they can be specified according to objective standards that can be promulgated and enforced, including staff/child ratios, group sizes, features of the physical facilities, and caregivers' training. Other features are more subjective and cannot be regulated, including the nature and frequency of caregiver-child interactions, the stability of relationships between children and their caregivers, teaching and learning styles, and the sensitivity of a program to the cultural heritages and preferences of the children and families it serves.

Regulatable Features of Care

For the regulatable features of child care quality, research and best practice provide reasonable ranges, which depend on the age of the children and on other characteristics of the child care setting (see Chapter 4). For example, appropriate staff/child ratios for 3-year-olds can range from 5 to 10 children per caregiver: the appropriate level in any particular setting depends on other related features of the setting, including group size, the availability of other adult caregivers, the arrangement of physical space, and the qualifications of the caregivers. Standards for the regulatable features of out-of-home child care, therefore, are expressed in terms of ranges rather than precise numbers.

Staff/Child Ratios Research shows that the staff/child ratio is most critical for infants and young toddlers (0 to 24 months). For those youngest children, the ratio should not exceed 1:4. For 2-year-olds, acceptable ranges are 1:3 to 1:6; for 3-year-olds, 1:5 to 1:10; and for 4- and 5-year-olds, 1:7 to 1:10.

Group Size   Children benefit from social interactions with peers; however, larger groups are generally associated with less positive interactions and developmental outcomes. Acceptable ranges are a maximum of 6 to 8 children during the first year of life, 6 to 12 for 1- and 2-year-olds, 14 to 20 for 3-year-olds, and 16 to 20 for 4- and 5-year-olds.

Caregiver Training and Experience   Caregivers in child care centers, family day care homes, and school-based programs should have specific training in child development theory and practice. In addition, research shows that more years of general education contribute to caregiver performance and children's developmental outcomes.

Physical Space and Facilities   Space should be well organized, orderly, differentiated, and designed for children's use. Specific activities should have assigned areas within a child care center or family day care home (e.g., an art table, a dramatic play corner, a block-building corner, a reading corner). Facilities and toys should be age appropriate for the children using them.

Unregulatable Features of Care

Research also suggests that the regulatable and unregulatable features of quality are highly correlated. Good things tend to go together, so that programs and arrangements that adhere to high standards on regulatable dimensions tend to maintain high standards on unregulatable dimensions as well. Programs that comply with appropriate staff/child ratios and group sizes and that hire and maintain well-qualified staff, for example, are very likely to also be programs in which children receive plenty of nurturant one-on-one attention, in which the balance between activities that emphasize cognitive and social development is appropriate and in which children are given opportunities to initiate and pace their own activities with appropriate caregiver support. Conversely, programs that do not maintain high standards on regulatable dimensions of care also frequently fail to achieve appropriate levels on unregulatable dimensions.

Daily programs in child care settings should include some learning activities that permit children to choose and initiate their activities and to pace themselves. Learning activities should foster both cognitive and social development. They should be structured, yet flexible enough to accommodate the developmental needs of individual children. Learning activities should be balanced by time for unstructured play and exploration.

Furthermore, if programs are able to pay staff at levels commensurate with their training, experience, and responsibilities, they are also likely to attract well-qualified caregivers, to avoid high rates of turnover, and to provide stability in children's relationships with their caregivers. Children benefit from stable relationships with caregivers over time. The assignments of caregivers to particular groups of children should be maintained in order to foster the formation of trusting, affectionate relationships between individual adults and children.

Importance of Quality Care

Throughout this report we have highlighted the fact that quality care can play a particularly important role in enhancing developmental outcomes among children from economically disadvantaged and highly stressed families, as well as those from middle- and upper middle-class families. Research shows that high-quality cognitive enrichment programs have positive implications for the intellectual development of children from low-income families who are at risk for school failure. And the effects are not only short term. Studies of the long-term effects of child care (although they are few) offer evidence that the quality of child care in the early years is related to later psychosocial and behavioral outcomes. Conversely, poor-quality child care threatens the health and development of children, especially those from poor and minority families.

Juggling jobs and childrearing responsibilities is difficult for most parents. Coordinating work and child care schedules, managing the demands of jobs and housework, being psychologically as well as physically available to children and to employers, and coping with the inevitable emergencies and unforeseen demands that arise in both domains create high levels of stress and anxiety. For single parents, especially those who are economically disadvantaged, the pressures are especially difficult. Quality child care that is reliable and dependable can help to alleviate parental stress and buffer children as well as parents from the problems associated with combining work and parenting roles.

Improving Poor-Quality Care

A great deal of available out-of-home child care appears to be of poor quality. Numerous studies of center care and family day care in this country have shown that many children are in programs that do not meet the fundamental standards of quality we have outlined, although it is impossible to calculate the precise number of inadequate programs and the number of children they serve. The regulatory policies of many states do not reflect knowledge from research and best practice about appropriate ranges for staff/child ratios and group sizes for children of different ages, about the organization and design of physical spaces, or about the desirable education and qualifications of staff. Even in states with regulations that establish high standards for care, many state regulating agencies have inadequate staff to appropriately and effectively monitor compliance, so that enforcement is all too frequently sporadic and ineffective. And as detailed in this report, many programs and providers are exempt from licensure and are unregulated. It also appears that many providers, especially those that operate outside the regulated system, lack the knowledge and economic resources required to improve their programs to acceptable levels of quality.

Relatedly, as we have discussed at many points throughout this report, child care workers are underpaid relative to their education and training, experience, and levels of responsibility. Low salaries have been shown to jeopardize the quality of care that children receive by contributing to high turnover rates and instability in child care centers and by discouraging many well-qualified caregivers from entering or remaining in the market. In states and localities that have launched special initiatives to increase salaries, staff recruitment and retention have improved. Raising wages for caregivers with more education has been shown to be especially effective in increasing the quality and stability of staff.

In the long run, achieving the levels of quality in out-of-home child care that are fundamental to support and nurture children's health and development will require action on several fronts. State regulations governing child care programs and settings will have to be changed to reflect what is known about the ways in which regulatable features of care influence quality. At the same time, alternative quality control mechanisms that reward regulated and unregulated providers for meeting performance standards will have to be developed and implemented. Incentives and opportunities for improving caregiver qualifications will have to be developed. And, finally, the salaries and wages of caregivers will have to be increased to levels commensurate with their training, experience, and responsibilities.

Goal 2: Improve Accessibility to Quality Child Care Services and Arrangements for Families in Different Social, Economic, and Cultural Circumstances

Regardless of their social, economic, or cultural backgrounds and circumstances, all families should have access to quality child care services and arrangements. If parents' right to choose freely from a diversity of options is to be the guiding principle for child care policy and the delivery of services, then parents must have options. For too many families, particularly low-income families, there are too few choices.

Is There a Shortage of Child Care?

Data on the supply of and demand for child care services are inadequate to allow us to reach a definitive answer to the question of whether there is a shortage of child care. The available national data on demand and the limited information on supply lead us to conclude that in a narrow economic sense there is no generalized shortage of child care services. That is, most parents who have ample financial resources and time to search can arrange the care they want for their children. But for parents without time and resources, choices may be severely restricted. Moreover, several specialized types of child care services are in short supply: organized infant and toddler care programs, before- and after-school care programs, child care and preschool education programs for children with disabilities, comprehensive care programs for economically disadvantaged children and those at risk of later school failure, and services for children whose parents do not work traditional daytime schedules. As difficult as many parents find it to arrange care for their 3- to 5-year-olds, parents who need out-of-home care for their younger and older children, as well as those who require care for children with special needs, often face long and frustrating searches that end with less than satisfactory results. For a variety of reasons the market has not independently responded to the needs of these parents and children, and in the absence of government intervention, it seems unlikely that it will.

There is also significant evidence of a shortage of quality child care. Even when the market functions well in a narrow economic sense, it often does not produce care of appropriate quality for the healthy development of children; for low-income families, this is a particularly serious problem. Studies show that children from economically disadvantaged families are less likely to be in quality programs in the absence of special access and subsidies.

Infant Care

Care for very young children is difficult and expensive to provide. Regulations that limit the number of children per caregiver (although in many states not to levels recommended by professional performance standards) increase the staff costs associated with infant care. Special caregiver training requirements and equipment also add to these costs. In centers that operate solely on parent fees, the tuitions of preschool-age children partially subsidize the costs of caring for infants and toddlers. If the supply of care for the nation's youngest children is to grow to meet the projected demand over the next decade, substantial additional public and private resources will be needed to establish facilities, train caregivers, and help subsidize the costs of care for children in low-income families.

Before- and After-School Care

Before- and after-school care is also in short supply in many communities (see Chapter 6). Barriers to the use of school buildings and staff have limited the opportunities to establish school-based programs, and although many proprietary and not-for-profit centers have established programs, these are usually most appropriate for 5- to 8-year-old children. Most of the programs that do exist require parent fees and therefore may limit the access for children in low-income families who cannot pay. From a cost perspective, relatively modest levels of public funding can benefit large numbers of children: school buildings that are not used during nonschool hours and when school is not in session provide well-equipped facilities. Coordination with other community-based programs and facilities, such as parks and recreation department programs, can widen the range of activities and options to meet the needs and interests of children aged 5 to 12. Although some states and communities have begun to develop exemplary before- and after-school care models, further experimentation and development are needed.

Care for Children With Special Needs

Federal programs for the development of child care and preschool programs for children with disabilities (including those under P.L. 99-457) make funds available to states to distribute to local schools or other community-based organizations that serve this population. Given the many needs of many of these children and their families, communities should be encouraged to develop and evaluate model programs that provide comprehensive health, education, and parent education services for children with handicapping conditions.

Out-of-home child care services are in short supply for mildly ill children and those whose parents work nontraditional schedules. The accessibility of care when children are sick and during evenings, nights, and weekends is generally limited and may affect parents' decisions to accept employment as well as time lost from work. For shift workers who earn low wages and who are single parents, the problems of arranging quality child care may be exacerbated. Accordingly, special services to meet the needs of these children and families are needed to facilitate parents' employment and to ensure that their children receive adequate care.

Improving Access to Child Care

In the broadest sense, improving access to child care means improving families' options for choosing arrangements that meet their needs and preferences. In part this requires that policies and programs be expanded to serve special categories of children and families who are currently unserved or underserved in the child care market: for example, infants and toddlers, school-age children, mildly and chronically ill children, children with disabilities, and children whose parents work nontraditional schedules. In addition, it requires that the existing market function more effectively in matching the providers and the consumers of care.

Parents need adequate information to weigh available child care options and knowledge of how to gain access to these out-of-home services. However, studies suggest that many parents are not well informed about the alternative programs and arrangements that are available and their administrative requirements (see Chapter 8). They also lack information about the availability of support to permit them to remain at home to care for their children or to rely on relatives. Moreover, many parents lack knowledge to effectively weigh considerations of program quality in relation to considerations of cost, location, and hours. Indeed, many do not know how to distinguish quality programs. Because of the newness and decentralized character of many child care services, it is often difficult for parents to obtain relevant information. Accordingly, services and administrative mechanisms to provide better information to parents who are child care consumers will help them locate and gain access to available services and make informed choices among them.

In this regard, it would be helpful to parents if child care programs were rated according to a standardized scale, much the way hotels and motion pictures are rated as a guide to consumers. The availability of information that distinguishes the quality of child care programs relative to professional standards would help parents understand the level of quality they are purchasing, and it may also encourage providers to improve the quality of their programs in order to achieve a higher rating. This approach is at the heart of the accreditation program for child care centers of the National Association for the Education of Young Children. Through a process of self-evaluation and external review and validation, programs that meet the NAEYC accreditation criteria are certified. Accreditation is intended as a process to foster program improvement by providers and as a guide to parent consumers.

Goal 3: Enhance the Affordability of Child Care Services, Especially for Low- and Moderate-Income Families

One of the most central child care problems confronting policy makers is that for the millions of low-income working families, paid child care services are simply unaffordable; others can only afford to purchase care of inadequate quality. For those who cannot afford to purchase the services they need and want, the human and financial costs can be significant both in the short and the long term. They are borne by children who receive inadequate and unsafe care; by parents whose employability and earnings potential are depreciated; by employers who experience work interruptions, absenteeism, and employee turnover; and by society, which is forced to bear the costs of welfare payments, lost productivity, and forgone tax revenues. As many observers have noted, the ultimate cost of unaffordable child care will be borne by an aging U.S. society three or four decades from now, when failure to meet the developmental needs of today's children will limit the potential of tomorrow's adults to support the social and economic institutions upon which larger and larger numbers of older Americans will be dependent. In short, an essential question to ask is whether, given the likely long-term costs of poor-quality care, high-quality care is too costly in today's market. This question cannot be answered empirically, but it is especially relevant in considering the special child care problems of low-income families.

Federal Child Care Subsidies

There has been a sharp shift in who benefits from federal child care spending over the past decade and a half (see Chapter 7). In the early 1970s, nearly 80 percent of federal funds that support child care went to low-income families. Today the figure is only about 50 percent. This change resulted in part from greater reliance on the dependent care tax credit, which largely benefits middle- and upper middle-income families. In its current form, its benefits do not go to low-income working families who do not earn enough to pay income taxes. In addition, the Social Services Block Grant program, which provides funds to the states to subsidize social services for low-income populations, including child care, was decreased during the 1980s. Its reduced income ceilings disqualify many working poor families. And Head Start, the largest federally funded child development program, is a part-day program and therefore does not meet the needs of most working parents for full-day care.

The Special Needs of Low-Income Families

There are special issues regarding child care for children in low-income families. The vast majority of poor families—many of which are headed by an unmarried mother—do not use market child care at all. Those mothers who are employed rely primarily on relative care or other informal unlicensed arrangements, including family day care. Although this may reflect their preferences, there is evidence that several barriers impede the use of more formal programs. The first is obviously cost. For many low-income families, especially those headed by single mothers, the cost of child care is quite high—usually matched only by food and housing as a proportion of family income. It represents an average of more than 20 percent of family income per child among all low-income families with employed mothers and an average of 30 percent of the mother's earnings. Among some families, especially those with more than one young child, the proportions are even higher. Although some subsidies are available, child care options are necessarily limited for poor families. And the fact that they are forced to rely on unregulated services raises questions about the quality of the care they purchase.

Second, many low-wage jobs involve nontraditional work schedules, which usually means that relatives and other informal arrangements are the only available options. In addition, proportionally more low-income parents work part time and, therefore, earn less than full-time workers. There is evidence that this pattern may also restrict child care options because most centers offer only full-day programs.

Care by fathers and by extended-family members continues to be an important component of current child care arrangements, especially for low-income families. Relative care has declined in the 1980s in comparison with family day care, center care, and school-based programs, and further declines are anticipated as many grandmothers and other female relatives who might otherwise serve as caregivers continue to enter or remain in the labor force in increasing numbers. However, the panel believes that public policies should not undermine the ability of relatives to serve as child care providers nor should they penalize parents who choose to rely on other family members rather than purchasing care in the market.

Making Quality Child Care Affordable

In the long term, making quality out-of-home child care available and affordable to low-income families will require major investments of public resources in the form of subsidies to providers who serve children from economically disadvantaged families or direct income subsidies to families with children. Child care is costly regardless of who provides the services and who makes the payments. Moreover, quality care is generally more costly than inadequate care (see Chapter 8). Without government support, many low-income parents will continue to have strong economic incentives to stay out of the labor force and to limit their incomes or to place their children in substandard out-of-home arrangements or add considerable stress to relatives who may be pressured to provide care. The Family Support Act of 1988 requires parents of young children to work as a condition of welfare receipt. Without generous child care or other income subsidies, however, children in low-income families, more than ever before, will be vulnerable to poor-quality care, if it is all that their parents can afford or all that public subsidies will cover. Yet highly constrained public budgets make it unlikely that the necessary level of new resources will be immediately available to subsidize the costs of quality child care for all children in low-income families in the United States.

RECOMMENDATIONS FOR
CHILD CARE POLICIES AND PROGRAMS

Achieving the goals we have established for developing a child care system will entail substantial public investments by government at all levels, as well as by employers, charitable organizations, and parents. Because the well-being of the nation's children is so critical to the well-being of society as a whole, we believe that these investments are necessary and justified. Yet in the short term, economic realities may limit the nation's ability to allocate major new funds for child care. Accordingly, we recommend pursuit of our goals by incremental steps. In developing our specific recommendations, three basic tensions were the subject of considerable debate in the panel's deliberations; their resolution required common sense as much as a reading of the scientific evidence.

The first of these tensions is the one between emphasizing breadth and depth of coverage: Should added public resources for child care be used primarily to improve the general availability of child care to all families, to support the full costs of high-quality preschool compensatory care for a modest portion of the most disadvantaged children, or to provide a small subsidy that would cover the full costs of lower quality care to a much larger portion of low-income families? The panel sees merit in all three approaches and believes sufficient public resources should be committed in the near term to permit meaningful advances in each. However, we conclude that depth should be emphasized over breadth: since the need for more high-quality child care is heavily concentrated among the most disadvantaged children, so should be public support for child care.

The second tension is between improving the quality of out-of-home child care services and improving their availability and affordability. Efforts to improve the quality of care—by improving the ratios of staff to children, increasing the education and training of caregivers, increasing caregiver wages and salaries, and improving the physical facilities of centers, family day care homes, and public schools—will substantially raise the costs of care. The higher costs incurred by providers will be passed on to consumers in the form of higher fees unless they are partially or wholly offset by employers or government. Thus, raising the quality and price of care will likely make it increasingly unaffordable to many low-income families. Faced with a shrinking consumer market, many providers may be forced to reduce their services or to close down, reducing the supply of child care services and making them inaccessible to families that are unable to pay. As Cherlin (1988) and others have suggested, a two-tiered system could well develop, consisting of a high-priced, high-quality regulated market for upper income families and a lower priced, low-quality unregulated market for those who cannot afford to pay for quality care. Therefore, it is important that any public initiatives to improve the quality of child care supplied in the market be accompanied by greater financial subsidies for those families for whom affordability is already, or will become, a major barrier.

The third major tension is between maximizing parental choice in child care and ensuring that all care meets some standards of quality. This tension has led the panel to a policy compromise that should be explicitly recognized. Parental choice is fundamental, and, therefore, no policies are acceptable that compel parents to place their child in any particular government-chosen setting. However, public policy should strive to make a range of child care options accessible to parents, and it should provide financial subsidies and incentives for services that meet standards of quality determined by research and practice so that those programs and arrangements are available and parents can use them.

On the basis of its review of the scientific evidence and the panel's best assessment of the costs, effects, and feasibility of selected alternative policy and programmatic actions, the panel recommends five immediate steps to improve the child care system in the United States. The first three will require substantially augmenting current government allocations for child care—by $5 to $10 billion annually. The other two can be implemented at much more modest cost, much of which could be borne by the private sector.

Some of the specific steps we propose would require actions by federal, state, and local policy makers to enact new legislation or direct the agencies under their jurisdiction to undertake new initiatives. Others would require the continuation or intensification of public- and private-sector efforts already under way. Many of our recommendations build on policies and programs already in place. Many reinforce the priorities of other individuals and groups that have addressed these issues.

1. **The federal government, in partnership with the states, should expand subsidies to support low-income families' use of quality child care programs and arrangements.**

The child care problems of low-income families have been a major focus of this report. For many parents in or near poverty, problems with child care can be a barrier to becoming and staying employed. Therefore, child care must be a central component of any policy to help poor families achieve economic self-sufficiency through employment. This idea is represented in the Family Support Act of 1988, although in light of the current constraints on public budgets, sufficient additional resources required to meet the needs of all low-income families and their children are unlikely to be immediately available. Nevertheless, there is an urgent need for federal and state governments to take steps to increase funds allocated to child care for this population. Implementation of the Family Support Act of 1988 is expected to give added impetus for such action by increasing the demand for nonparental child care by up to 10 percent (Kisker et al., 1989).

Several specific funding mechanisms are available to channel support for low-income families for child care, including: (1) changing the dependent care tax credit to meet the needs of low-income families; (2) expanding the earned income tax credit or converting the personal tax exemption for children to a refundable credit; (3) providing additional support for the purchase of services through grant programs such as the Social Services Block Grant program; and (4) allocating additional support for child care and early childhood education provided by the public school systems. As we discussed in Chapters 7 and 8, each approach has particular strengths and weaknesses.

The politically popular dependent care tax credit is the one federal child care program that has expanded substantially since the early 1980s. Intended to expand the choices available to employed parents who use out-of-home child care services, the credit currently provides an estimated $3.9 billion of financial assistance to working families. However, the credit largely benefits middle- and upper middle-income families. Working parents who do not pay income taxes because their wages are low cannot use the credit. In order to benefit those parents, the credit would have to be changed—to make tax benefits refundable to low-income families and to make benefits available to parents on a timely basis (rather than at the end of the year) to allow them to use the additional income to pay for child care services. Estimates of the added costs of making the dependent care tax credit fully refundable at current benefit levels are approximately $300 million. Estimates of the added costs of making the credit refundable and raising the benefit level to the projected average costs of purchasing quality care of $4,000 per child under age 6 per year and $2,000 per child aged 6 to 13 per year are as high as $10 billion. However, if the higher benefit levels were limited to low- and moderate-income families, the total additional costs would be much less, and they could be lowered further by eliminating the current subsidy for high-income taxpayers.

Since increasing the earned income tax credit would target additional funds to low-income working families with children without tying those funds specifically to the purchase of child care, this type of child allowance subsidy also increases families' options with respect to child care arrangements. In a similar vein, many advocates of policies that would encourage, or at least not discourage, mothers in two-parent families to remain at home and care for their children themselves have supported increasing the personal income tax exemption. The personal tax exemption provides a form of allowance to families with dependent children, but in its current form it provides little or no benefit to low-income families. If the exemption were converted to a refundable tax credit, it could effectively target needed assistance to economically disadvantaged parents regardless of their employment status.

Increasing the Social Services Block Grant program or other programs that subsidize child care providers who serve children from low-income families would also enhance the affordability of services for this population. At the same time, it could improve the availability of programs in low-income communities and neighborhoods where proprietary providers have few economic incentives for developing programs. The Social Services Block Grant program and similar programs also offer significant opportunities to link funding to compliance with performance standards that are likely to be associated with higher quality care. Funding for the Child Care Food Program, in particular, has been an effective mechanism for bringing family day care homes into the licensed system and for developing routine structures for monitoring compliance with regulations and standards of care.

The panel is neutral as to the specific funding mechanism for channeling general support for low-income families for child care. We strongly endorse the fundamental tenet that public policy should enhance parents' ability to choose programs and arrangements that meet their special needs and preferences, but we also recognize that quality programs will not develop in many poor communities unless providers are directly subsidized to serve those consumers. Existing scientific data and analyses shed light on the likely direction of effects of these alternative policies. But they do not provide a sufficient basis for recommending any particular mix among the various types of direct consumer subsidies, which provide income support to economically disadvantaged families (whether restricted to working parents and paid child care or not), and provider subsidies, which provide direct support to the individuals and institutions that care for poor children.

2. **In partnership with the states, the federal government should expand Head Start and other compensatory preschool programs for income-eligible 3- and 4-year-olds who are at risk of early school failure.**

Over two decades of experience with the federally funded Head Start program and major evaluation studies provide convincing evidence of the effectiveness of high-quality comprehensive early childhood education. These programs provide economically disadvantaged and at-risk preschool children an early educational experience that improves their chances of later academic success. Comprehensive care programs are costly, from $2,500 to $3,500 per child for a typical Head Start part-day program and more for more intensive academic or social services components or if the program is combined with extended-day child care services. Not all children require comprehensive services, nor should they receive them. But for children from very poor or disorganized families, these programs have a positive effect on their social, emotional, and cognitive development as well as on their physical health and well-being. Head Start has an impressive record of success, yet it currently serves less than 20 percent of the income-eligible population; and, as a part-day program, it is not responsive to the schedules and child care needs of many employed parents. Other privately sponsored programs in communities across the country have achieved similarly positive results, but they, too, serve only a small fraction of those children who need them and would benefit from participation in them.

Accordingly, the panel concludes that the Head Start program should be expanded to serve all income-eligible 3- and 4-year-olds in need of comprehensive child development services. In addition, Head Start programs should be integrated with community child care programs to provide extended-day care for children whose parents are employed. They should also be coordinated with other public and private school and child care programs serving children in low-income families and children with disabilities in this age group to ensure that appropriate services are accessible to all children and families who need them.

For low-income families who do not require intensive comprehensive child care programs that combine health, education, and social services, publicly provided compensatory education programs should be expanded. The majority of 4-year-old children now participate in an organized group program. For middle- and upper middle-income children, nursery and preschool programs have become a common experience. For economically disadvantaged children at risk of school failure, many public school systems are developing compensatory preschool programs to boost early social and cognitive development and to enhance children's ability to participate in regular elementary school classes at age 5 or 6. These programs have been shown to substantially improve school readiness for children from economically disadvantaged or disorganized families and those whose native language is not English. Although they are expanding, they are not currently available to all children who would benefit from participation.

Accordingly, the panel concludes that the federal government, in partnership with the states and local school systems, should coordinate funding for and the development of compensatory programs for 4-year-olds at risk of later school failure. In some communities, public schools could be the providers of these services; in others, services could be provided under the auspices of other community-based institutions and coordinated with programs provided by the schools.

3. Governments at all levels, along with employers and other private-sector groups, should make investments to strengthen the infrastructure of the child care system.

Improving the accessibility of quality child care to low- and moderate-income families will depend in part on developing a child care system that meets the needs of all children and families. The current uncoordinated patchwork of programs and arrangements provides services of varying cost and quality to some, but not all, who need and want them. Improving the capacity of the existing system to match consumers and providers, to offer information and referral to parents, to provide training and technical assistance to family day care providers, and to support effective planning and coordination of policies, programs, and resources at all levels would enhance the quality and accessibility of services to all families. The panel urges several specific steps to strengthen the infrastructure of the child care system.

a. Expand resource and referral services.

Public policy toward child care has been increasingly aimed at ensuring the right of parents to choose the form of care that best meets their needs and fits their values concerning childrearing, and a diverse and decentralized assortment of child care services and arrangements has evolved. But parents can only take advantage of the available choices if they understand what is available and practical and if they understand how to gain access to them. Resource and referral services, which have developed in several states and communities, provide an effective mechanism for matching consumers and providers, for providing information and consumer education to parents, for providing information and technical assistance to providers, especially family day care homes, and for providing information and support to state and local planning groups. They are not a panacea for all the ills of an incoherent and competitive child care system, but they can provide an essential part of the necessary infrastructure of a more coordinated system and can help the existing market function more effectively.

Accordingly, the panel recommends that government at all levels, in partnership with employers and the voluntary sector, support the establishment and operation of independent local resource and referral services.

Resource and referral services models should be further developed, refined, and evaluated as a basis for future decision making concerning the most effective means of organizing and delivering these essential child care support services.

b. Improve caregiver training and wages.

The quality of child care is inextricably linked to the qualifications and stability of caregivers. As we have discussed throughout this report, well-trained and consistent staff are an important ingredient of high-quality care. Caregivers who have had training in child development as well as basic health and safety practices are better able to meet children's fundamental physical and developmental needs, and the amount of formal education obtained by caregivers is a strong predictor of appropriate caregiving behavior. Specialized training is especially important for those who care for infants, children with disabilities, and children of diverse cultural backgrounds.

Quality child care also requires settings and conditions that value adults as well as children. Indeed, the quality of children's experiences in child care is directly linked to the well-being of their caregivers. Instability that results from high rates of staff turnover has been found to be directly attributable to low wages and poor benefits. Child care workers are underpaid relative to their education and training, experience, and levels of responsibility. But raising the wages of caregivers will inevitably raise the costs of care and result in fees for services that are beyond the means of many families. As the Child Care Staffing Study (Whitebook et al., 1989) reports, in the face of a rapidly growing demand for services, an increasing number of consumers with a limited ability to pay, and restricted government and corporate support, the United States has implicitly adopted a policy that relies on child care providers to subsidize the cost of care through their low wages.

The panel concludes that improving the quality of child care will inevitably require professional preparation and adequate compensation for caregivers. The federal and state governments should expand support for preservice and in-service training programs for child care providers, and they should take steps to increase salaries for qualified caregivers by earmarking state funds for increasing salaries and increasing reimbursement rates for publicly funded child care in order to reflect the full cost of care based on improved salaries.

c. Expand vendor-voucher programs.

Since the early 1980s the use of vendor-voucher programs has grown in many states as a way of subsidizing child care for low-income families and maximizing their options. Some employers are also beginning to offer vouchers as a fringe benefit. These initiatives have enhanced parents' ability to choose particular child care arrangements, if options are available in their communities, and they have created opportunities for many low-income parents to place their children in center care rather than relying solely on relative care and unregulated family day care. In this regard, vouchers represent an important policy tool for fostering integration of children from low- and moderate-income families in child care. Their effectiveness, however, depends on the availability of an efficient resource and referral system to inform parents of their options and to help them gain access to programs in the community.

The panel recommends that state governments and private community agencies expand support for vendor-voucher programs as a way of subsidizing child care expenses for low-income families and that employers be encouraged to support vendor-voucher programs as a benefit of employment. The provision of vouchers should be linked to use of licensed or other regulated forms of care. States should allocate funds to develop, refine, and evaluate models for linking vendor-voucher programs to effective resource and referral services.

d. Encourage the organization of family day care systems.

Networks or systems of family day care providers have expanded rapidly over the past several years, largely in response to requirements for receipt of Child Care Food Program subsidies. Although systems vary in size and in the types of supports and services they offer, they have been shown to be effective mechanisms for assisting providers to meet the administrative requirements for public subsidies, disseminating information concerning best practices, providing preservice and in-service training, sharing toys and other educational resources, organizing emergency backup care, and providing client referrals. In addition, family day care systems provide a potentially powerful mechanism for monitoring compliance with national standards for family day care and providing technical assistance to providers to improve the quality of their services. Networks and systems are currently sponsored by a variety of not-for-profit community organizations. The availability of public support would provide an incentive for the further expansion of these systems. Therefore, the panel recommends that the federal and state governments allocate funds for the establishment of family day care systems to provide training and support to family day care providers and to monitor their compliance with child care standards.

e. Improve planning and coordination.

The emergence of a diverse set of decentralized child care services has meant that in many communities there is little coordination among programs, providers, and agencies. They frequently do not share a set of common goals or purpose, and in the absence of a community infrastructure to link them, they are likely to compete for financial resources, staff, and space. The panel concludes that planning and coordination must occur at all levels of the policy process. At each level of government—federal, state, and local—there must be an institutional structure that can serve as the focal point for coordinating resources across agencies, for establishing priorities, and for designing and implementing policy. At each level, planning must involve the array of relevant public- and private-sector groups and must be based on systematically gathered data about children, their families, and available resources.

To be effective, state and local planning and coordination should not simply consist of another "blue-ribbon" commission or task force that outlines needs and announces goals, but fails to resolve the difficult issues of jurisdiction that exist among education, social services, welfare, economic development, and health and mental health programs, providers, and professional interests. Instead, planning and coordination must involve a process that will develop a long-term view of what the state's and the community's pattern of child care should be, how that view can be translated into legislative initiatives for policies and programs, and how administrative structures can be organized and empowered to carry them out. Developing and empowering effective institutional mechanisms for planning and coordination will inevitably be a lengthy process. There have been several effective models (see Chapter 6), and the panel concludes that steps should be taken to expand their development.

4. The federal government should initiate a process to develop national standards for child care.

The lengthy and painful effort to promulgate federal quality and safety standards or regulations for the delivery of child care services was terminated with the elimination of the Federal Interagency Day Care Requirements in 1982, and the states became the sole authority for establishing regulations and enforcing them. The content of state regulations varies dramatically across jurisdictions, not as a reflection of the different developmental needs of children but as a reflection of different views of the role of government in developing standards or regulations and the will and capacity of state systems to see that they are maintained. Within jurisdictions, different institutions that serve children of the same age are governed by different regulatory policies or are exempted altogether.

The panel concludes that uniform national child care standards—based on current knowledge from child development research and best practice from the fields of public health, child care, and early childhood education—are a necessary (though not sufficient) condition for achieving quality in out-of-home child care. Such standards should be established as a guide to be adopted by all states as a basis for improving the regulation and licensing of child care and preschool education programs. Unfortunately, there are few economic or political incentives for the states to take this step. Existing regulations have been established through a process of political negotiation, and in most states the systems for monitoring and enforcing regulations are not adequate for effective oversight of the rapidly growing array of programs and providers in their jurisdictions. Thus, incentives must also be created to encourage state involvement: for example, linking federal funding to compliance with national standards.

To develop national standards, the panel recommends that the federal government establish a national-level task force to bring together representatives of the states, the relevant professional organizations, service providers, and appropriate federal agencies. Current knowledge from child development research and existing professional performance standards can provide the basis for developing health and safety requirements, acceptable ranges for staff/child ratios, group size, caregiver qualifications, and physical facilities, as well as program content. Such a process should also address the practical considerations of states' adoption of standards, such as the cost of services to parents and the cost to states of ensuring compliance. These standards should reflect the common needs of children of different ages, from different cultural heritages, and with special needs, regardless of the setting in which they are served. At the same time, they should take account of the physical and administrative differences between child care centers, schools, and family day care homes.

5. The federal government should mandate unpaid, job-protected leave for employed parents of infants up to 1 year of age.

Child care is most demanding during the first year of a child's life. For parents, it is often a difficult period of personal and social adjustment, which is frequently exacerbated by the stress and lack of sleep that accompany a baby's arrival. For employed parents, combining work and family roles may compound the difficulties. The establishment of strong relationships between parents and children in the early months of life has been shown to have significant implications for children's later development. And these relationships are more likely to develop when parents have time and emotional energy to interact with their young children.

Parental leave policies that permit parents to remain at home to care for their own children for a defined period of time after birth or adoption have been implemented in many European countries and have been widely discussed in recent years in the United States. Researchers, professionals, and parents alike agree that too many children enter out-of-home care before they and their parents have "had a good start together" (Kahn and Kamerman, 1987). In many cases parents are unable to remain at home because they cannot afford the lost income or because they would have to forfeit their job to do so. Given the shortage of high-quality infant care services, many observers worry about the long-term effects of exposing very young children to inadequate care and of forcing their parents back to work before they are psychologically ready to return.

The panel has concluded that, in the current infant care market, some parents are forced to make choices they should not have to make. Often those who choose employment have difficulty finding quality infant care at a cost they can afford. And many of those for whom the pressure for employment is greatest—single parents and those employed in low-wage jobs—may be forced to place their very young children in poor-quality care. Research has shown that children from low-income and highly stressed families are especially vulnerable to the potentially damaging effects of poor-quality care.

Alternative polices to increase parental choice and improve the infant care market can take several forms. One option is to improve the supply of quality infant care. Although the panel favors policies to improve the accessibility of quality infant care, the inherent tensions among availability, affordability, and quality also lead us to recommend a complementary policy of parental leave to provide parents the opportunity to care for their very young children themselves.

After weighing the evidence on the estimated costs and benefits of alternative policies, the panel acknowledges that on narrow economic grounds the case for parental leave is inconclusive. Clearly there are a number of monetary and nonmonetary costs and benefits associated with such policies. For example, mandated parental leave would entail costs to some employers for recruiting and training replacement employees, and it may result in discrimination against women of childbearing age. But the potential benefits are also significant, including fostering equal opportunity for women workers by increasing their attachment to the labor force and their seniority in their jobs, increasing work force stability, and reducing welfare costs. The potential costs of not having parental leave are also significant, although they are less easily measured in monetary terms. An array of studies highlights the potentially detrimental developmental problems for young children, parents' stress in attempting to combine parenting roles and employment during the early months after the birth or adoption of a child, and women's lost wages (short and long term) and increased welfare costs if women have to quit their jobs. These considerations led the panel to recommend parental leave as one important component of a national child care policy.

Even among those who agree that parental leave policies should be implemented, there is little consensus about whether leaves should be paid or unpaid and, if paid, at what level of wage replacement, for what period of time, at whose cost, and with what assistance for the particular problems of small employers. Our conclusion, based on a review of the available research and the panel's professional judgment, is that, in the long term, policies should provide paid leave with partial income replacement for up to 6 months and unpaid leave for up to an additional 6 months, with job-related health benefits and job guarantees during the year.

We recognize, however, that the costs to employers and governments will make the implementation of paid parental leave impossible in the near term. Accordingly, as a first step, we recommend that the federal government mandate that employers ensure unpaid, job-protected leave, with continued health benefits, for up to 1 year for all parents who prefer to remain at home following the arrival of a new baby. We acknowledge that without wage replacement, parental leave will not be a viable option for many families, and we look forward to the eventual implementation of policies to provide paid leave.

In sum, in keeping with the panel's objective of enhancing families' choices among child care arrangements for infants, parental leave—as well as quality out-of-home care—should be an option regardless of parents' economic status.

CONCLUSION

As we stated at the beginning of this chapter, the panel's framework for policy and program development is organized around three fundamental goals: to enhance the quality of out-of-home child care services and arrangements; to enhance the accessibility of child care services and arrangements to families in different social, economic, and cultural circumstances; and to enhance the affordability of child care services for low-income families. Our five recommendations are intended as immediate steps to further these goals. It is important to recognize that none of our recommended policy and programmatic actions alone can solve the complex problems of child care in the United States; nor can any single strategy address the needs and characteristics of all children and parents. In presenting several strategies for achieving the goals, we have tried to take account of the diversity of children, families, employers, and communities—of different values, different social, economic, and cultural backgrounds, different ages and stages of development, and different community support systems. But the strategies, as well as the goals themselves, are interdependent: in the long term, they need to be pursued simultaneously and in a coordinated fashion, although in the short term they will inevitably require difficult tradeoffs.

As we have stressed throughout this book, there are no easy answers or quick fixes. Nor are there any cheap solutions. Developing a coherent child care policy and delivery system in the United States will require a major investment of new resources at all levels of government and continued support from employers and the volunteer sector. It will also require a sustained, coordinated commitment by policy makers, service providers, employers, and parents. Everyone is touched by the issue of child care, and everyone must contribute to the development of an effective child care system. Indeed, investments in child care must be viewed as investments in the health and development of all American children, the well-being of all American families, and the future productivity of the American work force.

REFERENCES

Cherlin, A., ed.
   1988   *The Changing American Family and Public Policy.* Washington, D.C.: The Urban Institute Press.
Kahn, A., and S. Kamerman
   1987   *Child Care: Facing the Hard Choices.* Dover, Mass.: Auburn House.
Kisker, E.E., R. Maynard, A. Gordon, and M. Shain
   1989   *The Child Care Challenge: What Parents Need and What Is Available in Three Metropolitan Areas.* Princeton, N.J.: Mathematica Policy Research.
Whitebook, M., C. Howes, and D. Phillips
   1989   *Who Cares? Child Care Teachers and the Quality of Care in America.* Executive summary of the National Child Care Staffing Study. Oakland, Calif.: Child Care Employee Project.

Appendix A
State Regulations for
Family Day Care and Center Care

The four tables in this appendix present information on state regulations for family day care and center care. The regulations are the minimum requirements under which programs are permitted to operate. The provisions are presented under four categories: general features, which include type of regulation and coverage as well as requirements for physical setting; group size, including caregiver/child ratios; caregiver qualifications; and "protective features," which include parental right to visit. The data in this appendix were drawn from G. Morgan (*The National State of Child Care Regulation, 1986.* Watertown, Mass.: Work/Family Directions, Inc., 1986) and the panel's survey.

315

TABLE A-1 State Regulation of Family Day Care: General Features and Group Size

State	General Features					Group Size	
	Type of Regulation [a]	Inspections per Year	Minimum Size Covered [b]	Square Feet Indoors [c]	Square Feet Outdoors [c]	No. of Children Under 2 Years Per Caregiver	Maximum Group Size Permitted
Alabama	Lic.	1	1	NS	NS	NS	6
Alaska	Lic.	1 per 2 yrs.	5	NS	NS	2 < 30 mos.	6
Arizona	None	–	–	–	–	–	–
Arkansas	Lic.	3-4	7	35	75	–	10
California	Lic.	10% sample	2	NS	NS	3	6
Colorado	Lic.	33% sample	2	35	75	3	6
Connecticut	Mand. Reg.	1 per 2 yrs.	1	NS	NS	2	6
Delaware	Mand. Cert.	1	1	NS	NS	4	6
District of Columbia	Lic.	1	1	NS	NS	2	5
Florida	Lic. (County) Reg. (State)	2	2	NS	NS	NS	5
Georgia	Reg.	3% sample	3	35	NS	NS	6
Hawaii	Reg.	1	3	35	75	2	5
Idaho	Vol. Reg.	1	1	NS	NS	NS	6
Illinois	Lic.	1	4	NS	NS	3	8
Indiana	Lic.	1	6	35	50	6	10
Iowa	Vol. Reg.	20% sample	1	35	50	4	6
Kansas	Lic.	NA	1	25	NS	1 < 18 mos.	10
Kentucky	Lic.	1	4	35	60	NS	12
Louisiana	None	–	–	–	–	–	–
Maine	Lic. or Reg.	1	3	35	NS	NS	10
Maryland	Reg.	1	1	NS	NS	2	6
Massachusetts	Lic.	NA	1	NS	75	2	6
Michigan	Lic.	0	1	35	400 total	NS	6
Minnesota	Lic.	NA	2	35	50	NS	6
Mississippi	None	–	–	–	–	–	–
Missouri	Lic.	2	4	35	75	2	10
Montana	Reg.	15% sample	3	NS	0	3	6

Nebraska	Reg.	5% per month	4	35	50	2 < 18 mos.	8
Nevada	Lic.	4	5	35	37.5	2 < 13 mos.	6
New Hampshire	Lic.	3 per 2 yrs.	4	35	50	2	6
New Jersey	Vol. Reg.	1 per 3 yrs.	3	NS	1	NS	8
New Mexico	Lic.	2	5	35	60	2	6
New York	Lic.	1	3	NS	NS	2	6
North Carolina	Reg.	NA	1	NS	NS	NS	5
North Dakota	Lic.	2	6	35	75	NS	7; 4 < 2 yrs.
Ohio	Cert.	2	1	NS	NS	NS	12
Oklahoma	Lic.	4	1	35	75	NS	5
Oregon	Vol. Reg.	0	1	35	NS	2	5
Pennsylvania	Reg.	20% sample	4	NS	NS	4 < 3 yrs.	6
Rhode Island	Cert.	1 per 2 yrs.	4	NS	NS	NS	6
South Carolina	Reg.	0	2	NS	NS	NS	6
South Dakota	Reg.	1-12	1	NS	NS	NS	NR
Tennessee	Lic.	2	5	NS	NS	4	7
Texas	Reg.	0	4	NS	NS	4 < 18 mos.	12
Utah	Lic.	1 per 2 yrs.	4	35	40	2	8
Vermont	Lic.	2	3	35	75	2	6
Virginia	Lic.	2	6	NS	NS	4	9
Washington	Lic.	0	1	35	1	2	6
West Virginia	Vol. Reg.	1	1	NS	0	NS	NR
Wisconsin	Lic.	Varies	4	35	75	4	8
Wyoming	Lic.	Varies	3	35	75	2	6

[a]Cert., certificate; Lic., license; Mand., mandatory; Reg., registration; Vol., voluntary
[b]Number of children
[c]Per child

Abbreviations:
NA, not ascertained
NR, not regulated: not mentioned in regulations
NS, not specified: mentioned, but not quantified (e.g., "adequate")

318

TABLE A-2 State Regulation of Family Day Care: Caregiver Qualifications and Protective Features

	Caregiver Qualifications			Protective Features		
State	Preservice Training Required	Criminal Records Checked	Child Abuse Registry Checked	Immunizations Required	Corporal Punishment Permitted	Parental Right to Visit
Alabama	Yes	Yes	No	Yes	No [a]	NR
Alaska	No	No	No	No	Yes	NR
Arizona	–	–	–	–	–	–
Arkansas	No	No	No	Yes	Yes	NR
California	No	Yes	Yes	No	No	Yes
Colorado	Yes	Yes	Yes	Yes-P	No	Yes
Connecticut	No	Yes	No	NA	No	L
Delaware	Yes	No	Yes	Yes	No	L
District of Columbia	No	No	No	Yes	NR	NR
Florida	Yes	Yes	Yes	Yes	No	NR
Georgia	Yes	Yes	No	Yes	No	NR
Hawaii	Yes	Yes	No	Yes	No	NR
Idaho	No	No	No	NA	NS	NA
Illinois	No	Yes	Yes	No	NS	Yes
Indiana	No	No	No	No	NS	NR
Iowa	No	Yes	Yes	No	NS	NR
Kansas	No	Yes	Yes	Yes	NS	Yes
Kentucky	No	Yes	No	Yes	No	NR
Louisiana	–	–	–	–	–	–
Maine	No	No	Yes	No	No	NR
Maryland	No	No	No	No	NS	NR
Massachusetts	Yes	Yes	No	Yes	NS	Yes
Michigan	No	Yes	Yes	Yes	No	NR
Minnesota	Yes	Yes	No	Yes-TP	No	NR
Mississippi	–	–	–	–	–	–
Missouri	No	Yes	Yes	Yes	No	NR
Montana	No	No	No	Yes	No	NR

State						
Nebraska	No	Yes	NA	No	Yes	NR
Nevada	Yes	Yes	No	Yes	No	Yes
New Hampshire	Yes	Yes	No	Yes	No	NR
New Jersey	No	No	No	NA	NA	NA
New Mexico	No	Yes	No	Yes	No	NR
New York	No	No	Yes	Yes	NR	Yes
North Carolina	No	No	No	Yes	No	NR
North Dakota	No	No	Yes	Yes	NS	L
Ohio	No	No	No	Yes	No	Yes
Oklahoma	No	No	No	Yes	No	NR
Oregon	No	Yes	Yes	No	No	NR
Pennsylvania	No	Yes	Yes	Yes	No	NR
Rhode Island	Yes	Yes	No	Yes	No	NR
South Carolina	No	No	No	No	Yes	NR
South Dakota	No	No	Yes	Yes	No[b]	NR
Tennessee	No	Yes	Yes	Yes	Yes	NR
Texas	No	Yes	No	Yes	Yes	NR
Utah	Yes	Yes	Yes	Yes	No	Yes
Vermont	No	No	No	No	No	Yes
Virginia	No	No	No	No	No	Yes
Washington	No	Yes	Yes	Yes	No	NR
West Virginia	No	Yes	No	Yes	NR	NR
Wisconsin	Yes	No	No	Yes	No	Yes
Wyoming	Yes	No	No	Yes	No	NR

[a]For children at least 3 years old
[b]For children at least 15 months old

Abbreviations:
  L, limited
  NA, not ascertained
  NR, not regulated: not mentioned in regulations
  NS, not specified: mentioned, but not quantified (e.g., "adequate")
  P, preschoolers
  TP, toddlers and preschoolers

TABLE A-3 State Regulation of Center Care: General Features, Staff/Child Ratio, and Group Size

	General Features				Staff/Child Ratio			Group Size		
State	Inspections per Year	Square Feet Indoors[a]	Square Feet Outdoors[a]	Permitted Age of Entry	≤1- Year- Olds	3- Year- Olds	5- Year- Olds	1- Year- Olds	3- Year- Olds	5- Year- Olds
Alabama	1	35	60	8 wks.	1:6	1:10	1:20	6	10	20
Alaska	1 per 2 yrs.	35	75	6 wks.	1:5	1:10	1:15	NR	NR	NR
Arizona	2	25	75	NR	1:5	1:15	1:25	NR	NR	NR
Arkansas	3-4	35	75	6 wks.	1:6	1:12	1:18	NR	NR	NR
California	1	35	75	NR	1:4	1:12	1:12	NR	NR	NR
Colorado	1 per 2 yrs.	30	75	6 wks.	1:5	1:10	1:15	NR	NR	NR
Connecticut	1 per 2 yrs.	35	75	NR	1:4	1:10	1:10	8	20	20
Delaware	1	3	50	NR	1:4	1:10	1:25	NR	NR	NR
District of Columbia	1	35	60	NR	1:4	1:8	1:15	8	16	25
Florida	4	20	45	NR	1:6	1:15	1:25	NR	NR	NR
Georgia	4	35	100	NR	1:7	1:12	1:18	NR	NR	NR
Hawaii	1-3	35	NR	2 yrs.	—	1:12	1:20	NR	NR	NR
Idaho	1	NS	NS	NR	1:12	1:12	1:12	NR	NR	NR
Illinois	1	35	75	3 wks.	1:4	1:10	1:20	12	20	20
Indiana	3	35	50	NR	1:4	1:10	1:15	8	NR	NR
Iowa	1	35	75	2 wks.	1:4	1:8	1:15	8	NR	NR
Kansas	NA	35	75	2 wks.	1:3	1:12	1:12	9	24	28
Kentucky	1	35	60	NR	1:6	1:12	1:12	NR	NR	NR
Louisiana	1	35	75	NR	1:6	1:14	1:20	NR	NR	NR
Maine	1	35	75	6 wks.	1:4	1:10	1:10	12	NR	NR
Maryland	1	35	75	8 wks.	1:3	1:10	1:13	6	20	26
Massachusetts	NA	35	75	4 wks.	1:3	1:10	1:15	7	20	30
Michigan	1	35	1,200 total	NR	1:4	1:10	1:12	NR	NR	NR
Minnesota	NA	35	50	6 wks.	1:4	1:10	1:10	8	20	20
Mississippi	2	35	70	NR	1:5	1:14	1:20	8	20	20
Missouri	2	35	75	6 wks.	1:4	1:10	1:16	8	16	16
Montana	1	35	75	NR	1:4	1:8	1:10	NR	NR	NR

State										
Nebraska	2	35	50	6 wks.	1:4	1:10	1:15	NR	NR	NR
Nevada	4	35	37.5	NR	NR	NR	NR	NR	NR	NR
New Hampshire	3 per 2 yrs.	35	50	6 wks.	1:4	1:8	1:15	8	12	NR
New Jersey	1 per 3 yrs.	30	50	NR	1:4	1:10	NR	NR	NR	NR
New Mexico	2	35	60	6 mos.	1:6	1:12	1:15	8	20	16
New York	1	35	NS	8 wks.	1:4	1:6	1:8	14	25	25
North Carolina	3	25	75	NR	1:7	1:15	1:25	NR	NR	NR
North Dakota	2	35	75	NR	1:4	1:7	1:12	12	24	28
Ohio	2	35	60	NR	1:6	1:12	1:14	12	24	30
Oklahoma	4	35	75	NR	1:6	1:12	1:15	8	24	30
Oregon	1	35	75	6 wks.	1:4	1:10	1:15	NR	20	NR
Pennsylvania	1	40	65	NR	1:4	1:10	1:10	4	15	25
Rhode Island	1	35	NR	6 wks.	1:4	1:8	1:12	NR	NR	NR
South Carolina	Varies	35	75	NR	1:8	1:15	1:25	20	20	20
South Dakota	1-12	35	50	4 wks.	1:5	1:10	1:10	10	20	25
Tennessee	2	30	50	6 wks.	1:5	1:10	1:20	14	20	25
Texas	2	30	80	NR	1:5	1:15	1:22	8	20	35
Utah	3	35	40	NR	1:4	1:15	1:20	8	20	20
Vermont	2	35	75	NR	1:4	1:10	1:10	8	20	20
Virginia	2	25	75	NR	1:4	1:10	1:20	NR	NR	NR
Washington	1	35	75	4 wks.	1:4	1:10	1:10	8	20	20
West Virginia	1	35	75	3 mos.	1:4	1:10	1:15	NR	NR	NR
Wisconsin	Varies	35	75	NR	1:4	1:10	1:17	8	20	32
Wyoming	1	35	75	NR	1:5	1:10	1:20	NR	NR	NR

[a]Per child

Abbreviations:

NA, not ascertained

NR, not regulated: not mentioned in regulations

NS, not specified: mentioned, but not quantified (e.g., "adequate")

TABLE A-4 State Regulation of Center Care: Caregiver Qualifications and Protective Features

| | Caregiver Qualifications | | | | | | | Protective Features | | |
State	Preservice Training Required Directors	Teachers	Assistants	Health Training Required	First Aid Training Required	Criminal Records Checked	Child Abuse Registry Checked	Immunizations Required	Corporal Punishment Permitted	Parental Right to Visit
Alabama	Yes	No	NA	No	No	Yes	No	Yes	No	L
Alaska	No	No	No	No	Yes	No	No	Yes	Yes	L
Arizona	Yes	Yes	No	Yes	No	Yes	No	No	No[a]	Yes
Arkansas	Yes	No	No	No	No	No	No	Yes	Yes	NR
California	Yes	Yes	No	No	Yes	Yes	Yes	Yes	No	Yes
Colorado	Yes	Yes	No	No	Yes	Yes	Yes	Yes	No	L
Connecticut	Yes	No	No	No	Yes	Yes	No	Yes	No	Yes
Delaware	Yes	Yes	No	No	Yes	No	Yes	Yes	NS	Yes
District of Columbia	Yes	Yes	No	No	No	No	No	Yes	NR	NR
Florida	Yes	No	No	Yes	Yes	Yes	Yes	Yes	No	Yes
Georgia	Yes	Yes	Yes	No	No	Yes	No	Yes	No	Yes
Hawaii	No	Yes	Yes	Yes	No	Yes	No	No	No	NR
Idaho	No	No	No	No	No	Yes	No	No	NS	NR
Illinois	Yes	Yes	No	No	No	Yes	Yes	Yes	No	L
Indiana	Yes	No	No	No	Yes	No	No	Yes	No	Yes
Iowa	Yes	No	No	No	No	Yes	Yes	Yes	No	Yes
Kansas	Yes	Yes	No	Yes	No	Yes	Yes	Yes	No	Yes
Kentucky	No	No	No	Yes	No	Yes	No	Yes	No	NR
Louisiana	No	No	No	No	No	No	No	Yes	No	NR
Maine	Yes	No	No	No	No	Yes	No	Yes	No	L
Maryland	Yes	Yes	No	Yes	No	No	No	Yes	NS	NR
Massachusetts	Yes	Yes	No	Yes	Yes	No	No	Yes	No	L
Michigan	Yes	No	No	Yes	No	Yes	Yes	Yes	No	L
Minnesota	Yes	Yes	No	Yes	No	No	No	Yes-TP	No	NR
Mississippi	No	No	No	No	No	No	No	Yes	NR	NR
Missouri	Yes	Yes	No	No	No	Yes	Yes	Yes	No	NR
Montana	Yes	Yes	No	Yes	No	No	No	Yes-TP	No	NR

State									
Nebraska	Yes	No	No	No	Yes	NA	No	No	L
Nevada	Yes	Yes	Yes	Yes	Yes	No	Yes	No	Yes
New Hampshire	No	Yes	Yes	No	Yes	No		No	NR
New Jersey	Yes	No	Yes	No	No	No	Yes-TP	No	Yes
New Mexico	No	No	No	Yes	No	Yes	Yes	No	Yes
New York	Yes	No	Yes	No	No	No	Yes	No	L
North Carolina	Yes	Yes	No	Yes	No	Yes	Yes	No	NR
North Dakota	Yes	Yes	Yes	No	No	No	Yes	NS	L
Ohio	Yes	No	No	No	No	No	Yes	No	Yes
Oklahoma	Yes	No	No	Yes	No	No	Yes	No	NR
Oregon	Yes	No	No	No	No	Yes	Yes	No	L
Pennsylvania	Yes	No	No	Yes	Yes	Yes	Yes	No	NR
Rhode Island	Yes	Yes	No	Yes	Yes	No	Yes	NR	L
South Carolina	Yes	No	Yes	No	Yes	No	Yes	Yes	NR
South Dakota	Yes	No	Yes	No	No	Yes	Yes	No b	L
Tennessee	No	Yes	No	Yes	Yes	Yes	Yes	Yes	NR
Texas	Yes	No	No	No	Yes	No	Yes	Yes	NR
Utah	Yes	No	Yes	No	No	Yes	Yes	No	Yes
Vermont	Yes	No	No	Yes	Yes	No	Yes	No	Yes
Virginia	Yes	No	No	No	Yes	No	Yes	No	Yes
Washington	Yes	No	Yes	Yes	Yes	Yes	Yes	No	NR
West Virginia	Yes	No	No	Yes	Yes	No	Yes	No	L
Wisconsin	Yes	NA	Yes	No	No	No	Yes	No	Yes
Wyoming	No	No	No	Yes	No	No	Yes	No	NR

a For children at least 3 years old
b For children at least 15 months old

Abbreviations:
NA, not ascertained
NR, not regulated: not mentioned in regulations
NS, not specified: mentioned, but not quantified (e.g., "adequate")

Appendix B
Professional Standards for
Early Childhood Programs

This appendix presents a comparison of the salient provisions of the six major sets of standards for early childhood programs. Two of them, the Head Start performance standards and the Federal Interagency Day Care Requirements (FIDCR), were established as criteria for federal program support. The Head Start standards still govern the operation of Head Start programs. The FIDCR, which governed the operation of child programs receiving federal support through Title XX of the Social Security Act, were suspended when Title XX became the Social Services Block Grant program in 1981.

The four sets of standards developed by professional groups and individuals demonstrate the practical application of research on out-of-home care. Compliance is voluntary. Each of the sets of standards was established for different reasons and at different times, but they have much in common. Two of them, the accreditation criteria of the National Association of the Education of Young Children's (NAEYC) and the standards for child care service of the Child Welfare League of America (CWLA), were established as guidelines for programs to assess and improve their own performance. The NAEYC standards are the criteria that are used for accrediting early childhood programs. The safeguards of the National Black Child Development Institute (NBCDI) were established as broad guidelines for public schools' initiating early childhood programs serving minority children. The Early Childhood Environment Rating Scale (ECERS) was established by child development scholars at the University of North Carolina as an instrument for assessing program quality for research purposes.

The first part of this appendix briefly notes the major purposes and intended audience of the six sets of standards. The second part compares

15 provisions of these standards, what the panel calls indicators of quality, grouped in five general categories: caregiver qualifications and roles; group sizes and staff/child ratios; curriculum content and structure; physical characteristics of programs; and parental participation.

PROFESSIONAL STANDARDS AND
REQUIREMENTS FOR FEDERAL FUNDING

Accreditation Criteria and Procedures of the National Academy of Early Childhood Programs, National Association for the Education of Young Children (NAEYC) The accreditation criteria were developed in 1984 to "improve the quality of life for young children." Center-based programs determine their compliance with the standards through a process of self-evaluation involving staff, parents, and a professional validator. Programs meeting the criteria are recognized with a certificate of recognition that is valid for 3 years. The standards are designed for programs serving children aged birth through 8 years in center-based programs serving 10 or more children. Compliance is voluntary. (S. Bredekamp, ed. Washington, D.C.: National Association for the Education of Young Children, 1984)

Safeguards: Guidelines for Establishing Programs for Four Year Olds in the Public Schools, National Black Child Development Institute (NBCDI) These guidelines were developed in 1987 to "offer clear and direct suggestions for ways of ensuring that early education programs in the public schools create a learning environment for Black children which is productive, effective and long lasting in positive outcomes." Center-based programs in the public schools can determine their compliance with the standards through a process of self-evaluation; however, one of the safeguards states: "Public school-based early childhood programs should be subject to a regular, external review by community members and early childhood development experts." There are no incentives for meeting the guidelines. The standards are designed for programs serving 4-year-olds in public schools. Compliance is voluntary. (Washington, D.C.: National Black Child Development Institute, 1987)

Early Childhood Environment Rating Scale (ECERS): These standards were developed in 1980 "to provide a basis for evaluation and planning." Center-based programs determine their compliance with the standards through a process of self-evaluation, which can involve staff, trainers, and outside professionals. There are no incentives for meeting the standards. The standards are designed for programs serving children at least 9 months of age in child care centers. Compliance is voluntary. (T. Harms and R.M. Clifford. New York: Teachers College Press, 1980)

Standards for Day Care Service, Child Welfare League of America (CWLA) These standards were developed in 1960 and revised in 1984 "to be goals for continual improvement of services to children and families. They represent practices considered to be most desirable . . . These are therefore standards for social welfare services for children, regardless of auspices or setting." Agencies, center-based programs, and family day care homes determine their compliance with the standards through a process of self-evaluation and community assessment. There are no incentives for meeting the standards. The standards are designed for comprehensive programs and urge planning of services to meet children's needs. The standards for center-based programs are designed primarily for programs serving children aged 3 and older, and the standards note that "family day care is suitable for all children and may be preferable for infants" (p. 18). Compliance is voluntary. (New York: Child Welfare League of America, 1984)

Federal Interagency Day Care Requirements (FIDCR) These requirements for federal funding were developed in 1968 and revised in 1980 in an effort to standardize the requirements of federally funded programs providing comprehensive services to children. However, the FIDCR were suspended in 1981. The basic responsibility for enforcement of the requirements lay with the administering agency. Acceptance of federal funds was an agreement to abide by the requirements. The requirements were designed for family day care homes, group day care homes, and child care centers. The requirements address the needs of children from infancy through 14 years of age, but no requirements were set for center-based care of children under 3 years of age. Compliance was mandatory for programs receiving federal funds. (Washington, D.C.: U.S. Department of Health, Education and Welfare, U.S. Office of Economic Opportunity, and U.S. Department of Labor [DHEW Publ. No. OHDS 78-31081], 1968)

Head Start Performance Standards These standards for federal funding were promulgated in 1975. They cover all Head Start programs, which are for children between 3 years of age and the age of compulsory school attendance unless the Head Start agency's approved grant provides otherwise. "While compliance with the performance standards is required as a condition of Federal Head Start funding, it is expected that the standards will be largely self-enforcing." (Washington, D.C.: U.S. Department of Health and Human Services [45-CFR-1304], 1984)

INDICATORS OF QUALITY:
COMPARISON OF STANDARDS

Caregiver Qualifications and Roles

INDICATOR: The potential for forming an affectionate relationship with a familiar caregiver.

NAEYC: Each staff member has primary responsibility for and develops a deeper attachment to an identified group of children. Every attempt is made to have continuity of adults who work with children particularly infants and toddlers. Infants spend the majority of the time interacting with the same person each day (p. 64).

NBCDI: Not covered.

ECERS: Not covered.

CWLA: Each child should have a particular teacher on whom he or she can depend for comfort, security, and protection. Young children need a warm, close contact with a friendly adult, especially when they are in a group and away from home for long hours (p. 45).

FIDCR: Not covered.

Head Start: Not covered.

INDICATOR: Frequent positive interaction between caregiver and children. Caregivers who are responsive, positive, accepting, and comforting.

NAEYC: Staff interact frequently with children. Staff express respect for and affection toward children by smiling, holding, touching, and speaking to children at their eye level throughout the day, particularly on arrival and departure and when diapering or feeding very young children. . . . Staff are available and responsive to children; encourage them to share experiences, ideas, and feelings, and listen to them with attention and respect (p. 8).

NBCDI: Not covered.

ECERS: Calm but busy atmosphere. Children seem happy most of the time. Staff and children seem relaxed, voices cheerful, frequent smiling. Adults show warmth in physical contact (i.e., gentle holding, hugging). Mutual respect exists among adults and children (p. 33). Child given help and encouragement when needed. Teacher shows appreciation of children's work (p. 23).

CWLA: Not covered.

FIDCR: Not covered.

Head Start: Provides environment of acceptance which helps each child build ethnic pride, develop a positive self-concept, enhance his individual strengths and develop facility in social relationships (p. 6). Promoting language understanding and use in an atmosphere that encourages easy communication among children and between children and adults (p. 7).

INDICATOR: Caregiver training related to child development.

NAEYC: The program is staffed by individuals who are 18 years of age or older, who have been trained in early childhood education/child development, and who demonstrate the appropriate personal characteristics for working with children as exemplified in the criteria for interactions among staff and children and curriculum. Staff working with school-age children have been trained in child development, recreation, or a related field. The amount of training required will vary depending on the level of professional responsibility of the position [see Table B-1]. . . . The chief administrative officer has training and/or experience in business administration. If the chief administrative officer is not an early childhood specialist, an early childhood specialist is employed to direct the educational program (p. 18).

NBCDI: Teachers in public school-based programs should be required to have specific training in preschool education and/or ongoing, inservice training provided by qualified staff (p. 8).

Premise The skills of the center teachers are key determinants of the quality of the school and of how and what the children learn. The creation of the entire learning atmosphere is largely dependent upon the teacher. Therefore, schools should employ highly trained individuals for these positions.

Suggestions

1. Center directors should have a masters degree in early childhood education or, in addition to a degree in elementary education or a related field, must have completed coursework in early childhood education equivalent to child development associate (CDA) training or equivalent to the requirements of the local or state department of education, whichever is higher. Directors should also have previous experience in child development and training in management and staff-parent relations.
2. Teachers should have at minimum a bachelor of arts degree in early childhood education, or a degree in a related field with a completion of certification courses required by the local or state

TABLE B-1 Staff Qualifications, NAEYC Accreditation Criteria

Title	Level of Professional Responsibility	Training Requirements
Early childhood teacher assistant	Pre-professionals who implement program activities under direct supervision of the professional staff	High school graduate or equivalent, participation in professional development programs
Early childhood associate teacher	Professionals who independently implement program activities and who may be responsible for the care and education of a group of children	Child development associate credential or associate degree in early childhood education/child development
Early childhood teacher	Professionals who are responsible for the care and education of a group of children	Baccalaureate degree in early childhood education/child development
Early childhood specialist	Professionals who supervise and train staff, design curriculum, and/or administer programs	Baccalaureate degree in early childhood education/child development and at least three years of full-time teaching experience with young children and/or a graduate degree in early childhood education/child development

department of education or CDA credentialing, or a combination of both if CDA provides more rigorous standards.

3. At least every three years, recertification should be required in order to help teachers keep abreast of changing trends and improvements in the field.

4. For principals at the public schools where programs for four year olds are located, there should be provisions made for basic training in early childhood education. There should also be proper orientation of other school personnel including lunchroom workers, aides, and guidance counselors. Staff development seminars at the district level could provide such orientation. Local colleges and technical schools could provide basic child development courses.

5. Every attempt should be made to make use of the experience of private day care personnel and other community day care workers. When qualified, these individuals should be given consideration as staff. Their training and/or recertification could be facilitated by utilizing CDA credentialing and/or by local school district staff development programs which are certified by the local or state department of education.

ECERS: Not covered.

CWLA: *Staff Required for Day Care Service.* In addition to an executive director, a day care service that offers both center care and family day care requires the following basic staff to carry out the program.

Management

- Director of Day Care Service (where day care is one of multiple services for children), with professional education in child development, early childhood education, or social work
- Center Director, with professional education in early childhood education, child development, or social work, and experience in working with children and on-site supervision of teaching staff
- Supervisor of Teaching Staff (when program is large), professionally qualified and experienced in early childhood education; for school-age programs, qualified in group work or in elementary education and experienced in out-of-school programs
- Social Work Supervisor (when group is large), with professional education and experience in social work (this responsibility may be carried by the director or through arrangements with another social agency)

Direct Delivery

- Social Worker(s), with professional education in social work and experience in social services for families and children
- Teachers of Preschool Children, at least one for each group in the day care center, with professional education and experience in early childhood education or child development, and with teaching experience
- Leaders for School-Age Children, at least one for each group of school-age children, with professional education in early childhood education, elementary education, or social group work, and experience in working with school-age children
- Aides, with some education, training, and experience with children and families, to work under the supervision of professional teaching or social work staff (p. 20)

FIDCR: Educational activities must be under the supervision and direction of a staff member trained or experienced in child growth and development. Such supervision may be provided from a central point for day care homes (p. 240). The persons providing direct care for children in the facility must have had training or demonstrated ability in working with children (p. 241).

Head Start: Not covered.

INDICATOR: Opportunities for caregiver training.

NAEYC: In cases where staff members do not meet the specified qualifications, a training plan, both individualized and center-wide, has been developed and is being implemented for those staff members. The training is appropriate to the age group with which the staff member is working (p. 18). The center provides regular training opportunities for staff to improve in working with children and families and expects staff to participate in staff development. These may include attendance at workshops and seminars, visits to other children's programs, access to resource materials, in-service sessions, or enrollment in college level/technical school courses. Training addresses the following areas: health and safety, child growth and development, planning learning activities, guidance and discipline techniques, linkages with community services, communication and relations with families, and detection of child abuse (p. 19).

NBCDI: Teachers in public school-based programs should be required to have specific training in preschool education and/or ongoing, inservice training provided by qualified staff. All districts should have an ongoing, inservice training program implemented by the center director and/or in conjunction with a larger,district-wide staff development program. This should include seminars, visits to other child development programs and classrooms and intra-district, access to resource materials and to college and technical schools offering coursework in Early Childhood Education and related field study, and videotaped sessions featuring the center staff and followed up by a constructive, critical sharing and evaluation component (p. 9).

ECERS: Good professional library, current materials on wide variety of subjects readily available. Regular staff meetings, which include staff development activities. Plans for orienting new staff members. Planned sharing of professional materials among staff. Inservice training includes workshops and courses available in community as well as training in staff meetings. Support available for inservice training (i.e., released time, travel costs, scholarships) (p. 37).

CWLA: Not covered.

FIDCR: The operating or administering agency must provide or arrange for the provision of orientation, continuous inservice training, and supervision for all staff involved in a day care program—professionals, nonprofessionals, and volunteers—in general program goals as well as specific program areas; i.e., nutrition, health, child growth and development, including the meaning of supplementary care to the child, educational guidance and remedial techniques, and the relation of the community to the child. . . . Staff must be assigned responsibility for organizing and coordinating the training program (p. 244). Nonprofessional staff must be given career progression opportunities which include job upgrading and work related training and education (p. 245).

Head Start: The plan shall provide methods for enhancing the knowledge and understanding of both staff and parents of the educational and developmental needs and activities of children in the program (p. 10). Staff and parent training, under a program jointly developed with all components of the Head Start program, in child development and behavioral developmental problems of preschool children (p. 11). Staff training in identification of and handling children with special needs and working with the parents of such children, and in coordinating relevant referral resources (p. 12).

Group Sizes and Ratios

INDICATOR: **Maximum group size.**

Child Age	NAEYC	NBCDI[a]	ECERS[a]	CWLA	FIDCR	Head Start[a]
0-12 mos.	6 - 8			--	--	
12-24 mos.	6 - 12			--	--	
2 yrs.	8 - 12			--	--	
3 yrs.	14 - 20			14	15	
4 yrs.	16 - 20			16	20	
5 yrs.	16 - 20			18	20	
6-8 yrs.	20 - 24			20	25	

[a]Not covered.

INDICATOR: **Staff/child ratio.**

Child Age	NAEYC	NBCDI[a]	ECERS[a]	CWLA	FIDCR	Head Start[a]
0-12 mos.	1:3-1:4		1:3	1:4		
12-24 mos.	1:3-1:4		1:3	1:4		
2 yrs.	1:4-1:6		1:3	1:4		
3 yrs.	1:7-1:10		1:7	1:5		
4 yrs.	1:8-1:10		1:8	1:7		
5 yrs.	1:8-1:10		1:9	1:7		
6-8 yrs.	1:10-1:12		1:10	1:15		

[a]Not covered.

Curriculum Content and Structure

INDICATOR: **Curriculum encompassing both socioemotional and cognitive development.**

NAEYC: Staff provide a variety of developmentally appropriate activities and materials that are selected to emphasize concrete experiential learning and to achieve the following goals:

a. foster positive self-concept.
b. develop social skills.
c. encourage children to think, reason, question, and experiment.
d. encourage language development.
e. enhance physical development and skills.
f. encourage and demonstrate sound health, safety, and nutritional practices.
g. encourage creative expression and appreciation for the arts.
h. respect cultural diversity of staff and children (p. 13).

NBCDI: Curriculum for preschool-age children in the public schools should be culturally sensitive and appropriate to the child's age and level of development (p. 10). The schedule should be well-balanced with provisions for both teacher- and child-oriented activities, taking into account the personality, interests, and varied strengths of individual children. Each day should be designed to facilitate cognitive, social, physical, cultural, and emotional development (p. 11).

ECERS: Not covered.

CWLA: *Social and educational goals.* The activities and experiences of each child, including relationships with other children and teachers, as well as the use of materials and equipment, should be planned according to individual needs.   The child should be able to enjoy the following experiences:

- emotional support, warmth, and caring
- exposure to adult models with whom to identify
- participation in work with tools or other objects from the natural environment, sometimes in play, sometimes in purposeful pursuits of the real world
- performance of a variety of tasks so as to have an opportunity to achieve competence in some skill areas
- a balance of freedom, of space, time, and choice
- a balance of independence from adults and dependence on adults
- assumption of individual and group responsibilities
- interaction with other children, making friends, and participation in group fun and planned activities
- affirmation of his or her own heritage and culture and an acceptance and appreciation of others
- work at his or her own developmental level and pace, yet with appropriate challenge
- learning to handle success and failure
- opportunity for exploring, inventing,and pursuing individualized ideas and interests (pp. 36-37).

FIDR: The daily activities for each child in the facility must be designed to influence a positive concept of self and motivation and to enhance his social, cognitive, and communication skills (p. 241).

Head Start: Provide children with a learning environment and the varied experiences which will help them develop socially, intellectually, physically, and emotionally in a manner appropriate to their age and stage of development toward the overall goal of social competence (p. 4).

INDICATOR: Children have opportunities to select activities.

NAEYC: Staff provide materials and time for children to select their own activities during the day. Children may choose from among several activities which the teacher has planned or the children initiate. Staff respect the child's right to choose not to participate at times (p. 13).

NBCDI: Curriculum for preschool-age children in the public schools should be culturally sensitive and appropriate to the child's age and level of development. There should be a variety of activities in which the children may choose to participate (pp. 10-11).

ECERS: Many materials present for free choice and supervised use. At least one planned activity daily. (Example: reading books to children, story telling, flannel board stories, finger plays, etc.) (p. 19).

CWLA: Not covered.

FIDCR: Not covered.

Head Start: Providing a balanced program of staff directed and child initiated activities (p. 7).

INDICATOR: Experience with cooperative group process.

NAEYC: Staff fosters cooperation and other prosocial behaviors among children (p. 10).

NBCDI: Not covered.

ECERS: Not covered.

CWLA: Not covered.

FIDCR: Not covered.

Head Start: Not covered.

INDICATOR: Curriculum is structured but not overly rigid.

NAEYC: The daily schedule is planned to provide a balance of activities on the following dimensions:

   a. indoor/outdoor
   b. quiet/active
   c. individual/small group/large group
   d. large muscle/small muscle
   e. child initiated/staff initiated (p. 12).

Staff are flexible enough to change planned or routine activities according to the needs or interests of children or to cope with changes in weather or other situations which affect routines without unduly alarming children (p. 14).

NBCDI: There should be some flexibility in the routine and daily schedule to allow for constructive spontaneity in experience, group mood and energy level changes, and changes in weather (p. 11).

ECERS: Schedule provides balance of structure and flexibility. Several activity periods, some indoors and some outdoors, are planned each day in addition to routine care (p. 29).

CWLA: The program should have *flexibility* as well as *continuity*, and should be related to the progressive developmental requirements of the children in the group. For all children, the program should provide a *rhythm* in the day, with intervals of stimulation and relaxation, and a *balance* between periods of active and quiet play, or rest. *Regularity* in day-to-day routines gives children a sense of stability and continuity and prepares them for what will happen next.

FIDCR: Not covered.

Head Start: Not covered.

INDICATOR: Recognition and appreciation of children's culture.

NAEYC: Developmentally appropriate materials and equipment which project heterogeneous racial, sexual, and age attributes are selected and used (p. 12).

NBCDI: Each day in the class there should be evidence of consistent, positive acknowledgment and appreciation of the cultural heritage of Black children through the use of well-chosen visual aids, books, records, and other learning material (p. 11).

ECERS: Cultural awareness evidenced by liberal inclusion of multiracial and nonsexist materials (i.e., dolls, illustrations in story books, and pictorial bulletin board materials). Cultural awareness is part of curriculum through planned use of both multiracial and nonsexist materials (i.e., including holidays from other religions and cultures, cooking of ethnic foods, introducing a variety of roles for women and men through stories and dramatic play) (p. 33).

CWLA: Not covered.

FIDCR: Not covered.

Head Start: Having curriculum which is relevant and reflective of the needs of the population served (bilingual/bicultural, multicultural, rural, urban, reservation, migrant, etc.). Having staff and program resources reflective of the racial and ethnic population of the children in the program (p. 8).

Physical Characteristics of Programs

INDICATOR: Physical environment is child oriented.

NAEYC: Age-appropriate materials and equipment of sufficient quantity, variety, and durability are readily accessible to children and arranged on low, open shelves to promote independent use by children (p. 26).

NBCDI: Not covered.

ECERS: Full range of learning activity furnishings regularly used plus provision for appropriate independent use by children (i.e., through picture-word labeling or other guidance) (p. 15). Variety of developmentally appropriate perceptual/fine motor materials in good repair used daily by children rotated to maintain interest. Materials organized to encourage self-help, activities planned to enhance fine motor skills (p. 23).

CWLA: The equipment, furnishings, and materials in the playroom should be selected on the basis of suitability for the children who will use them, durability, and adaptability for various uses (p. 92).

FIDCR: Each facility must have toys, games, equipment and material, books, etc., for educational development and creative expression appropriate to the particular type of facility and age level of the children (p. 241).

Head Start: The plan shall provide for appropriate and sufficient furniture, equipment and materials to meet the needs of the program, and for their arrangement in such a way as to facilitate learning, assure a balanced program of spontaneous and structured activities, and encourage self-reliance in the children. The equipment and materials shall be geared to the age, ability, and developmental needs of the children (pp. 13-14).

INDICATOR: Physical setting is orderly and differentiated.

NAEYC: Activity areas are defined clearly by spatial arrangement. Space is arranged so that children can work individually, together in small groups, or in a large group. Space is arranged to provide clear pathways for children to move from one area to another and to minimize distractions (p. 25).

NBCDI: Not covered.

ECERS: Three or more interest centers defined and conveniently equipped (i.e., water provided, shelving adequate). Quiet and noisy centers separated. Appropriate play space provided in each center (i.e., rug or table area out of flow of traffic). Easy visual supervision of centers. . . . Centers selected to provide a variety of learning experiences. Arrangement of centers designed to promote independent use by children (i.e., labeled open shelves, convenient drying space for art work). Additional materials organized and available to add to or change centers (p. 17).

CWLA: Furnishings, equipment, and materials should be arranged in orderly, clearly defined areas of interest, with sufficient space in each for the children to see the various activities available to them and to have at hand all the equipment and materials necessary for a particular activity (p. 93).

FIDCR: Not covered

Head Start: The plan shall provide for appropriate and sufficient furniture, equipment and materials to meet the needs of the program, and for their arrangement in such a way as to facilitate learning, assure a balanced program of spontaneous and structured activities, and encourage self-reliance in the children. The equipment and materials shall be accessible, attractive, and inviting to the children (pp. 13-14).

Parental Participation

INDICATOR: Parental involvement.

NAEYC: Parents are welcome visitors in the center at all times (for example, to observe, eat lunch with a child, or volunteer to help in the classroom). Parents and other family members are encouraged to be involved in the program in various ways, taking into consideration working parents and those with little spare time (p. 16).

NBCDI: The entire school atmosphere as well as organized activities should reflect respect for and welcome to parents at all times. Parents should know they can visit the school at all times, and every effort should be made to make parents feel part of the total program, erasing the air of intimidation and rejection that is often felt in public schools (p. 5).

ECERS: Parents welcomed to be a part of program (i.e., eat lunch with child, share a family custom with child's class) (p. 37).

CWLA: Not covered.

FIDCR: Opportunities must be provided parents at times convenient to them to work with the program and, whenever possible, observe their children in the day care facility (p. 245).

Head Start: Not covered.

INDICATOR: Parent-staff conferences and communication.

NAEYC: Conferences are held at least once a year and at other times, as needed, to discuss children's progress, accomplishments, and difficulties at home and at the center (p. 17).

NBCDI: Not covered.

ECERS: Parent/staff information exchanged at regular intervals (i.e., through parent conferences, newsletter, etc.). Parents made aware of approach practiced at facility (i.e., through information sheets, parent meetings, etc.) (p. 37).

CWLA: In addition to the daily informal contacts, periodic conferences with center staff members or the family day care provider and with the teacher in group day care should be scheduled for parents so they may discuss the child's progress, consider whether he or she is benefiting, and, if necessary, modify the plan or receive help in making a more suitable arrangement (p. 32).

FIDCR: Not covered.

Head Start: Participation in staff and staff-parent conferences and the making of periodic home visits (no less than two) by members of the education staff. (p. 11).

Appendix C

Participants in Panel Workshops

To complement its detailed review of the scientific literature, the Panel on Child Care Policy convened a series of workshops in 1988 to hear from a broad array of scholars, service providers, public officials, and representatives of key professional organizations and interest groups. The workshops covered five child care issues: policy implications of research, the child care market, standards and regulations, the delivery system, and international perspectives of policies and programs. This appendix presents the names of the presenters and observers who participated in those workshops.

WORKSHOP ON THE POLICY IMPLICATIONS
OF CHILD CARE RESEARCH

Presenters

Deborah Belle, Department of Psychology, Boston University

Jay Belsky, Division of Individual and Family Studies, Pennsylvania State University

Helen Blank, Director of Child Care, Children's Defense Fund

Donna Bryant, Frank Porter Graham Child Development Center, University of North Carolina at Chapel Hill

Alison Clarke-Stewart, Program in Social Ecology, University of California at Irvine

Judith F. Dunn, Department of Individual and Family Studies, Pennsylvania State University

Hillel Goelman, Department of Language Education, University of British Columbia

Ronald Haskins, Professional Welfare Assistant, Committee on Ways and Means, Minority Staff Committee

Carolee Howes, Graduate School of Education, University of California at Los Angeles

Michael Lamb, Laboratory of Comparative Ethology, National Institutes of Health - National Institute of Child Health and Human Development

Catherine C. Lewis, School of Medicine, Department of Pediatrics, University of California at San Francisco

Susanne Martinez, Legislative Assistant, Office of Senator Cranston

Deborah Phillips, Department of Psychology, University of Virginia

Sandra Scarr, Department of Psychology, University of Virginia

Michelle Seligson, School-Age Child Care Project, Wellesley College Center for Research on Women

Margaret B. Spencer, Division of Educational Studies, Emory University

Ann Turnbull, Professor of Special Education, Acting Associate Director, Bureau of Child Research, University of Kansas

Deborah Vandell, Department of Psychology, University of Texas at Dallas

Brian Vaughn, Department of Psychology, University of Illinois at Chicago

Gloria Zamora, Desegregation Assistance Center South-Central Collaborative, Inter-cultural Development Research Association, San Antonio

Observers

Wendy Baldwin, Chief, Demographic and Behavioral Sciences Branch, Center for Population Research, National Institute of Child Health and Human Development

Sarah Friedman, Health Scientist Administrator, Human Learning and Behavior Branch, National Institute of Child Health and Human Development

Patricia Hawkins, Child Care Specialist, Head Start Bureau

Margaret A. Lucas, Chief, Child Development Service, U.S. Army Community and Family Support Center

Nell Ryan, Executive Assistant to the Deputy Assistant Secretary for Human Development Services, Office of Human Development Services, U.S. Department of Health and Human Services

Heidi Sigal, Program Officer, Foundation for Child Development

Fredric Solomon, Director, Division of Mental Health and Behavioral Medicine, Institute of Medicine

Eleanor Szanton, Executive Director, National Center for Clinical Infant Programs

Betsy Ussery, Assistant Commissioner of Administration for Children
    Youth and Families, Head Start Bureau
Barbara Willer, Director for Child Care Information Services, National
    Association for the Education of Young Children

WORKSHOP ON THE CHILD CARE MARKET

Presenters

Diane Adams, Director, Community Coordinated Child Care
Joyce Allen, Senior Research Associate, Joint Center for Political Studies
Mary Jo Bane, J.F.K. School of Government, Harvard University
Robin Barnes, Research Associate, The Urban Institute
Lorie Brush, Consultant, Analysis, Research, and Training
Kathryn Ceja, Legislative Assistant, Office of Representative
    Nancy Johnson, U.S. House of Representatives
Rachel Connelly, Department of Economics, Bowdoin College
Peggy Connerton, Chief Economist, Service Employees International
    Union, AFL-CIO, CLC
Carol DeVita, Research Associate, The Urban Institute
Mark Freidman, Deputy Director of Administration, Maryland
    Department of Human Resources
Ruth Freis, Director, Resources for Family Development
Alan Gauld, Human Services Finance Officer, Bank of America
Walter Gunn, Senior Research Psychologist, Center for Disease Control
Sandra Hofferth, Health Scientist and Administrator, National Institute of
    Child Health and Human Development
Julie Isaacs, Analyst, Congressional Budget Office
Chris Iverson, Employment Policy Director, Committee on Labor and
    Human Resources, U.S. Senate
Susanne Martinez, Legal Counsel to Alan Cranston, U.S. Senate
Marsha Renwanz, Staff Director, Subcommittee on Children, U.S. Senate
Philip Robins, Department of Economics, University of Miami
Judy Simpson, Children's World Learning Centers, Inc.
Sharon Stephan, Congressional Research Service
Myra Strober, Department of Education, Stanford University
Linda Waite, Senior Sociologist, The Rand Corporation

Observers

Helen Blank, Director, Day Care Division, Children's Defense Fund
Deborah Bowland, Executive Assistant to the Assistant Secretary for
    Policy, U.S. Department of Labor

Ellen Galinsky, Project Director, Work and Family Life Studies, Bank Street College

Patricia Hawkins, Child Care Specialist, Head Start Bureau

Margaret A. Lucas, Chief, Child Development Service, U.S. Army Community and Family Support Center

Naomi Marshall, National Black Child Development Institute

Sharon McGroder, Intern, Division of Children, Youth and Family Policy, ASPE, U.S. Department of Health and Human Services

Roberta McKay, Economist, Women's Bureau, U.S. Department of Labor

William Prosser, Director, Division of Children, Youth and Family Policy, ASPE, U.S. Department of Health and Human Services

Barbara Reisman, Child Care Action Campaign

Nell Ryan, Special Assistant to the Assistant Secretary for Human Development Services, U.S. Department of Health and Human Services

Ann Segal, Executive Assistant to the Assistant Secretary for Planning and Evaluation, U.S. Department of Health and Human Services

Barbara Willer, Director for Child Care Information Services, National Association for the Education of Young Children

WORKSHOP ON STANDARDS AND REGULATIONS

Presenters

Roberta Aptekar, Child Welfare League of America, Washington, DC

David Beard, Texas Department of Human Resources, Austin, TX

Eugene B. Bardach, School of Public Policy, University of California at Berkley

Sue Bradekamp, National Association for the Education of Young Children, Washington, D.C.

Norris Class, Professor Emeritus, University of Southern California

Jack Clayton, American Association of Christian Schools, Fairfax, VA

Richard Clifford, Frank Porter Graham Child Development Center, University of North Carolina at Chapel Hill

Rory Darrah, California Resource and Referral Network, San Francisco, CA

Diane Dennis, Kinder Care Learning Centers, Falls Church, VA

Patricia Fossarelli, Johns Hopkins University Hospital

Austine Fowler, Early Childhood Office, District of Columbia Public Schools

Margery Freeman, National Council of Churches, New Orleans, LA

Sarah Green, Manatee County Head Start, Bradenton, FL

Karen Hill-Scott, Crystal Stairs, Inc., Inglewood, CA

Randy Hitz, Oregon State Department of Education, Salem, OR
Sharon Lynn Kagan, Office of Early Childhood Education, Office of the
    Mayor, New York City
Pauline Koch, Licensing Services for Children, Youth, and Families,
    Wilmington, DE
Patricia Levin, Community Services for Children, Bethlehem, PA
Margaret Lucas, Child Development Services, U.S. Army Community and
    Family Services, Alexandria, VA
Eula Miller, Northern Virginia Community College, Alexandria, VA
Karen Miller, Children's World Learning Centers, Inc., Golden, CO
Gwen Morgan, Work/Family Directions, Wheelock College, Boston, MA
Donald Peters, Individual and Family Services, University of Delaware
Carol Phillips, Council for Early Childhood Education, Washington, D.C.
Winona Sample, California Department of Education, Santa Clara, CA
Tutti Sherlock, National Association of Child Care Resource and Referral
    Agencies, Rochester, MN
Helen Taylor, National Child Day Care Association, Washington, D.C.
Nancy Travis, Save the Children, Atlanta, GA

Observers

Helen Blank, Children's Defense Fund
Patricia Hawkins, Head Start Bureau, U.S. Department of Health and
    Human Services
Chris Iverson, Senate Committee on Labor and Human Resources
Allen Jensen, Subcommittee on Public Assistance and Unemployment
    Compensation, House Committee on Ways and Means
Barbara Lipsky, Employment and Standards, U.S. Department of Labor
Naomi Marshall, National Black Child Development Institute, Inc.
Sharon McGroder, Assistant Secretary's Office for Planning and
    Evaluation U.S. Department of Health and Human Services
Gail Perry, House Committee on Education and Labor
Peggy Pizzo, National Center for Clinical Infant Programs
Billy Press, National Academy of Sciences
William Prosser, Division of Children, Youth, and Family Policy, ASPE,
    U.S Department of Health and Human Services
Anne Rosewater, House Select Committee on Children, Youth, and
    Families
Nell Ryan, Office of Human Development Services, U.S. Department of
    Health and Human Services
Thomas Schultz, National Association of State Boards of Education
Ann Segal, U.S. Department of Health and Human Services

Damian Thorman, Subcommittee on Human Resources, House
    Committee on Education and Labor
Betsy Ussury, Head Start Bureau, U.S. Department of Health and Human
    Services
Kate Wash-O'Beirne, U.S. Department of Health and Human Services
Susan Wilhelm, Subcommittee on Human Resources, House Committee
    on Education and Labor
Barbara Willer, National Association for the Education of Young Children

WORKSHOP ON CHILD CARE DELIVERY SYSTEMS

Presenters

Susan Abrams, Children's World Learning Centers, Inc.
David Allen, Resources for Child Caring, St. Paul, MN
Roslyn Anderson, Olsen Early Childhood Center, Minneapolis, MN
William Ashton, Forest T. Jones & Co., Reston, VA
Rebecca Maria Barrera, Niños Group, Inc., San Antonio, TX
Roberta Bergman, Child Care Answers, Dallas, TX
Douglas Besharov, American Enterprise Institute, Washington, D.C.
Joanne Brady, Educational Development Center, Inc., Boston, MA
Donna Bryant, Frank Porter Graham Child Development Center,
    University of North Carolina, Chapel Hill
Abby Cohen, Child Care Law Center, San Francisco, CA
Margaret Doolin, Governor's Office of Employee Relations, New York
Arthur Emlen, Regional Research Institute, Portland, Or
Suzanne Faulk, Wheezles and Sneezles, Berleley, CA
Ann Forsyth, Governor's Task Force on Work and Family, New York
Ellen Galinsky, Bank Street College and President, National Association
    for the Education of Young Children
David Gleason, Corporate Child Care, Inc., Nashville, TN
Sharon Kalemkiarian, Insurance for Child Care Project, San Diego, CA
Sheila Kamerman, Columbia University School of Social Work
Joan Lombardi, Child Care Employee Project, Alexandria, VA
Joyce Long, American Federation of State, County, and Municipal
    Employees
Fern Marx, Wellesley College
Gwen Morgan, Work Family Directions, Wheelock College
Clennie Murphy, Head Start Bureau, U.S. Department of Health and
    Human Services
Eleanor Nelson, Prospect Hill Parent's and Children's Centers, Waltham,
    MA
Roger Neugebauer, Child Care Information Exchange, Redmond, CA

Sister Geraldine O'Brien, East Coast Migrant Head Start, Arington, VA
Claudia Ostrander, Maryland National Bank
Diana Pearce, Women's Policy Research Institute, Washington, D.C.
Deborah Phillips, University of Virginia
Judith Rosen, Fairfax County Office for Children, Fairfax, VA
Barbara Roy, First Bank of St. Paul/St. Paul Area Chamber of Commerce
June Sale, U.C.L.A. Child Care Services, Los Angeles, CA
Michelle Seligson, Wellesley College
Patty Siegal, California Child Care Resource Referral Network, San
    Francisco, CA
William Swan, University of Georgia
Edward Zigler, Yale University

Observers

Helen Blank, Children's Defense Fund
Kathryn Ceja, Representative Johnson's Office
Jeri Eckhart, U.S. Department of Labor
Ruth Gardner, Senate Subcommittee on Children
Patricia Hawkins, Head Start Bureau, U.S. Department of Health and
    Human Services
Sandra Hofferth, National Institute of Child Health and Human
    Development
Chris Iverson, Senate Committee on Labor and Human Resources
Allen Jensen, Subcommittee on Public Assistance and Unemployment
    Compensation, House Committee on Ways and Means
Sally Kilgore, Department of Education
Margaret A. Lucas, U.S. Army Community and Family Support Center
Niobe Marshall, National Black Child Development Institute, Inc.
Shelby Miller, The Ford Foundation
Jay Noell, Congressional Budget Office
Gail Perry, House Committee on Education and Labor
Billie Press, National Academy of Sciences
William Prosser, Division of Children, Youth, and Family Policy, ASPE,
    U.S. Department of Health and Human Services
Anne Rosewater, House Select Committee on Children, Youth, and
    Families
Nell Ryan, Office of Human Development Services, U.S. Department of
    Health and Human Services
Thomas Schultz, National Association of State Boards of Education
Heidi Sigal, Foundation for Child Development
Frederic Solomon, Institute of Mediciane
Eleanor Szanton, National Center for Clinical Infant Programs

Richard Tarplin, Senate Subcommittee on Children
Betsy Ussery, Head Start Bureau, U.S. Department of Health and Human Services
Barbara Willer, National Association for the Education of Young Children

WORKSHOP ON CHILD CARE POLICIES AND PROGRAM: INTERNATIONAL PERSPECTIVES

Presenters

Bengt-Erik Andersson, Institute of Education, University of Stockholm, Sweden
Olga Baudelot, Institut National de Recherche Pédagogique, France
Glenn Drover, School of Social Work, University of British Columbia, Canada
Alfred Kahn, School of Social Work, Columbia University
Sheila Kamerman, School of Social Work, Columbia University
Soren Kindlund, Ministry of Health and Social Affairs, Sweden
Peter Moss, Thomas Coram Research Unit, Institute of Education, University of London, England
Jacob Vedel-Pedersen, Danish National Social Research Institute, Denmark

Observers

Marianne Ferber, Department of Economics, University of Illinois; Chair, Panel on Employer Policies and Working Families
Ulla Malkus, Harvard University
Billie Press, National Academy of Sciences
Betsy Ussery, Associate Commissioner, Head Start Bureau

Index

L